BEYOND THE REPUBLIC

The Key Centre for Ethics, Law, Justice and Governance

The Key Centre for Ethics, Law, Justice and Governance (KCELJAG) is the first nationally funded research centre in Law, Ethics, Governance or Criminology. It incorporates three centres – the Centre for Australian Public Sector Management, the Centre for Crime Policy and Public Safety and the National Institute for Law, Ethics and Public Affairs (NILEPA). It aims to provide a distinctive and significant response to the challenges posed by globalisation to the values and institutions of liberal democracy. It aims to do this through the application of the insights of academics and practitioners in law, ethics, politics and criminology. One of its prime publishing outputs is through the series Law, Ethics and Public Affairs. The patron of the Key Centre is His Excellency, Sir William Deane, AC, KBE, and the Chairman of the Advisory Board is Hon Justice Tony Fitzgerald. It is led by Professor Charles Sampford (Director) and Professors Pat Weller and Ross Homel (Deputy Directors). More information on the Centre is available on its website, <www.gu.edu.au>, and from the Centre Manager. One of the publication outlets is the series on Law, Ethics and Public Affairs, published by the Federation Press.

Law, Ethics and Public Affairs

General Editor: Charles Sampford

Interpreting Constitutions: Theories, Principles and Institutions
edited by Charles Sampford and Kim Preston

Rethinking Human Rights
edited by Brian Galligan and Charles Sampford

Justice for People with Disabilities: Legal and Institutional Issues
edited by Marge Hauritz, Charles Sampford and Sophie Blencowe

Ethics and Political Practice
edited by Noel Preston and Charles Sampford with C-A Bois

Beyond the Adversarial System
edited by Helen Stacy and Michael Lavarch

Educating Lawyers for a Less Adversarial System
edited by Charles Sampford, Suzanne Condlln and Sophie Blencowe

Through the World's Eye
Michael Kirby

Local Government, Public Enterprise and Ethics
edited by Patrick Bishop and Noel Preston

BEYOND THE REPUBLIC

Meeting the Global Challenges to Constitutionalism

editors

Charles Sampford

Tom Round

The Federation Press
2001

Published in Sydney by

The Federation Press
71 John St, Leichhardt, NSW, 2040
PO Box 45, Annandale, NSW, 2038
Ph: (02) 9552 2200 Fax: (02) 9552 1681
E-mail: info@federationpress.com.au
Website: http://www.federationpress.com.au

National Library of Australia Cataloguing-in-Publication data:

Beyond the republic
Includes index
ISBN 1 86287 377 1

1. Globalization – Australia. 2. Australia – Politics and government. I. Sampford, CJG (Charles JG). II. Round, Tom.

338.8/042

Typeset by The Federation Press, Leichhardt, NSW.
Printed by Ligare Pty Ltd, Riverwood, NSW.

CONTENTS

Contributors vii
Table of Cases xiii
Table of Statutes xvi

Introduction: Globalisation and Constitutionalism
Tom Round and Charles Sampford 1

Part I: W[h]ither National Sovereignty? 11

1 Reconceiving and Reinstitutionalising Liberal Democratic Values in a More Global World
Charles Sampford 11

2 The Decline of Sovereignty: Problems for Democratic Government
Sir Anthony Mason 27

3 The Empire Strikes Back: The Constitution, Sovereignty and 19th Century Globalisation
Helen Irving 47

4 The Changing Context of Australian Citizenship: The Case for Multiculturalism
Peter Wong and Violeta Brdaroska 56

5 The Constitution of International Civil Society
Aynsley Kellow 68

6 Democracy in a World of Global Markets
Tom Campbell 78

7 Democracy as Comparative Advantage
Roland Rich 93

8 Democracy: Its Survivability
Alun A Preece 107

Part II: Constitutional Theory and Structure 119

9 The Australian Constitution and the Challenge of Theory
John Williams 119

10 Dividing Power in a Federation in an Age of Globalisation
Cheryl Saunders 129

11 A Federation amid Global Imperatives?
Glyn Davis and Naomi Sunderland 146

12 The Role of Upper Houses: Is Washminster Washed Up?
Senator Helen Coonan 156

13 Washminster Revisited: The Role of the Upper House
Senator Andrew Bartlett 164

14 Government as a Public Trust: Crown Mystique, Unequal Laws, and Modern Democracy
Steven C Churches 173

Part III: Individuals, Minorities, and Their Rights **184**

15 Recognising Rights
Alice ES Tay 184

16 Constitutional Transformations: Universal Values and the Politics of Constitutional Understanding
Heinz Klug 191

17 Globalisation – the Bane of Popular Sovereignty?
John Pyke 205

18 Constitutional Cants
Gerald N Rosenberg 215

19 Law's Laws: The Demand and Supply of Rights
Neil Komesar 230

20 Recognition of Indigenous Rights: American Law, Australian Law and International Law
Garth Nettheim 241

21 First Peoples, Late Admissions: Recognising Indigenous Rights
Peter Jull and Helena Kajlich 257

22 Recognising Indigenous Law in Australia: Drawing on the African Experience
Bede Harris 270

23 Rights of Indigenous People and Conservation: Joint Management of National Parks in South Africa and Australia
Bertus de Villiers 279

24 Constitutional Dreaming
Christine Morris 290

Appendix 1: Promotion of the Right to Democracy 300
Appendix 2: Items Proposed for Framework Agreement and Political Negotiations Process 303
Bibliography 306
Index 327

CONTRIBUTORS

SENATOR ANDREW BARTLETT has been an Australian Democrat Senator for Queensland since November 1997 and is the Democrat spokesperson on Electoral Matters, Immigration and Multiculturalism, Social Security, Environment and Animal Welfare, Gay and Lesbian Issues, Veteran's Affairs, and Housing. Previously he worked with the Department of Social Security, with a community radio station, and as a researcher for Democrat Senators. He has held several party positions, including Queensland Branch President and National Campaign Director. He has a strong interest in environmental, social justice and animal welfare issues.

VIOLETA BRDAROSKA works as a parliamentary adviser to the Hon Dr Peter Wong AM MLC, in the NSW Parliament. She has an Honours degree in political science and a Master's degree in arts (international relations), both from the University of New South Wales. Violeta was born in 1972 in Ohrid, Macedonia, and migrated to Australia in 1991. She is active in the areas of political studies, international relations and social issues. She is currently conducting research in the areas of multicultural affairs, population migration and human rights.

PROFESSOR TOM CAMPBELL, BA (Oxford), MA and PhD (Glasgow), is Professor of Law at the Australian National University in Canberra.

DR STEVEN CHURCHES has been General Counsel to the Legislative Council of Western Australia since 1999. Before that he practised at the Bar in Sydney and Perth. He has a particular interest in the relation of government to the community, and was counsel to the High Court of Australia in such cases as *Teoh, Bropho, Webster v Lampard* (1993) 177 CLR 598(concerning the utility of statutory protections for statutory officers) and *Wilson v Minister for Aboriginal Affairs* (1996) 189 CLR 1 (concerning the separation of powers). He has published numerous articles on public law and legal history over the past 20 years.

SENATOR HELEN COONAN, a lawyer by profession, was elected a Liberal Senator for New South Wales in March 1996. In November 1998 she was appointed Deputy Government Whip in the Senate. Senator Coonan serves on a number of Senate and Joint Committees, including Public Accounts and Audit, Treaties, Legal and Constitutional Affairs, Socio-economic Consequences of National and Competition Policy, and Regulations and Ordinances. She has participated in inquiries into a important areas of public policy including the Multilateral Agreement on investment, legal aid, health insurance, childcare, Work-for-the-Dole, copyright, privacy, euthanasia, the Constitutional Convention, and electronic commerce. Senator Coonan has been involved in such recent issues as parliamentary reform, an international criminal court, the portrayal of women in the media, and the socio-economic impact of competition policy. She is a member of the Council for Equal Opportunity in Employment and the Board of the Centre for Asia Pacific Women in Politics.

DR GLYN DAVIS is Director-General of the Department of the Premier and Cabinet, Queensland. He was previously Professor of Politics and Public Policy at Griffith University.

DR BERTUS DE VILLIERS (BA Law, LLB, LLD) is Manager of the Goldfields Land Council's Native Title and Legal Section, and previously held senior posts in South African National Parks and the Centre for Constitutional Analysis of the Human Sciences Research Council (Pretoria). He has served as a consultant to South Africa's Commission on Provincial Government, and on the Executive of the Federalism Research Committee of the International Political Science Association. He has a special interest in environmental issues, the protection of human rights, federalism, intergovernmental relations, land rights and other constitutional issues.

DR BEDE HARRIS is a native of Zimbabwe. After reading history for his BA (Mod) degree at Trinity College, Dublin, he obtained an LLB at Rhodes University, South Africa, where his interest in customary law was fostered by Professor AJ Kerr, one of South Africa's leading scholars in the field. Dr Harris then taught constitutional law at the University of Natal, Pietermaritzburg, before migrating to New Zealand, where he taught at the University of Waikato and obtained his DPhil, his thesis being a comparative study of doctrines underlying freedom of expression in the United States, Canada and South Africa. After lecturing at James Cook University, where he participated in bridging programs for indigenous students run by the Centre for Aboriginal and Torres Strait Islander Participation Research and Development (CATSPRD), he moved to the University of Canberra, where he lectures in constitutional, corporate and human rights law.

DR HELEN IRVING is a Senior Lecturer in the Faculty of Humanities and Social Sciences at the University of Technology, Sydney. Her publications include *To Constitute a Nation: A Cultural History of Australia's Constitution* (Cambridge University Press, 1997/9) and, as editor, *The Centenary Companion to Australian Federation* (Cambridge University Press, 1999). She is a member of the Council of the Constitutional Centenary Foundation.

MR PETER JULL is an Adjunct Professor in the Department of Government, University of Queensland, and formerly a Senior Research Fellow and interim Director at the Australian National University's North Australia Research Unit, Darwin. He has been an adviser on northern hinterland and indigenous policy in the Canadian Prime Minister's Department; political and constitutional adviser to regional, national, and international Inuit organisations; assistant to successive heads of government in the Northwest Territories; and secretary to the Cabinet of British Columbia.

Ms Helena Kajlich, a Seattle-born Brisbane resident, is studying native title, human rights and constitutional reform in the Departments of Law and Government at the University of Queensland.

Professor Aynsley Kellow is Head of the School of Government at the University of Tasmania.

Professor Heinz J Klug is Assistant Professor of Law at the University of Wisconsin – Madison, and previously taught public international law, human rights law, post-apartheid law and introduction to South African law at the University of the Witwatersrand in Johannesburg. He has worked with the South African Ministry of Water Affairs and Forestry as well as the Ministry of Land Affairs on water law and land tenure issues. Professor Klug served on the secretariat and was a staff member of the African National Congress Land Commission. He was also a team member on the World Bank mission to South Africa on Land Reform and Rural Restructuring. He is the author of *Constituting Democracy: Law, Globalism and South Africa's Political Reconstruction* (Cambridge University Press, 2000).

Professor Neil K Komesar is Burris-Bascom Professor of Law at the University of Wisconsin. He holds BA, MA, JD and PhD (economics) degrees from the University of Chicago. He has written on subjects including constitutional theory, tort reform, land use, damages, criminal victimisation, public interest law, property rights, landlord–tenant law and class actions. He is the author *Imperfect Alternatives: Choosing Institutions in Law, Economics, and Public Policy* (University of Chicago Press, 1994), a comparative institutional analysis of law, and is completing his second book on the subject, *Law's Limits: The Role of Courts, the Rule of Law and the Supply and Demand of Rights* (in progress).

Sir Anthony Mason, AC, KBE, BA LLB (Syd), FASSA, was Chief Justice of Australia from 1987 to 1995, having been appointed to the High Court in 1972. From 1995 to 1999 he was Chancellor of the University of New South Wales, and is currently National Fellow in the Research School of Social Sciences at the Australian National University, Canberra.

Ms Christine Morris is a traditional matrilineal custodian of the Kombmerri clan and a traditional patrilineal (grandfather) custodian of the Mununjahli clan district, both in south-east Queensland. She currently holds the position of Research Fellow in the Australian Key Centre for Cultural and Media Policy at Griffith University. Her field of specialisation – Indigenous beliefs systems and their conceptual reality – has enabled her to contribute to the *First International Declaration on Indigenous Intellectual Property Rights* and to a similar Declaration for the wet tropics of far north Queensland. Her current research is in Indigenous intellectual property rights as these pertain to Arts Queensland's Indigenous cultural policies. Due to her interest in traditional stories and in the maintenance of oral tradition she served as guest editor on literature for the *Aboriginal and Torres Strait Islander Studies Encyclopedia.* Formally she was a specialist in Traditional Belief Systems for ABC Radio National, producing and presenting a collection of audio documentaries on the subject. She has also produced a video giving a socio-historical account of the Yugumbeh Language Programs.

PROFESSOR GARTH NETTHEIM is Emeritus Professor in the Faculty of Law at the University of New South Wales, and Chair of the Advisory Committee of the Indigenous Law Centre.

MR ALUN A PREECE is a Lecturer in the TC Beirne School of Law, at the University of Queensland. He received his MA and LLB from Cambridge and his LLM from the University of Queensland.

MR JOHN PYKE BSc (Syd), LLB (UNSW), LLM (Syd) is a Lecturer in the School of Law, Queensland University of Technology, and a barrister of the Supreme Court of New South Wales.

MR ROLAND RICH, born in 1951 in Paris, holds a BA and LLB (University of Sydney), and a Master's in International Law (Australian National University). After working as a barrister in Sydney, he joined the Department of Foreign Affairs and held diplomatic posts including Third Secretary, Paris; Delegate, Australian Mission to UNESCO; Second Secretary, Rangoon; First Secretary, Manila; and Australian Ambassador to Laos. In the Department of Foreign Affairs and Trade he held the positions of Legal Adviser and Assistant Secretary of the International Organisations Branch. He is now Director of the Centre for Democratic Institutions, based in Canberra at the Australian National University.

ASSOCIATE PROFESSOR GERALD N ROSENBERG is Associate Professor of Political Science and Lecturer in Law at the University of Chicago. Trained as both a lawyer and a political scientist, and a member of the Washington DC Bar, he writes on judicial institutions. He is particularly interested in the ways in which judicial institutions can further the interests of the relatively disadvantaged. His work has appeared in the *University of Chicago Law Review*, *University of Virginia Law Review*, *Law and Social Inquiry*, *NOMOS*, *Supreme Court Review* and other journals. He has contributed to multiple edited collections and is author of *The Hollow Hope: Can Courts Bring About Social Change?* (University of Chicago Press, 1991). From September 1995 to September 1996 he was a Visiting Fellow in the Law Program at the Research School of Social Sciences, Australian National University.

MR TOM ROUND gained degrees in arts (with first-class honours in government) and law from the University of Queensland. He has worked as a lecturer in the School of Criminology (formerly Justice Administration) at Griffith University, Queensland, and in the Commonwealth Department of Immigration and Multicultural Affairs, and is presently a Research Officer in the Key Centre for Ethics, Law, Justice and Governance (KCELJAG).

PROFESSOR CHARLES SAMPFORD gained a double first in politics and philosophy and the Supreme Court Prize in Law from Melbourne University, and then continued his law studies at Oxford. He was awarded a DPhil in 1984. He taught law at Melbourne University before being seconded to the Philosophy Department in 1990 to help establish the Centre for Philosophy and Public Issues as Deputy Director and Principal Research Fellow. In 1991, as the Foundation Dean of Law at Griffith University, he founded and directed the National Institute for Law, Ethics and Public Affairs. In 1997, he was elected the Visiting Senior Research Fellow at St John's College, Oxford, and in 1999 he was awarded a Senior Fulbright Fellowship, which he took up at Harvard in 2000. He has written some 60 articles and chapters in Australian and foreign journals and collections, and 12 books. He has also played a central role in the establishment of the International Institute for Public Ethics, an international association of public ethics practitioners, of which he is the Vice President. Professor Sampford has been the principal legal adviser for the Queensland Scrutiny of Legislation Committee since 1995. He has advised the Nolan Committee on Standards in Public Life and the Lord Chancellor's Committee on Legal Education and Professional Conduct in the United Kingdom. In September 1998, he went to Indonesia on a special mission for the World Bank to advise the Indonesian government on governance reforms to deal with corruption.

PROFESSOR CHERYL SAUNDERS is Professor of Law and Director of the Centre for Comparative Constitutional Studies at the University of Melbourne.

MS NAOMI SUNDERLAND, formerly of the Department of the Premier and Cabinet, now works as a research officer with the Brisbane Institute, and is undertaking doctoral work at the Queensland University of Technology.

PROFESSOR ALICE ERH-SOON TAY is Commonwealth Human Rights Commissioner and, previously, Challis Professor of Jurisprudence and Director of the Centre for Asian and Pacific Law at the University of Sydney. She has been a member of the Australian Law Reform Commission and the Australian Science and Technology Council, and President of the International Association for Philosophy of Law and Social Philosophy and of the National Office of Overseas Skills Recognition. She received her PhD from the Australian National University in 1964, and her LLD from Edinburgh in

1987. In 1986 she was awarded the Order of Australia for her contribution to teaching and research in law. With the late Eugene Kamenka she has authored and edited 19 books and over 110 articles on socialist legal systems and legal culture, comparative law, legal theory, jurisprudence and human rights. She specialises in jurisprudence, legal and social philosophy, comparative and communist legal systems, macro-sociology of law and human rights.

DR JOHN WILLIAMS is a senior lecturer in Law at the University of Adelaide. His published research is in the area of constitutional law and history. He is co-editor of the *Australian Journal of Legal History* and the *New Federalist.* His current research project relates to the collation and publication of the drafts of the Australian Constitution.

DR PETER WONG AM MLC is a general practitioner who has represented the Unity Party in the New South Wales Legislative Council since March 1999. Born in China in 1942, Dr Wong holds degrees in pharmacy and medicine from Sydney University. He has been a member of the NSW Ethnic Affairs Commission (1991–7), the Bureau for Immigration Research (1992–4), and the National Multicultural Advisory Council of the Department of Immigration and Multicultural Affairs. In 1990 he co-founded the Welfare Committee for Chinese Students, providing support for the PRC nationals in Australia after Tiananmen, and in 1991 he co-founded the Australian Chinese Charity Foundation. In 1992 Dr Wong was appointed first Chairperson of the NSW Ethnic Schools Board, and he is also a director of Sydney University's Herbal Medicine and Research Centre.

TABLE OF CASES

Abrams v United States 250 US 616 (1919): 219
Adarand Constructors Inc v Peña 515 US 200 (1995): 225
Advisory Opinion on the Legality of the Threat or Use of Nuclear Weapons, 8 July 1996, 35 ILM 809: 33–4
Alden v Maine 527 US 707 (1999): 132
Amalgamated Society of Engineers v Adelaide Steamship Co (1920) 28 CLR 129: 127
American Booksellers Association v Hudnut 771 F 2d 323 (7th Cir 1985), 475 US 1001 (1986): 225
American Communications Association v Douds 339 US 382 (1950): 220
Anastaplo, In re 366 US 82 (1961): 221
Atyeo v Aboriginal Lands Trust (1996) 136 FLR 47: 179–80
Australian Capital Television Pty Ltd v Commonwealth (1992) 177 CLR 106: 120, 137, 139, 206, 207
Australian Communist Party v Commonwealth (1951) 83 CLR 1: 142
Bangindawo v Head of the Nyanda Regional Authority 1998 (3) BCLR 314 (Tk): 277
Barenblatt v United States 360 US 109 (1959): 200
Beswick v Beswick [1966] Ch 538: 179
Blessing v Freestone 117 S Ct 1335 (1997): 132
Bradken v BHP (1979) 145 CLR 107: 178
Bradley v Commonwealth (1973) 128 CLR 557: 136
Brewster v Lash (1903) 2 Cases in the Court of Error, Barbados 72: 180
Bridgetown/Greenbushes Friends of the Forest Inc v CALM (1997) 18 WAR 126: 180
Bropho v Western Australia (1990) 171 CLR 1: 140, 179
Brown v Board of Education 347 US 483 (1954): 228
Buckley v Valeo 424 US 1 (1976): 225
Byrne v Ireland [1972] IR 241: 178
Cain v Doyle (1946) 72 CLR 409: 182
Chairperson of the Constitutional Assembly, Ex parte: In Re Certification of the Constitution of the Republic of South Africa, 1996 (4) SA 744 (First Certification Case): 195, 201–2
Cherokee Nation v Georgia 30 US (5 Pet) 1 (1831): 245
City of Cleburne v Cleburne Living Center Inc 473 US 432 (1985): 231ff
Coe v Commonwealth (1979) 53 ALJR 403: 271
Coe v Commonwealth (No 2) (1993) 118 ALR 193: 271
Cole v Whitfield (1988) 165 CLR 360: 134
Commonwealth v Tasmania (1983) 158 CLR 1: 137
Communist Party of Indiana v Whitcomb 414 US 441 (1974): 220
Conway v Rimmer [1968] AC 910: 208
Courtenay v the King (1311) YB 5 Ed II, 31 Selden Society 130: 180
Cunliffe v Commonwealth (1994) 182 CLR 272: 139
Davis v Commonwealth (1988) 166 CLR 79: 139
Dennis v United States 341 US 494 (1951): 219, 227
Department of Transport v Egoroff [1986] TLR 226: 182
Dingjan, Re; ex parte Wagner (1995) 183 CLR 323: 138
Downs v Williams (1971) 125 CLR 61: 182
Egan v Chadwick (1999) 46 NSWLR 563: 174–5
Egan v Willis (1998) 195 CLR 424: 174–5
Erie Railroad Co v Tompkins 304 US 64 (1938): 273
Fuzile v Ntloko 1944 NAC (C&O) 2: 274
Gitlow v New York 268 US 45 (1925): 219
Goryl v Greyhound Australia (1994) 179 CLR 463: 273
Gould v Brown (1998) 193 CLR 346: 141
Gregory v Ashcroft 501 US 452 (1991): 132
Ha v New South Wales (1997) 189 CLR 465, 71 ALJR 1080: 139
Hamlet of Baker Lake v Minister of Indian Affairs (1979) 107 DLR 513: 285

Hampton v Mow Sun Wong 426 US 88 (1976): 237
Hayes v Northern Territory [1999] FCA 1248: 245
Horne v Barber (1920) 27 CLR 494: 175
Hughes Aircraft Systems International v Airservices Australia (1997) 76 FCR 151: 177
Idaho v Couerd'alene Tribe of Idaho 117 S Ct 2028 (1997): 132
James v Valtierra 402 US 137 (1971): 212
Johnson & Graham's Lessee v M'Intosh 8 Wheat 543, 21 US 543 (1823): 244
Kable v Director of Public Prosecutions (NSW) (1996) 189 CLR 51: 140–1
Kartinyeri v Commonwealth (1998) 152 ALR 540, 72 ALJR 722: 251, 254
Konigsberg v California 366 US 36 (1961): 221
Korematsu v United States 323 US 214 (1944): 216, 237
Laird v Tatum 408 US 1 (1972): 221
Lamont v Postmaster General 381 US 301 (1965): 219
Lange v Australian Broadcasting Corporation (1997) 189 CLR 520, 145 ALR 96: 139, 140, 142, 207
Law Students Civil Rights Research Council v Wadmond 401 US 154 (1971): 221
Leask v Commonwealth (1996) 187 CLR 579: 139
Lerner v Casey 357 US 468 (1958): 220
Levy v Victoria (1997) 189 CLR 579, 146 ALR 248: 140
Lloyds Bank Ltd v Bundy [1975] QB 326: 179
Lucas v Colorado 377 US 713 (1964): 212
Mabo v Queensland (No 1) (1988) 166 CLR 186: 251
Mabo v Queensland (No 2) (1992) 175 CLR 1: 62, 246, 271, 285
McGinty v Western Australia (1996) 186 CLR 140, 70 ALJR 200: 120, 140, 206–7
Mbekushe v Dumiso 1941 NAC (C&O) 57: 276
Milirrpum v Nabalco Pty Ltd and the Commonwealth (1971) 17 FLR 141 (the Gove Land Rights Case): 294
Minister for Immigration and Ethnic Affairs v Teoh (1995) 183 CLR 273, 128 ALR 353: 55, 137, 162, 239
Minister for Justice (WA) ex rel Ansett Transport Industries (Operations) Pty Ltd v National Airlines Commission (1976) 138 CLR 492: 135
Minister of Local Government & Housing, Kwa-Zulu Natal 1998 (4) BCLR 399 (CC): 277
Minister of Native Affairs v Buthelezi 1961(1) SA 766 (D): 271
Minister of Native Affairs, Ex parte; In re Yako v Beyi 1948(1) SA 388 (A): 272–3
Mokoba v Langa 1952 NAC (S) 76: 274
Mvubu v Chilisa 1972 BAC 66 (NE): 273
National Bank of Boston v Bellotti 435 US 765 (1978): 225
Nationwide News Pty Ltd v Wills (1992) 177 CLR 1: 206
New South Wales v Commonwealth (1975) 135 CLR 337 (Seas and Submerged Lands Case): 205
New South Wales v Commonwealth (1990) 169 CLR 482 (Corporations Law Case): 138, 143
New State Ice Co v Liebmann 285 US 262 (1932): 131
New York Times Co v United States 403 US 713 (1970) (Pentagon Papers Case): 237
New York v United States 505 US 144 (1992): 132, 143
Nhlanhla v Mokweno 1952 NAC 286 (NE): 274
Port McDonnell Professional Fishermen's Association v South Australia (1989) 168 CLR 340: 140
Printz v United States 117 S Ct 2365 (1997): 143
Project Blue Sky Inc v Australian Broadcasting Authority (1998) 194 CLR 355: 162
Province of Bombay v Municipal Corporation of Bombay [1947] AC 58: 180
R v Brown [1994] 1 AC 212: 143
R v Duncan; ex parte Australian Iron and Steel Pty Ltd (1983) 158 CLR 535: 136, 142
R v Kirby; ex parte Boilermakers' Society of Australia (1956) 94 CLR 254: 136
Regents of the University of California v John Doe 117 S Ct 900 (1997)]: 132
Registrar of the Accident Compensation Tribunal v FCT (1993) 178 CLR 145: 179

Reitman v Mulkey 387 US 369 (1967): 212
Residential Tenancies Tribunal of New South Wales v Henderson, Re; ex parte Defence Force Housing Authority (1997) 190 CLR 410: 140
Rudler v Franks [1947] 1 KB 430: 35
S v Makwanyane 1995 (6) BCLR 665 (CC): 277–8
Scales v United States 367 US 203 (1961): 219
Seminole Tribe of Florida v Florida 116 S Ct 1114 (1996): 132
Shrimp Case (WTO): 40–1
Sonti v Sonti 1929 NAC (C&O) 23: 276
State Government Insurance Commission v Trigwell (1979) 142 CLR 617: 239
Stephens v West Australian Newspapers Ltd (1994) 182 CLR 211: 140, 207
Sue v Hill (1999) 163 ALR 648, 73 ALJR 1016: 205
Theophanous v Herald & Weekly Times Ltd (1994) 182 CLR 104: 121, 128
Thorpe v Commonwealth (No 3) (1997) 71 ALJR 767: 271
United States v Carolene Products 304 US 144 (1938): 233
United States v Lopez 514 US 549 (1995): 132
United States v Spock 416 F 2d 165 (1st Cir 1969): 221
Uphaus v Wyman 360 US 72 (1959): 220
Victoria v Commonwealth (1996) 187 CLR 416: 140
Wakim, Re; ex parte McNally (1999) 163 ALR 270, 73 ALJR 839: 119, 134, 138, 141, 143
Walker v New South Wales (1994) 182 CLR 45: 271
Western Australia v Commonwealth (1995) 183 CLR 373: 253
Whitney v California 274 US 357 (1927): 219
Wickard v Filburn (1942) 317 US 111: 135
Wik Peoples v Queensland (1996) 187 CLR 1: 180, 245, 265
Worcester v State of Georgia 31 US 530, 6 Pet 515 (1832): 245
Yates v United States 354 US 298 (1957): 219

TABLE OF STATUTES

Constitution: 1, 45, 47, 119ff, 164–5
- s 51(ii) (taxation power): 138
- s 51(xx) (corporations power): 138–9
- s 51(xxix) (external affairs power): 54–5, 137, 142, 212
- s 51(xxvi) (races power): 138, 251, 253, 260
- s 51(xxxv) (industrial relations power): 138, 143
- s 77: 134
- s 90 (excise): 135, 139–40
- s 92 (inter-State free trade): 127–8, 134, 135
- s 105a: 136
- s 106 (State Constitutions): 140
- s 109: 251
- s 121 (New States): 261

Commonwealth

Aboriginal and Torres Strait Islander Heritage Protection Act 1984: 251
Aboriginal Land Rights (Northern Territory) Act 1976: 247, 252
Constitution Alteration (Establishment of Republic) Bill 1999: 134, 160, 253
Constitution Alteration (Preamble) 1999: 253, 265–6
Environment, Protection and Biodiversity Conservation Act 1999: 146, 150ff, 169
Financial Agreement 1927: 136
Mutual Recognition Act 1992: 136
Native Title Act 1993: 158, 251–52, 293
Racial Discrimination Act 1975: 249, 251, 254
Re-establishment and Employment Act 1945: 182
Regional Forests Agreement Bill: 170
Trade Practices Act 1974: 293
Trans-Tasman Mutual Recognition Act 1997: 136

New South Wales

Evidence (Amendment) Act 1979: 208
Evidence (Crown Privilege) Amendment Act 1988: 208

Queensland

Freedom of Information Act 1992
- s 36: 207–8

Victoria

Audit (Amendment) Act 1997: 208

Western Australia

Aboriginal Affairs Planning Authority Act 1972: 179
Aboriginal Heritage Act 1972: 179
Wildlife Conservation Act 1950: 180

Canada

Canadian Charter of Rights and Freedoms: 198–9, 229

Columbia

Constitution (1991): 195

India

Constitution (1950): 195

Namibia

Constitution (1990): 195

Germany

Basic Law of the Federal Republic of Germany (1949): 195
Constitution (1949): 195, 201

South Africa

Black Administration Act No 37 of 1927: 271–2
Constitution of 1993 (Interim): 195, 200–3, 277
- s 22: 277
- s 25: 277
- s 28: 203
- s 96: 277

Constitution of 1996: 8, 276
- s 8: 276
- s 9: 276–7
- s 25: 202
- s 28: 201, 203
- s 36: 201, 276–7
- ss 211–212: 276
- Expropriation Act 1956: 282
- Law of Evidence Amendment Act 1988: 271–2

National Parks Act 1976: 280
- s 2b: 283
- s 8c: 282
- s 11: 281
- s 11a: 281

s 12: 281, 284
s 14: 281
s 14c: 280
s 17: 281
s 21: 281
s 29: 284
Restitution of Land Rights Act 1994: 282ff

Switzerland

Constitution
Art 25: 210

Turkey

Constitution (1982): 117

United Kingdom

Appellate Jurisdiction Act 1876: 49
Bill of Rights 1689: 177
Colonial Laws Validity Act 1865: 48, 53
Commonwealth of Australia Constitution Act 1900: 51
Crown Proceedings Act 1947: 182
Housing Act 1936: 182
Human Rights Act 1998: 188
Naturalization Act 1870: 49
Statute of Westminster 1936: 2

United States

Alaska Native Claims Settlement Act 1971 (ANCSA): 259
Alien and Sedition Acts (< 1798): 219
Alien Registration Act 54 Stat 670 (1940) (Smith Act): 219
Bill of Rights: 8, 12, 215–29
Child Online Protection Act 1998: 39
Communications Decency Act 1996: 39
Constitution: 1, 114–15, 119, 125, 127, 132
Eleventh Amendment: 132
First Amendment: 218–25
Fourteenth Amendment: 216, 231ff
Indian Appropriations Act 1871: 245
National Labor Relations Act 61 Stat 136 (1947) (Taft-Hartley Act): 219
Smith Act (Alien Registration Act, 1940): 219
Taft-Hartley Act (National Labor Relations Act, 1947): 219

International

Convention Against Torture and Other Inhuman or Degrading Treatment or Punishment 1984 (UN GA Res 39/46): 275
Convention on Biological Diversity (1993) 31 ILM 818: 30
Convention on Combating Bribery of Foreign Public Officials in International Business Transactions, Organisation for Economic Cooperation and Development: 103
Convention on the Rights of the Child (CROC): 32
Convention on Wetlands of International Importance (RAMSAR) 1971: 284
European Convention on Human Rights and Fundamental Freedoms (ECHR): 32, 189
Framework Convention on Climate Change (1992) 31 ILM 849: 30, 151
Friendly Relations Declaration (1970) (UN GA Res 2625 (XXV)): 249
International Convention for the Elimination of All Forms of Racial Discrimination (CERD) 1965: 32, 249, 251
International Covenant on Civil and Political Rights 1966 (UN GA Res 2200 A (XXI): 32, 211, 248, 270, 275
International Covenant on Economic, Social and Cultural Rights (ICESCR) 1966 (UN GA Res 2200 A (XXI)): 32, 248, 270
Montreal Protocol on Substances that Deplete the Ozone Layer (1987) 26 ILM 1541: 30, 74
Rio Declaration on the Environment and Development (1992): 30, 75
United Nations Charter: 70
United Nations draft Declaration on the Rights of Indigenous Peoples: 250, 255, 270
Universal Declaration of Human Rights (1948): 32, 70, 185

INTRODUCTION

Globalisation and Constitutionalism

Tom Round and Charles Sampford

This book began with an occasion and a need. The occasion was the 50th annual Symposium of the Fulbright Association for Australian–American Relations, hosted by the Australian Key Centre for Ethics, Law, Justice and Governance (KCELJAG),[1] and held at Brisbane from 29 September to 1 October 1999. The need was to re-examine the challenges that Australian constitutional law, theory and practice all face now that globalisation – the unimpeded movement of people, money, information and ideas across national boundaries – is eroding the sovereignty of nation-states.

Other writers have studied globalisation, but as a political, economic, social or environmental rather than a constitutional phenomenon. On the other hand, works on Australian constitutionalism tend to assume that the centuries-old tradition of national sovereignty, dating from the 1648 Treaty of Westphalia, will continue. This book may therefore be the first full-length Australian work to discuss *systematically* both topics in tandem, and to analyse how each affects the other.

Australian constitutionalism

The Australian Constitution adopts elements from both the UK and the United States. Although it has operated with a high degree of success since 1901, revisions are often advocated – usually to make it either more 'British' or more 'American'.[2] But now the Australian, British and United States Constitutions *all* face fundamental global shifts that erode some of the very basic assumptions on which those were established. This assumption, that

1 KCELJAG, established under the Australian Research Council (ARC) Research Centres Scheme, was formed from three Griffith University-based research centres – the Centre for Australian Public Sector Management (CAPSM), the Centre for Crime Policy and Public Safety (CCP&PS), and the National Institute for Law, Ethics and Public Affairs (NILEPA) – in December 1998.

2 For example, C Howard (1980) *The Constitution, Power and Politics*, Fontana/Collins; H Evans (1983) 'Questioning the Tyranny', *Quadrant*, April, 70–3.

nation-states are independent political communities in which most legal and political issues arise, and can be resolved, within the state,[3] faces strong challenges – from greater acknowledgment (in principle) of human rights and democracy as international standards; from libertarian and economic-rationalist critiques of government regulation; from globalisation of markets (itself subject to neo-protectionist criticisms); from the power of trans-national corporations; from growing appreciation of the role of civil society, particularly non-government organisations (NGOs); and from a shift from 'effective control' to 'popular consent' as the litmus of legitimate sovereignty. Although contested, these challenges suggest fresh answers – and new questions – in relation to certain long-standing Australian constitutional debates, and for contrasting differences between Australia's Constitution and the United States', and between the two countries' differing capacity to assert their sovereignty. Clearly the way that Australia (United States, Britain, Canada, South Africa, etc) relates to the outside world will have changed drastically between, say, 1959 and 2009.[4]

Themes

The chapters that follow are grouped into three parts, addressing shifts in power – along the 'horizontal', 'internal', and 'vertical' axes respectively – away from the executive governments of nation-states.[5] The first part,

3 J Austin (1832) *The Province of Jurisprudence Determined.*

4 The year 1959 was probably the high-water mark of 'Fortress Australia'. It was after the *Statute of Westminster 1936*, the appointment of Australian-born Governors-General, and the diminution of other colonial links to Whitehall; but before the advent of global economic deregulation, tariff reduction, homogenising Hollywood culture, the growth of international environmental and human rights law, Boeing 707s, and the linkage of Indigenous movements world-wide. Hilary Carey notes that Sir Robert Menzies, when elected Prime Minister in 1949, 'became the leader of a fortress Australia . . . more hostile to external influences than at any time in her history'. H Carey (1996) *Believing in Australia: A Cultural History of Religions*, Allen & Unwin, p 140.

5 It is useful to focus on national executive governments, for three reasons: first, traditionally the executive *is* the country in international law. (For example, a passport is in form a letter from one Head of State to others requesting safe passage.) Even republics like France and the United States soon decided that their President would, like a monarch, be nation's sole voice to the outside world.

Second, by definition every country has an executive (if it has any organised government at all), but not all countries have legislatures or judiciaries separate from the executive. The Hobbesian or Blackstonian view of the 'civil magistrate' as the primary organ of government, with legislators, judges and constitutions as either servants or obstacles to it, is descriptively accurate if not normatively appealing.

And third, over the last century it was assumed that executive power would continue to grow as nation-states became more unified. In Australia, the United States, Britain and other democracies, legislators have agreed to grant the executive wide financial and quasi-legislative powers, especially to deal with depressions, world wars and other crises. Paradoxically, both technological advances and the need for swift, decisive and confidential responses to international crises – factors that once helped aggrandise national

'W[h]ither National Sovereignty?', examines the declining 'horizontal' power of nation-states' executive governments relative to other nation-states, to international organisations, and to NGOs. The second, 'Constitutional Theory and Structure', considers the declining 'internal' power of nation-states' executive governments relative to their legislatures – especially Upper Houses – and to sub-national (ie, State, provincial and regional) governments. Finally, 'Individuals, Minorities, and Their Rights' discusses the declining 'vertical' power of nation-states' executive governments relative to the citizens they govern, against the rights that those citizens (as individuals, and as members of other minority groups – in particular, of Indigenous first nations) can invoke to 'trump' the policies of governing majorities.

Globalisation has many aspects, and admirers of some may well dislike others. Many of those who applaud the domestic application of international law are unenthusiastic about dismantling of trade barriers – and vice versa.[6] Some support internationalisation of law and markets alike, but a much larger bloc oppose both.[7]

Part I: W[h]ither national sovereignty?

These chapters discuss the advantages (or otherwise) of democratic governance in a world where nations – and fundamentally opposing ideologies – compete vigorously; and the nature of citizenship in a world where national borders have become porous. The Westphalian settlement held that, because aggressive wars and invasions were wrong, therefore other intrusions on a nation-state's sovereignty were impermissible too. Regarding national boundaries as 'watertight' was praised for extending the benefits of competition, as observed by Darwin and Adam Smith, to the international sphere. If countries experiment freely with different institutions, laws and *moeurs*, those deemed valuable will survive and be emulated; thus international diversity helps good eventually drive out bad. But now the effective (and ideological) hegemony of open world markets, while enforcing 'survival of the fittest' in the economic sphere, is said to erase diversity in *other* spheres – by pressuring governments everywhere to compete for the 'bottom line'; by exporting

---

(*cont*)

executive governments – now ***undermine*** that power. Developments like the Internet make national boundaries 'porous'; problems like the ozone layer make 'national sovereignty' seem irrelevant; and the sheer destructiveness and range of modern weapons makes war too horrible for rational and humane governments to embrace.

6 Two British Eurosceptics note the irony that 'those most sceptical of European federalism were often the greatest proponents of a federal Europe's purported objectives – free trade and strong defence': R Atkinson and N McWhirter (1995) *Treason at Maastricht: The Destruction of the Nation State*, Compuprint, p 117.

7 For example, supporters of Patrick Buchanan in the United States and Pauline Hanson in Australia.

a homogeneous US-derived consumer culture ('McWorld')[8] that overwhelms local communities and traditions.[9]

National sovereignty is often associated with the Hobbesian doctrine that citizens have only what rights their governments permit them.[10] But liberal democratic values also emerged in an era of 'strong states', states able to resolve almost all legal and political disputes within their own borders. Now these values – citizenship, democracy, welfare, community – lack clear application in a globalised world. Some claim this is a convenient reason for playing down those values. Charles Sampford (Chapter 1) advocates an alternative – that liberal democratic values should be neither abandoned, nor defended with outmoded weapons, but rethought. In particular, we must reconsider which institutions could uphold those values, and examine ways of building these values into such institutions through basic design, management, ethics regimes and integrity systems.

Sir Anthony Mason (Chapter 2) describes how globalisation has exposed the limitations of the doctrine of national sovereignty. Problems have proliferated which nation-states can no longer solve on their own, inducing them to waive their autonomy by embracing international standards. But globalisation and the economics of competition are in tension with liberal democratic government. The existing international decision-making infrastructure is inadequate, and so too are domestic governmental arrangements; both need renovating to overcome the democratic deficit.

Globalism includes, but is not limited to, inter- or trans-nationalism: 'There was a globalised economy between 1870 and 1914 – organised by empires rather than independent nation-states'.[11] Our 19th century ancestors considered themselves less 'Australians' or 'world citizens' than 'British subjects': despite (or because of) their proud membership in one trans-national empire, they were suspicious of other peoples. As Helen Irving notes (Chapter 3), the increasing prominence of international law is not unprecedented. Australia's understanding of sovereignty at Federation was shaped in an era when decisions in London had repercussions around the world. The Constitution itself was designed to accommodate both Imperial membership and emerging national sovereignty, as shown by its provisions on Privy Council appeals, treaty-making, and reservation and disallowance of legislation.

8 BR Barber (1995) *Jihad Versus McWorld*, Times Books.

9 G Redden (2000) '*The Beach*: A Tale of Two Freedoms', 19 *Social Alternatives* 30–4.

10 A Carty (1991) 'English Constitutional Law from a Postmodernist Perspective', in P Fitzpatrick (ed), *Dangerous Supplements: Resistance and Renewal in Jurisprudence*, Pluto Press, pp 182–206.

11 M Desai (2000) 'The Left is Wrong about Free Trade', *New Statesman and Society*, 17 April, 23–4.

Australia's original view of itself as a 'new Britannia'[12] is challenged not only by globalisation from without but also by multiculturalism, adopted as government policy, from within. Peter Wong and Violeta Brdaroska (Chapter 4) examine how Australian citizenship has evolved, and whether cultural uniformity is necessary for citizenship. They conclude that although originally focused on a particular ethnicity and culture (albeit one identified with a global empire, rather than a nation-state), Australian citizenship is now based upon multicultural national identity and an ethnically inclusive nation-state; Australia shares an evolving 'global citizenship' with the rest of the world.

If global citizenship exists, does it entail a global social contract? Aynsley Kellow (Chapter 5) analyses the 'constitution' of international civil society. If this 'constitution' enables NGOs to influence global decisions without sharing the costs such decisions impose, it is defective as allowing, in effect, 'representation without taxation'. Using environmental NGOs as an example, Kellow outlines two models that international civil society could follow. The first, 'corporatist' model involves a federation of national peak associations. The second, operating in the United Nations, requires NGOs to be transnational to gain official recognition, yet also allows creative ways of enabling groups with no transnational basis to participate in international negotiations.

Is it utopian to hope that democracy will triumph? Tom Campbell (Chapter 6) argues that two widespread beliefs – dissatisfaction with democracy, based on optimistic hope that better systems are available; and concern for democracy's health, based on pessimistic fear that global market forces leave little for voting to decide – both threaten the citizen participation on which democracy depends. So too does the application of market forces to the political sphere, by eroding barriers to the control of politics by finance.

Fortunately, democracy brings economic and military benefits. Roland Rich argues (Chapter 7) that transnational economic actors seek out comparative advantage around the globe. As well as traditional factors (skilled labour, raw materials, market proximity) a crucial new factor is emerging: good governance. This requires accountable government; the Rule of Law; transparent decision-making; a competent public service; and participation by civil society. Not only is democracy a universal value and a basic human right; we are also learning that democracy provides comparative economic advantage. Likewise, Alun Preece (Chapter 8) analyses the international 'survivability' of democracy, detecting the factors common to the seven nations that have maintained democracy continuously over the 20th century. Some of the most important advantages, like geographical isolation, are not (easily) copied by other countries' constitution-makers.

12 H McQueen (1976) *A New Britannia*, Penguin.

However, Preece concludes that democracy has survival value from a military perspective – by promoting peace among countries, it reduces the risk of foreign conquest and internal military coup.

Part II: Constitutional theory and structure

The chapters in the second part examine the 'internal' organisation of national governments, particularly relative to their legislative branch and to sub-national levels of government under the same Constitution.

In contemporary Australia, 'republicanism' means removing legal links to the British monarchy. John Williams (Chapter 9) contends that understanding of Australia's Constitution is often limited by failure to acknowledge that its clauses were animated by a definite theoretical ideal – one, moreover, with a trans-national pedigree: 'small-R' or civic republicanism, derived by Andrew Inglis Clark from the United States Constitution. Although the Australian document reads as a dry, practical framework for government, its forgotten republican heritage (expressed in its provisions for checking power and ensuring deliberation) offers ideals richer than either legalistic interpretation or bare anti-monarchism.

Although the national/regional and legislative/executive division of powers has been debated for a century or more in Australia, Britain and the United States, globalisation changes the debate radically. When national sovereignty was strong, the question was simply *which* branch or level of an all-powerful sovereign state would make a particular decision. But now that nation-states' power to regulate and tax is diminishing, *all* branches and levels of government find their writ runs less and their revenue cake is smaller. This makes the distribution of taxing powers more acute, and raises issues of whether the national and regional governments should compete for investment, or instead co-operate to ensure they all fare better in global competition.

Cheryl Saunders (Chapter 10) and Glyn Davis and Naomi Sunderland (Chapter 11) reassess the state of the Australian federal union, examining respectively its balance of legal and political powers. Saunders concludes that globalisation and other factors make it harder to allocate power legally among different governments. Decentralised federalism offers such benefits as democracy, checks and balances, economic performance, and peace for divided communities; but at the same time, centralisation promises impartiality, equality, broader vision – and, now, international competitiveness. Global standards on matters from trade practices to environmental pollution to human rights are a new, powerfully centripetal force. Saunders explores Australia's actual and potential responses to this dilemma, referring to comparative developments elsewhere, particularly United States Supreme Court judgments. Davis and Sunderland note that Australian federal practice has shifted from the balance intended by the original Constitution, as legislative and financial power gravitate to Canberra. While not necessarily bad (constitutional arrangements *should* be adaptive), this centralisation raises concerns. How can citizens and interest groups participate in policy choices if responsibility is shared among different governments? And what scope is left for local involvement if policy-making and implementation are enmeshed in complex intergovernmental and international agreements?

Since Federation, many have doubted whether Australia's powerful United States-style Senate can coexist with the Westminster tradition of executive responsibility to the Lower House. But despite its constitutional power, the Senate normally follows Westminster convention. The United States Senate has never sought to use its budget veto to remove the Executive, but asserts control over foreign relations through its power to reject treaties.

Two Australian Senators offer distinct views on the role their chamber should play in a globalised future. Helen Coonan (Chapter 12) asks whether Australia's 'Washminster' hybrid of United States and British constitutionalism is 'washed up'.[13] The Senate's powers and electoral basis make it hard for governments to ensure their legislation is passed. Many consider an unwieldy Senate, resistant to change, an institutional roadblock to Australia's progress – particularly with globalisation placing pressure on national governments. Coonan argues that an institutional overhaul is overdue, to better meet the challenges facing a modern democracy. Andrew Bartlett (Chapter 13) defends the Senate's role and record, arguing that the Senate has not been 'hostile' to the executive since 1975; that Senators review legislative proposals in good faith, seeking constructive improvements in the national interest; and that voters deliberately choose to give neither Government nor Opposition a majority of seats, instead using its proportional voting system to keep the Senate an independent watchdog.

Steven Churches argues (Chapter 14) that with Australian lower houses tightly controlled by governments (and able to veto upper houses), the function of keeping officials accountable falls by default on the judiciary. Yet our courts' reluctance to engage in 'judicial activism' means that unsound common-law rules – themselves the product of judicial creativity in centuries past – remain in force. In particular Churches critiques the traditional presumption that statutes are not intended to bind the Crown (a domestic analogy to Westphalian sovereignty), because this generates unequal laws unjustifiable in a modern democracy. He shows how constructive attention to precedents from other jurisdictions offers judges the guidance and legitimacy they need to keep government a 'public trust'.

13 The term originates in EV Thompson (1980) 'The Washminster Mutation' in P Weller and D Jaensch (eds), *Responsible Government in Australia*, Drummond.

Part III: Individuals, minorities, and their rights

The final part examines the 'internal' balance of power between a nation-state and its citizens, and the rights they can assert (as individuals or as minority groups) against their government. Too often the question of protecting rights is reduced to the single issue of importing United States-style constitutional rights. However, we must remember that the United States Bill of Rights guarantees only court-enforced restraints on governments; it was established before rights protection was considered an international issue; and before social, economic, cultural and environmental rights were articulated. Australia has pioneered alternative methods of protecting rights, particularly legislative scrutiny and specialised commissions.

Alice Tay (Chapter 15) offers a perspective drawn from her experience as both a legal academic and a practitioner in the concrete business of protecting rights, as President of Australia's Human Rights and Equal Opportunity Commission (HREOC). Tay argues that 'rights talk' is too easily cheapened when wants are presented as matters of right; and that laws are less important than supportive cultures for ensuring rights are respected in practice. Heinz Klug (Chapter 16) describes the drafting of the property rights clause in South Africa's Constitution to illustrate the complex ways in which 'universal' principles interact with the particular socio-economic, political, historical and legal cultures in which these principles find concrete application. International precedents frame the range of options available, but they must be moulded to suit domestic circumstances – and in turn, particular national adaptations provide further clarification of the principle, each offering one more interpretation of the principle's meaning.

Proposals for entrenched constitutional rights are often criticised as subordinating the sovereign people (more precisely, their elected representatives) to a wish list of 'natural rights' preferred by some elite, whether long-dead Founders or today's judges. John Pyke (Chapter 17) offers an alternative conception. Popular sovereignty (of the *whole* nation, not just of those in the majority) means one's sole 'fundamental' right is to participate equally in public decisions. Thus a Constitution should guarantee every citizen's right to vote, and ensure (eg, via petition- or convention-initiated referenda) that significant changes in public opinion are reflected in the Constitution. Voters may still decide to entrench non-participative rights, but any Bill of Rights so enacted would remain a subject of democratic debate and possible amendment. Pyke address two likely objections: that popular democracy is anachronistic in the light of countries' increasing subjection to international law and/or markets, and that populist mechanisms might be (ab)used to enact discriminatory laws with xenophobic intent – morally objectionable in any era, but especially unwise in a globalised world.

Two United States scholars are more pessimistic about the value of judicially enforced constitutional rights. However laudable its intentions, says Gerald Rosenberg (Chapter 18), the world-wide clamour for Bills of

Rights gives little critical attention to whether constitutions will achieve this goal. Supporters claim that entrenched guarantees plus independent courts will protect human rights and educate the electorate to respect them. But even in countries that (like the United States) meet these criteria, there is little evidence that this happens. Rosenberg argues that constitutional guarantees are neither necessary nor sufficient for advancing human rights. In fact, judicialisation poses risks – of giving veto power to the wealthy; of enervating public involvement in the civil liberties struggles; and of turning questions of justice into debates over abstract legal distinctions. Rosenberg suggests that ordinary legislation is a more prudent and effective way of protecting human rights.

Applying the 'dismal science' of economics to legal and political institutions, Neil Komesar (Chapter 19) offers conclusions that sound dismal to those tempted to believe that 'writing it down will make it happen'. Komesar argues that law – being the product of an adjudicative process involving complex litigation dynamics and limited physical resources – is itself subject to 'law's laws' of supply and demand. Judicial intervention is most needed when other decision-making mechanisms (political processes, markets and informal communities) work badly – but the same factors that 'clog' these other mechanisms, *numbers* and *complexity*, also make it difficult for courts to do any better. Globalisation increases complexity and therefore aggravates these problems. Defining a meaningful role for courts means facing these structural limitations.

While national sovereignty is challenged from 'above' through demands for open borders and greater international co-ordination, it also faces challenges from 'below'[14] – specifically, demands for self-determination and legal recognition for Indigenous peoples and other minorities, often inspired by international law declarations and by Indigenous campaigns in other countries. The rights of Indigenous peoples in Australia and the United States were long disregarded, but globalisation now amplifies the voice of minority groups who formerly were 'locked up' inside nation-states that claimed to 'represent' them.

Garth Nettheim (Chapter 20) contrasts Australia's and the United States' historical record of respecting Indigenous rights, and observes that Indigenous peoples around the globe share a remarkably similar agenda – particularly recognition of their equality with the non-Indigenous majority, and of their distinctive collective rights as the first peoples of their country. International human rights standards declare the rights of everyone to self-determination, to territory and culture, and to freedom from racial

---

14 '[T]he nation-state . . . is being squeezed by vice-like pressures from above and below. One set of forces seeks to transfer political power downwards from the nation-state to sub-national regions and groups. The others seek to shift power upwards from the nation to transnational agencies and organisations': A Toffler (1980) *The Third Wave*, Collins, p 322.

discrimination; while recent and evolving developments apply these standards in detail specifically to Indigenous peoples.

Peter Jull and Helena Kajlich, Bede Harris and Bertus de Villiers also examine comparative constitutional, statutory and administrative models of Indigenous policy from other nations, particularly Canada and South Africa. Jull and Kajlich (Chapter 21) examine Canada's progress and conclude that Australia may have better prospects than many today expect. They argue for a broader understanding of 'constitutional', because many options are available other than re-wording the Constitution itself; moreover, process and debate are valuable even if the document is not amended. Bede Harris (Chapter 22) notes that acknowledging the rights of its Indigenous peoples would require Australia to recognise their law, if not necessarily their sovereignty. If so, South African experience offers legal precedents for reconciling conflicts of Indigenous laws with each other, with general laws, and with fundamental human rights. Bertus de Villiers (Chapter 23) compares the systems adopted for joint management of national parks in Australia and South Africa, and their compatibility with international standards of Indigenous rights. Restoration of land rights is a key facet in the transformation of South Africa, yet its complexity is often underestimated, and the clash of interests can make the process drawn-out and emotional – especially when land claims affect national parks and other conservation areas held dear by the mainstream.

Finally, Christine Morris (Chapter 24) addresses common misunderstandings about what Aborigines and Torres Strait Islanders want when they call for recognition of their law and sovereignty. Far from demanding 'rights without responsibilities', as often caricatured, Indigenous Australians want to carry out their responsibilities under their law – a '*full* law' that acknowledges the sacred and unseen as well as the material world. To deal with globalisation, mainstream Australians could benefit by learning from pre-1788 Indigenous governance of this continent, with over 200 peoples and languages – as the United States Founders learned from the Iroquois.

Conclusion

Important questions about globalisation remain unanswered. At what crucial point (if any) did it begin? Can it be slowed, halted, or even reversed, by anything short of another dark age of technological regression? *Should* it be? These authors offer distinct perspectives, yet their chapters all confirm the rationale of this book – that globalisation requires, for better or worse, that we reconsider and re-justify our national institutions, if only to defend our decision to retain them unchanged. How fitting that a book and symposium so generously sponsored by the Commission bearing his name should seek to apply the vision of Senator James William Fulbright to the era of Albright.

Part I: W[h]ither National Sovereignty?

1

Reconceiving and Reinstitutionalising Liberal Democratic Values in a More Global World

Charles Sampford[1]

The institutional and ideological context of 'strong states'

Western legal, constitutional and political theory was built on the assumption that most polities are 'strong states' – states that largely pass Austin's test of sovereignty, according to which most legal and political issues arise, and can be resolved, within the state.[2] Such states emerged in Western Europe after the Treaty of Westphalia,[3] when the horrors of the Thirty Years War (1618–48) convinced many that the worst danger in international affairs was one state's intervention in another.[4]

Post-Westphalian states were originally highly authoritarian – justifying this by fear of internal chaos.[5] But these states were civilised by the North Atlantic Enlightenment in the 18th century and by social democracy in the 19th century. I use the phrase 'North Atlantic Enlightenment' not to flatter the Fulbright Commission, but to acknowledge that many of the institutional innovations for realising Enlightenment values were devised in

---

1 The assistance of Suzanne Condlln, Tom Round and Dr Cephas Lumina in preparing this chapter is gratefully acknowledged.

2 J Austin (1832) *The Province of Jurisprudence Determined.*

3 These saw themselves as part of an international community of nation-states. See GM Lyons and M Mastanduno (1993) 'International Intervention, State Sovereignty and the Future of International Society' 45 *International Social Science Journal* 519.

4 See A-M Slaughter Burley and C Kaysen (1993) 'Introductory Note: Emerging Norms of Justified Intervention', in LW Reed and C Kaysen (eds), *Emerging Norms of Justified Intervention: A Collection of Essays from a Project of the American Academy of Arts and Sciences*, American Academy of Arts and Sciences, p 8.

5 See, in particular, T Hobbes (1973) *Leviathan*, Dent.

America. Enlightenment liberals insisted that states justify themselves to their citizens by furthering citizens' rights and being accountable to them. Initially, the mechanism for accountability was the right to revolution, proposed by Locke and realised by the young American Republic. But revolution was a crude accountability mechanism; later developments such as checks and balances, bicameral legislatures, strengthened separation of powers, and entrenched constitutions enforced by judicial review were an improvement. Accountability was further secured through democratic legislatures and administrative law,[6] while social democrats sought to extend the range of rights the growing state guaranteed its citizens.[7] Those who did not place their hopes in revolution seemed to hold a basically 'Whig' view of history, excepting constant improvement towards a common destiny where the rights secured by liberal democratic societies were expanded and such societies covered the globe.[8] But all assumed the existence of a strong state. The debates were over *which* values should be applied to its governance – liberty, equality, rights, citizenship, democracy, community, welfare, and/or the Rule of Law.

Globalisation's challenge to liberal democratic values

A range of recent trends, popularly labelled 'globalisation',[9] have shaken the assumption that a world of strong sovereign states is the natural condition towards which humankind is evolving. The 350 years since Westphalia can be seen in a fundamentally different light. Rather than a process of politically crystallising/ossifying/entrenching distinct geographic areas as 'states', this period can now be reinterpreted as a relatively brief interlude in the

---

6 Including judicial review, freedom of information legislation, merits review tribunals, ombudsmen, investigative media and public interest litigation.

7 Political philosophy did not end its development with the US Bill of Rights; I argue elsewhere that the thinking of the last 200 years is not adequately reflected in the kinds of rights instruments drafted by today's constitutionalists. See 'The Four Dimensions of Rights' in B Galligan and C Sampford (eds) (1997) *Rethinking Human Rights*, Federation Press.

8 While sovereign states were conceived in, and initially seen as limited to, Western Europe, such statehood was extended to other states that could defend themselves and, after decolonisation, to all new states. See Lyons and Mastanduno (1993), p 521. The traditional view was that when societies reached a certain point of development they were catapulted into statehood. See J Chopra and TG Weiss, 'Sovereignty is No Longer Sacrosanct: Codifying Humanitarian Intervention' (1992) 6 *Ethics and International Affairs* 95–117.

9 For the purposes of this chapter, the definition used by Sir Anthony Mason (Chapter 2) is appropriate: 'globalisation' refers to the world systems in money, travel and communications, and the exchange of people, data and ideas. World systems, working through and across nation-states, are growing in importance and already a primary influence in every university. In fact universities are one of the main 'carriers' of globalisation.

development of political *communities* and political *institutions*. Sovereign nation-states are not the endpoint of constitutional development, merely a transitory phase.[10]

The political and economic forces of 'globalisation' undermine the assumption of the strong state as the background for political debates over balancing and realising liberal democratic values. Both supporters and opponents of globalisation query the continuing relevance of state-based theories and values. These values were formed in and for strong states. Citizenship, democracy, welfare, and community have clear meaning *within* sovereign states but lack apparent application in a broader, more diffuse, globalised world. The institutions that sustain, promote and realise those values are very much state-based. The rights, duties and 'sense of belonging' that citizenship carries are attached to state institutions. Democracy is realised through citizen participation in the national and sub-national legislatures of nation-states – and loses mileage if the real power and range of choice open to those legislatures is restricted.[11] Welfare rights like education and healthcare are only implemented through the institutions of strong, sovereign (and wealthy) states – and the capacity of even these institutions to do so is increasingly questioned.[12]

There have been two kinds of responses to such globalisation, from the libertarian Right and the traditional Left:

- The libertarian Right treats the decline of state institutions is a convenient excuse for limiting or playing down liberal democratic values. It sheds crocodile tears for the claimed demise of values that it always treated as inconveniences to the maximisation of individual wealth by the already wealthy.
- The traditional Left argues for protecting and bolstering strong sovereign states on the basis that only these can deliver those rights that cost money.

KCELJAG's goal

The Key Centre for Ethics, Law, Justice and Governance (KCELJAG) is founded on the view that the values of liberal democracy should be re-

10 SD Krasner (1995) 'Sovereignty and Intervention', in GM Lyons and M Mastanduno (eds), *Beyond Westphalia? State Sovereignty and International Intervention*, Johns Hopkins University Press, p 233.

11 PG Cerny, 'Globalisation and Other Stories: The Search for a New Paradigm for International Relations' (1996) 4 *International Journal* 620.

12 Even if values become impossible, or virtually impossible, to realise, this does not eliminate their worth (at least not in my reading of the facts/values relationship). However, if such values were *impossible* to achieve, it would have significant consequences for our actions on the values we should be *next* attempting to realise, and the balances we make between those values and their competitors.

thought – rather than abandoned using globalisation as a pretext, or defended by dogged attempt to recreate the strong states of the past. KCELJAG does not envisage the end of state-based institutions; these will continue to play important roles in realising liberal democratic values. But their role will be shared with government, corporate and non-government institutions at global, regional, national, and sub-national levels. As long as other institutions supporting liberal democratic values remain weak, state-based institutions will play a significant role.

Most Enlightenment values were claims for *all* human beings. The French Assembly declared 'the rights of *man*'; the United States Declaration of Independence found it 'self-evident' that '*all men* are created equal'.[13] But despite such universal claims, the institutions these states created were devoted exclusively to providing rights to their own citizens. A more globalised political philosophy could enable these values to be applied globally. The Westphalian pillars of sovereignty and non-intervention protected fledging liberal democracies from being crushed by authoritarian neighbours.[14] But the doctrine of sovereignty also erected barriers against liberal democratic values spreading to neighbouring states, whose citizens often had great need of them. KCELJAG's research efforts are premised on the hope that globalisation clears the way for wider application of liberty, rights, equality, democracy, citizenship and the Rule of Law. KCELJAG aims to contribute to national and international discussion on these issues, through a four-stage process:

(1) examining the challenges globalisation presents to the values of liberal democracy;

(2) considering how these values could be redefined for a world largely without strong states;

(3) assessing which institutions (local, national, regional and global) can realise these values (this inevitably raises questions of how such institutions will be funded); and

(4) analysing the means by which these values can be built into those institutions – through basic design, management, ethics regimes and integrity systems.[15]

Not world government

To be effective, reconceived liberal democratic values need institutions to support them. But these institutions should not be expected to mean a

13 Of course, today we would say all 'humans' or 'persons', but 'all men' was radically egalitarian for the 18th century.

14 Compare Alun Preece (Chapter 8).

15 This would involve examining *seriatim* and collectively the various techniques available for public governance (including contract, reward, punishment, direct control, budgetary or substantive approval, merits or process review) at a theoretical and practical level.

'world government'. To assume that creating a larger, global 'strong state' will solve the problems globalisation presents for *existing* strong states misses the point – the decline of sovereignty. Such a view remains stuck in the assumptions held during the period of strong states. More likely to emerge is a world where institutions cross previous national boundaries and, unlike sovereign states, do *not* claim jurisdiction over all areas of life.

The strong sovereign state was a Westphalian solution to the strife that preceded it. The solution to the problems of post-Westphalian strong states is unlikely to be the creation of a new, ever-more-encompassing version of the same kind of institution.[16] That would be to see the problems of post-Westphalian states as soluble by more and larger of the same.

Not simply universal adoption of 'Western', American (or Australian) values

The Cold War's end saw some unedifying bouts of triumphalism. Communism's collapse was taken as a vindication of what were claimed to be 'Western values', and the future was assumed to mean all countries copying these values. I say 'claimed' because the triumphalists tended to be those who advocated the more libertarian versions of capitalism, not the American liberals and European social democrats who had done so much to civilise capitalism and so help to survive. The triumphalists ignored many long-standing (and unanswered) criticisms of libertarian capitalism.[17] Communism was a failed response to those criticisms. American 'liberalism' and European social democracy have made more successful, although still tentative, contributions.

I am a universalist, in the sense that the process envisaged through KCELJAG's work involves the pursuit of values that can offer answers to the universal problems of human society as this becomes more globalised. I do not believe the answers will be culturally specific. Nor do I believe the sources of those answers will come from one single culture. I am absolutely certain that no culture currently provides all the answers. The values of the Enlightenment, as challenged, modified and developed by 250 years of legal,

16 This prediction could be incorrect. I am aware that the European Union (EU) was seen by some of its founders as a future European federation, while others saw it as having more narrow goals (and a few still think of it in narrower terms). It is possible that the idealism of global governance will prove successful and I will ruefully look back on my comments as the early musings of a global sceptic, rivalling the pronouncements of the Eurosceptics (see my comments above). However, it is my profound impression that the world is moving beyond Westphalian strong states that suggests to me that the future does not lie in an enlarged version of the past. See also Krasner (1995), p 235.

17 For example the *Reader's Digest* recently urged Russians not to reject capitalism merely because the first capitalists they encountered were mafias and local warlords. It is unlikely that the *Digest* would advocate further experiments with 'Socialism' on the ground that Stalin and Brezhnev are not representative of Socialists generally.

political and social philosophy, suggest an excellent starting point – not least because the Enlightenment, too, witnessed a fundamental shift in the relationship between state and citizen. Rather than concentrating on the duties of subject to sovereign, it emphasised that public institutions must be justified on the basis of how they serve the citizens. The North Atlantic Enlightenment held no monopoly on truth, but was an important step forward in the universal struggle to improve the human condition.

What we need now is an international search for new and revised values, a search to which everyone can contribute and in which everyone can learn from the ideas and failures of others. As in so many other areas, any claim to universality must be accompanied by a surrender to it.

The global search for answers will draw on different cultures' attempts to find answers to problems of the human condition. Within each culture, the process will begin by exploring its own culturally specific values, ideals, concepts and stories as ways by which that culture has addressed those problems. These can then be compared to the values, ideals, concepts and stories in other cultures, so that we can appreciate similarities and differences. Different cultures have much to learn from each other. For example, Anglo-American ideology has been strong on emphasising the importance of individuals but has tended to be weak on understanding institutions. Institutions are often reduced to matrices of interpersonal contracts, rather than viewed as organic wholes. This focus on individuals leads to myopia, even hostility, towards institutions – particularly 'public' ones. European and Asian cultures seem (to borrow Komesar's phrase) to 'take institutions [more] seriously', and to have a sounder understanding of their nature.[18]

Examples like this help us assess the significance of the Enlightenment. It certainly, and rightly, placed the individual at the centre of legal and political philosophy. Its fundamental point was that institutions should serve individuals, not vice versa. This does not mean institutions should be abandoned, but that the criterion for justifying them should be reconceived – as means of protecting, realising and furthering individual human rights.

Reinventing and recombining values

As mentioned, the values of liberal democracy were formed in and for strong states. Although these values were often based on long-standing ideals found in a wide variety of cultures, local contexts affected the ways in which those ideals were expressed, combined and reconceived as liberal democratic values[19] (for example, the direct democracy of Athens gave way to the representative democracy in modern states). Constitutional values for a more globalised world may be variations on the values of citizenship,

---

18 NK Komesar 'Taking Institutions Seriously: Introduction to a Strategy for Constitutional Analysis' (1984) 51 *University of Chicago Law Review* 366; cf Christine Morris (Chapter 25).

19 Cf Heinz Klug (Chapter 17).

democracy and welfare – or they might also be recombined into new values, within new concepts that speak more effectively to the problems of globalisation.[20] Sometimes the values will not be recombined, but reinvented in a different form that reveals more general principles of which liberal democratic values were merely one contemporary form. I will take one example – citizenship.

Post-Westphalian authoritarian states saw individuals as subjects. The Transatlantic Enlightenment saw them as citizens. What was new was the idea that institutions such as the state existed to serve individuals rather than the individual existing to serve the state. The concept of citizenship built upon earlier pre-Enlightenment values of family, tribe and ethnic group. At each stage of human development, membership in the most socially and economically powerful groups has been seen as a great advantage, and exclusion from such groups as a heavy punishment (eg, being disowned by family, expelled from the tribe or outlawed from the village). The Enlightenment elevated membership in the state, then the most significant and powerful social group. But now, as the sovereign state wanes in social significance, other memberships become more crucial – including those of work. The 'real' value may be the right to participate in the benefits of social life in the most significant social groupings, whatever forms these take.

The ever-present danger of regression

The hope behind KCELJAG's project is that the challenges of globalisation will be met with new values, informing new institutions, which together can civilise a world of weakened states – just as the North Atlantic Enlightenment helped civilise the absolutist states of post-Westphalian Europe. But this is by no means guaranteed. If globalisation produces destabilisation,[21] such benign results are unlikely. There are risks that, if Enlightenment ideals break down, instead of advancing beyond them societies may revert to *pre*-Enlightenment values such as tribal exclusivity, ethnic supremacy and religious fanaticism.[22]

If society breaks down, people will not buy books like this, or engage in sincere and open debate about new ideas for global society; they will seek refuge in some existing idea that seems to make sense. This could be extremist versions of libertarian capitalism (to which some Eastern European nations were briefly attracted, believing that the opposite of whatever they

20 Cf R Holton (1998) *Globalisation and the Nation-State*, Macmillan, p 43, who believes that the values can be combined but does not advocate it.

21 I sometimes wonder if globalisation is actually shorthand for 'global destabilisation'!

22 'People become "nationalistic" when they are afraid; when the only answer to the question "Who will protect me now?" becomes "my own people"'. M Ignatieff (1998) *The Warrior's Honor: Ethnic War and the Modern Conscience*, Chatto and Windus, p 45.

endured under Stalinism must be best).[23] It might be a half-baked version of American capitalism gleaned from soap operas broadcast by the former regime in the belief that such patent nonsense cannot affect people's intellects.[24] But it is more likely to be the revival of some other, older, more deeply rooted ideal, given ever more destructive power by modern technology. In the Balkans and some African countries, it has been ethnic supremacy or tribal domination – values especially damaging to multi-ethnic communities. In Afghanistan, Sudan, Timor and, to a lesser extent, in the Balkans, it has been religious intolerance. In some cases, the breakdown of sovereign states has seen a reversion to the worst features of tribalism and violence amplified by modern technology.[25] If countries in crisis cannot afford rational discussion of new ideas and values, the time for more fortunate societies to do so is now.

This problem is not confined to newly disintegrating states in the developing world. The West's response to the end of the Cold War *might* have been to transcend the competing global ideologies of capitalism and Communism; but the West has reverted to earlier ideals of global competition – what JK Galbraith calls 'primitive capitalism'[26] – instead of learning from the miseries generated by these ideologies, or developing new ideas about how countries can relate to one another, such as those expounded in the *Brandt Report*.[27]

A fundamental shift in the basis of constitutional legitimacy

The constitutional value most under threat is, of course, sovereignty itself. Its effect is weakened as globalisation ensures that forces outside the state's borders influence, and sometimes control, what goes on inside them. But

23 See C Sampford (1991) 'Dworkin's Claim to a Socialist Inheritance' 16 *Bulletin of the Australian Society of Legal Philosophy* 37, in which I predicted that this infatuation would be short-lived.

24 Ceausescu's regime reportedly screened old episodes of *Dallas* and *Dynasty* in the hope these would either be innocuous, or would show Romanians the evils of capitalism. However, it is reported, they were the most popular shows on television and led many to fall in love with Western capitalism.

25 Not only modern weapons, but also modern communications. Even though most of the Rwandan killings were by machete, the Hutu Government-run radio stations orchestrated the genocide of the Tutsis.

26 And what I have called 'vulgar capitalism': C Sampford (1991) 'Coups d'État and Law' in E Attwooll (ed) *Shaping Revolution*, Aberdeen University Press.

27 Note that the last two sets of revolutionary ideals – capitalism and Socialism – have been global; Independent Commission on International Development Issues (Chair: W Brandt) (1980) *North–South: A Programme for Survival* (The Brandt Report), MIT Press. The failure of the latter has amounted to a 'revolution' in the 16th century sense. We need a third set of revolutionary ideals – ideals that transcend Socialism, not retreat from it to the era that preceded Socialism with all the faults that spawned it.

sovereignty and its concomitant ban on intervention are also being challenged normatively. Dating from the Westphalian era, modern ideas of sovereignty are a century older than the Enlightenment. What would most erode sovereignty and its associated taboo against intervention would be the whole-hearted implementation of Enlightenment values.[28]

In domestic law and political theory, there has been a fundamental shift in the basis of political legitimacy – from what I call 'the prior successful use of force' to 'the consent of the governed' (a shift that was, of course, impelled by the North Atlantic Enlightenment). That shift occurred first in the United States and France, but is now almost universally acknowledged as a matter of domestic constitutional law and theory. International law, however, has continued to recognise states and governments solely by the criterion of who exercises effective political control over defined territories. Even if a democratically elected government is overturned by a *coup d'état*, the new regime's ambassadors are accredited by foreign powers, and allowed to take that country's seat at the United Nations and other international forums. This glaring inconsistency has been a constant feature of democratic nations and has caused much tension and soul-searching.

This inconsistency arises because the Enlightenment essentially concerned the internal workings of states, not their external relations. *It was addressed to the domestic aspects of sovereignty, not its international dimensions.* International law is still based on ideas of sovereignty formed a century before the Enlightenment. Enlightenment values were not addressed to international law or the external elements of sovereignty, and there have only been half-hearted attempts to do this since.

This inconsistency will not be sustainable in the medium term. Democracy enjoys almost universal popularity; communications are improving; sovereign states are weakening; international law and its agencies are gaining strength. My (very optimistic) prediction is that, within 10 to 20 years, 'prior successful use of force' will be as illegitimate as a claim to sovereignty under international law as it is today under the domestic constitutional law of democracies. Within two decades, it will be impracticable for authoritarians to overthrow democratic regimes because – they will be denied international recognition and, more tentatively, because the intervention of other states will be unequivocally legitimate.

A paradigm shift

The shift in domestic constitutional legitimacy to 'consent of the governed' reverses the direction of power, authority and accountability. Power is no longer seen as emanating from the all-powerful 'sovereign' but, instead, stems from the consent of the people. Domestically, this puts the people at the centre of constitutional jurisprudence. The traditional jurisprudential

---

28 Krasner (1995), p 247.

question about which leaders the people 'habitually obey' is reversed: instead, we ask 'Whom do the political leaders represent?' Internationally, this shift does not merely change the direction of authority and accountability; it also affects *which* units are recognised. Instead of asking 'Who habitually obeys them?', regimes will be acknowledged on the basis of 'To whom they are accountable?'

Full acceptance of this principle means a government only 'represents' internationally those whose consent it has sought and gained. This means little change for democratic regimes. But for undemocratic regimes, it means the government is acknowledged as 'representing' *only* those whose consent it has sought – be this a party, an ethnic group, a restricted electorate, or an officer corps. This allows undemocratic regimes to be recognised as representing one or some groups within their states' geographical area, and as having current capacity to dominate other groups. However, a government that has not sought a mandate from a particular group of its inhabitants is not accepted as speaking for the excluded group.

This leaves obvious lacunae for those whose consent the government has not sought. It opens the way for others to claim to represent them instead. In some cases, such credentials would be easily established. Where an elected government is ousted by a military coup, members of that government (or their accredited representatives) still at large would speak for that government and the majority who elected it.[29] Recent examples include Timoci Bavadra in Fiji (1987), Aung San Suu Kyi in Burma (1990) and Jean-Bertrand Aristide in Haiti (1991). The denial of recognition to Haiti's Cedras coup, and Aristide's eventual restoration, represented an enormous step forward. But the fact that SLORC and Sitiveni Rabuka were recognised by the international community for most purposes suggests that the shift described here is only just beginning. I would like to believe that Haiti in 1991 represented a sea-change, indicating that future coups will be resisted in similar fashion, but I must concede that Petersen's analysis based on states' interests is more plausible.[30]

Of course, in most cases, it is not nearly so clear who has the right to speak for those whose consent the government has not sought. It is the nature of dictatorships and oligarchies to use force to suppress any processes by which such credentials could be established. There are often a number of voices claiming to speak for the unrepresented, in a number of

---

29 In my earlier work on coups, I suggested that democratic governments should have clearly stated lines of authority in the case of coups to ensure that it is clear who speaks for them, even if the key leaders have been killed or imprisoned. See Sampford (1991) 'Coups d'État and Law', p 161; and C Sampford 'Coups d'État and Law' (1989) 13 *Bulletin of the Australian Society of Legal Philosophy* 253. These arguments will be expanded in my book *Dare to Call it Treason* (Dartmouth, forthcoming in 2001).

30 See FJ Petersen (1998) 'The Façade of Humanitarian Intervention for Human Rights in a Community of Sovereign Nations' 12 *Arizona Journal of International and Comparative Law* 871.

overlapping ways. Sometimes there is one body that represents the bulk of the people in one sphere of life, which comes to speak for most spheres – such as the Catholic Church in Communist Poland and COSATU in South Africa. This means that the excluded may not speak with a clear, unified voice. But that is no reason for not listening to them. In particular, those who want to suppress those voices have no standing to argue that lack of volume or clarity should count against those voices that can still be heard.

Consequences of this paradigm shift

This paradigm shift has fundamental consequences for the nature, content and practice of international law. As argued above, it might amount to nothing less than a new 'international Enlightenment' to civilise the institutions of global capitalism, just as the original Enlightenment civilised the post-Westphalian authoritarian state. It will lead to a whole new jurisprudence and political philosophy, with particular concrete ramifications in the following seven areas:

Who is liable for 'sovereign debt'?

At present, international legal personality gives those in power the right to contract on behalf of their state and the people within its territory. Even if a contract is beyond the rulers' legal power – even if it is entered into corruptly, and its benefits are corruptly expropriated – it still binds those rulers' successors. Too often sovereign debt is incurred by corrupt regimes, and its proceeds spirited away to bank accounts in the developed world. When a democratic regime replaces the former rulers, it must repay the debt to the lenders, while the corrupt former leaders enjoy the loan funds from the comfort and security of their First World exile.

The paradigm shift would fundamentally change the dynamics of such arrangements. If a government is not accountable to all of its citizens, then the people are not accountable for that government's actions. When the international debt collectors call, the people can legitimately claim: 'You did not contract with us; you contracted with them. Go recover your funds from those who borrowed them.' They could insist on the principle that governments cannot commit those whose consent they do not sought and to whom they are not accountable.[31]

---

31 '"Nicaragua" did not borrow the money; rather, some people within the Nicaraguan... dictatorship borrowed it, under the cloak of the legal personality of the state.... The people effectively called upon to repay the debts of Iraq incurred for military spending under Saddam Hussein again are the people who received no gain and much pain from the expenditure'. W Mansell, B Meteyard and A Thomson (1995) *A Critical Introduction to Law*, Cavendish, pp 126–8. By the same principle, an independent East Timor would be entitled to renegotiate the 1989 Timor Gap treaty: see D Lague (2000) 'Timor Call to Review Oil Treaty', *Sydney Morning Herald*, 8 May.

This would make international law more like domestic law. If hoodlums take over a house and hold the lawful owners in terror, they commit serious offences. If they seek to borrow from a bank on the security of the house, the loan is not only unenforceable against the owners, the bank is also guilty of some serious conspiracy offences – especially if they know or suspect the money is used to buy guns to terrorise the occupants. Far from recouping their loans from the liberated occupants, such banks would face enormous damages claims, prison sentences and almost certain closure. I am not suggesting that international bankers should suffer these particular penalties, but rather that, as a matter of international law, there should be no obligation on the new government to repay the loan. The inevitable consequence of this – that loan funds would dry up except for democracies, rendering dictatorial regimes economically non-viable – is fully intended!

Cheating does not count

In this and in all other matters, the government's title to claim to represent a group and to make commitments in their name would depend on its having gained that group's consent. Making recognition depend on such consent makes it the government's interest to gain it. It also has the excellent side-effect of ensuring that *cheating does not count.* Rigging elections would not be a clever strategy, but would merely ensure that those who do it cannot gain the consent that is the condition precedent of representing a people in the international community.[32] If they fail to gain the support of the people, they forfeit any right to speak for them, and others may claim that right.

There is a clear parallel in contract law. If you obtained the other party's consent by fraud or coercion, the contract is void. Indeed, it is even worse for the election-rigger. If, despite the election rigging, interference or intimidation, the other side wins, they are entitled to count the election result in their favour (as in East Timor (1999) where 78.5 per cent voted for independence despite systematic terror by Indonesian-funded militia). Again, this has a parallel in contract law: the *victim* may still enforce a contract against a party engaging in misleading and deceptive conduct.

Delegation of power

Once governments are seen as representatives of those whose consent they obtain, an entirely new question arises: *What powers have the people consented to delegate to their representatives?* To a constitutional lawyer, this issue is strangely

32 This assumes minimum standards for fair elections, currently being drafted for UN-supervised elections. These minimum standards could be developed in a number of ways: by practice developed in UN-supervised elections; by international NGOs like the Stockholm-based International Institute for Democracy and Electoral Assistance (IDEA); by formation of a 'Democratic League' with high membership standards, and; ultimately, embodiment in international law by such authoritative bodies as the UN General Assembly and the International Court of Justice.

absent from much international law. One of the core elements of constitutionalism is that a public body (unlike a private person) needs constitutional authorisation for every action. This is reinforced by the 'closure rule' in public law: 'whatever is not permitted is prohibited'. Domestically, this principle is often reconciled with sovereignty by viewing the people as sovereign: the only power a public body has is whatever has been specifically authorised by the constitution, which in turn is agreed (or at least accepted) by the sovereign people. Raising such questions means the international community would have to take domestic constitutions seriously. A state's international representatives would be seen as just that: representatives, with only those powers they have been given. In some cases, different constitutionally endorsed bodies might be authorised to exercise different elements of the people's sovereign power.

Towards the unification of public law with public international law

Once such issues are taken seriously in international law, public (ie, constitutional and administrative) domestic law and public international law will begin to fuse, methodologically and doctrinally. Methodologically, the question of what powers public bodies exercise will become a matter of international as well as domestic constitutional law. This will automatically introduce critical elements of domestic constitutional content and doctrine into international law.

In the other direction, the actual limitations on state power caused by globalisation and the increasing domestic reach of treaties will mean that international doctrine and methodology will infuse domestic law in all forms. As the walls between states break down, so will the walls between domestic public law and public international law.

By the same token, the growing reach of international business and the growing recognition of international agencies means that public and private international law will be increasingly linked. Domestic corporate law (which elsewhere I have termed the 'constitutional and administrative law of corporations')[33] will be at least linked, and probably fused, with the new emerging global public law.

Elimination of the conflict between sovereignty and human rights

Reconceiving the basis of international constitutional legitimacy this way eliminates most of the conflict between sovereignty and protection of human rights.[34] Such conflict is always possible when the international com-

33 See C Sampford (1992) 'Law, Institutions and the Public/Private Divide' 20 *Federal Law Review* 185.

34 This does not deal with problems of human rights abuses by democratic states.

munity recognises, as sovereign, any group gaining effective political control over a territory through 'prior successful use of force'. This formula does not rule out the risk that such force might be used to violate the human rights of excluded groups. If anything, it positively *encourages* rights abuses by rewarding the successful use of force to secure dominion over a country. It rewards those who mount anti-democratic coups. It rewards those who rig elections. It rewards those who intimidate the population, or who rule through and for one ethnic or social group against others.[35]

But if sovereignty is seen as binding only those to whom the sovereign power is democratically accountable, this gives members of any group over which such sovereignty is asserted a right to democratic participation. It also accords a right to those who have been excluded to democratic participation in that or another state. Sovereignty is no longer the recognition of a power over a people but the collective right of a people to participate in, and benefit from, an independent political community, participating as an equal in the community of nations. To put it another way, (liberal democratic) sovereignty *becomes* a human right.[36]

International legal personality

The fact that the group in power only 'represents' those whose consent it seeks has important consequences for international legal personality. Originally, only states had such personality. But the paradigm shift outlined here would change this. Any excluded groups whose consent is not sought have a right to demand full participation in the processes of seeking consent and ensuring accountability. If that right is denied, the group in power has no right to represent them in the international community. The excluded group has the right to fill this gap through 'self-help', which gives those representing that group a particularly important right to be heard. Such representatives must be accorded a form of international legal personality. If the group in power suppresses such groups, their right to be heard is not extinguished; individual members of the group retain it. Any attempt to silence the

35 This reconception overcomes the problem Steven David observes. Although some elites in developing countries represent little more than themselves, use state power for their own ends and interests, and have come to power by illegitimate means (including foreign support), they enjoy all the benefits of sovereignty, including a veto over intervention. SR David (1987) *Third World Coups d'État and International Security*, Johns Hopkins University Press, pp 4–6.

36 Krasner (1995), p 231. Some would leave this as a collective right of the people. Others might like to conceive it in terms of individual rights – as a right of all persons to take part in a sovereign government, to be a part of the group to whom a government is accountable: see C Sampford (1997) 'The Four Dimensions of Rights and Their Means of Protection', in B Galligan and C Sampford (eds), *Rethinking Human Rights*, Federation Press; cf John Pyke (Chapter 18). Either way, the point is that every human being on the planet has the right to participate in such a community and denying that right is a violation of human rights.

group's representatives would only have the effect of giving every member of the excluded group a right to be heard in international forums.[37]

Legitimating intervention in certain cases

If governments represent only those whose consent they have sought, preventing them oppressing those whose consent they have *not* sought ceases to count as 'intervention' in the traditional sense. Those who protect the oppressed group are not interfering in the internal workings of a sovereign territory or trying to disrupt the integrity of a sovereign state. Instead they are assisting in a conflict between international legal entities. What would previously have been called 'intervention' takes on a different character, more like action taken to assist the self-defence of a sovereign government. It might still be called 'intervention', as it will still involve 'coming between' other person, but this label will lose its normative stigma.

Of course, this does not mean that all such 'interventions' will be justified. Key questions remain: when is intervention justified? Who may intervene? What processes should be required before intervention can be justified? But these are questions for another time and place.[38]

Conclusion

I have referred to the 'North Atlantic Enlightenment'. This is not just in deference to the fact that the paper on which this chapter is based was delivered to a Symposium in the memory of United States Senator Fulbright. The words of the North Atlantic Enlightenment ring out over the centuries as among the finest statements of human aspiration in any language. There have been many echoes and restatements by Abraham Lincoln, Woodrow Wilson, Franklin Roosevelt, Earl Warren, John Kennedy, Martin Luther King – not to mention Bill Clinton's Normandy speech on 6 June 1994.

But its moral achievement was not limited to articulating values. Americans in particular were aware of the temptations of power. They did not rely simply on training public officials to avoid those temptations. Saints are in short supply, and no training program can ever deliver enough saints to fulfil all the important public positions of a modern liberal democracy. They realised, better than most, that the point is to design institutions that do not need saints to run them. The United States Founders sought to

37 The US Declaration of Independence similarly asserts that, if legislatures are dissolved without new elections following, 'the Legislative Powers, incapable of Annihilation' thereby return 'to the People at large'.

38 These were the central issues canvassed in a paper delivered to the final plenary session of the World Congress of Legal and Social Philosophy in New York (29 June 1999). They will be developed in a book forthcoming in 2001.

establish checks to prevent the abuse of power, rather than trying to ensure its saintly exercise.

We are now witnessing a sea-change as fundamental as that which followed the Treaty of Westphalia. The forces of globalisation are fundamentally weakening the strong sovereign states that were civilised by the North Atlantic Enlightenment. We need a new 'Global Enlightenment' to avoid the dangers and to crystallise the opportunities of globalisation. This new enlightenment must involve the reconceiving of liberal democratic values for a more global world and the development of institutions that can realise those values.

2

The Decline of Sovereignty

Problems for Democratic Government

Sir Anthony Mason

Introduction

My purpose in this address is to sketch the developments which have given rise to globalisation, to describe the effect which it has had on national sovereignty and autonomy and to present the problems which thereby arise for democratic government and constitutionalism.

Globalisation

The term 'globalisation' is generally used to denote the greater interconnection or integration between different societies or activities in different parts of the world such that an effect or activity in one part of the world is more likely to have an effect in another part of the world. Globalisation is not new in the sense that the history of humanity records a steady, even if interrupted, progress along a globalised path. What is remarkable is the speed of that progress in very recent years and how it now extends to the totality of our activities and interests.

Very little of what we do is untouched by the phenomenon of globalisation. Communication, opinion, information, learning, culture, economics, trade, finance, politics and human rights are in the process of transformation. So much so that our patterns of thought are already changing from a national perspective to an international perspective.

What happens in one part of the world has repercussions elsewhere – a comment by Alan Greenspan of the Federal Reserve Bank in Washington can, within hours, generate a rise or fall on the Australian Stock Exchange. The television screen brings us close together as citizens of an instant world, making us eyewitness observers of the Kosovo tragedy, the India-Pakistan conflict and the earthquake in Turkey, thereby creating a public opinion that transcends national boundaries. By courtesy of the television screen, CNN's recycled news programs take us on our daily round from an interview with President Clinton in the White House, on to an encounter with President Putin in Moscow and then to a confrontation in Aceh or East Timor.

Globalisation, as we know it, is the product of a variety of factors. First and foremost globalisation is an economic process. It has created:

> permissive conditions for a range of distinct but inter-twined structural trends – that is, it expands the playing field within which different market actors and firms interact. It transforms the international economy from one made up of holistic national economies interacting on the basis of *national* 'comparative advantage' into one in which a variety of '*competitive* advantages' are created in ways which are not dependent on the nation-state as social, economic and/or political unit.[1]

Globalisation reflects the triumph of the philosophy or ideology of economic rationalism, the theory that society and its institutions must be so ordered as to generate the most efficient economic outcomes. Economic rationalism sees as one of its major goals the establishment of an integrated world economy, including world markets. To that end, barriers to free trade, such as quotas, duties and colourable quarantine, health and safety requirements, restrictions on the flow of capital and fixed exchange rates, as well as subsidies for home production, are to be eliminated.

The rise of the doctrine of economic rationalism has had a devastating impact on national sovereignty. Economic rationalism, with its emphasis on free trade and freedom of competition, with its hostility to the welfare state and monolithic trade unionism, created a climate of thought in which the new technological advances could be fully exploited. Economic rationalism has succeeded in promoting the desirability, indeed the inevitability, of a world market. Economic rationalism has also played a part in the elimination of tariff barriers, though significant elements of protectionism remain in the world's largest economies. At the same time fixed currency rates have been replaced by floating exchange rates which are vulnerable to the hazards of the markets. The markets can be manipulated by financial operators, corporations and funds whose resources exceed those of many nation-states. The dismantling and privatisation of State owned monopolies have resulted in many instances in the foreign ownership of utilities by multi-national corporations.

The creation of a world market has been driven by the United States, the world's most powerful economy. One example is the Trade-Related Aspects of Intellectual Property Rights (TRIPS) Agreement reached at Marrakesh in 1994. It was the outcome of a United States initiative. By that Agreement, developing countries traded off increased protection for the intellectual property rights of owners in the United States for greater access to markets for primary products. And it has been said that 'At least on the

---

1 PG Cerny (1996) 'Globalisation and Other Stories: The Search for a New Paradigm of International Relations' 51 *International Journal* 617 at 626.

money markets, globalisation so far means little more than the Americanisation of the world'.[2]

A second factor has been the technological revolution and the consequences it has brought in its train. Information technology, through the Internet and other means, has enabled electronic communication to take place instantly throughout the world across national boundaries. Increasingly, transactions and communications, commercial and non-commercial, pay little regard to national boundaries. These developments have enabled multi-national corporations to so organise their activities that they can harness capital, technology, materials and labour at locations throughout the world. In this way, they can locate units of production in jurisdictions where costs are low and governments are willing to provide them with infrastructure and tax advantages.

The capacity of electronic communication to generate a visual signal from anywhere to everywhere has had wide-ranging consequences not only for international commerce and finance but also for the transmission of news, information and opinion around the world. We think in terms of global images. The very clothes we wear are dominated by worldwide designer labels. Ermenegildo Zegna and Gianni Versace are names that dog our every footstep in high-class shopping malls. More down-market, the food we eat is offered by McDonald's and the beverage we drink is produced by Coca-Cola. So McLuhan's prediction of the global village may be transformed into reality.

A third factor has been the internationalisation of politics and the near-universal acceptance of human rights protection. On the one hand, the emergence of world opinion, in which the television screen has played a prominent role, has been instrumental in the development of world politics. The same can be said for human rights. The television footage from Kosovo, East Timor, Sri Lanka and Africa has given great momentum to human rights protection. On the other hand, there is a tension between economic rationalism and human rights. The paramountcy of efficient outcomes promoted by economic rationalism, which has led to an increasing gulf between rich and poor and rich and poor nations, is at odds with the protection of human rights.

A fourth factor, which is an aspect or offshoot of the economic process, is that nation-states now compete with each other for investment. As investment looks for low tax regimes, there is worldwide pressure to lower taxes. The proposal to reduce capital gains tax in Australia is put forward as necessary to attract foreign investment. Similar comments have been made in support of the goods and services tax. Uniformity in approach to taxation is a characteristic rather than a cause of globalisation.

---

2 H-P Martin and H Schumann (1997) *The Global Trap*, Pluto Press, p 74.

A final factor has been the emergence of a major threat to the world environment as a consequence of pollution, arising mainly from industrialisation and use of chemicals and fertilisers.[3] Pollution has adversely affected not only seas, rivers and waterways, but also the air and the atmosphere. The depletion of the ozone layer is a matter of major concern, as is the prospect of global warming.

The threat to the environment is a striking example of the problems that confront the modern world because it is a problem that requires an international solution, indeed a solution in which the entire world participates. Although progress has been slow, we have seen a number of international developments on the environment. They include the 1987 Montreal Protocol on Substances that Deplete the Ozone Layer,[4] the 1992 Rio Declaration on the Environment and Development, the Convention on Biological Diversity,[5] the Framework Convention on Climate Change,[6] the establishment of the Commission on Sustainable Development and the recent Kyoto Conference.

Other illustrations of problems incapable of a national solution are cross-border and international criminal conduct and tax avoidance, notably by multi-national corporations, some of which are reputed to pay relatively little by way of tax.

The pace of globalisation owes something to the demise of Soviet Communism. The end of the Cold War and the arms race gave market capitalism a symbolic triumph, and left the United States free to enforce human rights (albeit selectively) by international intervention without fear of starting a Third World War. NATO intervention in Kosovo would have been unthinkable two decades ago.

The onward march of globalisation does not mean that nationalism is a spent force. The break-up of Yugoslavia, the fragmentation of Soviet Russia, the African upheavals and East Timor/Indonesia indicate that age-old ethnic antagonisms remain with us.

Perhaps the most important consequence of the technological revolution is the development of the knowledge economy, that is, the emergence of global trade in knowledge as a commodity in its own right. According to Professor Ron Johnston:

> The two defining characteristics of the global knowledge economy are the increased knowledge intensity of the process of creation, production and distribution of goods and services, and the fact that economic processes are becoming increasingly integrated on a global basis. Neither of these two elements

3 In February 2000, a cyanide spill by an Australian company operating in Romania soon reached Hungary and Serbia.

4 (1987) 26 ILM 1541.

5 (1993) 31 ILM 818.

6 (1992) 31 ILM 849.

> is new to the world, but both their rising intensity and their mutual interaction are of a new order.[7]

The rise of the knowledge economy has many implications for the world in which we live. Knowledge knows no boundaries. And it lends itself to innovation and development, which is bound to occur at an exponential rate as a result of the greater accessibility of knowledge. One implication is that national governments and supra-national authorities have a responsibility to take measures to ensure that knowledge is reasonably accessible and is not locked up by multi-national corporations. Co-operative use of knowledge by researchers and others, working across national boundaries, is the key to further advances.

Another implication is that national regulation of access to knowledge and of communication is quite inadequate in this brave new world. That is why the law of intellectual property, most notably copyright law reform, has become a contentious issue not only in Australia but also in other parts of the world. Later this chapter refers in a little more detail to the inadequacy of our existing arrangements in terms of achieving a satisfactory regime for decision-making and regulation in the new global society. In other words, the problems call for a solution evolved at the international level and that is what the 1996 WIPO Conference at Geneva attempted to achieve in relation to copyright law reform.

The existing world institutional order

The institutional arrangements presently in place are not well adapted to the global world. The foundation of these arrangements consists of the world's nation-states. They are legally sovereign states which are autonomous in the sense that they cannot be compelled to act in any particular way. Nation-states are loosely joined together in the United Nations Organisation. By joining the UN, a nation-state undertakes certain obligations, just as it does when it becomes a party to an international or regional convention or treaty, whatever the subject matter of the convention may be.

The assumption that underlies this world of legally sovereign nation-states is that each state is entitled to, and will act, in its own self-interest. That is why the United Nations (and earlier the League of Nations) were formed so as to ensure that the nations of the world would co-operate with a view to preserving peace and avoiding war. In the 19th and early 20th century era of the Great Powers, the assumption was a valid assumption. Its validity was not thrown into question by the ratification of conventions, such as the Geneva Conventions, which sought to regulate the conduct of

---

7 R Johnson (Professor, Engineering Faculty, University of Sydney) (1999) 'The Challenge of the Knowledge Economy: Managing Knowledge', presented at *Australia's Information Future Innovation and Knowledge Management for the Twenty-First Century*, Australian National University, 3–4 March.

nation-states *inter se* or to deal with matters of international concern, such as shipping, and, at a later stage, international air navigation. But the validity of the assumption has become increasingly problematic as the forces behind globalisation have come into play and generated international conventions and treaties which seek to regulate activities and conduct within nation-states and limit the policies in which the nation-state can pursue internally in the exercise of its autonomy.

The human rights revolution has spawned a wide range of international instruments, including the Universal Declaration in 1948, continuing with the International Convention for the Elimination of All Forms of Racial Discrimination (CERD) 1965, the International Covenant on Civil and Political Rights (ICCPR) 1966, the International Covenant on Economic, Social and Cultural Rights (ICESCR) and the Convention on the Rights of the Child (CROC). These instruments impose obligations on ratifying states to exercise their sovereign powers so that the exercise will conform to the human rights standards protected by the instruments. Some instruments provide a specific mechanism for monitoring and enforcing compliance with the obligations so imposed. Enforcement may take the form of a complaint made to a Committee set up by the instrument, as it does under the First Optional Protocol to the ICCPR but, even in that case, the form of enforcement is much weaker than that generally available under domestic law.

The absence of a court or tribunal with general jurisdiction to enforce obligations so created is no doubt attributable to the fact that enforcement is against states. Likewise, the weakness of the specific enforcement mechanisms actually provided for is attributable to the same fact. The point remains that although ratification by many states of the plethora of international conventions has effectively reduced the area of state autonomy, enforcement of the conventions remains weak.

An exception must be made for the European Convention on Human Rights and Fundamental Freedoms, which is rigorously applied by the European Court of Human Rights.

In the case of international trade agreements, similar comments can be made, though in this area enforcement is stronger and more effective. International and regional trade agreements restrict the capacity of a state to protect its own industry, its producers and service providers against outside competition, thereby limiting the autonomy of the state. In the case of regional free trade agreements, such as the North American Free Trade Agreement and the Treaty of Rome, the enforcement mechanisms are stronger and more effective.

International institutions have been created to meet needs as and when they have arisen. The World Bank, the International Monetary Fund (IMF) and the World Intellectual Property Organisation and regional banks such as the Asian Development Bank, have been with us for some time. So also OECD and the various UN Commissions. The World Trade Organisation (WTO) and the War Crimes Tribunal (to be followed by the International Criminal Court) are more recent entrants upon the stage. There are many other international and regional organisations which are the product of international co-operation. That co-operation arises from a recognition that the regulation of the world calls for an institutional foundation over and above that offered by nation-states acting in their own self-interest.

All these organisations are indicative of a movement away from the nation-state as the dominating player on the world stage. In 1997, the World Bank stated:

> The state still defines the policies and rules for those within its jurisdiction, but global events and international agreements are increasingly affecting its choices. People are now more mobile, more educated, and better informed about conditions elsewhere. And involvement in the global economy tightens constraints on arbitrary state action, reduces the state's ability to tax capital, and brings much closer financial market scrutiny of monetary and fiscal policies.[8]

The decline of sovereignty

The doctrine of sovereignty

Traditionally the primary concern of nation-states was to maintain their independent sovereignty. The recognition of the independent sovereignty of the nation-state was founded upon its capacity to control things and events within its own borders. The nation-state was, for practical purposes, the unit of organisation capable more or less of ordering its own destiny, depending upon the extent of its size, population, resources and position. Globalisation has undermined the position of the nation-state as the unit of organisation by bringing into existence a new world in which borders are no longer the barrier they once were. The nation-state's capacity to control events within its own borders is 'challenged by transnational corporations, economic globalisation and trade, international crime and the rise of global communications and technology'.[9]

The various challenges – economic, environmental, political – have demonstrated the incapacity of the nation-state to resolve both national and international problems. But although globalisation undermines the sovereignty of the nation-state, it also offers a solution to the problems of the nation-state.

---

8 World Bank (1997) *World Development Report 1997*, Oxford University Press, p 12.

9 CJ Vachon (1998) 'Sovereignty Versus Globalisation: The International Court of Justice's Advisory Opinion on the Threat or Use of Nuclear Weapons' 24 *Denver Journal of International Law and Policy* 691 at 695.

> Globalisation increasingly offers incentives to nation-states to surrender bits of their sovereignty consensually through treaties to fashion advantageous economic arrangements.[10]

One instance of such a limitation of sovereignty is acceptance by a nation-state of the jurisdiction of the International Court, of the Rule of Law that it enunciates and enforcement of its decision. The reluctance of a number of states to accept the compulsory jurisdiction of the International Court or to accept it without reservation or qualification is an indication that sovereignty is still a force to be reckoned with, notwithstanding the onward march of globalisation.

A similar comment may be made about the International Court's Advisory Opinion in the *Nuclear Weapons Case*.[11] The Court's refusal to declare outright the illegality of nuclear weapons in any circumstances must be seen as subordinating humanitarian concerns and the survival of the planet to the sovereignty of the nation-state and matters of national military security.[12]

On the other hand, the very recent past has provided us with two traumatic illustrations of the decline of sovereignty. The first is the NATO intervention in Kosovo where sovereignty and the principle of non-intervention were no barrier to NATO intervention to prevent crimes against humanity and violations of human rights. If the rhetoric of the Kosovo intervention is to be taken at face value – and that is a big question – it could be the harbinger of a very serious erosion of the doctrine of sovereignty. The second was the application for extradition of General Pinochet from the United Kingdom to Spain in order to meet charges of torture and crimes against humanity arising from his rule in Chile. Sovereign immunity was not seen as a sufficient answer to part of that application, although there can be little doubt that as recently as the 1960s it would have been.

Loss of sovereignty or autonomy

The brief sketch I have given of the wide range of international conventions and trade agreements that attract ratification by many states is also a telling illustration of what is seen as a loss of sovereignty. In truth, it may not be a loss of sovereignty in the strict sense, at least according to our domestic law, because Australia, like some other nations, retains the power under its domestic law to repudiate any international obligations. But, in practice, most nations would not wish to do so at the price of courting international disapproval with the possibility of retaliatory action, particularly in matters of trade.

---

10 JB Attanasio (1996) 'Rapporteur's Overview and Conclusions: Of Sovereignty, Globalisation and Courts' 28 *New York University Journal of International Law and Policy* 1 at 26.

11 *Advisory Opinion on the Legality of the Threat or Use of Nuclear Weapons*, 8 July 1996, 35 ILM 809.

12 Vachon (1998), p 720.

Further, it may be said that, when a state assumes an obligation to exercise its powers in a particular way because it is thought appropriate to undertake that obligation either as a matter of self-interest or in the interests of the community of nations, it is wrong to say that the assumption of the obligation involves a loss of sovereignty.

Nonetheless, globalisation in its various forms has effectively reduced the capacity of the nation-state to exercise its sovereign powers. The emergence of large economic zones or blocs and the world market have perhaps done more to bring about this result than anything else has. The imperative that confronts states, such as Australia, which are not members of the European, North American and Latin American blocs, is to become a constituent member of such a bloc with the consequence that adhesion to the structural framework of the bloc becomes mandatory.

The creation of an economic bloc necessarily entails some degree of union or integration. Just how much is a matter of choice, although modern experience points to more rather than less. One can have a simple customs union with uniform tariffs designed to give preference to member states as against outsiders, with appropriate safeguards against discriminatory protective practices. Even such a union requires an institutional infrastructure incorporating regulatory and supervisory bodies with the vesting of necessary jurisdiction in courts and tribunals.

The most notable and sophisticated example we have is the European Community or the European Union, to give it its political name. The Treaty of Rome provided, in the very beginning, for European economic co-operation which could develop into economic integration with the potential for political integration. The history of the Community has been one of increasing integration with the European Commission, with the support of the Council, and the European Court of Justice leading the way. The structural framework of the Union is significant. It has a very strong Executive in the form of the Commission, over which there is the Council consisting of the Ministers of national governments, the members of the Commission being effectively appointed by governments. The European Parliament lacks the power to effectively control the Commission and is much weaker than national legislatures.

The United Kingdom's resistance to the drive towards European integration, economic and political, arises from a deep-seated concern about the erosion of national sovereignty. That concern has been heightened by the bureaucratic nature of European decision-making which, granted the weak role of the European Parliament, contrasts sharply with the UK's tradition of democratic parliamentary sovereignty.

If the European model is to serve as a pointer to the future, we might wish to strengthen the role of the European Parliament. Whether such a move would satisfy Eurosceptics is doubtful, to say the least of it. Satisfying 'globo-sceptics' would be even more problematic. In other words, it may well be that the substance of the resistance to the decline of sovereignty is that decision-making by international and regional authorities represents decision-making by strangers who are not alive to the sentiments and aspirations of the national and local communities. Reluctance to accept external centralised decision-making is a matter of the utmost importance because it is a manifestation of the strong sentiment that we have lost meaningful self-government, namely government that reflects a real sense of community input. That sentiment, in turn, lies behind popular cynicism about politicians and the political process, and alienation from society.

Recognition of the strength of that sentiment is to be seen in the way in which national politicians, when speaking to their electorates about world market issues, do so in terms of national interest. In other words, people are distrustful of globalisation. They associate the term and all it stands for with an erosion in standards of social security (which they accept only grudgingly, if at all), and with the shaping of their destiny by strangers and external forces. So, in order to make globalisation acceptable it is necessary to represent that there is no alternative to it or that it is in the national interest.

The rhetoric of national interest is employed to justify government decisions to take us down a globalised path. Despite a widespread belief that globalisation is a force which sweeps us along helplessly in its wake, the transformations which have taken place have been linked to government and legislative decisions. For example, participation in TRIPS and in the negotiations relating to the Multilateral Agreement on Investments (MAI) were government-based decisions.

The comment has been made that MAI:

> was a vivid illustration of just how keen [s]tates are to surrender their discretionary powers to the markets. OECD members were offering to restrict voluntarily their own ability to discriminate against foreign capital.[13]

Participation in MAI was thought to be inevitable because foreign investors would look askance at non-participants, notwithstanding that MAI involved a substantial democratic deficit in the sacrifice of national capacity to discriminate in favour of domestic investors and domestic production. Ultimately MAI came undone, despite the secrecy surrounding its deliberations, when the draft became known and the public in countries such as Canada and Australia became aware of its shortcomings. Four criticisms were made of MAI, each legitimate. Firstly, the negotiations were designed to advance the interests of international investors; secondly, the negotiations were secret; thirdly, they lacked democratic input and failed to concede to the host state regulation of legitimate interests such as control of capital flows (flight of capital), the environment and protection of disadvantaged groups; fourthly,

---

13 S Burchill (1999) 'In-your-face Globalisation Yields "Democratic Deficit"' *Australian Financial Review*, 12 August, p 19.

MAI's dispute settlement procedure was weighted in favour of foreign investors.

Europe has another message for us. The economic co-operation that led major European states to embrace the Euro shows that increasing economic integration has political consequences that aggravate the decline of sovereignty. Indeed, United Kingdom reluctance to embrace the Euro is a recognition of that fact. The stabilisation of a regional currency will impose on regional member states an economic discipline that will severely constrain the financial and budgetary options that would otherwise be available to them as a matter of economic policy.

Yet so volatile have been national currencies, especially in Asia and Latin America, that there has now emerged a movement favouring the integration of currencies in smaller states within a major currency. Integration of this kind would promote stability. So, it has been suggested that Mexico and New Zealand, to take two instances, should 'dollarise' their currencies. Mr Paul Volcker, former Chairman of the Federal Reserve Bank, said only recently that there may well be a move towards the adoption of three major international currencies, namely the Euro, the United States dollar and perhaps an Asian unit. This move, if it does take place, would be a striking demonstration of the force of economic imperatives and the potential which they have for eroding the autonomy of the nation-state.

Another by-product of globalisation and economic rationalism is the trend in favour of central bank independence and freedom from democratic political control. The European Central Bank is a notable example. It is responsible for setting interest rates and managing the Euro. The independence of the European Central Bank has been acclaimed by the *Financial Times* and *The Economist*. Yet it represents an extraordinary sacrifice of autonomy by the European nation-states and a marked democratic deficit. In the case of both a national and a regional central bank, such independence constitutes a serious democratic deficit. This trend illustrates that globalisation is not only a threat to sovereignty; it is an even greater threat to liberal democratic government. In any event, the superiority of the independent central bank model to the model which subjects the central bank to political control has by no means been demonstrated.[14]

The international institutional deficiency

The United Nations has not proved effective in responding to the various outbreaks of hostilities in Africa, the Middle East, the Balkans or in East Timor. In some of these conflicts, it has been left to the United States and

---

14 S Berman and K McNamara (1999) 'Central Banks: A Withdrawal of Accountability', *Australian Financial Review*, 14 May, pp 3–5. But for a contrary view, see A Lijphart (1999) 'Australian Democracy: Modifying Majoritarianism?' 34 *Australian Journal of Political Science* 313 at 314.

its allies (including NATO) to take action. The existing institutional infrastructure falls short of what is required. The response of the World Bank and the IMF may have been adequate to meet the Asian economic meltdown, though critics would dispute that concession, but that is not to say that the institutions can solve a more serious economic catastrophe.

There has been a reluctance to accede to the compulsory jurisdiction of the International Court. The United States has opposed the establishment of the International Criminal Court. And the WTO tribunals exercise jurisdiction between member states rather than at the suit of individuals.

That is because international law and international regulation is predominantly directed at states and at the conduct of states. The jurisdiction of international courts and tribunals is not uncommonly confined to states. Only a state can initiate a complaint in the WTO tribunals, a limitation which was fatal to the Australian rice growers who alleged that the Japanese Government was guilty of discrimination against them in its endeavour to protect its own producers. The Australian Government refused to take the matter to the WTO on the ground that to take the matter up might prejudice other trade interests with Japan, which were more important to Australia. It was reported that Japanese Government officials had raised the possibility that retaliatory action could be taken against Australian wheat imports to Japan if Australia lodged a formal objection to WTO against the Japanese decision to impose a 390 per cent tariff on rice imports over and above existing quota limits.[15]

There are three deficiencies here. The first is one of access – the individual and the corporation cannot invoke the jurisdiction. The second is that the interests of the individual and the corporation depend, for their protection, on the willingness of the state to institute proceedings and seek enforcement. So the relationship which exists between the courts and the citizen in the modern democracy has no parallel at the international level. At that level, inaccessibility prevails. International law has failed to reach out beyond states and to provide a system of law and regulation that can be invoked and enforced at the instance of those who are not states.

What has been said already conveys some idea of the inadequacies of the existing system. Globalisation has not been accompanied by the creation of an appropriate decision-making infrastructure. That infrastructure consists largely of the institutions established on or after the end of the second World War in the era of the nation-state, in particular the United Nations, the International Court (with the limitations on its compulsory jurisdiction), OECD and GATT, out of which the WTO has emerged. There are, of course, the ad hoc bodies and tribunals for which specific conventions and agreements provide but their powers and jurisdiction is sometimes quite

15 B Pearsen (1999) 'Paying the Price over Rice' *Australian Financial Review*, 30 April, p 16.

limited and they operate for the most part, as between governments. Often they are inaccessible to individuals and corporations.

Remarks of the Minister for Foreign Affairs to which reference will be made later identify the problem, namely that the forces of globalism require decisions to be taken at an international level if action is to be effective in responding to world problems, whether those problems relate to the peace-keeping initiatives, environment, trade, commerce, technology or human rights. The problem of regulating what is put on the Internet is a good example. How do we regulate the availability of illegal and pornographic material? How do we deal with defamatory material? National responses may not be effective and may deter service providers. An internationally agreed regime is obviously desirable, even though it may be one dictated by the United States which is the greatest contributor to the Internet and is subject to its own constitutional requirements.

In 1997 the Supreme Court of the United States declared invalid the *Communications Decency Act* 1996 which attempted to regulate material on the Internet, the statute contravening the constitutional guarantee of freedom of speech. Congress enacted the *Child Online Protection Act* 1998 in a second attempt to protect children from Internet pornography. It was challenged by civil libertarians and others who regard the Act as threatening adult access to legitimate material.[16] This only serves to highlight the point that Australian democratic input may perhaps count for little in a struggle the outcome of which may be influenced by American and European imperatives, in this case notably United States constitutional law. An international Internet Content summit held in Germany in December 1999 considered recommending filtering software in the hands of the Internet user and industry self-regulation.[17]

Another point to be made is that in the fora in which international decisions are made powerful corporate and business interests generally exercise greater power than they can exercise in true democracies. That is partly due to the fact that international decision-making, as already mentioned, often takes place behind closed doors.

International tribunals

One outcome of the 1994 Uruguay Round discussions was the bringing of international disputes relating to intellectual property within the jurisdiction of the WTO. A standing Appellate Body was set up with power to give binding decisions. The new tribunal has jurisdiction to rule that governments must amend or repeal domestic laws that are inconsistent with world norms. Otherwise the governments are exposed to trade sanctions. This

16 'Net-porn Law Faces Challenge' (1998) *Brisbane Courier-Mail*, 24 October, p 29.

17 *Sydney Morning Herald* (1999) 25 August, p 25.

means that the intellectual property legislation of not less than 130 member States (including Australia) is subject to review by the WTO Appellate Body.

Ms Gail Evans has made the point that:

> the apparent consent of members to the judicial review of their legislation by an international organisation must continue to raise issues of political and legal legitimacy. Democratically elected parliaments and the citizens who elected them should still be concerned for the autonomy of their decision-making, because in the absence of a unified image of global sovereignty, a clear chain of representative political action is not discernible between member states and the WTO.[18]

In the recent case *India – Patent Protection for Pharmaceutical and Agricultural Chemical Products*,[19] the Appellate Body upheld a recommendation that India bring its legislation for patent protection of those products into conformity with TRIPS. The Appellate Body held that India had not complied with its obligation under Article 70.8(a) to establish a 'means' that adequately preserves novelty and priority in respect of applications for product patents in respect of pharmaceutical and agricultural inventions and that India had not complied with its obligations under Article 70.9 of TRIPS with respect to the grant of exclusive marketing rights.

One problem with the trade tribunal is that it reflects an international law model; jurisdiction is limited to member States with very limited participation by private parties. In the *Shrimp Case*,[20] the Appellate Body held that it had the right to accept or reject any information or advice which it may have sought or received and that a party may attach to its submissions briefs provided by NGOs. The decision in the *Shrimp Case*, while expanding the sources of information and advice, does not overcome the problem of inaccessibility.

The problem is that the international tribunal according to the traditional international law model is unlikely to provide the degree of satisfaction to the individual litigant that is provided by national courts and tribunals. Lack of accessibility and inability to focus on individual interests rather than considerations of economic efficiency and world trade mean that they are unlikely to be regarded as an adequate substitute for national courts and tribunals.

Another serious problem is the marked tendency of the WTO to discount environmental concerns because the WTO invariably favours free trade over the environment. This tendency was exhibited in the recent ruling against Australia's quarantine provisions protecting the Australian salmon industry against the possibility of disease from imported Canadian salmon.

---

18 'Intellectual Property Disputes and the Supercourt of the World Trade Organisation: The Case for a New Model of Dispute Resolution' (1998) 16 *Prometheus* 395 at 397.

19 Ibid, pp 398–9.

20 World Trade Organisation (WTO) (1998) *Report of the Panel on United States: Import Prohibition of Certain Shrimp and Shrimp Products* 37 ILM 832 (*Shrimp Case*).

The susceptibility of Australian bird life to Newcastle disease, which has decimated the poultry industry in parts of New South Wales, is indicative of the potential risks that globalisation presents to the Australian environment. As one commentator has said:

> Much of our sovereignty over trade has now been ceded to the WTO. In disputes over trade rules, the WTO views environmental arguments as devious means of restricting trade and always favours free trade over environment. Disputes are heard in secret and decided by trade specialists – not environmental scientists, and certainly not citizens who can take a broad view of the national interest.[21]

Following the decision in the *Shrimp Case*, NGOs have claimed that the WTO has 'a bias against environmental policies',[22] based on its criticism of United States import controls which were designed to protect turtles in prawn fisheries.

International treaty-making and the democratic deficit

More important than that shortcoming is the prescription by international conventions and agreements of obligations and standards with which nation-states must comply. The prescription of those obligations and standards proceeds not from a democratic choice made by the peoples of the world but rather from a choice made by executive governments. It is that prescription which in effect reduces the capacity of the nation-state to exercise a choice whether to depart from the obligations and standards otherwise than at the price of violating its international obligations. By reducing the nation-state's capacity in this way, the nation-state is effectively deprived of its capacity to make effective choices it might otherwise make in the interest of its citizens. That means that, in the case of democracies, there is a democratic deficit.

That expression is sometimes used to convey two different ideas. One is the notion that entry into the commitment involves effectively, for the future, a loss of choice. The second is the notion that the commitment that an executive government makes to the international obligation or standard is not necessarily approved by the democratically elected legislature and that has been the case in Australia.

The second notion has been the subject of controversy in Australia, largely because the Federal Executive Government had exercised its treaty-making power without the benefit of wide-ranging consultation with State

---

21 C Hamilton (1999) 'Native Wildlife under Threat' *Australian Financial Review*, 13 May, p 21.

22 *Inside Trade*, 13 November 1998; quoted in G Shaffer (1999) 'International Decisions: United States – Import Prohibition of Certain Shrimp Products' 93 *American Journal of International Law* 514.

governments and relevant interest groups. In 1996 the Federal Government introduced new procedures to regulate its treaty-making activities. On 2 May 1996, the Minister for Foreign Affairs, when announcing the new procedures, said:

> it is vital to note that trade flows, environmental concerns, human rights, to name only a few of an increasing array of such issues, can only be effectively managed . . . through international agreement. This means that treaties, the fundamental instruments of international law, are an increasingly important component of contemporary international relations and of Australia's own legal development.[23]

The new procedures entail the tabling of a treaty before it becomes binding on Australia. The tabling of the treaty is accompanied by a National Interest Analysis (NIA) which is to reveal the impact the treaty will have on Australia.

The Joint Parliamentary Committee on Treaties now considers tabled treaties, the Analysis and any other question relating to an international instrument referred by either House or a Minister. The role of the Committee is to provide detailed scrutiny and bring forward reports for consideration by Parliament. A Treaties Council, acting as an adjunct to COAG, has an advisory function.

However, the absence of provision for parliamentary approval of a treaty is a matter of legitimate concern. A treaty once ratified imposes an obligation to legislate in conformity with its requirements in that respect and in effect deprives Parliament of its freedom of choice, otherwise than by violating the treaty. Why should Parliament not be specifically required to approve the treaty, particularly if its provisions amount to regulation or standard setting? The government regards this as unnecessary and as leading to inefficiency. This response attracts the celebrated Mandy Rice-Davies retort 'It would, wouldn't it'. The requirement of Parliamentary approval would elevate the matter to the level of public debate and enhance deliberative democracy.

In any event, the efficacy of the new procedures in remedying the democratic deficit depends in part on the range and depth of consultation in Australia and the responsiveness of the government to that consultation. Here there is a need for co-operation between levels of government if effective democratic input is to play a worthwhile part. According to the government report 'Review of the Treaty-making Process'[24] consultation has become effective as a result of the work of the Parliamentary Joint Standing Committee on Treaties (JSCOT) which has sought and obtained submissions from a wide range of parliamentary, government, industry and community groups. The States and Territories have reservations about this.

---

23 House of Representatives (1996) *Hansard*, 2 May, p 231.

24 August 1999.

The Review notes that States and Territories have expressed some concern about the adequacy of the time made available for consultation with the Commonwealth agency preparing the NIA. The government says that it will continue to ensure that Commonwealth agencies will consult promptly so that States and Territories can make the best possible use of Ministerial Councils and consultation mechanisms.

There is a further question whether consultation results in bringing to the surface significant issues for national and international public debate. One promising development, arising out of the Review, is the acknowledgment that there are two stages before tabling of a treaty when JSCOT could consider a treaty. The first is during negotiations, before the text and Australia's position is finalised.[25] The second is when the Minister refers a treaty to JSCOT.

Viewed from a democratic perspective, international treaty-making conducted by diplomatic processes suffers from a want of openness. Fortunately the Department of Foreign Affairs and Trade recognises this problem. The same comment cannot be made about the Treasury, which has, in the past, thrived, on a culture of secrecy. It was this culture that led to grass-roots public opposition to MAI and to a bizarre lack of co-operation with JSCOT, which was inquiring into MAI. The culture of secrecy in Australia appears to in fact be strengthening. Auditors-General have forcefully drawn attention to the problem and to the consequences that it has for democratic accountability.[26] Their remarks relate to the domestic scene. The same problem arises at the international level though the context is rather different.

The Review acknowledged that States and Territories often participate in treaty negotiations and provide the delegation with expert technical assistance. The government supports State and Territory-funded participation in treaty negotiations.

The Melbourne Constitutional Convention in March 1998 resolved in favour of Parliamentary approval of treaties before ratification by Australia.[27] That would be a distinct advance. But for the reasons already given, that advance would not adequately safeguard the democratic process. Detailed public information statements concerning negotiations are necessary, unless the subject matter is of such a nature to require confidentiality.

---

25 This happened in the case of MAI.

26 See, for example, Editorial (1999) 'No Secrets', *Sydney Morning Herald*, 24 August, p 24.

27 Co-sponsored by the Victorian Government and the Constitutional Centenary Foundation, this Convention was separate from the Commonwealth's Constitutional Convention held in Canberra in February 1998.

Problems for the future

Some of the problems arising from globalisation arise from the excesses of economic rationalism. In some cases, the rational answer to the problem lies in the assertion by the nation-state of its autonomous power. For example, there is no reason why a nation-state should encourage short-term portfolio investment capital with its potential for instability and refrain from regulating its repatriation in case of emergency. Nor is there any reason why a nation-state like Australia should treat foreign investors more favourably than its own investors. Nation-states have been deferential to the markets to the point of being supine, ever craving market endorsement of the nation's economic and financial policies via the coveted AAA rating.[28]

However, even granted rational answers to some of the problems and a stronger assertion of national sovereignty, globalisation is here to stay, with its many challenges.

Globalisation presents not only a challenge to the sovereignty and autonomy of the nation-state; it presents also a challenge to liberal democratic values. Globalisation offers no satisfactory replacement for the nation-state as the unit of organisation for the ordering of world affairs. Globalisation has not brought into existence an international infrastructure which is yet capable of regulating and supervising the global activities which are beyond the management capability of the nation-state.

The result is that there is a democratic deficit. The democratic deficit arises in two ways. The international decision-making infrastructure is government-based, not popularly based, and the democratic governance of the nation-state does not carry through to the international infrastructure. It follows that international decision-making is bureaucratic rather than democratic in character. It is often secret rather than open and public and it therefore provides a fertile field for lobbying and influence by powerful interests.

The European experience is perhaps the best pointer to the future that we have. It confirms the existence of the problems identified above without providing answers that are all immediately acceptable. It does, however, suggest that it should be possible to construct international institutions that are more efficient, more open, more accountable and more accessible than those presently in existence. Whether they are to be linked to the United Nations is an open question. If so the UN would require substantial restructuring. The jurisdiction of courts and tribunals would need redefinition and to be made compulsory. The jurisdiction should not be confined to states.

At the same time it is difficult to see that, at this stage, it would be practicable to establish a world legislature, even with the limited powers of the European Parliament. And that means that international institutions

---

28 See F Argy (1998) *Australia at the Cross-Roads*, Allen & Unwin, p 138.

must be government based in the sense that they are responsible to the governments and, through governments, to the legislatures of nation-states. Ultimately, accountability of international institutions to democratically elected legislatures, if it could be achieved, would be a significant advance.

The Australian Constitution

The Australian Constitution was formulated long before the modern process of globalisation got under way, even before Australia became a member of the community of nations. But the Constitution enables Australia to participate fully in international affairs as a sovereign state. It might be said that the Constitution does not make adequate provision in relation to human rights and the rights of citizens. That is a matter of debate into which I shall not venture, except for the concluding comments that follow.

Of more relevance to the present topic is the Constitution's division of powers between the Commonwealth and the States, a division fashioned when globalisation, as we know it today, was at best a speck on the horizon. That division of powers brings about disconnections, even antagonisms, where co-operation, if not unity of purpose, should prevail if Australia is to make its way in the new world. It does not follow that constitutional amendment is necessary. The structure of COAG and intergovernmental Councils may be enough, so long as they are invigorated and subject to rigorous public scrutiny.

Concluding comments

In order to ensure democratic input into international and regional decision-making, it is essential that national governments raise for discussion and debate issues that will arise for determination at international and regional levels. To that end, national governments should provide relevant information to legislatures and the public to enable national governments to ascertain the informed views and opinions of their communities. The Australian experience does not suggest that governments and politicians recognise that they have such a responsibility. There is, accordingly, a strong case for saying that the Australian Constitution and, for that matter, State Constitutions should be amended so as to impose on government an enforceable obligation to provide information and information which is truthful. It is obvious that Freedom of Information statutes have not created a sufficient climate of openness and accountability. And spin-doctors have honed the art of misinformation to the point of deception. Likewise, consideration should be given to the creation of an obligation to consult interested parties, notwithstanding the difficulty in framing such an obligation. Parliamentary approval of treaties has already been mentioned.

We should aim also to establish a statutory framework for the regulation of COAG and intergovernmental Ministerial Councils so that there is informative disclosure of their existence and their activities with appropriate reporting obligations so that Parliaments and the public know what these bodies are doing and have an opportunity to form views and provide an input. The Review of Treaty-Making Process made in August 1999 makes it clear that Ministerial Councils are an important source of inputs into treaty negotiation.

Unless we take the necessary steps to ensure that our own institutions give effect to liberal democratic values and are responsive to their communities, we have little hope that international and regional institutions will do so. Above all else, we should comprehensively reject the 'mandate' theory of government and the pervasive notion that 'government knows best', a notion which has so often been falsified by the historical record.

3

The Empire Strikes Back

The Constitution, Sovereignty and 19th Century Globalisation

Helen Irving

If 'globalisation' refers to a world system in which supra-national and trans-national institutions – economic, legal, technological and even cultural – shape the policies of nations and challenge their sovereignty, it has all been seen before. Over the years between 1865 and the 1890s – the decade in which the Australian Constitution was written – global markets and financial systems, internationalised law and information networks, all expanded dramatically. Decisions made, and events occurring in distant imperial centres, were increasingly and rapidly felt in the remotest parts of the globe, assisted by a revolutionary acceleration in the speed of transport and new communications technologies.[1] By 1872, the overland and submarine telegraph cable stretched from Britain to Australia via a dozen or more Middle Eastern and Asian ports, and worked so efficiently that a message could be sent from London to Hobart and returned in the same evening.[2] By the end of the 19th century, the telegraph network was truly 'global'. Its expansion both represented and facilitated the new era of imperial globalisation.

The new Imperialism

Empires have always operated along global lines of command and economic exploitation. But what characterised this era was a shift in approach to imperial policy, most strikingly within the British Empire. Colonial self-government and control of domestic matters had already been conceded in many cases by the 1870s, but in a rather ad hoc, pragmatic fashion. While self-government was commonly based on demands for democracy within

---

1 See T Standage (1998) *The Victorian Internet: The Remarkable Story of the Telegraph and the Nineteenth Century's On-Line Pioneers*, Weidenfeld & Nicolson.

2 KS Inglis (1980) 'The Imperial Connection: Telegraphic Communication between England and Australia, 1872–1902', in AF Madden and WH Morris-Jones (eds), *Australia and Britain: Studies in a Changing Relationship*, Sydney University Press.

the colonies themselves, it was often also a response on the part of Britain built around the difficulties of maintaining control at such great distances.

Britain's 'new imperialism' was 'launched' with a speech by Benjamin Disraeli in June 1872, predicting the disintegration of the Empire unless a new world-vision was constructed, with a 'great policy of Imperial consolidation'.[3] With Disraeli in power, a new phase began of expansions and annexations of territory, and the regularisation of imperial control, as well as the clarification and strengthening of the ideology of imperialism. It was not simply a matter of occupation and control of territory as had tended to characterise the 'old' imperialism. It included strategies to keep the colonies loyal, making certain concessions to them, creating new institutions that reflected both these concessions and sought to maintain the paramountcy of Britain.

Britain in the second half of the 19th century was increasingly in a position where effective control of its Empire was technically possible. But, centralised control as such was neither economically viable nor a necessity for those colonies thought capable of self-government. Nor was it considered a desirable strategy. Colonial self-government would now become a deliberate, albeit controlled, policy. In return, the colonies were themselves adapting and employing strategies that would maximise domestic autonomy, at the same time as maintaining their ties within the Empire. These shifts in policy were witnessed in new legal instruments and institutions around which imperial relations were shaped for more than half a century.

In 1865, the *Colonial Laws Validity Act*[4] was passed by the Imperial Parliament. It laid down a common rule for British disallowance of colonial legislation. Colonial statutes could be invalidated by Britain, as before, but no longer on the grounds of repugnancy to British policy. A colonial law would now only be disallowed where it was inconsistent with or 'repugnant' to British laws extending to the colonies 'by the express words or necessary intendment of any Act of Parliament'.[5] The *Colonial Laws Validity Act* was regarded as a 'charter of colonial independence' which 'removed all doubts as to the powers of colonial Legislatures to alter or repeal the general mass of English law . . . not made operative, by Statute, throughout the Empire'.[6] In the Australian colonies over the years between 1865 and 1900, very few Bills were not assented to, and five alone were actually disallowed.[7] In almost every case, these Bills were subsequently amended or simply re-enacted in their colony of origin, coming into force within a matter of a few years for the majority.

---

3 JFC Harrison (ed) (1965) *Society and Politics in England 1780–1960*, Harper & Row.

4 28 and 29 Vic (1865) c 63.

5 J Quick and R Garran (1901) *The Annotated Constitution of the Australian Commonwealth*, Angus & Robertson, p 348.

6 Ibid.

7 Ibid, pp 695–7.

In 1870, Britain's first *Naturalization Act*[8] was passed; it regularised the procedure for naturalisation within Britain and provided for the British colonies to pass their own naturalisation laws. British subject status could now be conferred upon foreign-born applicants not only within Britain, but also in the colonies outside Britain. Significantly, subject status by naturalisation was not portable. All those born within the British Empire, or on board a British ship were British subjects, regardless of their parentage, free, in law, to move and live and exercise the rights and privileges of subjects within the Empire. Subject status by birth was inalienable. But subjects by naturalisation remained subjects only within the colony in which their certificate of naturalisation was issued. Once they crossed its borders, they ceased to be subjects. This anomalous situation was to prove, in practice, useful in the Australian colonies, as an extra means for regulating immigration on racial grounds, by preventing 'coloured' subjects crossing colonial borders in search of work or residence. It was a local application which, paradoxically, the British themselves were consistently to oppose.

In 1876, the *Appellate Jurisdiction Act*[9] was passed in Britain, virtually assimilating the membership of the Judicial Committee of the Privy Council with the judicial membership of the House of Lords. These two appeal courts, the first hearing appeals from Britain's colonies and the second hearing domestic appeals, were now almost identical in composition, although not entirely in procedure and not, many felt (especially in the colonies), in prestige. The 1876 Act reflected a compromise between those in Britain who called for their merger into one joint Judicial Committee for the whole Empire, and those wanting to maintain the traditional powers of the House of Lords.[10] After 1895, it became possible (although it was rare) for there to be limited colonial representation on the Judicial Committee of the Privy Council, sitting in appeals from the member's own colony.

British finance and colonial Depression

The impact of imperial integration (rather than domination) was not confined to legal institutions. It was experienced in quite a different way (if not necessarily with a qualitatively different outcome) in the economic sphere. In the late 19th century, 'international financial penetration of the UK and other economies (in terms of openness to capital flows) was *greater* . . . than it was in the late 1980s, and . . . the international economy was hardly less integrated . . . than it is today'.[11] The last three decades of the 19th century were characterised by recession, in which short-lived booms alternated with

8 33 and 34 Vic (1870) c 14.

9 39 and 40 Vic (1876) c 59.

10 PA Howell (1979) *The Judicial Committee of the Privy Council, 1833–1876*, Cambridge University Press, p 69.

11 P Hirst and G Thompson (1996) *Globalisation in Question*, Polity Press, pp 196–7.

down-turns, and saw the beginning of the erosion of Britain's status as world leader in industrial power and of its dominance of world trade. Britain's economy, however, remained 'cushioned' for many years, through its financial power in insurance, banking, shipping and investments.[12] Much of this investment, indeed very heavily so in the 1880s, went into the colonies.

In November 1890, four months before the first Australasian Federal Convention was to meet in Sydney, the London-based Barings Bank crashed. It brought down with it one of the largest holders of Victorian government bonds. With that failure, came the rapid collapse of several dozen 'land banks' and other banks in Melbourne and Sydney. Liabilities to depositors amounted to £72 million. British investments dried up and creditors called in their debts. Victoria's Premier, James Munro, was personally ruined, as were half his Cabinet (and also Victorian backbencher, Alfred Deakin). Although they did not yet know its consequences, the shadow of Depression hung over the Federal Convention in 1891 at which many of these men were delegates. It would be one of the main reasons for the failure of their efforts, and for the fact that it would take another six years, during which policies of economic reconstruction became a priority, before work on drafting a new Constitution was commenced.

The policies of British financial institutions were not the single reason for Australia's Depression in the 1890s, but they were the dominant cause. In 1893, the British Treasury prepared a report on the crisis, placing the blame on the overheated ties of credit between Britain and the colonies. British loans during the 1880s, especially in Victoria, had induced the colonies to undertake rapid, grand schemes of public works, and had encouraged private investment and speculation on an unprecedented and irresponsible scale. When British financial institutions collapsed, the global impact was immediate. The outcome of the Depression in Australia was a legacy of wariness, both in trusting Britain as the sole source of overseas investment and in depending upon the 'mother country' for assistance. A greater commitment and capacity within the colonies to responsible financial management also emerged.

Sovereignty without statehood

The Depression strengthened the desire for Federation, and with it came the renewed goal of retaining imperial membership while expressing Australian nationalism and maximising domestic self-government. The processes of writing and negotiating an Australian Constitution would take the better part of the 1890s, but at its completion, the Constitution's 'genius' – partly deliberate and partly fortuitous – was to provide for national sovereignty in an

12 L James (1995) *The Rise and Fall of the British Empire*, Abacus, p 202.

Empire context, in which full nation-statehood was not yet desired and not yet available.

Sovereignty without statehood may seem a contradiction, and it might have been. In practice, however, it worked effectively. In 1901, Australia was a nation, having a sense of distinctive, cultural community and 'destiny', combined with the infrastructure of domestic sovereignty and the capacity for future full international personality.[13] Australia in 1901 would, indeed, almost have qualified as a state under Max Weber's famous definition, having 'a monopoly of the legitimate use of force' over a given territory. But it was unable to perform an Act of State: it could not declare war, or enter treaties, or invade another nation's territory, without Britain's authority or without the risk of its actions being overturned or repudiated by Britain. Although it rapidly acquired this status, it was not yet a full nation-state on the international scene.

The power to disallow colonial legislation was retained in the Commonwealth Constitution, as were the institutions of vice-regal office, appeals to the Privy Council, and imperial control of international affairs. By the time of Federation, however, these institutions were already attenuated and the colonial authorities were, effectively, reluctant to employ the powers they wielded, to curtail the sovereignty of the self-governing colonies. We turn now to a more detailed discussion of these constitutional questions.

In 1895 the Conservative Party returned to power in Britain. The new Colonial Secretary, Joseph Chamberlain, was the greatest proponent of the new imperialism. It was Chamberlain who engaged in negotiation and debate with Australian leaders in the final years of Australia's Constitution-framing. It was Chamberlain who guided the Commonwealth of Australia Constitution Bill through the Imperial Parliament in mid-1900. It was he who insisted upon the crucial amendment to s 74 of the Constitution, giving Australians access to Privy Council appeals.[14] But he also agreed to a workable compromise. It is now well known, because of Alfred Deakin's account of it, that the Australian delegation in London greeted the compromise formula with jubilation.[15] Section 74 opened up appeals to the Privy Council, but limited them in such a way that the bulk of constitutional questions would go no further than the High Court.

The Australian colonies had been the most ardent to challenge the power of the Judicial Committee of the Privy Council before Federation and the Commonwealth continued this challenge after 1901. As early as 1871, a

13 H Irving (1999) *To Constitute a Nation: A Cultural History of Australia's Constitution*, Cambridge University Press.

14 According to one view, despite the heavy petitioning from British and Australian investors and bankers on this matter, Chamberlain was in fact prepared to yield the point if all the Australian Premiers had stood firm: PA Howell (1999) 'Chamberlain', in H Irving (ed) *The Centenary Companion to Australian Federation*, Cambridge University Press.

15 A Deakin (1944) *The Federal Story*, Robertson & Mullins.

Victorian Royal Commission had reported critically on the delays in getting a decision in appeals and recommended their limitation.[16] The attempt in the 1890s by the Constitution's framers in the drafting of the Constitution to restrict appeals from all Australian courts and in virtually all classes of matter, was a continuation of this Australian attitude, and for the better part of the decade it had been treated by the British with resignation. Within the Colonial Office, the appeals provision in the 1891 draft Constitution was greeted with the comment: 'if Australians by their Parlts wish to shut themselves out of the Privy Council, we shall have to accept it' and the provision in the 1898 Constitution Bill by the note: 'The restriction is an instance of the peculiar Australian jealousy of anything like Imperial interference in local matters, and it would be useless to object to it.'[17]

Joseph Chamberlain, by 1900, thought otherwise. Among other things in his campaign to amend s 74, he held out to the Australians the enticement of a single Imperial Court of appeal, and subsequently introduced a proposal into the Parliament which included the creation of colonial 'Law Lords' holding the right to sit on United Kingdom and colonial appeals, as well as the right to sit in the House of Lords. Both the British and the Australians objected to Chamberlain's scheme, however; the Australians in particular on the grounds that a colonial judge should not have a seat in any Parliament. Britain's interest in creating an alternative court to the Judicial Committee ended there, and the Committee remained confined to colonial appeals.

Powers of disallowance

Other provisions of the Constitution also raised the issue of balancing national sovereignty within an imperial context. The power of the Queen to disallow Acts of the Commonwealth Parliament within one year of the Governor-General's assent was included in s 59. There was little debate in the Federal Conventions on this Section, but what there was, is instructive. The draft Bill, as it stood in 1891 provided for a two-year period for disallowance. Dr Cockburn, one of the South Australian delegates, moved that the period should be reduced to one year; he thought in fact that as little as six months would be adequate, given the rapid means of communication now available. Against objections that '[w]e are not all agreed on the question of the establishment of a republic!', Cockburn insisted that 'there is nothing more irritating than vetoing of domestic legislation'.[18] He proposed the provision that 'disallowance shall be exercised on such subjects as affect

16 DB Swinfen (1987) *Imperial Appeal: The Debate on the Appeal to the Privy Council, 1833–1986*, Manchester University Press, p 55.

17 Ibid, pp 59–60.

18 *Official Report of the National Australasian Convention Debates, 1891* (1986) Legal Books, p 763.

imperial interests' and that these subjects should be specified in a schedule. New Zealand's representative, Sir George Grey, pointed out that this had, effectively, been the arrangement between New Zealand and Britain for many years (until the relevant law, providing for 'the actual subjects upon which acts need to be sent home', was 'accidentally' repealed),[19] and that it had worked well, with no threat of rupture with Britain.

Only two more speeches were made. Samuel Griffith, Queensland's Premier, favoured the retention of the two-year period on the grounds that it permitted full communication of all interests affected by a law to be made to Britain prior to a decision to disallow. And one Western Australian delegate commented that '[u]nder this Bill the connection between the British Crown and Australia generally is so very slight, that we ought not to do anything calculated to weaken it. The time will possibly arrive quite soon enough for the connecting link to be cut altogether and we should at any rate do nothing in this Convention to hasten that time'.[20] Cockburn's proposal was defeated but, in the event, this Section was ultimately amended in the drafting processes of the second Federal Convention in 1897 to reduce the disallowance period to one year, and it passed without debate.

The *Colonial Laws Validity Act* was to apply to the Constitution, but there appears to have been no clear exploration of the relationship between disallowance under the Constitution and the provisions of the Act. Section 59 refers to the disallowance of 'any law' but does not state the grounds for disallowance. It does, clearly, limit the power of disallowance, confining it to within a year of the Governor-General's assent. Beyond one year, the law, unless otherwise invalid under the Constitution (and that would be, at least in the first instance, determined by the High Court), could not be overruled. In the view of contemporary constitutional authorities, Quick and Garran, the disallowance power would be 'sparingly exercised, in accordance with the rule long established, that Her Majesty's Government refrains from interfering with any colonial legislation which is consistent with colonial constitutional law, except in cases involving Imperial and international relations'.

The Governor-General's power to reserve a Bill for the Queen's pleasure, provided for in s 58, would be, Quick and Garran state, 'probably' exercised where a proposed law was in conflict with Imperial legislation applicable to the colonies, in other words, on similar grounds to the repugnancy test under the *Colonial Laws Validity Act*, or where it was inconsistent with treaty obligations of Her Majesty's Government.[21] We may assume that their analysis was sound, although we shall now never know: while 15 Bills were reserved between 1906 and 1975 by the Governor-General pursuant to

19 Ibid, p 764.

20 Ibid, p 765.

21 Ibid, pp 693–4.

s 58 (all having the character described by Quick and Garran, or under the particular provisions of s 74), the disallowance power was in fact never used at all. These provisions are now all obsolete.

External affairs

Section 51(xxix) – the 'External Affairs' power – is also illustrative of the balance between national sovereignty and imperial paramountcy in the era of empire globalisation. As the draft Constitution Bill stood in 1891, the placitum extended to 'External affairs and Treaties'. What is now Covering Clause 5 of the Constitution also included 'treaties made by the Commonwealth' (in addition to the *Commonwealth of Australia Constitution Act* itself and all laws made by the Parliament) as 'binding on the courts, judges, and people of every State and of every part of the Commonwealth'. Both references to treaties were struck out in the course of debate in the 1897–8 Convention, on the grounds that the Commonwealth could have no power to enter treaties in its own right. The sole treaty-making power was the Crown of the United Kingdom. The Commonwealth could enter trade agreements with other countries, but not conclude treaties.[22]

This arrangement was an accepted part of the imperial order, in which Britain controlled international policy, including defence policy, and attempted to maintain imperial uniformity or cohesion in law, but allowed colonial or dominion sovereignty in matters that were regarded as internal or domestic. The prospect that British treaties, entered into without Australian consultation or ratification, would have an immediate impact on Australian law, was in fact weak. As was recognised in debate in 1897, there was then (as now) no automatic incorporation of treaties into law in the United Kingdom, and treaty obligations were often overlooked or neglected. All of the Australian colonies except Queensland refused to adopt the 1895 Anglo-Japanese Treaty, for example, and the Treaty continued to have virtually no legal, or indeed, even moral impact upon Australia's anti-Asian policy in that era.

Although some concerns were expressed during the Constitution's drafting about limiting the powers of the Commonwealth, the relevance of treaties, and therefore the need for an express treaties power, appeared slight. The power remained for the colonies and subsequently the Commonwealth to pass legislation giving effect to treaties concluded by Britain. But Australia did not have or seek an independent international identity at that time. The word 'treaties' was removed from the Constitution; at the same time, there was no suggestion from any source that the statement 'the sole treaty-making power is the Crown of the United Kingdom', should be included in the Constitution. And nothing prevented the Executive power and

22 *Official Report of the National Australasian Convention Debates, 1897* (1986) Legal Books, p 239.

the external affairs power simply evolving, without any difficulty and indeed very quickly after the First World War, into treaty-making and implementing powers in their own right. Similarly, nothing in the Constitution prevented Australia from ultimately adopting its own citizenship law and abandoning the status of British subjects for its nationals, or from gaining ultimate control over all avenues of legal appeal.

Conclusion

Shaped in this climate, Australia's Constitution was well equipped to balance the competing demands of national sovereignty and imperial paramountcy. Now that the British Empire no longer exists, but other global forces do, it retains this character. There is no automatic incorporation of treaty obligations into domestic law (the over-reaction to *Teoh*'s *Case*[23] on the part of governments notwithstanding). There is a healthy, indeed sometimes over-vigorous, control of national citizenship through increasingly confining citizenship rights and entitlements to legal citizens as opposed to residents, and to exclusive Australian citizenship, as opposed to dual citizenship. There is a fully developed and distinctive system of Australian courts and Australian law. If globalised markets and information systems have, as everywhere, penetrated Australia's economy and culture, there are no constitutional impediments as such to their regulation.

The novelty of globalisation at the turn of the 21st century is often exaggerated, and the vulnerability of the nation-state to global forces may be similarly overstated. This is not to say that significant differences between the 'globalisation' of the past, and that of the present do not exist. While the British Empire was vast, the boundaries of its influence and control were less fluid, operating within a world of several imperial systems. The consciousness of Empire membership was far stronger, and far more integrated, shaping military, cultural, trading and legal loyalties and affinities in a manner that would be quite unfamiliar today. Many of today's nation-states were still in an embryonic stage, with sovereignty under construction rather than erosion. Ultimately, by encouraging the growth of national sovereignty in the colonies, as these were transformed into 'dominions' in the first decades of the 20th century, the new imperialism would itself assist the erosion of the Empire. Without overstating the similarities between the old and the new globalisation, the processes by which this paradoxical outcome was achieved are worthy of greater attention.

---

23 *Minister for Immigration and Ethnic Affairs v Teoh* (1995) 183 CLR 273.

4

The Changing Context of Australian Citizenship

The Case for Multiculturalism

Peter Wong and Violeta Brdaroska

When discussing multiculturalism and citizenship, it is relevant to refer to a story that a fellow candidate during the NSW State election told me. He asked an eight-year-old boy where he was from, wanting to find out whether the boy knew which electorate he lived in. The boy answered 'I was born in Australia, but I come from Lebanon'. This example illustrates not only the cultural diversity of Australia, but also the complexity of understanding citizenship and 'belonging' in contemporary times.

The traditional system of states that was the world order has been fundamentally altered by intensification of cross-border political, economic, social and cultural relations. The new system is characterised by interconnection of people, organisations, states and regions through migration, multimedia, financial markets and international organisations. The world has become economically homogenous, while its composing local, national and regional units have become multicultural.

Diversity is a central theme of this 'new world order', where the concept of local and global have merged. On one side, the international human rights regime, which promotes diverse political, social and cultural rights, has created a sense of belonging to a universal entity – heralding a notion of global citizenship. On the other, recognition of cultural diversity and self-determination at local level has become a crucial element of national citizenship. These changes call for redefinition of the traditional relationship between the state and the citizen. How successful this relationship becomes, depends on how well it accommodates two prominent features manifested by globalisation – universalism and diversity.

At first glance, universalism and diversity appear to be contradictory – the former meaning 'unity in all things' and uniculturalism, and the later promoting multiculturalism. Their assumed mutual exclusion heralds the 'doomsday' effects of globalisation that we continue to hear from different corners. At closer analysis, the contradiction is only superficial, in the context of global functioning, these two features become complementary and productive. The requisites for unity are not ethno-cultural homogeneity, but the recognition of how diverse we are as individuals and groups and how common are the goals of humanity.

'We are united by what makes us human' is a broadly utilised slogan, even by those who think that our ethno-cultural, racial and religious characteristics make us human. History shows us how nation-states have been 'humanised' by adopting ethno-cultural characteristics and promoted homogeneity in the name of national unity. To a large extent, the early nation-state demanded this process of uniculturalism for its existence and strength. On the other hand, a globalised world (where the national level is no longer the whole story), demands a process of recognition, respect and even promotion of difference. National strength is no longer defined through unicultural existence, but through the ability of the nation to interact with other units within all their diversity. By setting up standards that all (or most) cultures can aspire to meet, multiculturalism makes practical unity more attainable.

This chapter examines the relationship between the individual and the state within the context of the Australian nation. It explores the changing nature of citizenship as a result of both Australian historical experiences of managing diversity, and more general globalising trends. It is argued here that entrenchment of cultural diversity at all levels of citizenship is the most appropriate way to achieve unity. The imperative for culturally diverse societies such as Australia is redefining the traditional notion of citizenship. The new form of citizenship is multicultural and multi levelled, where civic pluralism represents the relationship between citizen and state in a globalised world.

Australia's historical process produced a set of structures and agencies in which multiculturalism operates, and where Australia meets the challenges of globalisation. The predominant argument of the chapter is that the more democratic the existing structures are, and the more they allow active citizenship, self-determination and respect of diversity, the more multiculturalism in Australia will succeed in meeting the globalisation challenges. Australian citizenship, based on multiculturalism, heralds optimistic possibilities for achieving social cohesion that is removed from homogenous and nationalistic boundaries of past constructs of citizenship.

Multiculturalism is an Australian reality. The 1996 Census classifies 282 major languages, including 170 Aboriginal and Torres Strait Islander languages and 92 religious denominations. The challenge is for Australian national 'imagining' and citizenship to become this reality.

Arguments questioning the merits of multiculturalism highlight the difficulty of achieving social cohesion through recognising diversity, flagging examples of multicultural societies collapsing into warring parts.[1] These ar-

1 M Dixson (1999) *The Imaginary Australian: Anglo-Celts and Identity: 1788 to the Present*, UNSW Press.

guments follow the conventional theory of the nation-state, nationalism and civic society, which equates cohesion with homogeneity. This is a theory describing a world of independent states where inter-state relations are conducted purely on national interests, and becomes increasingly ephemeral in the reality of cross-border activities common to the new, globalised system. The theoretical understanding of multiculturalism calls for re-examining the traditional notions of national belonging and citizenship and questions their relevance in a world where recognition of identity is of major significance.

The proposal here is to see multiculturalism not only as a policy of social justice for minorities, but as an ideological stance that claims 'unity within diversity'. Its pretension should be nothing less than the cornerstone of Australian national identity. Multiculturalism stands not only for legal and political equality, that is, formal equality as expressed by traditional liberal democratic theory. It means substantive equality, an equality of outcome in all forms of human interaction at all levels of social, political, economic and cultural life – it is a 'liberating recognition of the de-facto heterogeneity of the cultural and ethnic make-up of contemporary . . . societies'.[2] In this form, multiculturalism does not mean 'sameness of treatment' for all; it would not mean different laws for people from different cultural background. Multiculturalism calls for recognition of differences and particular needs when constructing laws and policies. As it aims to recognise particularities so that it minimises the inadequacies that have formed around them, multiculturalism encourages activism of all within the society, reduces the possibility of cultural, political and social domination of one group. As multiculturalism opens possibilities for mutual accommodation between different social groups and individuals, it is the most effective strategy of maintaining social cohesion in a culturally diverse democratic society.

Multiculturalism, to this extent, is both politics of identity, and practicality of citizenship. It provides the basis for a more inclusive relationship between the individual, groups and the state. Multiculturalism presumes 'active involvement in the political, social and legal aspects of citizenship. Kalantzis pictures this relationship between the individual and the state as consisting of four main processes: 'Symbolic Representation (the process of creating senses of belonging through representations of identity in the media, arts, educational practices and so on); political participation (representation in local, State and Federal Government); work (equitable access to employment and employment mobility) and social services (health care, local government services)'.[3]

---

2 T Turner (1994) 'Anthropology and Multiculturalism: What is Anthropology that Multiculturalists Should be Mindful of It?' in DT Goldberg (ed) *Multiculturalism: A Critical Reader*, Blackwell, p 407.

3 M Kalantzis (1995) *The New Citizen and the New State: An Australian Case for Civic Pluralism*, Occasional Paper No 9, Centre for Workplace Communication and Culture, p 27.

This form of citizenship would enable most stability and efficiency of a system that is challenged by new forces, such as the international and local implications of globalisation. Kalantzis's main processes are employed here as central standards to evaluate Australian democracy and citizenship, and particularly their ability to 'negotiate' future globalisation challenges to an outcome where the rights of all will be protected.

The entitlements of citizenship, its rights and obligations, are subject to constant change, along with the shifting basis of how 'belonging' to the national family is determined. Globalising circumstances bring diversity and universal human issues into the perspective of civic culture and national identity; citizenship becomes more inclusive and open. On the other hand, economic globalisation is prone to weakening the link between the state and the citizen. Provision of services, including those which are purely linked to the civic and social aspect of citizenship are evaluated in terms of their short-term economic benefit. The effect is that state functions that aim to protect the rights of citizens are reduced or transferred to the private sphere; existing democratic processes and structures are redefined to conform to these changes and the 'traditional' notion of citizenship is compromised.

In these circumstances, continuity and prosperity of the system depend on how effectively it absorbs the challenges of globalisation. A historical account of Australian nation-building reveals processes and structures that are necessary for progressive, balanced link between state and citizen.

Shifting of Australian citizenship and implications for the future

Australian citizenship is conceptualised on the basis of geographical and cultural fragments. Australian nation and citizenship have evolved across shifting foundations, incorporating experiences of colonialism; achievement of an independent nation-state status through a strong influence by the British empire; immigration; attempts for social and cultural integration of all Australian population; and finally, multiculturalism and rapid economic globalisation.

The foundations for Australian nation building were laid on the memory of the former sovereign, the British Empire. The drafting of the first Australian constitution did not mobilise a popular movement; it failed to define Australian citizenship in terms of positive core values, and presented the beginning of a 'citizenship void' in Australia.[4] This 'void' represents an anomaly in the democratic political process in Australia. On the one hand, the principles of democracy prescribed the rights and obligations of their

4 B Galligan and J Chesterman (1999) 'Australia's Citizenship Void' in A Davidson and K Weekly (eds), *Globalisation and Citizenship in the Asia-Pacific*, Macmillan, p 73.

citizens, notions of freedom, equality, and free political participation. On the other, their realisation was deficient in practice either because the citizens were not fully aware or practising their citizenship rights, or because a large portion of the population were regarded as foreigners or the 'other'. The first Constitution was created with little reference to the liberal democratic thought of contemporaries such as Rousseau, and was therefore far removed from analysis and thinking about the entitlements of citizenship.[5] Belonging to the Australian nation was codified in 'subject', rather than 'citizen', terms, entrenching the requirement of Anglo cultural homogeneity in the understanding of the entitlements of citizenship.[6] This enabled the severe limitation of the rights and lives of Indigenous peoples and immigrants. After 1901, intricate legislative and administrative instruments created at federal and State levels, excluded Aborigines from full citizenship rights and put them in the protection of the state which controlled their lives, employment, movement, association and forcefully removed their children.[7]

Although the Australian nation continued to be imagined along the lines of a white, Anglo-colonial sense of kin and community, an important tenet developed with the notion of Australian citizenship – the rejection of a class system and the high regard for egalitarianism.[8] These enabled a development of civil society, which enabled openness to post-war immigration programs and the subsequent development of multicultural policies.

With the adoption of multiculturalism in the early 1970s, the homogenous nature of the Australian basis of citizenship started to dissolve and opened ways for inclusion of all non-Anglo Saxon cultures and values. The Labor Party in the 1970s saw the growing immigrant working class as a strong political base. Immigrant workers, who as a result of assimilation policies were culturally and socially segregated into lower socio-economic areas, were included in Gough Whitlam's new egalitarian welfare and educational system. The emphasis was on recognition of diversity as predominantly a social justice measure, rather than a political and identity issue. Social services were to aid migrants and Indigenous peoples to integrate better into the national family.

Active policies to include diverse societies into the mainstream evolved to fuller recognition of cultural and linguistic diversity as the basis of Australian national identity. In November 1981, Prime Minister Fraser described the underlying principles and approach to multiculturalism:

> Multiculturalism involves respect for the law and for our democratic institutions and processes. Insisting on a core area of common values is no threat to multi-

---

5 A Davidson (1997) *From Subject to Citizen: Australian Citizenship in the Twentieth Century*, Cambridge University Press, p 224.

6 Galligan and Chesterman (1999), p 73.

7 Davidson (1997), pp 191–201.

8 EV Thompson (1994) *Fair Enough: Egalitarianism in Australia*, UNSW Press, p 46.

> culturalism but its guarantee, for it provides the minimal conditions on which the wellbeing of all is seated. Not least, multiculturalism is about equality of opportunity for the members of all groups to participate in, and benefit from Australia's social, economic and political life. Both morality and hard-nosed realism dictate this concern with equality of opportunity. I am talking about basic human rights. . . . No society can long retain a commitment and involvement of groups that are denied these rights.[9]

From these beginnings, the term 'multicultural' has been increasingly used to describe the cultural and ethnic diversity of contemporary Australia.

This statement offers a criterion for assessment of the effectiveness of the Australian system in protecting citizenship and furthering multiculturalism. Colonial experience resulted in transferring of a liberal democratic tradition into the Australian system, which essentially promotes freedom, respect of human rights, self-determination of the individual against the state and the Rule of Law. However, as is the case in many democracies, particular forms of nation-building, economic development and historical power structures, may negatively influence democracies to the detriment of their own citizens. Fundamental to the principles of democracy is the need for constant re-evaluation and reaffirmation of the democratic process itself.

Australian political and economic structures: challenges from the past and present

Current political, economic and social structures within the Australian system present both limitations and opportunities for multicultural civic pluralism. These relate to the challenges of globalisation and how they are managed at national political and social level; the political and democratic structures and the extent to which they allow 'active citizenship' and civic pluralism.

Firstly, Australia is challenged by the negative effects of globalised market, exhibited in processes of 'economic rationalism'. As these specifically target the social justice sphere, egalitarianism and equity are giving way to 'sameness of treatment' that pays little regard to specific needs. The Australian political sphere in the last few years demonstrates what happens when economic imperatives take over cultural and social imperatives. There has been a recent move towards building a nation where all citizens are the same, where community relations happen on an equal footing between all groups and individuals. Slogans such as 'for all of us' used in the 1996 federal election, and subsequent moves to downplay diversity, carry connotations that reject minority needs in favour of the Anglo-white mainstream. The process has given rise to an 'economic nationalist' conservatism with

---

9 National Multicultural Advisory Council (NMAC) (1999) *Report: Australian Multiculturalism for a New Century: Towards Inclusiveness*, April, p 25.

strong elements of intolerance and racism. The rise of One Nation was not an isolated phenomenon in Australian history. It was encouraged and legitimated by this process of economic imperatives and imprudent policies of governments at all levels which seemed to have abandoned active policies of cultural diversity.

Other possible limitations to progressive Australian multicultural citizenship are evident in the political and institutional structures and democratic processes. 'Active citizenship' – the civic and political awareness and efficient relationship between the citizen and the state – is limited by past exclusionist legacies and current inaction to address them. The political system is still dominated by highly educated, highly organised political elites where the cultural homogeneity of the early Australian nation is entrenched. They are not representative of the cultural diversity of the Australian nation. People from non-English speaking backgrounds, Indigenous people, women and other 'minority groups' are still underrepresented at all levels of political representation and in positions of major decision-making. While people born in non-English speaking countries make up close to 14 per cent of Australia's population, their participation in policy-making institutions is around 6.7 per cent.[10]

How does the current base of Australia's citizenship, multiculturalism, exist in such a system? How are we to face the future where globalisation threatens to impose even higher challenges? The answer is: by an examination of the past, the recognition of past wrongs and rethinking of our national and social basis – about what makes us citizens. The relationship between the state and the citizen must be enhanced. Defining of citizen rights and obligations must be sensitive to the diverse population. Diversity must become part of the mainstream.

National self-examination requires revisiting history and correcting its negative repercussions in the present. However limited the reconciliation process is becoming, it has nevertheless made a drastic progress with the recognition of land rights in the *Mabo* decision.[11] Active social policies have been put in place which aim at improving Aboriginal health, encourage better education for Indigenous people, improving quality of life and increasing the level of participation and employment in the public sector.

Although the government is refusing to genuinely apologise for wrong of the past, including the Stolen Generations, its recent statements of a qualified apology is a slow procession towards reconciliation. Citizenship based on multiculturalism depends on the success of the reconciliation process. By honouring human rights and international covenants, by creating the legal and social structures that would address issues of the Indigenous

---

10 J Jupp (1999) *The Political Participation of Ethnic Minorities in Australia*, Centre for Immigration and Multicultural Studies, p 9.

11 *Mabo v Queensland (No 2)* (1992) 175 CLR 1.

population and by fostering a civic culture that is in tune with diversity, the reconciliation process will have a positive future.

The Australian system has improved its stance on issues pertaining to migrants and the ethnic communities in general. Numerous policies for ethnically diverse workplace aim at addressing the disproportionate participation of people from non-English Speaking Backgrounds in areas of employment and political participation. The Access and Equity Policy requires all government department and agencies to show how service delivery is responding to the cultural diversity of the population. Numerous organisations and government advisory bodies, such as the Prime Minister's Australian National Multicultural Advisory Council provide key advice and policy to all levels of government. The work of the Department of Immigration and Multicultural Affairs, the Human Rights Commission and State Commissions contribute to entrenching policies of cultural diversity in the public sphere, areas of employment, health, education and media. As a consequence, Australian civic culture is increasingly accepting of cultural diversity.

Australia's future depends on how successfully it forgoes past ideas of a homogenous nation and develops ' a genuinely post-nationalist sense of common purpose'.[12] It depends on whether Australia completes its shift towards a multi-levelled, multi-dimensional citizenship, where diversity is consolidated in civic culture. Primarily, it depends on whether the new social contract is compatible with globalism.

Globalisation and multiculturalism

The nation-state, civic culture and the entitlements of citizenship are challenged to cope with rapid internationalisation of every aspect of life. Facing these challenges, the following questions must be asked: how are myths of national identities sustained in face of constant immigration, and challenged by demands for full citizenship rights by immigrant diaspora communities and Indigenous peoples? How can shared mentalities withstand the incursions of a global information super-highway, or of technologies that can connect directly local minority groups? How can a shared national future be voiced when sub-national regions can deal directly with the world?

Australia's policy of multiculturalism, which establishes a balance between separatism along lines of diversity, and cohesion of society as a whole, seeks to address these contradictions. The context of multiculturalism 'departs from the idea that all citizens are simply equal individuals, and instead sees them simultaneously as having equal rights as individuals and different needs and wants as members of groups with specific characteristics

12 Kalantzis (1995), p 31.

and social situations'.[13] It is therefore a policy which defines citizenship across different levels of conception: the local community – through group self-determination and participation, the national belonging – through legal and political representation, and global openness – through the notion of recognition of difference and human rights. The conception of multicultural Australian citizenship is therefore appropriate to highly diverse societies and contemporary economic needs.

There are two main ways in which the Australian multicultural nation meets the challenges of globalisation. Firstly, by recognising that Australian economic and political future depends on its fullest integration into the world. Secondly, in doing so, it must build on its internal cultural diversity so that it becomes a mainstream issue. These processes are an outcome of policies in recent decades, based on Australia's democratic tradition. As Australia faces the journey of globalisation through these two processes, Australian citizenship is rethought and redefined to consolidate cultural diversity as part of national identity. The predominant emphasis of these processes is that multiculturalism and globalisation and symbiotic and complementary.

The efficient work of the international human rights regime serves as evidence for the complementarity between multiculturalism and globalisation. International legal instruments and institutions have created a system that explicitly puts legal obligations on states, multinationals and even individuals to respect human rights. National policies for protection of human rights are implemented under the influence of the international legal regime. In the past 20 years, according to international covenants, Australia has also established legislative instruments and organisations for the protection of human rights and equality of its citizens, protection from racial, gender and other discrimination.

Economic perspectives of globalisation have been elementary in Australia's movement towards multiculturalism. Australia is integrating into the world market and into the Asia-Pacific Region. Cultural diversity is increasingly negotiated on grounds of economics and productivity. Current economic and technological developments of globalisation, give particular relevance to the economic potential of all the characteristics that the individual carries to the workplace – diverse cultural and linguistic skills, life experiences, communication knowledge, country knowledge and international networks.

The dividends of Australian multiculturalism, identified as 'Productive Diversity', are stressed in the recent report by the National Multicultural Advisory Council:

---

13 S Castles (1995–6) *Research Paper No 16: Multicultural Citizenship*, Commonwealth Parliamentary Research Service, p 11.

> The Australian model contains opportunities for the advancement of Australia's strategic international interests . . . because there is no language on earth that is not spoken in Australia, and no economy in which an Australian has not worked, we are uniquely placed to take advantage of the globalisation of world markets . . . When we engage any nation socially, politically or economically, we can draw on the knowledge and expertise of Australians from the same background to help make the engagement more beneficial to our national interest.[14]

The emphasis is still on an Australian national unit operating in a globalised world, but there is a significant shift from the notion of recognition of cultural diversity for purposes of social justice for minorities, to its recognition as part of the mainstream.

Facing the challenges of globalisation through incorporating into the global requires managing the local level. Australia's shift to the global sphere has predisposed its national level to a more inclusive management of diversity – incorporating multiculturalism at all layers in the relationship between state and citizen. As seen earlier, the relationship rests on four main spheres: symbolic representation of diversity in the processes of creating identity – the media, arts, educational practices; political participation at all levels of government; work and social services. As these spheres are the pillars of citizenship, successful representation of cultural diversity in all of them would guarantee a progressive Australian citizenship.

Active recognition of cultural diversity is taking place in work and in public areas of life. In the workplace, the Australian model of work and management adopts intercultural competencies as the 'core competencies for managers and workers in an era when homogenous workforces and monocultural and monolingual marketplaces are fast disappearing'.[15] In the public arena, through multimedia and supermedia channels, subcultural and different ethnic identities are provided with growing opportunities to find autonomy and realise their own ways of participation into the national and global. Public space is reshaped to allow for cultural diversity into planning and delivery of institutional and public service frameworks. Multiculturalism has reconfigured Australian citizenship so that it embodies civic pluralism – entrenchment of diversity within the realisation of citizen rights and obligations.

Multicultural citizenship will be successful in meeting the challenges of globalisation and ensuring civic pluralism by following four main principles. The first is achieving equality of rights for every citizen, including equality before the law and social justice services. Secondly, recognising that formal equality of rights must be accompanied by equity strategies that recognise group differences. It is the recognition that equal treatment in circumstances of disadvantage and discrimination can only exacerbate current inequalities. Thirdly, multicultural citizenship happens through establishing

---

14 NMAC (1999), p 64.

15 Kalantzis (1995), p 6.

mechanisms for group representation and participation through means of institutional arrangements to ensure the participation of people directly affected, wherever important decisions are made. This seeks to establish more units of democratic participation, at more places of operation, and to make the centralised government more accountable to those units. The fourth principle is state intervention through active policies and programs to break up existing barriers that create disadvantage over difference, such as gender, ethnicity, Aboriginality.[16] This requires that there would be differential treatment of these groups, the emphasis is on equitable services that address specific needs.

There is also an imperative on governments to engage in an effective evaluation of the impact of economic decisions upon the social sphere, which requires a reversal of the direction of the traditional process of decision-making. At the basis of this strategy is an understanding that recognition of the importance of a strong and culturally diverse civic society is not about 'tolerance of minorities' or a matter of compassion. The importance of multiculturalism rests on the idea that 'cultural and linguistic diversity is a productive resource, of immediate value locally and the basis of Australia's ability to link into global networks'.[17]

Evolving forms of Australian identity, sociality and citizenship must adopt these principles of multicultural citizenship. Civic pluralism should become the norm in the four spheres of relationship between the state and the citizen. In this way, Australia will negotiate with local and global diversity. Australia's citizenship, being based on cultural diversity and aiming towards a more inclusive civic pluralism, represents a unique national and international resource.

Conclusion

Australian citizenship has evolved through various stages – colonialism, creation of culturally homogenous nation, immigration and multiculturalism. Early consciousness of membership in a larger empire left a tradition of democracy, and political and legal symbolism that presents a contemporary framework for Australian citizenship. Immigrant experiences and the way the Australian nation managed ethnic diversity had left another legacy of cultural diversity and social justice, which also set the frameworks for operation of multiculturalism. Building on these structures, multicultural Australia tackles the challenges of globalisation.

In order to address changes posed by globalisation, a fundamental rethinking of social element is needed. Local communities coexist well with global issues, as they both centre on recognition and respect of diversity

16 Castles (1995–6), p iii.

17 Kalantzis (1995), p 25.

while working in a wider and cohesive environment. To this extent, a fragmented basis of citizenship, ie a different basis for conceptualisation of a civil society, presents endless opportunities for Australian multiculturalism.

However, the Australian system must seek the fine balance between unlimited openness to the global and restricting the national. On one side, the imperative is opening the economy and the socio-political system so that the benefits of globalisation (cultural diversity, universalism and economic benefits) are allowed to enter the national and therefore benefit the principles of multicultural Australian citizenship. On the other hand, proper structures must be placed that will restrict the negative sides of globalisation – economic rationalism and destruction of the civic communitarian base of citizenship. Higher civic awareness, together with increased government transparency and regulative structures are needed to limit their impact on the society.

The principles of multiculturalism are complementary with the notions of openness and interconnectedness presented by globalisation. The same challenges that globalisation presents to the traditional nation-state system, also offer optimistic possibilities for multiculturalism. These are increased migration and population integration across national boundaries, loosing validity of the notion of homogenous national identity and the work of international legal organisations which promote respect of cultural diversity and human rights, together with transnational communication and economic links. These aspects of globalisation have contributed to an improvement of the democratic standards of the Australian system and have opened opportunities for multicultural functioning. Australian citizenship has shifted from the original homogenous and exclusive basis, onto a multi levelled, multicultural basis, where citizens from diverse communities at local and national levels share common rights and responsibilities. Central to the success of the new, redefined Australian citizenship is the understanding that its pluralist basis does not denote fragmented citizenship. Rather, it is an united, inclusive, and globalised citizenship.

Australian citizenship is conceptualised across different spatial, economic and cultural aspects, which have shifted and fragmented through its history. Multiculturalism represents an embodiment of all these facets. It links different geographical and cultural components, links the local with the national and global. By seeking a non-artificial, post-national foundation for the citizen, multiculturalism projects Australian diversity into the future.

5

The Constitution of International Civil Society

Aynsley Kellow

Non-governmental organisations (NGOs) have been granted access to the OECD and many international treaty processes, and (with some support from the Clinton Administration, responding to environmentalist and union demands) are now demanding entrée to the World Trade Organisation. Scholars often regard international civil society as fundamentally democratic in nature, although some are more sceptical. Some champion civil society as heralding the 'fading away' of the anarchic, Realist state-centred view of international relations, replacing it with a norm-governed system rooted in world-wide capitalist consumer culture (reflecting states' perceived inability to deal with certain problems), and with new forms of social identity which challenge the hegemony of statist world politics.[1]

Civil society is seen as existing in 'new political spaces', delineated by networks of economic, social and cultural relations, and occupied by conscious associations of geographically separated actors linked in networks for particular political and social purposes. These networks interact with states and governments, but extend themselves across state borders and are not constrained by the state system.[2]

This transnational dimension makes many uneasy about claims of *global* civil society'.[3] The members of domestic interest groups are subject to the obligations of citizenship, and the groups themselves are bound by the laws of their host nation. Groups claiming to represent civil society arouse the same unease as do transnational corporations: often they are unaccountable, sometimes because of deliberate strategies on their part. Greenpeace International, for example, is one transnational private corporation that has exploited transnational legal structures to evade liability for its actions.

---

1 RD Lipschutz (1992) 'Reconstructing World Politics: The Emergence of Global Civil Society' 21 *Millennium: Journal of International Studies* 389–420 at 392.

2 Ibid, p 393.

3 P Willetts (1988) 'The United Nations as a Political System' in P Taylor and AJR Groom (eds), *International Institutions at Work*, Pinter, p 29.

To believe that civil society represents the democratic side in global society reflects scepticism about states' ability to provide democratic governance, and places considerable faith in the representativeness of NGOs. But there are good reasons for doubting that NGOs necessarily represent grassroots democratic values suppressed by national governments, and there are serious questions about the accountability of some NGOs, which enjoy the rights of 'global citizens' but are not bound by the corresponding duties that normally accompany citizenship within the nation-state.

This chapter suggests that that credence should be given only, or mainly, to groups based in those societies where the impact of their lobbying will be felt. In other words, the case for NGO activity is strongest where 'democratic blockage' prevents fair participation in policy-making. Any other endeavours to pressure a state – including changing its stance in international negotiations – in the absence of such democratic blockage amounts to representation without taxation, because such NGOs need not live with the negative consequences of their intervention.[4]

Global civil society?

The anti-statist flavour of much writing on civil society reflects the fact that the groups comprising it usually champion such issues as the environment, human rights, and Indigenous peoples and so lack the 'privileged position' which Lindblom attributed to business interests in politics.[5] Not only do such groups society tend to make moral rather than interest-based claims, they have few weapons *other* than moral claims in their arsenal. They tend to be what Lipsky termed 'relatively powerless groups',[6] which create the bargaining resources they lack by engaging in protest activity. Many have succeeded so well that they can no longer be classed as 'relatively powerless'.

One problem is that normative political campaigns rarely succeed on their merits. There is intense competition on the political agenda, not just between norms-based and economic issues, but between different normative issues. Often, those that succeed in imposing sanctions coincide with economic interests that reinforce them.[7]

The 'privileged position of business' in domestic politics stems from three factors: superior ability to raise resources; government reliance on business expertise; and (perhaps most significantly) the structural power it enjoys because governments depend for their fiscal existence upon

4 A Kellow (1999) '"No Representation Without Taxation": A Sceptical Look at the Case for Global Civil Society', paper presented to the 4th Annual Conference on International Trade Education and Research: 'The WTO Millennium Round', Melbourne, 16–18 September.

5 CE Lindblom (1977) *Politics and Markets*, Basic Books.

6 M Lipsky (1968) 'Protest as a Political Resource' 62 *American Political Science Review* 1144–58.

7 B Yandle (1989) *The Political Limits of Environmental Regulation*, Quorum Books.

continued business viability. Sub-national governments are often especially vulnerable to fears of industrial relocation, so environmental groups frequently appeal instead to national governments and international organisations. Thus '[t]he state is read as the problem and global civil society is read out as the solution'.[8]

Business's advantages do not, however, translate well to the transnational arena. International organisations do not depend directly upon business profitability and are indifferent to its location. They are not directly responsible for implementing multilateral agreements (that is left to nation-states) and do not depend on business expertise.[9] At the same time, NGOs have more power at transnational level. Their ability to mobilise resources can equal or exceed that of business groups. They can help poorly resourced international organisations overcome their capacity deficit (UNEP's annual core budget is less than that of WWF or Greenpeace) and can perform functions that international organisations often cannot. The United Nations Charter prohibits UN organisations from engaging in domestic politics, so they cannot lobby at the national level in support of treaty negotiations. But NGOs can – and do.[10]

At the international level, NGOs often pressure industries or individuals in civil society rather than national governments or international organisations.[11] Human rights campaigns have targeted corporations as a way of pressuring non-democratic governments immune to international opinion.[12]

Such interventions depend for their legitimacy upon some moral claim, usually 'some universalising discourse'[13] such as 'world citizenship'. (Anthony Giddens claimed, for example, that we can speak of universal values.)[14] The UN Declaration on Human Rights and the ILO Conventions are important sources of such norms, all the more legitimate because backed by international law. Norms can constrain actions and even reconstruct national interests. Sociological institutionalist theorists[15] claim their research

---

8 RBJ Walker (1994) 'Social Movements/World Politics' 23 *Millennium: Journal of International Studies* 669–700 at 696.

9 DL Levy and D Egan (1998) 'Capital Contests: National and Transnational Channels of Corporate Influence on the Climate Change Negotiations' 26 *Politics and Society* 337–61.

10 See A Kellow (1999) *International Toxic Risk Management: Ideals, Interests and Implementation*, Cambridge University Press.

11 P Wapner (1995) 'Politics Beyond the State: Environmental Activism and World Civic Politics' 47 *World Politics* 311–40.

12 KA Rodman (1998) '"Think Globally, Punish Locally": Nonstate Actors, Multinational Corporations, and Human Rights Sanctions' 12 *Ethics and International Affairs* 19–41.

13 RBJ Walker (1994) 'Social Movements/World Politics' 23 *Millennium: Journal of International Studies* 669 at 689.

14 A Giddens (1994) *Beyond Left and Right: The Future of Radical Politics*, Polity Press, p 20.

15 M Finnemore (1996) 'Norms, Culture, and World Politics: Insights from Sociology's Institutionalism' 50 *International Organisation* 325–7.

provides 'powerful evidence of global cultural homogenisation'.[16] Global cultural norms may make similar behavioural claims on dissimilar actors. But the power of such claims appears to be stronger at some stages of the international policy process than at others.[17]

A norm of racial equality played a crucial role in reconstituting United States interests, causing it to favour sanctions against South Africa in the mid-1980s.[18] Yet the key change was domestic legislation reflecting the coming of age of African-American politics and its long-standing linkages with African liberation politics. This was the triumph of a *domestic* norm that was shared internationally, but by no means universally.

What is problematic is whether shared *global* norms are possible. Citizenship, racial equality, human rights, progress are common enough norms in Western culture but receive different emphasis in other societies. Environmental norms, for example, are not universally shared between, or even within, societies;[19] indeed, they appear unable to produce unanimity *among* environmentalists.[20] As Walker notes: 'who has the authority to act in the name of rainforests and dolphins, is . . . difficult to specify'.[21]

Although unlikely to be shared universally, norms can be shared widely enough to generate campaigns on a global basis. How representative are such campaigns? The ease of global communications makes them relatively easy to co-ordinate, but it also facilitates the co-ordination of soccer hooliganism. We must consider critically whether, and when, such campaigns should be accorded legitimacy in national and international politics.

This might seem carping when we are considering NGOs like Amnesty International; but should we grant the same legitimacy to 'People's Global Action', organisers of the 'Carnival Against Capitalism' riot in London on 18 June 1999? This was part of an Internet co-ordinated action in 43 countries, repeated over ensuing months in Seattle, Davos and Bangkok, organised and funded by a group of aristocratic youth playing anarchist. Why should we accept destruction of private property by Greenpeace if we would not accept destruction of Greenpeace's property by the French secret service?

---

16 Ibid, p 328.

17 See K Hanf and A Underdal (1998) 'Domesticating International Commitments: Linking National and International Decision-Making' in A Underdal (ed), *The Politics of International Environmental Management*, Kluwer.

18 A Klotz (1995) 'Norms Reconstituting Interests: Global Racial Equality and US Sanctions against South Africa' 49 *International Organisation* 451–78.

19 D Lal, 'Eco-fundamentalism' (1995) 71 *International Affairs* 515–28.

20 P Jokinen and K Koskinen (1998) 'Unity in Environmental Discourse? The Role of Decision-makers, Experts and Citizens in Developing Finnish Environmental Policy' 26 *Policy and Politics* 55–70. See also RBJ Walker (1994) 'Social Movements/World Politics' 23 *Millennium: Journal of International Studies* 669 at 699.

21 Ibid, p 675.

We must look sceptically at groups representing civil society and examine the legitimacy of their activities. Globalisation has raised questions about whether the current 'constitution' of civil society opens the door to undemocratic influence. This chapter focuses on actions aimed at imposing trade bans, and others such as the 'social tariffs' proposed by United States unions; these are probably the strongest actions being advocated, and so test the boundaries of legitimacy.

The case for civil society

How, then, civil society should be constituted in a political sense? If we talk about 'world citizenship', we must remember that citizenship carries not only rights to participate, but also corresponding duties – for example, to military service, and to be 'taxed' by the outcome of the political process.[22] Representation without taxation is no more fair than taxation without representation.

If accepted, this has important consequences, because global civil society offers many opportunities to engage in political activity that imposes 'taxes' on those who do not participate in the decision-making. Indeed, trade bans might actually *advantage* some interests. We can therefore ask: 'Under what circumstances should we grant legitimacy to NGOs' campaigns for trade bans or other sanctions?'

One case at least has some normative justification. Keck and Sikkink's descriptive 'boomerang' model of NGO activity also provides a useful *prescriptive* test of when NGOs ought to be regarded as acting legitimately.[23] In this case, 'democratic blockage' denies a group effective participation in its own country's politics. The group then appeals to an NGO in another, democratic nation which brings pressure to bear either directly on the non-democratic country, on an economic actor with investments in that country, or on its own national government. Action by NGOs in other countries can thus have democratic legitimacy.

This is what legitimated the campaign for sanctions against South Africa. The black majority was denied participation; and the African National Congress, which could claim to represent it, supported sanctions, and was willing to accept their consequences. But when campaigns for trade bans do not satisfy these conditions – a representative organisation supporting sanctions against its own government – they are much harder to justify. Bans and sanctions are such blunt instruments that we should be suspicious of calls for their imposition when these conditions are not met.

This suggests a criterion for judging the 'constitution' of civil society: if it permits actions that disadvantage the citizens of a society against their

22 I am grateful to Baogang He for suggesting this point.

23 ME Keck and K Sikkink (1998) *Activists beyond Borders: Advocacy Networks in International Politics*, Cornell University Press.

wishes, by groups which are themselves not 'taxed' by the consequences of these actions, such a constitution errs in granting participation rights without imposing countervailing obligations.

We will now examine how three different international organisations constitute participation by NGOs representing civil society, then assess each 'constitution' to determine how far it precludes 'representation without taxation'.

Three 'constitutions' for global civil society

The UN Charter (Article 71) provides that 'suitable arrangements' may be made for consultation with NGOs on matters within the UN's competence. Economic and Social Council (ECOSOC) Resolution 1296 (XLIV) of 23 May 1968 regulates these arrangements, which apply not only to environment, aid and human rights groups, but also to liberation movements such as the Palestine Liberation Organisation.[24] To qualify, organisations must have activities falling within ECOSOC's competence; an established headquarters, administration, and policy-making body; and branches in at least two countries.[25]

Importantly, according NGOs formal consultative status in ECOSOC enables UN agencies to deal with bodies other than national governments without violating Article 2(7) of the Charter, which forbids intervention in a state's domestic matters, if the UN agency only communicates formally with the NGO's *international* headquarters. NGOs can also serve the interests of international institutions by conducting consultancies. Such institutions are usually free to consult non-governmental bodies whether or not the latter 'exist' in a legal sense, or are appropriately representative.[26] Extra-budgetary funding from member states allows them to use such NGOs to advance their agendas, with the UN 'laundering' both the money and the influence at the price of a 15 per cent deduction.

NGOs have helped make up the 'governance deficit' of international agencies like UNEP.[27] In 1974 an Environment Liaison Centre (ELC) was established in Nairobi by NGOs to maintain contact with UNEP and the UN Centre for Human Settlements. By the 1980s, ELC had about 200 members and in February 1981 was recommended for Consultative Status

24 See, eg, P Willetts (1982) 'The Impact of Promotional Pressure Groups on Global Politics' in P Willetts (ed), *Pressure Groups in the Global System: The Transnational Relations of Issue-Orientated Non-Governmental Organizations*, Frances Pinter.

25 P Willetts (1982) 'Pressure Groups as Transnational Actors' in Willetts, p 12.

26 AJN Judge (1994) 'NGOs and Civil Society: Some Realities and Distortions – The Challenge of "Necessary-to-Governance Organisations" (NGOs)', paper presented to a seminar on state and society at Russian Public Policy Centre, Moscow, 6–8 December.

27 See B Gosovic (1992) *The Quest for World Environmental Cooperation: The Case of the UN Global Environmental Monitoring System*, Routledge.

within ECOSOC by its NGO Committee.[28] NGO participation in developing the 1987 Montreal Protocol was actively encouraged by UNEP,[29] and the same pattern may be seen with other conventions. Third World members of the UN's Committee on NGOs (CONGO) became more favourably disposed towards NGOs after they realised, from the Brundtland Report, that NGOs were useful 'in promoting bigger international development assistance and a new international economic order'.[30]

Each of the 'big three' environment NGOs (ENGOs) – Friends of the Earth (FOE), the World Wildlife Fund (WWF) and Greenpeace – has constituted itself differently in response to these opportunities:[31]

- FOE was formed in the United States in 1969.[32] Initially, founder David Brower simply appointed friends living outside the United States as his representatives, to give FOE an 'international' dimension.[33] FOE International was later able to gain recognition as an NGO, then consultative status at the Intergovernmental Maritime Consultative Organisation (IMCO), and observer status at the International Whaling Commission.[34]
- WWF also had its origins in the need of IGOs for support, not in some spontaneous upsurge of international civil society. Formed in 1962 to support the International Union for the Conservation of Nature, as its fund-raising wing,[35] WWF continues this role, also receiving substantial funding from national governments.
- Greenpeace appears the strongest exception to this scepticism, because it has a global reach with branches in 33 countries, including developing nations. However, its growth has reflected the needs of UNEP, and its base is quite narrowly concentrated in a few Northern

28 T Burke (1982) 'Friends of the Earth and the Conservation of Resources' in Willetts (1982), p 117.

29 T Princen and M Finger (1994) *Environmental NGOs in World Politics: Linking the Local and the Global*, Routledge, pp 5–6.

30 O Dahlén (1982) 'A Governmental Response to Pressure Groups: The Case of Sweden' in Willetts (1982), p 162. The utility of the development/environment nexus is increasingly coming into question; see R Sandbrook (1997) 'UNGASS Has Run Out of Steam' 73 *International Affairs* 641–54.

31 See P Wapner (1996) *Environmental Activism and World Civic Politics*, State University of New York Press.

32 T Burke (1982) 'Friends of the Earth and the Conservation of Resources' in Willetts (1982).

33 Ibid, p 106.

34 Ibid, p 108.

35 J McCormick (1993) 'International Non-governmental Organisations: Prospects for a Global Environmental Movement' in S Kamieniecki (ed), *Environmental Politics in the International Arena: Movements, Parties, Organizations, and Policy*, State University of New York Press, pp 133–4.

> European nations.[36] Greenpeace underwent rapid growth in the latter 1980s, when it went from being one of the smallest ENGOs, smaller than FOE and a mere fifth of the size of WWF, to being the largest, with twice the number of supporters of FOE and one-and-a-half times that of WWF.[37] UNEP's weakness as an intergovernmental organisation was a key factor in the further development of Greenpeace and other NGOs in the late 1980s, since such NGOs were able to enhance UNEP's influence.

Both generally, and specifically in relation to ENGOs, non-governmental actors have grown largely because *a role was provided for them* in international governance regimes – although this is not to deny that they have, on occasion, transformed decisional arenas and affected outcomes as a result.[38] The G-77 nations were careful to ensure that opportunities for NGO participation were carefully circumscribed at the Stockholm and Rio summits, and even more so in the Commission for Sustainable Development established after Rio.[39]

NGOs therefore operate in a political space delimited by international institutions; they are useful to IGOs precisely because they can put pressure on national governments. But the way in which NGOs like Greenpeace have constituted themselves to evade the control of national governments is reason for concern. This is especially so because of the recent innovation of creating networks, like the Basel Action Network and the Climate Action Network, that are accorded NGO status in UN proceedings. This innovation enables actors with *no* transnational status (and which therefore do not qualify as NGOs) to participate in international meetings. The Climate Action Network, which co-ordinated NGO participation in negotiations on the Kyoto Protocol, lists among its members the Australia Institute – a think-tank rather than an NGO, and one which (as its name suggests) operates in one country only. While it may have an established headquarters and an administration, it is disputable whether a think-tank can have a policy-making body. The Australian Conservation Foundation is also a member and because it is usually invited to participate as part of the Australian national delegation also, it gets to participate twice. Devices like these are increasingly used to circumvent the 'constitution' of

36 See A Kellow (2000) 'Norms, Interests and Environment NGOs: The Limits of Cosmopolitanism' 9(3) *Environmental Politics* (Autumn).

37 A Hansen (1993) 'Greenpeace and Press Coverage of Environmental Issues' in A Hansen (ed), *The Mass Media and Environmental Issues*, Leicester University Press, pp 152–3.

38 See, eg, L Elliot (1994) *International Environmental Politics: Protecting the Antarctic*, St Martin's Press.

39 See P Willetts (1996) 'From Stockholm to Rio and Beyond: The Impact of the Environmental Movement on the United Nations Consultative Arrangements for NGOs' 22 *Review of International Studies* 57–80.

international civil society, seemingly with the collusion of IGOs seeking greater independence from national actors.

In the OECD, too, NGOs can participate through national delegations, but they can also participate separately via two parallel structures, essentially corporatist in nature. The OECD's founding brief focused essentially on macroeconomic issues, and so its participation is structured through councils representing peak labour and business bodies – the Trade Union Advisory Committee (TUAC) and the Business and Industry Advisory Committee (BIAC). The OECD has become involved in regulatory issues that tend to split peak associations along sectoral lines.[40] When this occurs, various sectoral committees become the relevant players. Significantly, BIAC and TUAC are federations of national associations, in marked contrast to NGOs like Greenpeace.

The OECD made no provision for participation by NGOs other than business and labour, such as consumer groups and environmental groups. Increasingly, environmentalist NGOs have been granted observer status and invited to take part in proceedings beside BIAC and TUAC (and the Commission of the European Union), with rights of audience and debate. In contrast to the structure of TUAC and BIAC, however, such rights have usually been granted to the three major transnational NGOs (Greenpeace, WWF and FOE), rather than to federations of national associations.

At the opposite end of the scale to the UN, the WTO in the past has not granted NGOs rights to participate in its deliberations. Only the WTO's members, the contracting parties bound by the terms of its trade agreements, are allowed to take part. WTO agreements are widely considered more effective than most multilateral environmental agreements (MEAs), arguably because all who take part in making those decisions (including dispute-settlement panels) are bound by them. WTO proceedings are not slowed by rhetoric from those who enjoy 'representation without taxation'. But the WTO is regarded with suspicion by NGOs (witness Seattle) precisely because of this feature, because the national route favours business representation.

Conclusion

The way in which participation by representatives of civil society is constituted in international politics varies between regimes. The UN offers the most scope for obligation-free, non-democratic action; the WTO, the least.

This suggests caution about proposals to make the WTO more like the MEAs by granting any significant participation to non-parties. The *absence* of such participation has been key to the success of the trade agreements. If we want to build effective international regimes, we should be

40 TJ Lowi (1964) 'American Business, Public Policy, Case Studies, and Political Theory' 16 *World Politics* 677–715.

making MEAs more like the WTO instead, and channelling the representation of civil society primarily through nation-states, or (as with TUAC and BIAC in the OECD) through federations of national associations. We should invite participation by democratic, nationally based environmental groups like the Australian Conservation Foundation when developing national positions, rather than granting unaccountable private companies like Greenpeace representation in the WTO. The original intention of the UN 'constitution' – to restrict recognition to NGOs with branches in at least two countries – has been circumvented by such devices as 'networks' allowing single-nation groups to participate through multiple channels, or (to provide for recognition of groups like liberation movements) relaxing insistence on democratic structures. Similarly, we must decide whether environmental groups should be represented by federations of national organisations, or directly by international NGOs, in the OECD.

All this indicates the need to consider whether and how civil society should be represented, not just in the WTO but in other international arenas. There is a clear case for revisiting the 'constitution' of global civil society; for insisting on adherence to established rules for participation either at national level or through the UN; and for considerable scepticism where groups claim to act on behalf of others – except where 'democratic blockage' makes this legitimate.

6

Democracy in a World of Global Markets

Tom Campbell

Dissatisfaction with electoral democracy is often based on the optimistic belief that there is something better on offer, such as 'mixed' systems of governance (incorporating substantial elements of judicial oversight, managerialism or delegation to international and transnational organisations). Contemporary concerns for democracy are more and more associated with the pessimistic belief that, due to global market forces, there is little of significance that sovereign states, especially liberal democracies, can decide for themselves.[1] This combination of beliefs is dangerous for a system of government that depends on a degree of citizen participation, and even enthusiasm.

Equally insidious is the deleterious effect of global market ideology on the operative models of democracy. By implication, these increasingly incorporate market analogies, such as depicting the voter as consumer and the politician as salesperson, and thus condone the acceptance of actual market forces in the political sphere, so that there are fewer and fewer barriers to the control of politics by financial power.

By way of resistance to false optimism as to alternative systems, unnecessary pessimism as to the powerlessness of states and the ideological imperialism of global markets, this chapter reaffirms electoral democracy as a desirable and potentially effective way of institutionalising collective power for the purpose of self-protection. The particular focus is on a legally (but not judicially) oriented theory of democracy in which citizen are legislators and jurors rather than merely political consumers and thereby often economic pawns.

---

1 S Sassen (1996) *Losing Control? Sovereignty in an Age of Globalisation*, Columbia University Press.

Traditional battle lines

Classic theories of democracy can be divided into self-determination or autonomy models on the one hand and self-protection or utilitarian models on the other. The former stress the independent significance of people deciding their own destiny, whether or not they govern effectively; the latter stress the importance of having mechanisms whereby people, as individuals or groups, do in fact protect and further their interests. For self-determinationists, democracy is a matter of peoples making choices for themselves, shaping their own lives and making their own mistakes, while for the self-protectionists it is about citizens having effective means to defend and benefit themselves politically and economically.

In meta-moral terms, self-determinationism smacks of deontology, particularly rights associated with autonomy and freedom, while self-protection has the flavour of consequentialism, particularly the minimisation of harm. Self-determinism is readily associated with the language of inalienable rights, while self-protectionism is more at home with notions such as the common good and the general interest. Such contrasts can be expatiated copiously. Thus, the supporters of self-determination regard voting as an expressive act manifesting autonomy, and government as an embodiment of their will, while self-protectionists look upon voting as a power or instrument, and government as an external force, perhaps a necessary evil, which requires surveillance and containment.

The present conflict

To many contemporary commentators the conflict between self-determination and self-protection models is yesterday's war fought with outmoded and ineffectual weaponry over terrain that no longer has strategic import. Few people nowadays, it is said, have reason to voluntarily engage in voting either as a means of self-affirmation or as a significant self-protection. Democratic politics as a vocation is discredited to the point of ridicule. People look in fear or hope to wider, generally economic, factors in order to understand the insecurity of their presents and discern the shape of their futures.

Moreover, the more academic amongst the democratic theorists point to the phoney aspects of a conflict in which competing ideologies falsely highlight their alleged differences whereas in fact they represent rather similar forces engaged in a messy, confused and maybe unnecessary domestic conflict. After all, real self-determination, if it is to have any significance, must involve the successful exercise of power to achieve chosen objectives. Politics is not token self-expression but achievement of social and economic goals against or with other people.

Further, if there are any genuinely deontic rights, then the right to self-defence must be amongst the more foundational of these, and the successful exercise of the power of voting may be seen as the archetype of minimal self-determination.[2] This reduces the contrast between the two models largely to one between bungling self-determinationists and effective self-protectionists. This cannot be a satisfactory analysis, although there is point to the contrast between the idealism of self-determinationism and the more realistic goals of self-protectionism, which makes self-protectionism simply a particular form of self-determination.

In any case, the emerging consensus is that the choices presented to contemporary electorates are minimal, whatever their normative political rationale may be. The policies of parties with any chance of electoral success differ only at the margins, and the power of governments to implement their policies is greatly exaggerated. This is where the discourse of globalisation enters into the analysis. The freedom of sovereign states is said to be so diminished, in the face of powerful global economic forces that compel conformity to transnational market realities as the price of sustaining acceptable level of economic productivity and consumption, that the states' primary role of economic management is usurped. Countries have to compete for the favours of global economic organisations on terms that are set by the economically dominant states whose governments are, in turn, dependent on private corporate conglomerates.[3]

Contemporary analysts do not, however, agree as to either the novel armouries or the revised objectives for what pass as postmodern democracies. Indeed, it is exciting to note that at a time when globalisation is said to be a homogenising force, there is still some divergence in the competing political philosophies on offer. First in line, is the human rights approach. Although human rights philosophies have their modern origins contemporaneously with the institution of representative democracies they are now viewable as offering an alternative path to what is seen as a 'majoritarian' and hence oppressive system of government. Based on a powerful critique of winner-take-all political systems and backed up my extensive evidence of the plight of identifiable minority groups, the human rights movement seeks to pinpoint those individual interests which have fundamental moral status and to institutionalise their protection and furtherance in ways that counter elective dictatorship and systemic discrimination. Hence the enthusiasm for entrenched individual rights being placed in the institutional hands of

2 A point constantly and lucidly made by Jeremy Waldron: See J Waldron (1999) *Democracy and Disagreement*, Oxford University Press, Part III.

3 For balanced discussions of these trends, see D Held (1989) *Political Theory and the Modern State*, Polity Press, ch 8, and D Goldblatt, D Held, AG McGrew and J Perraton (1998) *Global Flows and Global Transformations: Concepts, Arguments and Evidence*, Polity Press.

judicial guardians who are believed to be above the political brawl.[4] This strategy accords with the global trend to link the idea of universal human rights to judicial rather than legislative or political authority.

It is impossible to be opposed to human rights in the context of efforts to counter state terrorism and inhumanity, yet there is much that is troubling about adequacy of human rights philosophy. In particular, there is the embarrassing persistence, indeed exponential increase, of disagreement as to their content at the level of precision at which they have to be applied to concrete situations. The particularisation of human rights reveals that abstract slogans do not offer operationalisable rights and duties, and the process of concretising abstract rights reveals that this is all too evidently a matter of politically contentious moral judgment.[5] All can agree, for instance, that there is, or should be, a right to life, but disagreement abounds over capital punishment, voluntary euthanasia and the duty of states to provide the prerequisites of a healthy existence.

At this point we encounter twin and complementary strategies. One is an apparent retreat into purely procedural human rights, which are then seen as means for both restraining and democratising government procedures. By confining human rights to the function of maintaining democratic process, either through identifying and entrenching political equality of speech, association and participation, or through the Rule of Law and the constitutional separation and even division of powers, issues of substance are avoided and left to the procedures of the properly constituted electoral system.[6] This move comes at the cost of dissociating human rights from the criterion of those rights which are not only universal but protect the most important human interests, and hence the exclusion of some of the traditionally most prized human rights. This may not be a price worth paying if procedural rights turn out to be as contentious in their detail as substantive rights.

The other strategy is the intellectualisation of democratic process by taking the focus of democratic government away from the instrumental power of the vote and towards public debate aimed at articulating an agreed content to basic rights and establishing legitimate discursive mechanisms for reaching consensus as to the common good. The deliberative focus goes with a general revival of the classical republican participatory ideal of a citizenry that is actively engaged in political life. This second strategy is particularly germane to that postmodern irony of a globalised world, the phenomenon of normative pluralism, that is, the recognition of the di-

4 RM Dworkin (1996) *Freedom's Law: The Moral Reading of the American Constitution*, Harvard University Press.

5 T Campbell (1999) 'Human Rights: A Culture of Controversy' 26 *Journal of Law and Society* 6–26.

6 In recent times, this mode of reading the Constitution of the United States stems from JH Ely (1981) *Democracy and Distrust: A Theory of Judicial Review*, Harvard University Press.

vergences of incompatible group-centred world views which are, in the tradition of liberal toleration, to be accorded equal respect.[7]

The promise of discourse

Discourse democracy offers a number of encouragements that transcend the dichotomies of rights and consequences on the one side, and of self-determination and self-protection on the other. First of all, deliberative democracy opens up the prospect of mutual accommodation based on working agreement rather than ideological unity, an enterprise that is associated with the notions of incompletely theorised agreement[8] and overlapping consensus.[9] Dialogue may lead to a *modus vivendi* amongst political opponents, which generates temporary acquiescence to a working agreement between the divergences that abound in pluralist societies.

No doubt this working agreement is soiled by a measure of bargaining in which advantages are traded not only on an equal basis, but also in recognition of the inescapable realities of existing economic and other social inequalities. Nevertheless, realistic political accommodation produces a *modus vivendi*, which can be a marginal improvement if not a just outcome for all parties. Partly in response to moral disquiet at the legitimisation of agreements reached between unequal parties, some discourse democrats brings in a second and more epistemological rationale for fundamental procedural rights, namely the function of dialogue in furthering the causes of truth and justice.[10] The arguments are familiar and to some extent enticing. Freedom of speech, especially where each person affected by a decision actually makes an equal input, leads to the pooling of information and the rational, empirically based critique of claims to knowledge, so that the outcome of an open and equal debate amongst all those affected by a decision is likely to at least increase the chances of a decision being taken on the basis of reliable information.[11]

Further, in a dialogue approaching to the Habermasian ideal speech situation, each person has to justify to every other his or her views as to what collective decision, if any, should be reached. This procedure is derived from what is involved in according a person equal respect, a basic equality which requires that we seek to reason with each other. This is said to have the effect of excluding evidently partial viewpoints and purely self-serving

7 Thus, J Habermas (1996) *Between Facts and Norms*, Polity Press.

8 C Sunstein (1996) *Legal Reasoning and Political Conflict*, New York University Press.

9 J Rawls (1993) *Political Liberalism*, Columbia University Press, 1993.

10 C Nino (1994) *The Constitution of Deliberative Democracy*, Yale University Press.

11 The classic statement of this thesis is JS Mill (1859) 'On Liberty' in JS Mill (1910) *Utilitarianism, Liberty, Representative Government*, Dent.

demands.[12] Just as no scientific view is correct merely because a particular person holds or believes it, so no political view is acceptable simply because it is the view of a particular person. In dialogue – scientific or political – reasons must be given, reasons which could be accepted by any person and which therefore exhibit impartiality, even objectivity, the hallmarks of justice as well as of truth.[13]

There are practical and epistemological difficulties here. The practical difficulties relate to the unrealisable nature of the ideal speech situation in contemporary market societies in which there is great inequality of capacity to engage in such debate and generally insufficient time and opportunity to do so. Of course, this can be rectified by radical egalitarian changes and the attainment of a civic culture in which dialogue is a common practice for all citizens, a program that has the happy requirement of adding economic to political equality. While there are technological developments which may be conducive to such communicative egalitarianism, it is clear that the current market trend is towards commodifying the means of communication, a development which is highly inegalitarian. Further, if the economic prerequisites of the ideal speech situation are to be written into fundamental rights, this involves the awkwardness of expanding the scope of human rights beyond procedural formalities and into the social and economic spheres, thus landing us with the political disagreements from which we were seeking to extricate ourselves by retreating into traditional civil and political rights.

The epistemological difficulties of deliberative democracy centre on the fact that there is much more to moral and political disagreement than disconfirmable information and self-referential partiality. What this something more amounts to, how significant it is, and what can be done about it, are the sleeping and unanswered issues which cast doubt on the moral sufficiency of democratic dialogue. Some disagreement can be overcome by adopting a point of view that is impartial in that it seeks to take the interests of everyone equally into account. Some moral views can be dismissed for their evident partiality. There are moral disagreements which can be overcome because they rest on factual disagreements that are corrigible, at least to the extent that evidence is available to settle the matter at issue (eg, urgency of combating ozone-layer depletion). Consequentialist moral beliefs are particularly subject to revision in the light of changes of empirical beliefs. Even deontic claims can be undermined by demonstrating that the nature of the actions praised or condemned are not in themselves what the holders of these beliefs take them to be. All moral judgments have an element of supervenience in that they are evaluations of some empirically describable

12 An effect that Jon Elster praises as the 'civilising force of hypocrisy': (1995) 'Strategic Uses of Argument' in K Arrow, R Mnookin, L Ross, A Tversky and R Wilson (eds), *Barriers to the Negotiated Resolution of Conflict*, Norton, pp 236–57. See Williams (Chapter 9).

13 A Gutmann and DF Thompson (1996) *Democracy and Disagreement*, Harvard University Press.

phenomena. Change your comprehension of what is involved in autonomous action, free trade, capital punishment or homosexuality and you may well change your deontic assessment of such phenomena. Or, then again, moral judgment may not respond to the clarification of factual issues for empirical information, even when viewed from a non-personalised perspective, does not necessitate or even always contribute to moral agreement.

Many philosophers have argued that factual agreement does generate moral consensus, but such positions depend on outmoded beliefs in a uniform human nature made up of basic emotional responses, which, in the absence of identifiable distorting circumstances, produce universal responses of acceptance or rejection to identified forms of conduct, motive and even belief.[14] Such views are not simply pre-postmodern; they are pre-latemodern, pre-Marx, and pre-social science. It matters not whether the diversity of human responses to similar fact situations is based on individual genetic differences, group culturation or the differential exercise of capacities for moral reason or rooted in profound differences in epistemological capabilities, the result is the same: there is more to moral judgment that impartiality plus information.

Democracy as collective self-protection

All this does not entirely demolish the pretensions of deliberative democracy. Even the elimination of some bases of moral mistake must be seen as advantageous. Moreover, there is the empirically testable claim that an increase in consensus derives from the right sort of deliberation in the right sort of setting, and consensus on political matters, however it comes about, is generally seen as a moral plus. Whether or not that consensus is a sign of objective truth and justice, it is at least a way of avoiding either coercive intervention or acquiescence in an unjust status quo.

The insufficiency of deliberation with respect to epistemological justification does, however, deflect attention back to the exercise of power in politics, that is the imposition of a binding requirement on a non-consenting minority. It is natural to analyse such situations as involving the unwarranted imposition of majority over minority interests, but, outside total consensus, we have no way of deciding if the minority is morally in the right, or represents a different but equally valid moral position, or is defending vested interests and unjustifiable self-preferences. In this context 'minority' does not analytically refer to disadvantaged and deprived groups, of which there are multitudes, but simply those aggregates that happen to be outside the

---

14 Such efforts may be traced in, for instance, A Smith (1759) *The Theory of Moral Sentiments* (6th edition 1790), Clarendon Press, 1979; and J Rawls (1974) *A Theory of Justice*, Oxford University Press.

majority consensus. Indeed, such aggregates normally include the most privileged and wealthy persons in any society.

At this point there are grounds for a reassertion of the self-protection model of democracy, enlarged, perhaps, to take into account not only protection against the partiality or ignorance of the current holders of economic and political power, but against the moral values of others mediated through the apparatus of state, church, media, law and authorised education.[15] It is important to assert that this majority protection function of electoral democracy is of fundamental importance not simply because of the dialogue model does not live up to its prerequisite of free, equal and informed dialogue, but because, even if it did realise these utopian prerequisites of the ideal speech situation, it could not deliver a consensus based on objectively justified moral agreement. Even so, majority rule can still be justified as a way of maximising the protection of people's interests, including the protection of what they morally value, including their conceptions of justice.

The import of this analysis is wide ranging and fundamental. Political debate should be conducted in a way that recognises that not all disagreement is based on illicit self-preference or misinformation. Therefore politics should not be conducted on the basis that debate can replace the exercise of decisive power through majority decision-making procedures. Further, there is no methodology of impartial informed dialogue, no form of routinised reflective equilibrium, no form of interpreting the history of law as the best that it can be, and no impartial decision-making procedure that can be taken to justify removing or diminishing the power of majorities to protect themselves against the evils and incompetences of governments, courts and employers. This renders problematic efforts to curb the power of majorities so that they do less harm to oppressed minorities: these same measures diminish the capacity of majorities to protect themselves against those minorities which are neither poor, nor oppressed, nor benign.

This is not to deny that there are important ways in which a social culture and a set of political institutions cannot be adjudged better or worse with' respect to maximising the extent and effectiveness of self-protection. Nor does it diminish the particular concern that has to be attached to protection of vulnerable minorities. The democratic ideal is, after all, self-protection for all, not just the self-protection of a majority. Majorities are, in this respect, always second-best devices. But the problem of moral epistemology does mean that we have to see democratic systems as primarily mechanisms for the generation and utilisation of power on the part of the bulk of the people. This means that our efforts should be directed to maximising the causal efficacy of a vote and providing the means whereby votes can be used for the effective protection of the interests of voters. Hence the

---

15 For example the landslide victory for reformists over fundamentalists in Iran's February 2000 parliamentary elections.

absolute centrality of information, not primarily to reach a rational consensus, but to give citizens a basis on which to assess the impact of government conduct on their lives.

That said, it is clearly imperative to develop a political culture in which it is recognised that the interests of all count equally and that the value of each individual person is not diminished simply by being in a minority. This involves the acceptance of such platitudinous truths as that not all self-protection is morally defensible and that everyone's morally justifiable self-protection is equally important. This is the stuff of a sense of justice. It is a virtue of majoritarian self-protection theory that if votes are cast not on the basis of a view of justice but with a view purely to maximising the amoral interests of the voter, then the result may still be better than one in which the amoral preferences of a minority triumph. But majoritarian protectionism is more defensible if it operates in a culture in which votes are cast on the basis of self-interest moderated to the point of moral justifiability, that is, with a view to a fair assessment of the impact of the outcome of the interests of all others, impartially considered by giving their interests equal weight. Moreover, this model can be extended to incorporate a regard not simply for different interests but for different values, or, what amounts to the same thing in many respects, the interests of others as they rather than we conceive of these interests.

At this point in the analysis we can accept the full force of the dialogue model as an element in a morally admirable form of electoral democracy. Such a dialogue encourages voters to put their self-interest in a context that enables them to judge its comparative worth and to exercise their voting power in the light of this judgment.[16] The outcome could be less discrimination against vulnerable minorities without diminishing the protection of majority interests and values.

In this context, we must emphasise the significance of the subject matter of democratic choice, or that which the voting is actually about. One of the traditional ways of seeking to ensure that majorities have regard to minority interests is to require that they choose general rules rather than make particular decisions directly bearing on what happens to identifiable individuals. This is part of the complex Rule of Law ideal, which serves many different functions. One of these functions is that political choices of *rules* are more satisfactory than individual political determinations because they are less likely to be discriminatory. Most effective in this regard are universal general rules which apply equally to all citizens, especially in societies where citizens are, as in Rousseau's republic, in essentially similar circumstances.[17]

16 This approach rejects both the public choice axiom of voter self-preference (JM Buchanan and G Tullock (1962) *The Calculus of Consent*, University of Michigan Press), and the Dworkinian downgrading of 'external' or other-directed preferences (RM Dworkin (1985) *A Matter of Principle*, Harvard University Press, pp 234–6).

17 T Campbell (1996) *The Legal Theory of Ethical Positivism*, Dartmouth, pp 58–61.

Currently, it may be argued, it is an obstacle to democratic power that voters get to choose only representatives who become members of a legislative assembly and occupy high executive office, thus leaving citizens at the mercy of whatever those elected persons come up with by way of executive action and legislation, with only a generalised and periodic opportunity to alter the rulers and thereby only indirectly the rules. One of the great democratic opportunities of new communication technologies is that voters might be given more direct access to debate on and choice of legislation, as Rousseau envisaged.[18]

Global victory

Yet all this, it will be said, is beside the point, or, at least, beside the points raised by globalisation as to the emptiness of the choices left to political procedures of any sort. The essentials of our lives are decided in the boardrooms of the multinationals, the power politics of World Trade Organisation 'agreements' and the exigencies of the laws of supply and demand in global markets.

This critique deserves a multiple response. First it needs to be said that there have been few states that have ever had political sovereignty in the sense of an actual capacity to successful pursue their prime objectives. The limitations on the achievements of politics may now be more global than local but they are not necessarily greater. The argument for democracy does depend on there being open-ended possibilities as to what can be achieved politically. Further, there is a tendency to overlook the potential for interstate co-operation for the protection of their mutual interest in not being at the mercy of a system of international competition that favours existing economic powers.

Secondly, the inevitability of global capitalism on current conceptions of the free trade model may be perceived as a legitimating ideology on a par with 'iron tendencies' identified in Marx's *Communist Manifesto* as leading to the inevitable downfall of capitalism and the equally determined emergence of Communism. The same arguments applied to Marx's historical determinism can be applied to liberal capitalist historical determinism. Both are effective propaganda; neither is it established hypothesis.

Thirdly, and relatedly, the propaganda of 'no real choice' is posited on a circular affirmation that the people's preference is always and inevitably for increased productivity and increased consumer goods, rather than better lives and happier communities. This may be ridiculed by saying that, of course, countries are free to be poor, but this again assumes that we all agree

18 J Fishkin (1991) *Democracy and Deliberation*, Yale University Press.

as to what constitutes poverty and how much consumer goods contribute to human happiness.

Nevertheless, we have to take cognisance of the fact that states are no longer sovereign in even the legal sense that they are free to extricate themselves from international law, particularly international trade law, a law which is almost entirely detached from any form of democratic control, and rides along on the coat-tails of the globalisation of 'human rights'.

The eventual way forward in this situation may be no different in principle from the way forward within undemocratic polities in general, in that the weak must gather their strength collectively against the individually strong through the development of institutions which provide an equal say for all affected parties, independent of wealth, race, gender or age. Here we have to discover the essentially collectivist element in democracy, albeit with an eye to redrawing the boundaries of the relevant polities to take account of increasing economic inter-dependence. Cosmopolitan theory points down this path to globalising democracy.[19]

Evidently, there are multitudes of problems confronting the development of global democracy. One concern is the amplification of existing problems of public choice theory. Individualistically oriented theorists of democracy, especially, it must be said, utilitarian self-protectionist theorists, have always been foxed by the connection between voting and individual interest. Voting, it is said, is an irrational activity, because one person's vote almost never affects the outcome and therefore there is no causal connection between voting and protecting interests.[20]

We should note that a similar form of argument can be used against many other examples of apparently irrational individual conduct, like joining an army to fight a just war, or paying taxes when you could evade detection if you did not. The standard justification to the model is to admit an element of moral fairness into the domain of rationality, but we need not go that far. The logic of collective action can be based on the ineffectiveness, not the immorality, of an individual approach to politics. Majorities in democratic theory have to be seen as more than the sum of the largest number of aggregate preferences, but as a form of collective action whereby 'the people' jointly rid themselves of unwanted rulers or rules.

The rational choice model cannot be simply translated to the international sphere, because of the disparate sizes of independent polities and the differences between the ontology of persons and that of states. However, the international vision of democracy can be of a system whereby the interests of the most numerous collectivities, taking account of their divergent

19 D Held (1995) *Democracy and Global Order: From the Modern State to Cosmopolitan Governance*, Stanford University Press.

20 R Wollheim (1969) 'A Paradox in the Theory of Democracy', in P Laslett and G Runciman (eds), *Philosophy, Politics and Society*, Blackwell.

sizes, can be brought to bear on those powerful minorities whose interests are given disproportionate weight in a world which is globalised in the sense that economic power is less and less cabinable and economic inequality is irrationally dependent on the accident of birthplace. And so, even if globalisation in the sense of interconnectedness of states is largely irreversible, something which is doubtless greatly exaggerated, there are no *a priori* reasons why democratisation of the globe should not feature as part of the solution to less palatable consequences of globalisation. Meanwhile, there is always the possibility of inter-state co-operation, a form of solidarity among poorer nations which echoes the unionisation of industrial workers in capitalist systems.

Yet such far-sighted hopes have little prospect of success if democracy does not regain credibility within the nation-state. This takes us to one of my initial points, the – on balance – pernicious global impact of the market model on democratic politics. I say 'on balance' because there are undoubted benefits to viewing citizens as political consumers in so far as this both affirms that it is citizen preferences that count, and in presenting the vote as a power to be utilised by its possessor. Indeed, at first sight, and in its historical development, the self-protection model can be viewed as a market model. The Benthamite vision of artificially harmonising the interests of citizen and ruler by making the latter subject to re-election by the former, with free speech as a prerequisite of informed electoral choice, is at the core of the self-protection model. Modern developments which stress that, in a pluralist society, winning a constitutionally sufficient majority requires governments to appeal to as many different interests as possible enhance the market flavour of the reigning theories of democracy.

The flaw in any acceptably precise application of the market theory of democracy has always been the fact that, in an electoral outcome, there is only one purchase, one elected government, and in relation to the goods provided by the elected government between elections, not everyone does or can receive that for which their vote might reasonably be considered sufficient payment. Elections are collective purchases. Indeed they cannot be properly regarded as purchases at all, since the resulting political establishment is a public good, enjoyed or suffered by those who did not pay for it as well as those who did. Governments are not owned, at least not by voters.

Moreover, the market model can be viewed as corrupting in so far as it legitimates voting as a form of self-preference, indeed requires it as a necessary prerequisite of the outcome. Hence the normative attractiveness of the deliberative counter-theories which foster impartiality and other moral attitudes in the democratic citizenry. By moving away from the idea that a vote is a means of obtaining personal benefit towards seeing the vote as an expression of opinion as to the general interest – as an interim decision-making process which temporarily interrupts a free and equal debate between all those affected by the decision in question – deliberative democracy gains the moral high ground.

Further, the market model encourages the acquiescence in the assumption that the goods to be fought for and won in the political arena are economic goods, either by way of redistribution, or in relation to facilitating the attainment of wealth through economic activity. Democratic politics is the pursuit of economic advantage by other means. It encourages the view that the worth of a vote to citizens is what they can purchase with it by way of economic advantage. This means that it is in effect acceptable to 'buy' and 'sell' votes both analogically and literally.

This viewpoint extends to the basic accoutrements of democratic politics. Political office is not only a source of gainful employment to the elected representative, but a means for the disbursement of economic favours. Information is needed by voters to make the instrumentally best choices and is therefore a valuable commodity to be created for gain, bought and sold, borrowed and lent. Speech as the instrument of persuasion in an essentially economic process must be available to all citizens, but its availability can be at a price, for speech is as much a commodity as the vote itself. And so we enter the world of highly rewarded opinion leaders with hidden paymasters, lobbyists on contract, public relations experts paid by results, political party fund raising, advertising expenditure, media owners and payments for asking parliamentary questions as a natural mode of democratic politics. Some of these activities are legal and others illegal, depending on where you are and when. Some of them are little more than a necessary economic base for non-economic political activity. But, in total, they amount to a commodification of available and effective political discourse, which carries the idea of a vote as a purchase to its logical conclusion.

If this is the democracy that is being globalised, then representative democracy is in real trouble since the market theory itself requires that economic and political currencies not be interchangeable. Democracy is a system of political equality, and political equality is unobtainable where the exercise of the equal rights involved can be bought and sold. Hence the understandable concern about campaign finances, political advertising, economic gerrymandering and media ownership.

In theory we can look to procedural human rights for assistance here, but the values of freedom have overcome the values of equality with respect to the human rights which are being globally prioritised. In particular, freedom of the market makes any real measures to control political advertising and media ownership unrealisable. Consequently deliberative democracy is in no position to sustain its preconditions of equal access and participation in the relevant debates. Despite its many attractions, therefore, the market model is inevitably implicated in the commodification of politics in ways that must depress democratic expectations.

There are, however, some positive lines of thought yet to be explored, some of which take us to some crucial connections of law and democracy. Thus, there is scope for a rapprochement between self-determination, self-protection and deliberative theory. To achieve this we must first curb the pretensions of deliberative democracy to be the only theory which does not simply take preferences as given and seek a mechanism to turn private into collective decisions, but involves a developing interaction of views which progress towards a novel outcome. For instance, in utilitarian theory freedom of expression has long been ascribed the role of rendering individual preferences and beliefs more rational and more co-ordinated. There is no problem in principle in developing this openness to include debate as to what constitutes a just agreement between participating parties. The self that is expressed or protected can be a self that cares about others as well as itself and is capable of giving equal consideration to the interests of others. Such self-interest can involve tolerance of the different values of others, but cannot be expected to endorse those values. Nor, as we have seen, is it to be expected that good faith and well-informed debate can resolve such value disagreements as remain. Hence the need to retain the vote as an exercise of equal power which minimises the inevitable harm arising from the fact that not everyone can get their own way in a polity. Nevertheless, informed and impartial dialogue can serve to improve self-protectionism in terms of its own objectives, without being able to resolve basic value disagreements. Having lured elements of deliberative democracy into the self-protection camp we are then faced with the utopianism of seeking to approximate to an ideal speech situation in a world of globalised markets. Two suggestions may be made in this respect, one relating to the form and the other to the content of law.

The Rule of Law is essential to democracy for a variety of reasons. One reason is that, where law is the prime object of democratic deliberation and choice, there is a greater chance of self-preferences rising to a measure of impartiality simply by dint of the fact that the matters at issue are presented in terms of categories and classes rather than individuals and particulars. At its most artificial, a universal law which applies equally to all citizens with respect to a matter in which they are all similarly situated, even selfish self-interests will, as Rousseau notes, opt for that law which is in the general interest. At its most aspirational, having decisions generalised, and the categories of choice explicit, makes the citizen face up – preferably in public – to the moral choices involved in selecting relevant criteria.

If this has merit, the radical implication is that citizens should participate in debate and choice of rules directly rather than via their elected representatives, a procedure that also has the advantage of reducing the current slippage between what parties promise and what they actually deliver, thus diminishing the power of political parties, the influence of well-financed pressure groups and the opportunities for corruption.

The second positive suggestion, which responds to the charge of utopianism against deliberative democracy, has to do with the content of democratic law. It concerns, contra the tendencies of globalised market parameters, the strict separation of politics from financial inputs designed to influence the outcome in favour of one party or policy. All political choices must be made in the light of their economic consequences, *inter alia.* This does not mean that economic power should be permitted to influence those choices. Such a policy requires draconian restrictions on party political finance, political donations, availability of paid advertising and ownership control of media outlets including editorial content. Without such measures, even the limited potentials of deliberative democracy are unrealisable and the self-protective function of the vote is vitiated by absence of reliable information and adequate debate.[21]

Taken together – choice of law, not choice of law-makers; and financially uncorrupted information and opinion flow – this may seem a taller than feasible order. However, there is one aspect of globalised markets that potentially works in their favour, namely the ever-increasing availability of economical and efficient means of communication. The Trojan horse of economic market power may turn out to be the information technologies it has spawned. With a multimedia communication system in every home, the prospect of widely viewed debate between and with random selected representatives, and electronic voting, there could exist the means if not the will for a shift to a more direct form of municipal democracy. This in turn may enhance the chances of democratising the international order so as to redirect global markets to serve the well-being of those vast populations who do not share in the creation and consumption of the goods that are and could be available to them rather than the profitability of transnational companies and the governments who, increasingly, serve them.

21 C Sunstein (1993) *Democracy and the Problem of Free Speech*, Free Press.

7

Democracy as Comparative Advantage

Roland Rich

> 'Democracy is a very nice thing but, you know, the world would be a much better place without it.'[1]

I am fond of this quote not just because it is such nonsense but because of its provenance. It comes from the late George Papadopoulos, the unrepentant leader of the junta of colonels who ruled Greece from 1967 to 1974. It was obtained by a journalist who was one of his last visitors in his prison cell where he was serving his sentence of 'life imprisonment plus ten years', imposed by President Karamanlis after he commuted the sentence of death passed by the courts. It is fitting that such criticism of democracy come from a dictator who did his country so much harm, a country that had otherwise contributed the very word 'democracy' to our language.

My argument here – the very antithesis of the Papadopoulos dictum – is that democracy itself can make the world a better place. While democracy is not a sufficient condition, it is a necessary precondition for sound and sustainable growth and good governance. This chapter will begin with some brief comments on global markets and will then examine the universal values embodied in democracy, concluding with the observation that democratic governance gives a nation an economic advantage over competitors following forms of governance such as one-party rule. I will also look briefly at constitutionalism the part it must play in the democratisation process in our region.

The global village

'Globalisation' has become a controversial term leading some commentators to portray it as an economic philosophy bolstering the strong against the weak. The anti-globalisation forces had their greatest victory in the coalition they were able to bring to bear against the OECD's proposed Multilateral Agreement on Investment. And unlike the violent coalition of the angry at

1 *Financial Times* (1999) 10–11 July.

Seattle, the blow against MAI was achieved through rational argument over the Internet. In a 1998 paper, I applauded this victory not on grounds of substance but because of the process it developed.[2] In terms of substance, I believe a document such as a Multilateral Agreement on Investment would be a valuable tool to create as much of an international level playing field as possible. It would be of most benefit to small and medium sized companies who do not have the clout of the world's corporate behemoths. An MAI would be a logical successor to the thousands of existing bilateral investment protection agreements that attempt to achieve similar ends. My admiration for the process of the defeat of the MAI is due to the fact that it showed the strength of global civil society.

We readily accept the indispensable role of civil society in liberal democracies. Criticism of governments by NGOs and civil society activists is a healthy corrective in modern societies. As the world develops into a global marketplace spawning global rules and practices, it is as necessary to develop global civil society that will adopt the same role as played by civil society in the domestic context. The process began through the human rights movements such as Amnesty International and was consolidated through the environmental movement in the groundbreaking work of Greenpeace and others. The MAI debate showed that global civil society exists wherever there is a phone line and an Internet terminal.

One of the aspects of the MAI debate I found curious was that the most resolute opponents of the OECD's draft treaty often happened to be among the staunchest advocates of international rules in the field of human rights and the protection of the environment. They criticised the MAI for limiting the rights of governments of developing countries to regulate foreign investors while at the same time insisting that those same countries become party to a raft of international treaties prohibiting trade in endangered species, protecting the ozone layer and fostering human rights. So while they purported to oppose globalisation, they were nevertheless supporting one of its most prominent manifestations, the acceptance of global rules and practices on a growing list of subjects.

The way globalisation has been dealt with in the media has tended to give it a mercantile character. Yet each one of us has stumbled upon examples of the human face of globalisation. I recall a rather striking example. When I served at the Australian Embassy in Vientiane, I was looking into the fate of the upland people of Laos who are predominantly Hmong villagers. The Hmong live in inhospitable upland forests and they practice hunting and shifting agriculture, perhaps better known as slash and burn farming. There may have been a time when low population densities and high child mortality would have kept the environmental impact of slash and

2 R Rich (1998) 'Non-State Actors and Development Assistance', Australia New Zealand Society of International Law, Proceedings of the 6th Annual Conference, CIPL (available at http://www.law.anu.edu.au/).

burn practices to sustainable levels with the forest being given 40 or 50 years to regenerate between the succeeding cultivations. Those days are past: now the environmental impact is clearly negative and is perhaps most clearly evident in the high siltation of Laos's major rivers.

The Lao Government's response has been to move the Hmong out of the safety of their beloved mountaintops to settlements in the lowlands. The only other solution is to find some form of sustainable livelihood in the upland areas. An Australian scientist investigating options was focusing on two products. It seems that the diseased bark of certain species of agarwood is in such demand in the Middle East, where it is used for funeral incense, that cultivating this tree may provide considerable income. And perfume manufacturers are always looking for exotic new rainforest plants. So the way in which the Hmong may be able to retain their upland lifestyle is to sell renewable forest products to customers they have never met, living thousands of kilometres away and using the products for purposes that have no connection with the Hmong lifestyle.

It is because globalisation has a human face that I have always been more comfortable with Marshall McLuhan's term 'the Global Village'. The Global Village seems better to imbue the meaning of the term with more human features and a manageable size whereas the term that succeeded it, globalisation, seems to conjure up forces beyond human understanding with a gestalt power beyond human control. But whatever name we give it, we need to describe a process that has well and truly begun and the effects of which we continue to grapple with. To reject globalisation is about as useful as rejecting the industrial revolution. The challenge is in understanding the phenomenon, harnessing its virtues and minimising its vices.

It is curious that the modern processes of globalisation and democratisation have both been described as occurring in three waves. Professor Samuel Huntington describes the three waves of democratisation as follows.[3] The first long wave begun in the 19th century led to the triumph of democracy in some 30 countries by the 1920s, though the rise of fascism reduced the number of democracies to no more than a dozen by the 1940s. The second wave began after the war leading to some 30 countries becoming liberal democracies. The third and most impressive wave has occurred in the last decade, although Huntington traces the process from the collapse of authoritarianism on the Iberian Peninsula in the 1970s. I will say more about this phenomenon below.

The analysis of the three waves of economic globalisation has tended to owe more to journalistic descriptions.[4] The first wave was the growing support for trade liberalisation after the Second World War. This was rein-

3 SP Huntington (1991) *The Third Wave: Democratization in the Late Twentieth Century*, University of Oklahoma Press.

4 Most recently in Rajiv Lall's article (1999) 'Time to get Wired', *Far Eastern Economic Review*, 19 August.

forced by successive rounds of trade liberalisation, helping to create a global marketplace. International trade became the means whereby developing countries could grow their economies and take advantage of their various trade advantages. The second wave occurred because of the worldwide opening of financial markets reacting to the oil crisis of the 1970s. Currencies were allowed to float and restrictions on capital flows were progressively eased thus unleashing the phenomenal growth of cross-border capital flows. Australia was to jump aboard this bandwagon in the early 1980s with the result that the Aussie dollar became the sixth most-traded currency in the world. And it was the flow of short-term capital or 'hot money' that was to become a lightning rod for criticism of globalisation after the 1997 Asian financial crisis.

The third wave of globalisation can be seen in the free flow of information around the world especially since the end of the Cold War. Television makes every crisis seem like a local crisis. Culture and language are driven around a borderless world by the news and entertainment industries. The effect of the Internet is still not completely clear. Its significance is indisputable. Its anarchic nature and democratic disposition augur well, though an important problem the gap remains between the haves and have-nots of the information age. It is the Internet that will be pushing the third wave of globalisation in the coming century, empowering individuals and corporations while minimising the role of governments. Nations of the world will be left with a stark choice of joining the global village or embracing forms of autarky, which are becoming the last refuge of authoritarianism and which we can witness in our own region in the lamentable regimes of Burma and North Korea.

The growth of democracy in the 1990s

Huntington's Third Wave of democracy describes a historical process. Larry Diamond has attempted to quantify it. Writing in 1996, Diamond embarked upon a process of definition and categorisation to measure the extent of the Third Wave.[5] This is not a simple process in that democracy is not easy to define for practical purposes. Diamond points to research from Berkeley that identified 550 subtypes of democracy. We are familiar with 'democracy with adjectives' in our own region including the various forms of people's democracy as in Mao's China, the ill-fated guided democracy of Indonesia's New Order under Suharto and the questionable social engineering democracy practised in Lee Kuan Yew's Singapore.

Diamond therefore begins with an important distinction between electoral democracy and liberal democracy. The former describes a system where electoral competition exists complemented by universal adult suf-

5 L Diamond (1996) 'Is the Third Wave Over?' 7 *Journal of Democracy* 20–37.

frage. The latter adds to that definition the existence of civil and political freedom. And, of course, therein lies the next definitional dilemma.

Liberal democracies extend beyond minimalist electoral democracies in a number of ways including the absence of significant 'reserved domains' for the military of other groups, horizontal accountability in a constitutional system of institutional checks and balances, and extensive civic freedoms leading to genuine pluralism. Diamond goes on to list nine specific features of liberal democracy, thus setting a high benchmark.[6] Having argued the theory, Diamond employs the Freedom House annual survey of freedom around the world as his measuring stick.[7] While there is inevitably a degree of arbitrariness in any scorecard, the Freedom House index has the advantage of many years of refinement and considerable international support. Diamond's next step is to measure the growth in both electoral and liberal democracies.

The growth of electoral democracies in the course of the Third Wave is impressive. At the commencement of the process in 1974, there were 39

---

6 Ibid, pp 22–3:

(1) Real power lies – in fact as well as in constitutional theory – with elected officials and their appointees, rather than with unaccountable internal actors (eg, the military) or foreign powers.

(2) Executive power is constrained constitutionally and held accountable by other government institutions (such as an independent judiciary, parliament, ombudsman, and auditor general).

(3) Not only are electoral outcomes uncertain, with a significant opposition vote and the presumption of party alternation in government over time, but no group that adheres to constitutional principles is denied the right to form a party and contest elections (even if electoral thresholds and other rules prevent smaller parties from winning representation in parliament).

(4) Cultural, ethnic, religious, and other minority groups, as well as traditionally disadvantaged or unempowered majorities, are not prohibited (legally or in practice) from expressing their interests in the political process, and from using their language and culture.

(5) Beyond parties and intermittent elections, citizens have multiple, ongoing channels and means for the expression and representation of their interests and values, including a diverse array of autonomous associations, movements, and groups that they are free to form and join.

(6) In addition to associational freedom and pluralism, there exist alternative sources of information, including independent media, to which citizens have (politically) unfettered access.

(7) Individuals have substantial freedom of belief, opinion, discussion, speech, publication, assembly, demonstration, and petition.

(8) Citizens are politically equal under the law (even though they are invariably unequal in their political resources), and the above-mentioned individual and group liberties are effectively protected by an independent, impartial judiciary whose decisions are enforced and respected by other centres of power.

(9) The rule of law protects citizens from unjustified detention, exile, terror, torture, and undue interference in their personal lives not only by the state but also by organised anti-state forces.

7 Freedom House, *Freedom in the World 1995* (available at http://freedomhouse.org/).

electoral democracies among the world's 142 countries. They were concentrated in Europe, the Americas and Oceania. This figure remained fairly static until 1990 when the figure jumped to 76 out of 165 – the percentage leap is a spectacular 27.5 per cent to 46.1 per cent. The process continues throughout the period under review:

1974 – 39 out of 142 or 27.5%
1990 – 76 out of 165 or 46.1%
1991 – 91 out of 183 or 49.7%
1992 – 99 out of 186 or 53.2%
1993 – 108 out of 190 or 56.8%
1994 – 114 out of 191 or 59.7%
1995 – 117 out of 191 or 61.3%

The leap of electoral democracies in the 1990s reflects the end of Cold War ideological competition. One system of government had 'won' and countries were quick to take note. Many of the conversions to electoral democracies were based on deep-seated and informed national will that gave the systems the sustainability to endure economic downturns. Among this category of countries one can certainly list those central European States like Hungary, Poland and the Czech Republic that had some national memory of democracy and whose people had secretly admired the achievements of the West European democracies. There were also gains in Latin America and in central Asia where, for example, Mongolia took to liberal democracy with gusto.

Yet for all the self-congratulatory achievement in the growth of electoral democracy, the qualitative analysis of these democracies shows a more sober picture. The trend line in relation to the growth in liberal democracies has not been nearly as impressive as demonstrated in Diamond's next table which shows the number of liberal democracies out of the total number of electoral democracies;

1990 – 65 out of 76 or 85.5%
1991 – 76 out of 91 or 83.5%
1992 – 75 out of 99 or 75.8%
1993 – 72 out of 108 or 66.7%
1994 – 76 out of 114 or 66.7%
1995 – 76 out of 117 or 65.0%

The number of liberal democracies is a relatively stable figure and it accounts for some 40 per cent of all the world's nations. This is a significant achievement in itself. It would also provide an interesting research project to compare the economic performance of the 76 liberal democracies with the other categories of countries including the electoral democracies, the pseudo-democracies and the shrinking but still significant 20 per cent of nations that refuse to allow any form of multiparty competition. My guess would be that there is a strong correlation between liberal democracy and economic success.

Yet, as Diamond points out, the picture is not as rosy as it might be. There have been many examples of the resurgence of authoritarian practices under elected civilian presidents.[8] Other states that turned to systems of electoral competition have allowed the process to degenerate into electoral charades.[9] Diamond is particularly concerned at the situation in Africa and he lists 10 countries whose electoral systems are so flawed as to put them among the pseudo-democracies.[10]

While perhaps not sufficient to balance this disturbing trend of countries reverting to old authoritarian ways, there have been a number of particularly felicitous developments in the past year or two. Free and fair elections have been held in Indonesia and Nigeria, significant countries by any measure. South Africa has maintained its commitment to democracy even with the transition from its national leader to his successor. Fiji has seen a change in government under its constitution whereby the non-Indigenous people will have greater influence than in the past and on this occasion, to its great credit, the outgoing government played to the rules. Thailand has adopted an innovative and progressive constitution aimed at eliminating the worst aspects of money politics in their electoral and parliamentary system. The Philippines had its second constitutional and peaceful change of leadership by electoral means since the fall of Marcos. And the recent change of government in Papua New Guinea holds out the prospect of that country finally trying to come to grips with its deep-seated electoral and governance problems.

Also on the positive side we are seeing a greater reluctance on the part of militaries to seize power, as was particularly evident in Indonesia where the military has accepted its diminished role and must now participate in the national debate about *dwifungsi* which is likely to see its eventual return to barracks. In Africa the terrible consequences brought about by military leaders in countries such as Liberia, Sierra Leone and the then Zaire, has left the elites and the wider public with little appetite for military coups.

So I think we can conclude with a positive scorecard on the gains of democracy in the 1990s. Indeed, I would quibble with Huntington's argument that the Third Wave began with the Portuguese overthrow of fascism in 1974. I think this and the return of Spanish democracy is better viewed as a late denouement of the consequences of the Second World War and thus part of the Second Wave, rather than triggering a new historical development. Surely the fall of the Berlin Wall and the collapse of Soviet ideology and Cold War competition should be seen as the commencement of the Third Wave.

---

8 Diamond (1996), p 29, lists Peru, Russia and Venezuela in this category.

9 Diamond lists Kazakhstan, Turkmenistan, Tajikistan, Armenia and Azerbaijan: ibid.

10 Senegal, Côte d'Ivoire, Burkina Faso, Ghana, Togo, Cameroon, Zimbabwe, Kenya and Ethiopia: ibid.

I do agree with Diamond, however, that the challenge before the international community, and in particular the world's liberal democracies, is to consolidate the gains of the Third Wave and help entrench the process of democratisation in the recently reformed countries. If I may be allowed a small plug for my Centre, this work is the very rationale of the establishment of the Centre for Democratic Institutions by the Foreign Minister, Mr Alexander Downer.

Democracy and universality

In facing the challenge of propagating democratic reform and consolidating democratic change, democracy activists have a significant advantage. The international community as a whole appears to have accepted the universal value of democracy. There does not appear to be any significant battle left to fight on the theory involved. I base this assertion on two grounds. Firstly, I review the arguments put forward by Nobel laureate Amartya Sen in his seminal work on democracy. Secondly, I draw our attention to an important resolution passed by the United Nations Commission on Human Rights in April 1999 entitled 'Promotion of the Right to Democracy'.

I had the privilege of hearing Professor Sen deliver his address on 'Democracy as a Universal Value' at the World Movement for Democracy conference in New Delhi in February in 1999. It has since been published in the *Journal of Democracy*.[11] He argues that a significant change has come to pass in the course of this century whereby the idea of democracy as the 'normal' form of government to which any nation is entitled became established. In the 19th century, theorists asked whether a certain country was ready for democracy. In the 20th century the paradigm shifted. The question was seen to be wrong. It is not right to ask if a country is fit for democracy but rather to see that a country can become fit through democracy.

Sen argues that unanimity of opinion should not be the test of a universal value. If that were the test, there would be no universal values. Rather he puts forward a different test noting that 'the claim of a universal value is that people anywhere may have reason to see it as valuable'.[12] He concludes that we have come to the point where there is now 'acceptance of democracy as a universally relevant system',[13] and that the onus for rejecting this claim has now passed to its opponents.

He sees in democracy a number of essential functions to the healthy functioning of a nation. Political and social participation has intrinsic value. To be prevented from such participation is a major deprivation. Sen also sees an instrumental value in democracy because it allows people a hearing

---

11 AK Sen (1999) 'Democracy as a Universal Value' 10 *Journal of Democracy* 3–17.

12 Ibid, p 12.

13 Ibid, p 4.

and helps direct political attention to their claims and needs. Thirdly, democracy has a constructive value in that its necessary dialogue allows citizens to learn from each other and thus allows society to develop. The point I wish to emphasise is that the intrinsic, instrumental and constructive values of democracy are universally applicable. All societies will benefit from allowing democracy to operate in this way.

Professor Sen deals in some details with criticisms of democracy that have been advanced at various points. He dismisses the notion that authoritarian systems of government are better at fostering development as lacking empirical support. Further, he counters the argument by drawing on his analysis of famines in which he concludes 'no substantial famine has ever occurred in any independent and democratic country with a relatively free press'.[14] This is because famines are preventable and a government in a democratic country facing criticism and elections will do all it can to prevent them. The contrast with the government of the Democratic People's Republic of Korea is striking.

The East Asian economic crisis brings out, according to Sen 'among other things, the penalty of undemocratic governance'.[15] The lack of transparency in business matters prevented public participation in reviewing financial arrangements. Once the economic hardships began to bite, the protective power of democracy was badly missed. I am pleased to note that the two examples given by Professor Sen in this regard, Indonesia and Thailand, both appear to be heeding the warning and moving purposefully towards establishing stronger democratic institutions.

I should also note that Professor Sen deals in some detail with the argument that 'Asian Values' provide an exception to his description of democracy as a universal value. He talks about the diversity within the various cultures and the religious and intellectual bases for democracy in both Asian and Western culture.

Support for Professor Sen's work was provided in April 1999 by the United Nations Commission on Human Rights. The UNCHR adopted Resolution 1999/57 on the Promotion of the Right to Democracy. It is of great interest and I annex it to this chapter. It certainly provides weighty evidence in support of the proposition that democracy is a universal value and indeed goes one step further in employing the language of entitlement.

In its preambular paragraphs, the Resolution recognises 'that democracy, development and respect for all human rights and fundamental freedoms are interdependent and mutually reinforcing' and resolves 'to take all measures within [the Commission's] power to secure for all people the fundamental democratic rights and freedoms to which they are entitled'. The second operative paragraph lists many of the fundamental features of demo-

14 Ibid, pp 6–7.

15 Ibid, p 8.

cratic governance including freedom of expression, the protection of the Rule of Law, universal suffrage, the right of political participation and the right of citizens to choose their governmental system through constitutional or other democratic means.

As we know, United Nations resolutions are persuasive but not binding. In this instance they are an expression of the opinion of governments of the international community on the issue of democracy. The weight to be accorded to the resolution will be determined in large part by analysing the voting pattern of the 51 members of the UNCHR. The first point to note is that no delegation voted in the negative. This in itself is a remarkable piece of evidence in support of Sen. Of the 51 delegations only two, China and Cuba, abstained, leaving the remaining 49 countries, from all corners of the earth, in support. It now remains for us to follow the passage of the concept of the right to democracy through the other organs of the United Nations such as the General Assembly to see if the balance of the international community also accepts this notion and to see if other one-party states are the only delegations that decide to abstain.

Democracy as comparative advantage

One of the reasons why democracy is a universally applicable system is that in the global economy it gives a country a comparative advantage. I do not wish to downplay the importance of the traditional factors. Proximity to markets remains important. Quality and dependability of supply are essential ingredients. Needless to say, price is critical and thus the cost of labour and raw materials remain just as relevant as ever. I would argue, however, that these traditional economic factors are no longer sufficient to judge competitiveness. These days, economic decision-makers are looking for a further factor: good governance.

To put this issue into practical terms one need but look at the various international market actors. Investors are the first to come to mind. Their importance to the international system and in particular to the economies of developing countries can be seen from the following World Bank chart,[16] showing official and private flows and then private flows as a percentage of total flows:

1990	\$56b/\$44b	44%
1993	\$53b/\$167b	75%
1996	\$32b/\$276b	89%
1998	\$48b/\$295b	82%

It is quite clear that to mobilise the external funds needed for development purposes, the governments and private sectors of developing countries must

16 World Bank Group, *Global Development Finance 1999* (available at http://www.worldbank.org).

change their traditional focus from Official Development Assistance and International Financial Institution loans to the private sectors of the nations of the industrialised world. But the private flows are not distributed evenly among developing countries. To attract Western investors one needs to demonstrate not only the prospect of strong returns but also security of investment. So investors look at issues such as the strength of the legal system, the transparency of government decision-making and the freedom of movement of people, money and ideas. It may have been argued in the halcyon days of East Asian growth not too long ago, that investors preferred sweetheart deals concluded on the quiet with strong governments. I believe one lesson of the 1997 crisis has been to disabuse us of these notions. Investors prefer openness and transparency and to act with certainty within the confines of clear laws. They prefer countries with good governance.

The manufacturer investing in a foreign country has a particular need for good governance. As producers and employers within a foreign jurisdiction, manufacturers have a particularly close relationship with local officialdom. They need the certainty and consistency that only good governance and the Rule of Law can provide. Increasingly, in our global village, manufacturers need to meet the expectations not only of local rules but also of international civil society I described above. Labour standards and working conditions that do not meet the expectations of international civil society may well face a consumer backlash.

Similar issues arise for traders. Although their relationship with the foreign country is not as intimate as that of the investor, they still need to deal with the banking sector, the customs bureaucracy and with counterparts in the private sector or the state trading companies. Their preference is also for good governance.

Economic actors also have another concern in common. They prefer to deal with countries with minimal corruption. I believe there has been a basic re-evaluation of this issue in the course of the decade. What was once seen as an inevitable part of economic life that perhaps even had the benefit of cutting red tape and facilitating progress on projects, is now seen as a terrible drain on a country's economic effort. The industrialised world has accepted its responsibility in the process, as, after all, for every bribe taker there is a bribe giver. The drafting and entry into force of the OECD Bribery Convention[17] was the signal that the battle against bribery and corruption was joined. The best means of dealing with corruption is through good governance. And the best means of assuring good governance is through the transparency and accountability and representation that parliamentary, liberal and secular democracy assures.

---

17 Organisation for Economic Cooperation and Development (OECD), *Convention on Combating Bribery of Foreign Public Officials in International Business Transactions* (available at http: //www.oecd.org).

Thus has democracy become comparative advantage. Democracy is clearly not a sufficient condition but it is a necessary precondition. The power of democracy to shape institutions and to protect individuals has its economic complementarities. A developing country with a democratic form of government will have an advantage over its non-democratic competitor in attracting investors, manufacturers, traders and probably even tourists. In a global economy this is a considerable advantage.

It is also my view that a democracy will have a comparative advantage in managing a market economy, another necessary precondition for success a global economy. This is a difficult assertion to justify. The economic success of China over recent years needs to be taken into account. But it remains my view that an authoritarian state will not feel able to allow the freedoms necessary to fuel a market economy over the long haul. I do not believe it is possible to sustain a system that grants individuals economic freedoms but continues to deny them civil and political freedoms. And I have doubts about the economic decision-making process in an authoritarian country where politics has always had priority over economics. It strikes me as a formula for corruption and crony capitalism.

A good example of the freedom needed in a market economy is freedom of information. Decisions in the corporate and financial worlds are based on the speed and accuracy of information. It is analysis based on information and risk based on that analysis which may well give one company a competitive edge over another. Freedom of expression, artistic freedom, the right to impart and receive information, freedom of the press, transparency and access to government and corporate decisions are all therefore critical to the success of a market economy, particularly in a situation of competition in a global market. Authoritarian states find it impossible to grant that freedom. They consider the political necessity to control the flows of information paramount. China's battle against the Internet is a fascinating case study.[18]

Another freedom critical to the success of a market economy is an individual's freedom of movement. Innovation often comes from outside influences and meeting new people. The most cosmopolitan societies are best at innovation and cultural renewal. As the global economy moves further into the information age, this aspect of economic competitiveness will become ever more crucial.

A further example of the essentiality of freedoms guaranteed by the civil and political rights to the fate of national markets in a global economy is the freedom of association. We have seen that democracy encourages good governance and an essential aspect of democracy is the right to meet and act together in civil society organisations. These noisy and difficult groups hounding governments and corporations on a host of different

18 *Reporters sans Frontieres* (1999) Press Release, 9 August (available at http://www.rsf.fr).

issues provide a necessary corrective for good national and corporate governance. A national economy will be weaker without the benefits of criticism from the NGO movement.

Constitutionalism

In the context of democracy as comparative advantage, a particular mention of constitutionalism is required and it seems appropriate to include a comment on recent developments in Asia in relation to constitutionalism. Constitutionalism is virtually a universal concept: only six states do not have a single documentary constitution.[19] And of these six, several would argue that their constitutions may be partly in documentary form and partly in the form of custom. Laos, for example, meandered through the first 15 years of Communist rule without a constitution and, indeed, without law. It was ruled by party decree. When the limits of this system became evident, the first law drafted was the 1991 Constitution. This near-universal acceptance is because 'constitutionalism ultimately aims to provide legal form to such aspirations as justice, the Rule of Law, and equity'.[20]

Yet we all accept that constitutionalism is insufficient of itself to safeguard broad aims such as justice and Rule of Law. Stalin's constitution read well but gave virtually no tangible support to the people of the Soviet Union. Constitutionalism that is not part of a system of rule by law will have limited benefits as it will not be able to hold accountable the rule-makers and rule-enforcers. In modern Asia, constitutionalism draws from various strands including Confucian ethics, Islamic morality and Kingship in tune with the cosmos.[21] Comparative analyses can therefore be difficult. From the standpoint of democracy, one important observation is open. There is a great difference between constitutions drafted by the ruling power and handed down to the people and those drafted in a democratic way by a constitutional assembly whose debates are reported in the media.

In modern Asia there are two striking examples of the latter type. The first was the Philippine Constitutional Commission of 1986, which drafted the post-Marcos constitution, and the second is the 1997 Thai constitution. Both were settled only after vigorous and open debate fully reported in the media. The final voting was subject to public scrutiny and in Thailand, the National Assembly was pressured into adopting the Constitution by popular demand and against the vested interests of many of its

19 L Nottage (1998) Book Review 9 *Public Law Review* 78. The six are Israel, Libya, New Zealand, Oman, Saudi Arabia and the United Kingdom.

20 G Hassall (1997) 'Constitutional Trends in Asia' in V Taylor (ed), *Asian Law through Australian Eyes*, LBC, p 131.

21 LW Beer (1992) *Constitutional Systems in Late Twentieth Century Asia*, University of Washington Press, p 17.

members.[22] Both the Philippine and Thai Constitutions are documents particular to their country and its social and political traditions, yet both have a very strong commitment to democracy and human rights as universal values.

There is guidance in the constitutional history of these two countries that could well assist Indonesia. Throughout the turbulence of the past several years in Indonesia, the country has maintained a certain adherence to constitutionalism. The resignation of President Suharto, the succession of President Habibie, the adoption of electoral laws and the holding of elections, and even the surrender of East Timor maintained adherence to the broad letter of the 1945 Constitution. Yet the Constitution of itself did not guarantee the Rule of Law as demonstrated by the excesses of the military in recent times. Indonesia is currently undergoing a significant debate about the future shape of the country dealing in particular with issues such as decentralisation and possible federalism. The lesson from the Philippines and Thailand is that the debate on constitutional amendment must be open and responsive so that the result will have the confidence of the Indonesian people.

22 A Panyarachun (1999) 'Democracy in Thailand', CDI Annual Address (available at http: //www.cdi.anu. edu.au).

8

Democracy

Its Survivability

Alun A Preece

Democracy as a large-scale phenomenon is very new in human history. Until the late 19th century, only isolated examples existed at infrequent intervals. This chapter assesses the survivability of democracy, drawing particularly on the experience of those countries that have maintained it the longest. Particular features of societies and governments have demonstrable survival value; they help those societies to adapt, survive, and thrive and those features (where replicable) to be copied by others.

At first glance, the world's most successful democracies show very wide diversity in those institutional features that are within a constitution-maker's control. These include federal or unitary structure, republic or monarchy, presidential or parliamentary executive, winner-take-all or proportional voting systems, rigid or flexible constitutions, and unicameral or bicameral legislatures.

However, these democracies do share certain features in common, which appear to have helped them maintain democracy. Unfortunately for the institutional designer, these features are either impossible to reproduce at all (eg, geographical isolation), or at least are very difficult to copy in the short term (eg, working class repudiating Marxism). But even so, avoiding certain known constitutional defects (eg, unreviewable emergency powers) can help any country achieve better governance.

Even long-successful systems of government can be extinguished by overwhelming catastrophe like conquest, famine, or plague, just as an asteroid strike may have made the dinosaurs extinct. However, in more evenly balanced struggles, having democratic governance will usually help a society to survive and retain its sovereignty. Democracy has three crucial advantages over absolutist forms of government in this regard:

- it provides governments with valuable feedback on mistaken policies;[1]
- it tends to motivate its citizens to fight harder to defend it; and

1 See Roland Rich (Chapter 7).

- it is better able to forge successful and enduring alliances with other democratic nations.[2]

Therefore societies should seek to preserve and replicate, as far as practicable, those features that are characteristic of successful democracies and which therefore presumably embody 'world's best practice'. This chapter examines the characteristics of those countries that have maintained democracy longest.[3]

A decade after the Berlin Wall fell, with military coups virtually extinct in South America, the 'end of history' belief – that democracy has finally triumphed – is tempting. Unfortunately, we have been there before. A century ago there was a similarly optimistic outlook, but democracy lost much ground in the dark events of a few decades later. In similar vein, much earlier, the democracy of the ancient world was overwhelmed by military defeat and internal tyranny, not to re-emerge for centuries. Even the past century and a half – the only period in history when democracy has been other than an isolated phenomenon – has seen a cycle of democratic advances, followed by retreats.

Rarity of uninterrupted democracy

Only seven countries – Australia, Canada, New Zealand, Sweden, Switzerland, Britain and the United States – have not lost democracy by suffering a change of government through force at some time during this century. And even these countries survived close calls, especially from 1939 to 1945. In the late 1960s most major American cities suffered devastating civil disorder, and Canada has periodically endured unconstitutional disruptions by Quebec separatists. Britain has employed emergency powers in parts of Ireland, and faced major problems from Communist-inspired industrial disruption in the 1970s. Australia faced a Communist union threat in the late 1940s.

Reasons for failing to maintain democracy

Colonialism

Many countries or territories fail to make the list because they were colonies for part of the 20th century. However, few countries are likely to become or remain colonies in future.

---

2 Immanuel Kant famously predicted that democratic countries would never war against one another. Although this has been disputed, it does seem that countries will ally with others they identify as sharing their values, and also that allied dictators will often fall out over the spoils, to the point of supporting military action against each other – eg, Hitler versus Stalin, Pol Pot versus Viet Cong, Brezhnev versus Tito and Mao, Galtieri versus Pinochet.

3 Space does not permit detailed analysis of what 'democracy' means. For present purposes, a society is classed as 'democratic' if its people have the effective ability to change their government at regular elections.

Invasion and conquest

The biggest single reason for countries losing 'democratic continuity' since 1900 was invasion by Axis powers before and during the Second World War. Nazi occupation is the only reason why Denmark, France, the Netherlands and Norway do not qualify. Belgium and Luxembourg would qualify but for German occupation during both World Wars.

Military coup

Military coups (defined as overthrow of the government by the state's official armed forces, with or without civil war) are the most common cause of democracy's demise. All South and Central American countries have experienced coups at some time this century, as have many former colonies in Africa, the Middle East and Asia. Even Europe has not been immune, with most of Eastern Europe falling prey to this disease between the wars, together with Portugal (1926), Spain (1936) and Greece (1967).

Insurrection/civil war

Democracy can also fail due to civil war in which authoritarian insurgents overthrow the government. For example, in Russia (1917) the Bolsheviks toppled Kerensky, although their control of the country was not complete for several years. Most military coups succeed quickly with little bloodshed, but some do not, leading to civil war as in Spain (1936–9).

Subversion of democratic institutions by those who originally come to power by virtue of these institutions

This was a significant cause of collapse of democratic institutions in Europe between the World Wars. It happened quickly in Germany between Hitler's ascent to the Chancellorship in 1933 and President Hindenburg's death in 1934. In Italy, Mussolini was at first merely Prime Minister under the monarchy, but gradually made himself dictator. However, he fell from office when King Victor Emmanuel II withdrew his support in July 1943, after the Allies invaded Sicily. In Japan, which had an elected parliament, militarist forces came to dominate the government in the 1930s. Similar events occurred in much of Eastern Europe at this time.

Subversion of a former colony's post-independence democracy has been very common, especially in Africa, although Asian former colonies have a somewhat better record. India and Sri Lanka have remained democratic with a few blemishes, but Malaysia and Singapore have had major deficiencies, and Pakistan has fallen under military rule several times. Democracy, it seems, must usually be home-grown to have the best chance of survival.

Miscellaneous revolutions

Some revolutions do not fall neatly into any of the categories above, and may not follow or precede democracy. A coup may arise from a combination of military force (internal or external) and elements of the existing government; for example, the 1948 Communist takeover of Czechoslovakia. Or the existing constitutional authorities may be pressured to appoint a particular government, for example, Mussolini in Italy (1922) after his supporters' 'March on Rome'. Spontaneous revolution may occur, as in Iran (1978) when Shah Reza Pahlevi went into exile leaving in office the moderate Dr Bakhtiar, whose government dissolved when Ayatollah Khomeini returned from exile.

'Democratic' abolition of democracy

There are *no* clear examples of a reasonably securely established democracy developing into a dictatorship by constitutional means.

Situation at the end of the 20th century

Although only seven countries have maintained uninterrupted democratic rule throughout the 20th century, the situation has been much better in recent decades. At the century's end, democracy has reached an all-time high – as measured by the number of countries espousing it. Since the Berlin Wall fell in 1989, the number of democracies worldwide has nearly doubled, growing (according to the United States State Department) from 66 to 117 in less than 10 years.[4] Moreover, military coups have gone out of fashion in South and Central America. During the 1990s there were almost none, with the whole continent (except Cuba) under democratic rule.

Comparison with earlier centuries

Democratic institutions were not widespread before the European revolutions of 1848. Only Britain maintained substantial elements of democracy throughout the 19th century, as it had during the 18th (apart from the upheaval of the American War of Independence, which can be viewed as a secession). Likewise, the southern provinces of the Netherlands (where democratic traditions existed since the Dutch Republic of the 16th century) seceded to become Belgium in 1831. American democracy, dating from the 1776–89 founding, was blemished by the Civil War (1861–5). Sweden has had continuous democratic credentials since its 1809 revolution, which produced a constitution containing the Freedom of the Press Law. Switzerland's credentials date from 1848 – or even as early as 1291, the only unambiguous interruption being during Napoleon's conquest (1797–1802).

4 See Roland Rich (Chapter 7).

Impact of particular factors on development and maintenance of democracy

Religion

How many divisions has the Pope? – Josef Stalin

With these sarcastic words Stalin dismissed the influence of the Catholic Church, perhaps even of religion in general, on international affairs. But they haunted his successors when the 1978 election of the Polish Pope John Paul II triggered events which played a major role in the collapse of Communism in Europe after 1989.

Before 1945 Protestant countries generally developed democracy earlier, as after the Reformation Calvin reorganised his Genevan church on democratic lines, while the Catholic Church tended to hold more authoritarian views. Although the seven countries enjoying longest democratic rule also happen to have been Protestant-dominated after the Reformation (or when later founded), religion and democracy may *both* be consequences of a single cause – geographic isolation, discussed below. Since 1945 and the Second Vatican Council, the difference has been much less significant.

Democracy historically had little impact on Islamic nations, other than Turkey and (to a lesser extent) Egypt and Indonesia. Fundamentalism, on the rise, is opposed to democratic pluralism. India's maintenance of democracy since independence (1947) has been helped by its largest religion's lack of stringent opposition to democracy, and by the existence of many minority religions. Pluralism in religion tends to favour a pluralist political system.

Geographic isolation

Geographic isolation has long been recognised as crucial to national independence, protecting a society from challenge by outside forces.[5] Of the seven countries that have remained democratic throughout the 20th century, *all* enjoy this advantage in some form. When radical new ideas (religious or political) emerge, the *status quo* elsewhere feels threatened and tries to suppress the experiment – if it can. Thus in the 13th and 15th centuries the Church eradicated French Albigenses and Bohemian Husites who challenged its hegemony, but in the 16th century failed to extirpate Protestantism from its

5 'This fortress built by Nature for herself / Against infection and the hand of war, / . . . Against the envy of less happier lands'. William Shakespeare, *Richard II*, Act 2, Scene 1 (John of Gaunt).

'The importance of isolation is . . . great in preventing, after any physical change in the conditions, . . . the immigration of better adapted organisms; and thus new places in the natural economy of the district will be left open to be filled up by the modification of the old inhabitants. Lastly, isolation will give time for a new variety to be improved at a slow rate. . '. Charles Darwin, *The Origin of the Species*, ch IV.

isolated strongholds in Britain, Scandinavia and the Alpine redoubt of Switzerland. Geography helped democracy survive when it was a new, minority experiment in a world of absolutism. Once democracy became dominant, at the beginning of the 20th century, the tables were turned. The Russian Revolution challenged both democracy and capitalism, so it provoked Western military interventions. However, the Russian heartland has geographical advantages, being uniquely immune to naval power and placing barriers of distance and climate in any invader's path.

What do the seven surviving democracies have in common?

Examining the factors discussed shows that many are interrelated.

Geographic isolation/military preparedness/factors tending to prevent military coup

Geography makes military conquest harder. When democracy is lost, it is usually by military overthrow – invasion and conquest, or internal coup. Subversion of a pre-existing democratic system also requires military or paramilitary elements (eg, Hitler's Brownshirts). Inevitably the military/security apparatus of the State is strengthened in readiness for the final takeover, for the overthrow of democracy must be backed by force.

Military preparedness and/or strong alliances appear more effective than long traditions of neutrality as shown by the wartime fates of Denmark and the Benelux countries. Democracy has survived more successfully under the umbrellas of comprehensive post-war military alliances of the major democratic countries than in the inter-War era, when such arrangements were largely lacking. Only the British Empire and Commonwealth had such arrangements before 1941 and its democracies survived comparatively unscathed in 1939–45. The North Atlantic Treaty Organisation (NATO) was formed in 1949, the Australia, New Zealand and United States (ANZUS) pact in 1951 and the South-East Asia Treaty Organisation (SEATO) around the same time.

A long tradition of religious toleration

Pluralism in religion favours a pluralist political system.

Labour/workers' movements not embracing Marxism

This factor is relevant only from 1917 to 1989, and is largely confined to Anglo-Saxon and Scandinavian countries, which again are mainly Protestant. This may be because Catholic countries usually have two separate sets of labour organisations – one set Catholic and conservative, the other unions dominated by Socialists and Communists. In a unified union movement, Marxist views are less likely to be in the majority.

Long democratic tradition

The seven nations include the five oldest constitutional monarchies and the two oldest republics. Democracy is usually the result of historical evolution, and its existence and form both depend on each country's own experience. Significantly, none of the seven has radically changed its constitutional arrangements since it first became an independent democratic nation.[6]

Very advanced economies and comparatively tolerant social and political systems

It is much easier to maintain democracy with such advantages. At the same time, democracy brings about and reinforces such conditions.

Few lessons can be drawn from the constitutional system

These seven constitutional systems vary so widely (see Table 8.1) as to suggest that the precise form of democracy is not crucial. (In federal systems, the data relates primarily to the national level.)

It seems that federalism helps, but 'paper' entrenchment of other constitutional protections does not. Four of the seven are federations, and there are not many federal nations beside these four.

Conclusions: factors conducive to democracy

These factors, demonstrated by the above examination of features common to the seven longest enduring democracies, mirror the reasons why democracies fail.

Barriers against external overthrow of democracy

(a) Adequate defence arrangements should prevent conquest, military coup or successful insurrection or civil war, which together are responsible for most overthrows. The military forces' organisation and traditions are also vital factors. Strong military alliances of democratic countries are crucial as few societies can withstand all external threats alone. The paradox is that whilst a strong military is needed to defeat or deter invasions, it increases the risk of military coup. Antidotes are:

---

6 All changes were made constitutionally, the most major being the adoption of unicameralism in Sweden (1970) and New Zealand (1950), and reduction of the upper house's powers in Britain (1911) and Canada (1982).

Table 8.1: Features of the world's seven oldest continuous democracies

	Britain	United States	Australia	New Zealand	Canada	Sweden	Switzerland
First became independent democracy	1688 (possibly 1660)	1776	1900 (1850 for Colonies/States)	1852 (1907)	1867	1809	1291 (1848)
Head of State	Monarchy	Republic	Monarchy	Monarchy	Monarchy	Monarchy	Republic
Structure	Unitary	Federal	Federal	Unitary	Federal	Unitary	Federal
Revolution	1688	1776	Never	Never	Never	1809	Never
Civil war	1642–51	1861–5	Never	Never	Never	Never	1848
Foreign conquest	1066	Never	Never	Never	Never	Never	1797–1802
Military coup	Never	Never	Never	Never	Never	1809	Never
Constitution	Uncodified	Codified	Codified	Partly codified	Codified	Codified	Codified
Entrenched constitutional provisions	None	All	All	Few	Most	All	All (but no judicial review)
Amendment	Ordinary statute	Ratification by legislatures of three-fourths of States	Referenda (majority of votes and of States)	Ordinary statute	Usually, ratification by legislatures of two-thirds of Provinces (representing 50% of population); all Provinces for some matters, ordinary statute for others	Statute re-passed after intervening parliamentary election: some amendments may be passed immediately by three-fourths or five-sixths majority	Referenda (majority of votes and of Cantons)

Guarantees of rights	Mostly ordinary law	Entrenched (1791, 1865)	Mostly ordinary law	Mostly ordinary law	Entrenched (1982)	Entrenched (1975)	Mostly ordinary law
Legislature	Bicameral	Bicameral	Bicameral	Unicameral	Bicameral	Unicameral	Bicameral
Powers of upper house	Delay only	Full veto	Veto, unless double dissolution and joint sitting	–	Delay only	–	Full veto
Proportional representation	For EU and devolved regional elections only	None	Mostly upper houses only	Yes, since 1996	None	Yes	Yes
Executive	Cabinet responsible to legislature	President elected by direct vote, separate from the legislature	Cabinet responsible to legislature	Cabinet responsible to legislature	Cabinet responsible to legislature	Cabinet responsible to legislature	All-party Cabinet elected (but not removable) by legislature
Elective terms	Five years	Two, four or six years	Three or six years	Three years	Five years	Four years (three years 1970–94)	One or four years
Judicial removal	Parliament (majority both houses)	Impeachment (two-thirds of Senate)	Parliament (majority both houses)	Parliament (majority)	Parliament (majority both houses)	Removable only by court decision	Six-year terms

(b) ***Well-established traditions*** of non-involvement in politics by the armed forces.

(c) ***Alliances with other democracies.*** These have a twofold advantage: the armed forces need not be as strong, and the alliance can help put down a rebellion or counter an invasion (and deter either from occurring).[7]

(d) ***Numerous military reservists*** in comparison with the regular cadre, as in Switzerland. Such forces are unlikely to act in defiance of popular opinion.

(e) ***Reliance mainly on naval power for defence*** – another advantage of geographical isolation. Without a large army, risks of military coup or oppression of the populace are minimised. The classic example is England which, as feudal levies gradually ceased to be relevant, developed a strong tradition of no standing army in peacetime without Parliament's consent (although the Navy could be operated under Royal prerogative), a tradition praised by the *Federalist Papers.* It seems no coincidence that the great sea powers, Britain and the United States, have been more democratic than the great land powers of Russia, China and Central Europe.

Sweden and Switzerland have backed up their post-1815 neutrality with strong military preparedness, being the only two of the seven to have maintained military conscription throughout. In these countries there is a firm tradition of military non-involvement in politics and of efficient police forces and legal systems with traditions of independence and impartiality.

Prevention of internal subversion of democracy

This is more complex, but the existence of constitutional checks – and, even more, strengthening of democratic traditions – seem the most successful in the long run. The following certainly seem to assist:

(a) ***Existence of a healthy middle class.*** Aristotle's faith in the middle echelons of society being those most likely to support stability and reasonable government has proved far-sighted. Those near the top of society (eg, mediaeval nobles) so often aspire to leadership that they are prepared to stir upheaval in the hope that they can seize power amidst the chaos. By contrast, those at the bottom may be tempted (eg, by Marx's *Communist Manifesto* or Hitler's *Mein Kampf*) to overthrow the established order to secure themselves a better lot. Social

7 There are no examples of attempts to invade NATO or SEATO member countries. Other members of SEATO, notably Britain and Australia, came to Malaysia's aid in the 1948–60 Communist insurgency. No NATO countries have faced sufficiently serious threats of internal rebellion to require outside assistance, and there was widespread co-operation in countering Communist subversion during the Cold War.

mobility is important. If many members of society feel permanently deprived of any chance to improve their lot, they are unlikely to feel loyalty to the established order.

(b) ***Smooth development of democratic institutions.*** Secure democracy seems to draw its greatest strength from long tradition. This is probably why, despite monarchy's hierarchical symbolism, five out of the seven are monarchies, albeit constitutional ones. Likewise, military coups are less likely to be attempted where there is no tradition of their being attempted or succeeding.

(c) ***Economic success.*** Most democracies have enjoyed economic success during most of their emergence. Apart from tiny or oil-rich states (eg, Liechtenstein or Kuwait), Switzerland has had the highest Gross Domestic Product (GDP) per capita for many years, as did the United States for most of the preceding two centuries. Sweden, Britain, Australia, New Zealand and Canada have also been among the top few. Although this is to some extent a 'chicken and egg' relationship, it does seem democracy has caused good economic performance, rather than *vice versa.* Switzerland and Sweden were both poor until late in the 19th century, but became democratic before they became richer.[8]

(d) ***Impact of Precise Form of Constitutional Arrangements.*** This does not loom large among the reasons for long maintenance of democracy, probably because more democracies are overthrown by military *force majeure* than by exploiting constitutional loopholes. However, constitutional checks and balances probably do make a difference in more finely balanced cases.[9] Federalism seems to help,

8 Interestingly, among these seven countries, there appears to be some correlation between retention of an upper house with considerable powers and remaining near or attaining the best economic performance, particularly, when account is taken of the longish time lag present in effects of this nature. For example, Britain was much nearer the top in economic performance before powers of the House of Lords were drastically curtailed in 1911. Similarly, Sweden has dropped drastically from its position near the top since the adoption of unicameralism in 1970, as has that on Canada since constitutional changes in 1982. Similarly New Zealand was second only to the US in per capita income in the period immediately after World War II, but has since sunk to below 20th. Its Legislative Council was abolished in 1950.

9 An interesting example is India under Mrs Gandhi's Emergency rule (1975–7). The failure of her attempts – against the opposition of an independent judiciary – to oust judicial review of constitutional amendments can be seen to play a major role in maintaining Indian democracy. On the other hand, others might claim she was not an incipient dictator anyway, as she ultimately lifted the Emergency and called elections, which she lost.

Likewise, in Turkey the Constitutional Court in recent years outlawed an Islamic fundamentalist party as threatening the secular nature of the Turkish Constitution. This may have averted an otherwise-likely military takeover – as did occur in Algeria not long afterward – in the name of 'saving democracy'. Checks and balances probably help prevent situations reach the stage where extra-constitutional intervention is seen as necessary to protect democracy.

making it harder for one section to gain total control. 'Winner take all' electoral systems with few legal constraints seem particularly vulnerable to takeover, but Britain and New Zealand have used them for long periods.

Postscript: lessons from historical trends

> In the long history of the world, only a few generations have been granted the role of defending freedom in its hour of maximum danger. – President Kennedy, Inauguration Address (20 January 1961)

Since its evolution in the 18th century modern democracy has successfully seen off such challenges as:

- Napoleon and his technocrats;
- Unrestrained 'robber baron' capitalism of the industrial revolution – countered by expanding education, the franchise and anti-trust legislation;
- The unprecedented crisis caused by the rise of Fascism and Nazism; and
- Communism and a prolonged Cold War.

Democracy's survival may most of all be attributable to the combined military power of the two leading democratic countries, Britain and the United States. Significantly, the most disorderly period of the present century (1914–45) occurred when Britain's power was waning, but before Britain and the United States forged their enduring alliance.

Part II: Constitutional Theory and Structure

9

The Australian Constitution and the Challenge of Theory

John Williams

Theory and the Australian Constitution

Australia's Constitution is a much-studied document. It has accumulated a canon of classic texts and commentaries discussing its establishment and interpretation since Federation. Technical studies of its operation are now widely available. As Justice Kirby has noted, there are rarely, if ever, new 'brilliant flashes' of light to be shone into the 'dark corners of the Constitution'.[1] Yet one aspect of our constitutional landscape has gone unexplored: the theoretical nuances that underpin its operation and interpretation. Australian constitutional lawyers have been reluctant to debate the theoretical foundations of the constitutional arrangements we live under. As Cheryl Saunders notes, this is 'not a debate that we are accustomed to having'.[2]

Like theory, globalisation is also important but unexplored in Australian constitutionalism. Globalisation encompasses a multitude of relationships and movements, usually associated with the transmission of trans-national, indeed universalising, ideas. For instance, in rights jurisprudence the dominant norms of the United States or United Nations have been copied around the globe. While some fear globalisation means the end of constitutional diversity, this is unlikely. Firstly, because that outcome would require a homogenous signal 'at source'. This is clearly not so in the United States, where competing constitutional interpretations are intensely debated.

Secondly, universal concepts are inevitably expressed at a high level of abstraction. Thus they must be implemented through some cultural 'filter'. And if a concept lacks cultural relevance, its transplantation is unlikely to be successful. Paradoxically, then, globalisation may actually

1 *Re Wakim; ex parte McNally* (1999) 73 ALJR 839 at 876 per Kirby J.

2 C Saunders (1998) 'Oration: Sir Daryl Dawson' 20 *Adelaide Law Review* 1 at 7.

strengthen the local by promoting firmer expression of indigenous values in the face of universalising trends.[3]

It is here that theory remains relevant amidst globalising constitutionalism. Constitutions are expressed in broad and general terms, yet they operate in increasingly complex societies. No longer can judges simply rely on 'strict and complete legalism' to deflect political scrutiny of the judicial process.[4] Instead, every new decision faces political and legal criticism. Although there is rarely one unchallenged theory of the Constitution, the intellectual rigour offered by theoretical justification is more satisfying than relying on unpromising text alone. Republicanism, it is argued, provides a good theoretical platform for understanding the Constitution.[5]

Yet the text as the sole source of interpretation has been the persistent view in Australian constitutional law. Viewed as a mere Imperial statute, and reading using the normal methods of statutory interpretation, the Constitution is portrayed as vulnerable to vandals who would rewrite the text to fit their theories.

In *McGinty v Western Australia*, Justice McHugh quoted with approval Judge Richard Posner's rejection of 'top-down' or theoretical reasoning.[6] In contrast, McHugh considered 'bottom-up' or pragmatic reasoning more compatible with Australia's constitutional heritage, because '[a]ny theory of constitutional interpretation must be a matter of conviction based on some theory external to the Constitution itself'.[7]

The lure of theoretical illumination has also been resisted by many of Australia's constitutional scholars. George Winterton warns against judicial use of 'extra-constitutional notions', that is, 'claims of constitutional implications [that] are really too tenuous to be sustained, so that the relevant precept must be regarded as extra-constitutional'.[8] This seems, with respect, to be tautological. Something is constitutional because it can be seen to be constitutional. To be fair, Winterton acknowledges that the boundary between 'constitutional' and 'extra-constitutional' notions is a fine one and opinions will differ. However, what Winterton's distinction offers are two categories of results. If a result can be justified using constitutional methods, it can be accepted as a 'constitutional' notion. But otherwise, it must

---

3 See Klug, Chapter 17: S Choudhry (1999) 'Globalisation in Search of Justification: Toward a Theory of Comparative Constitutional Interpretation' 74 *Indiana Law Journal* 819.

4 O Dixon (1952) 'Address on Being Sworn in as Chief Justice' 85 CLR xi at xiii–xiv.

5 GN Rosenberg and JM Williams (1997) 'Do Not Go Gently into That Good Right: The First Amendment in the High Court of Australia' *Supreme Court Review* 439.

6 (1996) 186 CLR 140 at 230; RA Posner (1992) 'Legal Reasoning from the Top Down and from the Bottom Up: The Question of Unenumerated Constitutional Rights' 59 *University of Chicago Law Review* 433.

7 (1996) 186 CLR 140 at 230.

8 G Winterton (1986) 'Extra-Constitutional Notions in Australian Constitutional Law' 16 *Federal Law Review* 223 at 225.

invariably be 'extra-constitutional'. The problem is, this categorises some approaches as the product of 'normal and natural' reasoning but others as 'theoretical' and therefore somehow exotic.

Even so, Australia has recently witnessed the willingness of some senior judges to countenance some theoretical debate.[9] Sir Anthony Mason has noted that once purely textual constitutional interpretation is recognised as inadequate, 'a variety of theoretical approaches to constitutional interpretation begin to open up'.[10] It is noteworthy, though, that in his survey of constitutional theories, Mason cites only one Australian theorist.[11]

One well-known early comment on Australia's preference for the practical over the theoretical was Albert Métin's description of Australia a century ago as pursuing 'Socialism without doctrine': 'Demands on government are for practical concessions rather than declarations of principle. Western Europe is richer in theory, Australasia in practice'.[12] Métin noted what has proved a recurring theme in Australian governance. Our analogous tradition of a 'Constitution *without* theory' can be traced in large part to the Framers themselves.

The Constitution's drafting did not begin with a theoretical blank page. The United States Constitution and Canada's *British North America Act* were critical influences. Given the prominence of these precedents, the lack of comparative theoretical discussion of the Australian Constitution in the 1890s, or indeed since, is surprising.

The United States Constitutional model came with a wealth of theoretical baggage. *The Federalist* and *Anti-Federalist Papers* analysed the very foundations of the governance system it established. In turn, these accounts drew explicitly upon earlier theoretical texts.[13] Yet although Madison considered the 'celebrated' Montesquieu the 'oracle who is always consulted and cited'[14] on the separation of powers, Australians were less impressed. Sir Samuel Griffith observed at the 1891 Sydney Convention that the 'wisdom' of Montesquieu's analysis was 'very open to doubt'.[15]

How did the Australian Framers become so resistant to the theory behind the United States model? Partly because they inherited responsible government from Westminster. Yet there may be another explanation: the way the Framers were introduced to the United States Constitution. For

9 *Theophanous v Herald and Weekly Times* (1994) 182 CLR 104 at 180 per Deane J.

10 A Mason (1996) 'The Interpretation of a Constitution in a Modern Liberal Democracy' in C Sampford and K Preston (eds), *Interpreting Constitutions: Theories, Principles and Institutions*, Federation Press, pp 13–14.

11 Ibid, citing MJ Detmold (1985) *The Australian Commonwealth*, LBC; and MJ Detmold (1994) 'The New Constitutional Law' 16 *Sydney Law Review* 228.

12 A Métin (1977) *Socialism Without Doctrine*, Alternative Publishing, p 180.

13 J Madison, A Hamilton and J Jay (1987) *The Federalist Papers*, Penguin Books, Nos 47, 78.

14 Ibid, p 303.

15 *Debates of the Australasian Federal Convention*, Sydney 1891, Government Printer, p 35.

most of them, their main source – in La Nauze's term, their 'bible'[16] – on the American system was James Bryce's *The American Commonwealth*.

In his introduction, Bryce stated that although it seemed 'natural' for him to 'tread in the steps' of de Tocqueville, he rejected that temptation, because what de Tocqueville wrote was 'not so much a description of the country and people as a treatise'.[17] Bryce, on the other hand, assured his readers that he simply presented the facts, 'letting them speak for themselves'.[18] The Framers never questioned Bryce's choice of facts and their description. Bryce's implied conclusions encouraged the Framers to make particular constitutional choices without seeing any need for theoretical amplification. For instance, Griffith's 'doubt' about strict separation of powers echoes Bryce's sceptical description of the United States model.[19]

The Framers' copying of various constitutional precedents (but not of their theoretical underpinnings) was rarely questioned during the Conventions. Thus they copied federalism, the Senate and the separation of powers without debating possible improvements to which a theoretical road-map could have alerted them.[20] True, most Framers were practical colonial politicians not given to philosophising, but they were not ignorant of theory; many knew the classic works of political and legal theory well.[21]

With its American and British heritage, Australia's Constitution draws upon many republican templates. Often this, our *other* republican tradition, is overlooked when we discuss the 'capital-R' Republican future of Australia.[22] This tradition is not the simple anti-monarchism that Australians voted on in November 1999, but a comprehensive theory of government.[23]

This kind of republicanism, so important to Inglis Clark,[24] has been disallowed by some scholars as an 'extra-constitutional' notion. They reject it particularly because 'constitutional law . . . must be seen to incorporate an intellectually sustainable framework that does not depend upon the arbitrary shifts . . . of political thought'.[25] Must our search for an 'intellectually sustainable framework' be postponed because it shifts over time? Must Australian constitutional law wander forever through an a-theoretical wonderland?

---

16 JA La Nauze (1972) *The Making of the Australian Constitution*, Melbourne University Press, p 273.

17 J Bryce (1995) *The American Commonwealth*, Liberty Fund, p 3.

18 Ibid, p 4.

19 Ibid, p 260.

20 F Wheeler (1996) 'Original Intent and the Doctrine of the Separation of Powers in Australia' 7 *Public Law Review* 96.

21 H Evans (1998) 'The Other Metropolis: The Australian Founders' Knowledge of America' 2 *The New Federalist* 30.

22 T Keneally (1993) *Our Republic*, William Heinemann, p 156.

23 P Pettit (1997) *Republicanism: A Theory of Freedom and Government*, Oxford University Press.

24 JM Williams (1995) '"With Eyes Open": Andrew Inglis Clark and Our Republican Tradition' 23 *Federal Law Review* 149.

25 G Williams (1995) 'A Republican Tradition for Australia?' 23 *Federal Law Review* 143.

On the contrary: every one of our Constitution's fundamental features – the Rule of Law, separation of powers, federalism, deliberative democracy – is strongly consistent with republicanism. Far from being foreign to Australia's constitutional tradition, republicanism is central to it.

The juridical republic

Republican governance is most often associated with absence of a hereditary monarch – the interpretation that dominates Australia's current 'republican debate'. But beyond this narrow concept, we can distil what is more fundamental to the republican goal: maximisation of liberty. Anti-monarchism is a sub-theme that derives from a more central tenet, that arbitrary or absolute rulers threaten the liberty of the ruled.[26] The dilemma of the corruptibility of both ruler and ruled has prompted republican writers to trust the coercive power of the law to restrain both.[27] Machiavelli noted that 'hunger and poverty make men industrious, and . . . laws make them good'.[28]

To republicans, laws are justified if they promote liberty.[29] But in doing so, they must abide by two constraints, lest the law itself becomes a threat to liberty. The first constraint is that the government must be what James Harrington memorably called an 'empire of laws and not of men';[30] the law must be so structured as not to threaten its own primary goal. Secondly, the law's substantive content must aim to advance the common good of liberty.[31] This first limb of republican law has two sub-divisions – the Rule of Law and the separation of powers.

Rule of Law

At its core, the Rule of Law means the restraint of arbitrary power. As Algernon Sidney noted, its virtue is to protect citizens from their rulers' arbitrary whims: ''Tis not . . . upon the uncertain will or understanding of a prince, that the safety of a nation ought to depend.'[32]

Certain themes recur in descriptions of the Rule of Law by Sidney and other republicans. The law needs a high degree of predictability so that it does not vary with any official's personal dislikes. It must be applied in a dispassionate manner 'void of desire and fear, lust and anger', and must

26 P Pettit (1992) 'Republican Themes' 6 *Legislative Studies* 29.

27 Q Skinner (1990) 'The Republican Ideal of Political Liberty' in G Bock, Q Skinner and M Viroli (eds), *Machiavelli and Republicanism*, Cambridge University Press, p 305.

28 N Machiavelli (1975) *Discourse*, Routledge & Kegan Paul, p 217.

29 Pettit (1997), pp 35–41.

30 JGA Pocock (ed) (1977) *The Political Works of James Harrington*, Cambridge University Press, p 401.

31 Pettit (1997), pp 35–41.

32 T West (ed) (1990) *A Sidney, Discourses Concerning Government*, Liberty Classic, pp 400–1.

apply universally, to ruler and ruled alike.[33] Although the Rule of Law has a deeply republican source, it is a well from which many rival ideologies have drawn.[34]

Of course, the Rule of Law is not immune from critique; but republicans support it in order to defend the weak against the strong – that is, to prevent domination. Even Marxists have acknowledged that the law 'may be rhetoric, but it need not be empty rhetoric'.[35] Although disputed,[36] this conclusion supports modern republicans' insistence that law must advance the 'common good' of all, not just the sectarian or class interests of some.

Separation of powers

Equally essential is the separation of powers. For the Rule of Law to be supreme, power to make, enforce or interpret laws must not be concentrated in any one person or group, which would endanger liberty. As Montesquieu stated: 'When legislative power is united with executive power in a single person or in a single body of the magistracy, there is no liberty.'[37]

The institutional mechanism developed to prevent this emerged from the 18th century idea of the 'separation of powers'.[38] Montesquieu's analysis in *The Spirit of the Laws* became the popular understanding of this doctrine,[39] although there is disagreement over what meant by it.[40] Much of the debate over the doctrine's 'pure' and 'functional' aspects can be found in the *Federalist* and *Anti-Federalist* Papers.

In essence, the separation of powers is an institutional arrangement motivated by the imperative of protecting liberty.[41] WB Gwyn argues that the phrase 'separation of powers' is not taxonomic, that is, not self-explanatory.[42] Historically, it connoted both a normative ideal and a description of governmental functions or powers.[43]

33 Ibid.

34 AV Dicey (1920) *Introduction to the Study of the Law of the Constitution*, Macmillan, p 179; B Fine (1984) *Democracy and the Rule of Law: Liberal Ideals and Marxist Critiques*, Pluto Press; G de Q Walker (1988) *The Rule of Law: Foundation of Constitutional Democracy*, Melbourne University Press.

35 EP Thompson (1975) *Whigs and Hunters: The Origin of the Black Act*, Allen Lane, p 263; *accord* Fine (1984).

36 G Pearson (1976) 'Eighteenth Century English Criminal Law' 3(1) *British JLS* 115; MJ Horwitz (1977) 'The Rule of Law: An Unqualified Human Good?' 86 *Yale Law Journal* 561.

37 C Montesquieu (1989) *The Spirit of the Laws*, Cambridge University Press, p 157.

38 K Von Fritz (1954) *The Theory of the Mixed Constitution in Antiquity*, Columbia University Press.

39 Montesquieu (1989); Madison et al (1987), p 303.

40 MJC Vile (1967) *Constitutionalism and the Separation of Powers*, Clarendon Press, p 85.

41 Ibid, p 13.

42 WB Gwyn (1965) *The Meaning of the Separation of Powers*, Tulane University Press, p 8.

43 Ibid, p 5.

Federalism

While federalism offered a practical compromise for uniting Australia,[44] it also has theoretical value for republicans: decentralising political power 'makes perfect sense in a system premised on the fear of, and the desire to avoid, tyranny'[45] – even if only the tyranny of distance.

Federalism has ancient origins, but its modern form began with the United States Constitution.[46] In setting up a democratic federal republic, the American Framers had to overcome the historic criticisms of 'confederacies', particularly the weakness of the government and its viability over a large community. The American solution was to combine an extension of democratic notions of representation with institutional design. Its value was to check power and to guarantee the rights of smaller communities, as well as a basis for democratic government. It was a design based, as Madison noted, on expectations that '[t]he different governments will control each other, at the same time that each will be controlled by itself'.[47] Because federalism offers another method of protecting liberty by checking and dispersing power, it is a key element in republican statecraft.[48]

The deliberative republic

These institutional checks are all negative restraints against arbitrary rule. But republican institutions also seek to promote a positive value – democratic deliberation.

Faith in deliberation assumes that decisions binding the whole society should be based upon reasons broader than narrow or sectarian self-interest. As Sunstein notes, deliberation is 'designed to ensure that political outcomes will be supported by reference to a consensus (or at least broad agreement) among political equals'.[49] Crucial to a properly deliberative process is that alternative, or even unpopular, views will be fully heard – a vision normatively superior to mere majoritarianism.

One cost of introducing 'new' and unheard voices into public debate is that inevitably they challenge the existing consensus on public policy. Historically republicans have disagreed over the value of diversity (or discord) in decision-making. To Machiavelli, 'tumult' in a republic's political life was itself a virtue.[50] Others like James Harrington feared such divisions

---

44 L Zines (1989) 'A Legal Perspective' in B Galligan (ed), *Australian Federalism*, Longman Cheshire, p 16.

45 MH Redish (1995) *The Constitution as Political Structure*, Oxford University Press, p 25.

46 B Galligan (1995) *A Federal Republic: Australia's Constitutional System of Government*, Cambridge University Press, p 39.

47 Madison et al (1987), p 321.

48 C Sunstein, 'Beyond the Republican Revival' (1988) 97 *Yale Law Journal* 1539 at 1562.

49 Ibid, p 1550.

50 Skinner (1990), p 135; Machiavelli (1975), p 218.

might threaten public order.[51] However, at the founding of the American republic, the value of discord was reconsidered. To the Anti-Federalists, the ideal republic was based on heterogeneity: 'In a republic, the manners, sentiments, and interests of the people should be similar.'[52] But Madison's Federalists realised the advantage that heterogeneous 'factions' could check one another.[53]

The 'republican revival' in United States constitutional theory over the past decade has reopened this debate on the merits of republican theory.[54] Its proponents point to the value of deliberation in politics and jurisprudence,[55] while detractors fear it could undermine the Lockean liberalism traditionally considered fundamental to American law.[56]

The deliberative ideal makes both modest and ambitious claims. The most modest is that public deliberation tests the *veracity* of the opposing arguments in policy debates. Secondly, deliberative helps us quantify the relative *weight* we should give the competing positions. More ambitiously, the deliberative model promotes what Jon Elster calls the 'civilising force of hypocrisy'.[57] To be heard in debate, proponents must at least couch their appeals in the language of the 'public good'; and this encourages them eventually to *think* in terms broader than their own self-interest. The most ambitious claim is that deliberation will foster civic virtue and participation, helping the populace become better citizens.

The deliberative republic has been praised for what it can offer public policy.[58] However, to republicans the value of deliberation depends on other conditions being met. The first is a high degree of political equality. Republicans are suspicious of wide disparities in political influence, and favour democratic intervention to equalise them – for example, by redistributing wealth or widening access to the media.[59]

The second condition is universalism – the ideal that, through deliberation and mediation, we can establish some view of the 'common good'.[60] Republican theorists insist that such deliberative outcomes *not* be the prod-

---

51 See Pocock (1977), pp 66–7.

52 HJ Storing (ed) (1981) *The Complete Anti-Federalist*, Chicago University Press, p 369.

53 Madison et al (1987), No 10. See John Pyke (Chapter 24).

54 See RH Fallon (1989) 'What is Republicanism, and is it Worth Reviving?' 102 *Harvard Law Review* 1672.

55 C Sunstein (1985) 'Interest Groups in American Public Law' 38 *Stanford Law Review*.

56 RA Epstein (1988) 'Modern Republicanism: Or the Flight from Substance' 97 *Yale Law Journal* 1633.

57 J Elster (1995) 'Strategic Uses of Argument' in K Arrow (ed), *Barriers to Conflict Resolution*, cited in C Sunstein (1995) *Democracy and the Problem of Free Speech*, Free Press, p 243. See Tom Campbell (Chapter 7).

58 J Uhr (1998) *Deliberative Democracy in Australia*, Cambridge University Press.

59 Rosenberg and Williams (1997), p 439.

60 Sunstein (1988), p 1554.

uct of bargaining or 'deal-making' where the strong purchase the compliance of the weak. Rather, republicans seek to promote discussion among political equals in deciding collective policies.[61]

Losing the signal

As shown, Australia's Constitution has very republican 'credentials'. Although republican theory was available to the Framers in the 1890s, most regarded the Constitution's terms simply as governmental arrangements that could be operated without need for abstract philosophising. Because they relied on Bryce's supposedly 'neutral' description of the 'American Commonwealth', their *Australian* Commonwealth copied the drafting work of their United States counterparts without fully appreciating the theoretical richness behind it.

Although the Framers were, in one sense, republicans, they were not fuelled by anti-monarchical fervour. Indeed, when choosing the very title of their new nation, many hesitated at 'commonwealth', considering it too Cromwellian:[62]

> For both Parkes and Barton the choice of the word 'Commonwealth' was the achievement of one type of republic. It was not the republic of Lawson or Black but it was Parkes' 'true' republic none the less.[63]

But the republican nature of our Commonwealth goes further than its title. Because they drew so heavily upon the United States precedent, our Framers (often unknowingly) incorporated by reference the republican theory that inspired the United States clauses.

So how did this republican signal from America become lost since then? The *Engineers' Case* of 1920 redirected Australian jurisprudence from the American Constitution back to the British.[64] This judgment, Richard Latham argued,

> cut off Australian constitutional law from American precedents,... in favour of the crabbed English rules of statutory interpretation, which are... particularly unsuited to the interpretation of a rigid constitution.[65]

Around this same time, the rise of liberalism obscured the Constitution's republican heritage. Nowhere is this better seen than in the interpretation of s 92. The requirement of 'absolutely free' interstate trade has generated

---

61 F Michelman (1988) 'Law's Republic' 97 *Yale Law Journal* 1493; but *contra* R Epstein (1988), p 1639.

62 *Debates of the Australasian Federal Convention*, Sydney 1891, Government Printer, pp 551–2.

63 M McKenna (1996) *The Captive Republic*, Cambridge University Press, p 192.

64 *Amalgamated Society of Engineers v Adelaide Steamship Co* (1920) 28 CLR 129.

65 RTE Latham (1937) 'The Law and the Commonwealth' in W K Hancock (ed), *Survey of British Commonwealth Affairs*, Oxford University Press, p 564.

heated debates between the 'laissez-faire philosophy'[66] and the more interventionist 'New Deal' vision of government.[67]

But the republican 'signal', or indeed the use of theoretical inquiry generally, has not been lost entirely. Although more a 'movement' than a theory, Legal Realism has become a powerful influence on Australian legal culture.[68] The antecedents of Llewellyn and Pound have been traced to Holmes and his famous *The Common Law*. Holmes articulated a non-legalist vision of how law and theory operate. In Australia the Legal Realist movement is usually traced to Julius Stone, a student of Pound. Stone's classic *Province and Function of Law*[69] influenced generations of Australian students, and ultimately Australian legal education.[70]

To see the earlier links between American Legal Realism and Australia, one need only look to Andrew Inglis Clark. In 1892 he wrote to Oliver Wendell Holmes Jr that:

> Your book on the Common Law continues with renewed charm to supply me with an annual course of instruction in first principles, and the whole substance of a lecture I delivered . . . last autumn was taken from it and Maine's *Ancient Law*.[71]

Inglis Clark, the 'primary architect of our constitution',[72] realised the links between republicanism and Legal Realism at the same time he put his constitutional pen to paper. It would be extraordinarily misleading to imagine that merely changing the Head of State would introduce a republican tradition to Australia. Before, rather than beyond, the Republic *is* the republic.

66 L Zines (1997) *The High Court and the Constitution*, Butterworths, p 110.

67 Compare Chief Commissioner Piddington (1914–15) *Commonwealth Parliamentary Papers* No 69 Vol 2, p 1113.

68 KN Llewellyn (1931) 'Some Realism about Realism: Responding to Dean Pound' 44 *Harvard Law Review* 1222.

69 J Stone (1946) *The Province and Function of Law*, Associated General Publications.

70 See M Coper (1983) 'Interpreting the Constitution: A Handbook for Judges and Commentators' in AR Blackshield (ed), *Legal Change: Essays in Honour of Julius Stone*, Butterworths, p 52.

71 Inglis Clark to Holmes, 20 January 1892, Holmes Papers, Harvard, Box 39, E-19.

72 *Theophanous v Herald and Weekly Times Ltd* (1994) 182 CLR 104 at 172 per Deane J.

10

Dividing Power in a Federation in an Age of Globalisation

Cheryl Saunders

Introduction

It is clear that globalisation has implications for federal systems and for the federal division of power. It is less clear what these implications are.

Globalisation has different facets. In general, it refers to the dramatic increase in transnational activity of all kinds, facilitated and given greater impetus by the end of the Cold War. Much of this activity is commercial and financial. From this perspective, the most striking manifestation of globalisation is the interdependence of national economies in matters of finance, manufacturing and trade. In addition, globalisation can refer to the movement of people, through migration and tourism and for professional purposes, giving rise to a range of organisations, institutions, movements and groups that transcend national boundaries. From a different perspective again, globalisation is associated with dramatic developments in technology and communications, which are part of the general phenomenon and also provide a vehicle for it.

Internationalisation is both a response to globalisation and the product of similar forces, in the public sphere. Famously, it is manifested by a proliferation of treaties and other agreements between governments, responding in part to an acceptance that many new issues are international in character. International agreements now establish norms with which domestic compliance is expected across fields from trade to human rights to environmental protection. Some are accompanied by mechanisms for international scrutiny and effective enforcement. The influence of the international community is felt by domestic systems in other ways as well, from economic and other forms of sanctions to peacekeeping and election monitoring.

Some specific effects of both globalisation and internationalisation, on the nation-state, can be identified through reasoning and observation. Global geo-political conditions at the end of the 20th century have widened and deepened international economic competition. The interdependence of the world's economies has helped to dictate the form that competition takes. A global economy, global problems and mobility of capital and skills combine to weaken the capacities of governments to respond to national demands. Globalisation and internationalisation offer alternative sources of law over which governments may have little effective control, but which nevertheless may influence domestic activity. In theory and practice, national sovereignty thus is eroded, to a degree. Citizenship is weakened as an exclusive bond between people and their state. To the extent that the public realm is diminished through deregulation and privatisation, constitutional institutions and practices developed by reference to earlier assumptions about how government is conducted are displaced. The mechanisms of the market and private law are not necessarily a satisfactory substitute for them.

Despite a huge and growing literature, however, the longer term and more lasting implications of these developments for the nation-state and for the structure, functions and objectives of government are unsettled. The nation-state remains the principal building block of the international community, albeit now joined by a variety of non-state actors as well. The increase in international mobility notwithstanding, the great proportion of the world's people in fact are firmly and permanently located in the country of their own nationality. If anything, reaction against globalisation favours attachment to nations and regions, still largely dedicated to the interests of their own peoples and still largely within popular control. At the end of the 20th century, globalisation carries mixed messages for the conduct and goals of states. Different incentives variously suggest that states should minimise their own operations, in the interests of efficiency; or act positively to facilitate markets; or erect barriers to outside encroachment on the national interest; or play a constructive role as state citizens in the world community.

To a degree, the outlook for federalism is tied to that for the nation-state and is correspondingly difficult to predict. Federalism for this purpose is understood as a system of government in which power constitutionally is decentralised, as an alternative to unitary government. Where the alternative to federalism is disintegration, different considerations arise,[1] that are not pursued here. Even cursory consideration of the competing forces demonstrates the degree of ambiguity. To the extent that international economic competitiveness requires efficiency, deregulation, and maximisation of markets it suggests the need for stronger national or central authority. Global policy-making in response to global problems and pressures implies effective central capacity as well. On the other hand, there are respectable arguments that economic competitiveness also can benefit from decentralisation. Effective subnational government has some potential to maximise local strengths, to encourage experimentation and to stimulate improved

1 C Saunders (1995) 'Constitutional Arrangements of Federal Systems' 25 *Publius* 1–19.

local performance, through competition between jurisdictions. In the face of the powerlessness that is a product of globalisation, federalism also offers a prospect of enhanced democratic participation and greater responsiveness of government in relation to those issues that remain within local control.

This is the traditional analysis. There is a real question whether it is anchored too closely to present expectations of behaviour. In this event, it may not adequately reflect the reality of government in a globalised world. This position has been argued forcefully by Professor Alfred Aman, in the context of the United States.[2] Aman analyses three modes that a nation-state might adopt to deal with the circumstances that it faces at the end of the 20th century, voluntarily or involuntarily. He characterises the first as the 'strong' state seeking to defend the national interest through the familiar, if opposing, techniques of laissez-faire or regulation. He dismisses both: leaving the field to the market disadvantages the weaker members of the community, while a regulatory approach increases transaction costs to a degree that ultimately will prove uncompetitive.[3] His 'efficient' state, by contrast, is more interventionist but uses techniques for the purpose modelled on those of the private sector. It involves a change in discourse and process, but not necessarily in the conception of the task of government. In this sense, it represents a transition to a third mode, the 'globalising' state, which Aman believes more closely approaches the mark. It differs in both kind and degree from the others. The boundary between the global and the local is blurred. The state itself is dynamic, contributing to and being formed by the processes of globalisation. It no longer claims a monopoly on law and power in what previously had been the public sphere. It may seek to use what influence it has in essentially private ways. One of the greatest challenges faced by the state in this mode is to establish new mechanisms for democracy and public accountability in decision-making to replace those irreparably lost.

Aman is sceptical of the larger claims made for federalism as a solution or partial solution to the challenges of globalisation. In his view, these claims fail to take account of the 'interconnectedness' of subnational units with each other, with the nation-state and with the rest of the world. In practice, he argues, the forces of globalisation diminish the scope for experimentation that federalism claims as a strength.[4] If anything, the pressures for efficiency through deregulation and privatisation have a homogenising effect.[5] Nor does federalism necessarily overcome the democratic deficit that accompanies globalisation. The mobility and diversity of citizens diminishes

2 AC Aman Jr (1998) 'The Globalising State: A Future-Oriented Perspective on the Public/Private Distinction, Federalism and Democracy' 31 *Vanderbilt Journal of Transnational Law* 770.

3 At 803-08.

4 *New State Ice Co v Liebmann* 285 US 262 (1932) per Brandeis J at 311.

5 Aman (1998), p 860.

their links to more local communities. Instead, federalism impedes new democratic solutions by weakening choice at the national level, through which there is at least a chance of securing participation in and accountability for international decision-making. Fragmentation of power through federalism also impedes the capacity of the nation-state to contribute to the international control of global phenomena including, for example, the activities of transnational corporations. It thus detracts from the capacity of government to serve the interests of people. Aman acknowledges that the trend in the private sector towards smaller, more efficient business units might suggest that comparable advantages could be secured for government through a process of devolution.[6] He notes, however, a counter-argument that this may be no more than an indication of the advantages of decentralised management.[7]

Aman's is not an argument against federalism on any terms. His concern is with a form of federalism in which courts draw 'bright lines' between federal and State power (or public and private power) impeding the flexibility of the national political process to adapt to the unique global conditions in which it now must operate. Against that background, he is critical of a series of pro-State decisions of the United States Supreme Court in recent years, both for their outcome and for the reasoning on which they are based. The cases in question[8] variously limit the scope of federal regulatory power;[9] restrict federal capacity to regulate through the States;[10] protect State institutions from federal law;[11] and preserve the 'sovereign immunity' of States from suit under the Eleventh Amendment.[12] A repeated theme across all categories is the dual sovereignty of the nation and the States under the Constitution of the United States, rationalised by reference to the advantages of federalism for enhanced local participation, the greater responsiveness of government, and opportunities for experimentation and innovation. Aman is critical of the reasoning, charging the majority with treating States 'as if they were billiard balls rather than interconnected entities in a global web of economic and political activity'.[13]

---

6 Ibid, p 850.

7 Ibid, citing EL Rubin and M Feeley (1994) 'Federalism: Some Notes on a National Neurosis' 41 *UCLA Law Review* 903 at 914–26.

8 See also the discussion in B Swinford and EN Waltenburg (1998) 'The Consistency of the US Supreme Court's "Pro-State" Bloc' 28 *Publius* 25.

9 *United States v Lopez* 514 US 549 (1995).

10 *New York v United States* 505 US 144 (1992); *Printz v United States* 117 S Ct 2365 (1997).

11 *Gregory v Ashcroft* 501 US 452 (1991).

12 *Seminole Tribe of Florida v Florida* 116 S Ct 1114 (1996); *Idaho v Couerd'alene Tribe of Idaho* 117 S Ct 2028 (1997); *Regents of the University of California v John Doe* 117 S Ct 900 (1997); *Blessing v Freestone* 117 S Ct 1335 (1997); *Alden v Maine* 527 US 707 (1999).

13 Aman (1998), p 857.

For argument's sake, in this chapter I accept the potential implications of globalisation for governance as identified by Aman, in order to use his argument against 'bright lines' between federal and State power as a foil to explore questions of the division of power in the Australian federation. To this end, the next part begins by analysing the characteristics of Australian federalism in contrast to those of the United States. I then consider whether the pro-State trend in the United States Supreme Court is matched in any way in Australian jurisprudence, either as a response to the perceived demands of globalisation or as a phase in the normal swings and roundabouts of constitutional adjudication. In the final part I draw some conclusions. In general, these are that the lines prescribed by the federal division of power are at least as bright in Australia as in the United States. Their impact is diminished, however, by other differences in the constitutional systems of the two countries that aid Australia's capacity to respond to globalisation in other ways.

Characteristics of Australian federalism

Purposes

Federalism in Australia was a pragmatic response to the need to design a system of government that would bring together six self-governing Australian colonies, voluntarily, at the end of the 19th century. For the first three decades at least, there was a widely held view that federalism was an interim phase through which Australia necessarily must pass on the way to unitary government.[14] Even after that view was discredited, as it became accepted that federalism was here to stay, a tendency to bemoan the fact remained. The argument that Australia is 'over-governed' and that three levels of government are at least one too many in a country with a population of less than 20 million is often heard, although much less so outside the south-east corner of the mainland.

Despite the virtual absence of principle in the establishment and maintenance of federalism as a pillar of Australian Government, it is easy enough to justify it now. Australia has a small population, but geographically it is vast. It is difficult to imagine effective governance, much less democratic government, without substantial local autonomy of some kind. The small but viable number of relatively powerful States offers some potential for experimentation, maximisation of local strengths and constructive inter-State competition, whether that potential is realised or not. Arguably, the experience of federal governance equips Australia better to operate in a multi-layered global environment with federal characteristics of its own. And, in a theme to which I will return, Australian federalism offers a check

14 This was an issue that divided the first comprehensive inquiry into the Australian Constitution, in 1927–9: *Report of the Royal Commission on the Constitution* (1929).

and balance in a system of government that in other respects tends to concentrate power. Absent good reasons to the contrary, these considerations suggest that Australia should persevere with a federal form of government, even if it had the choice not to do so.

Structure

Outwardly, the Australian federal system is similar to that of the United States on which, manifestly, it was modelled. The manner of the division of powers is the same, conferring largely concurrent express powers on the national sphere of government, leaving the unexpressed residue to the States, subject to the paramountcy of valid federal laws.[15] The substance of the powers thus conferred is similar also, although the commercial powers are spelt out in greater detail in Australia and some additional powers have been added, to meet Australia's own perceived needs. Economic union is conceived along broadly similar lines: a customs union and restrictions on impediments to inter-State trade.[16] An upper house of the Australian Parliament, the Senate, represents the original States equally and to that extent is patterned on the United States model.[17] As in the United States, institutionally each level of government is discrete, with its own Constitution, its own legislature, executive and judiciary and its own administration. And in Australia each jurisdiction has its own representative of the Crown as well in the position of Governor, performing the role of constitutional Head of State, largely independent of the others. During the debate on a republic in 1999 this arrangement was reflected in the possibility that, if the referendum was approved nationally, one or more States nevertheless might retain their links with the Crown, at least in the short term.[18]

There were significant differences between United States and Australian federalism even in 1901, however, and others have emerged over time. A major structural difference concerns the courts. Unlike the United States Supreme Court, the Australian High Court is a final court of appeal in matters of State as well as federal law. Most relevantly for present purposes, this has had a homogenising effect on the common law and, to a lesser degree, on statute law. In addition, the Australian Constitution provides authority for federal jurisdiction to be conferred on State courts,[19] avoiding the establishment of two separate court systems. For the first 75 years of federation, all major courts below the level of the High Court were in the

---

15 Australian Constitution ss 51, 106, 109.

16 *Cole v Whitfield* (1988) 165 CLR 360.

17 By contrast, the Upper Houses of some other federations reflect population distribution, to a degree, in their composition.

18 *Constitution Alteration (Establishment of Republic) 1999*. In the event, the referendum was lost.

19 Australian Constitution s 77(iii).

State sphere, exercising both State and federal jurisdiction. This changed in the 1970s, with the establishment of the Federal Court of Australia and the Family Court. The hierarchy of federal courts was extended further in 2000, with the establishment of the Federal Magistrates' Service. It has now been established that there is no reciprocal implied authority for State jurisdiction to be conferred on federal courts.[20] Nevertheless, the potential for merging both streams of jurisdiction in the same courts is a factor that has contributed to the characterisation of the Australian judicature as 'integrated' and of Australian law as 'united'.[21] Apart from these initial differences between the federal structures of the United States and Australia, others have developed over time.

Most obviously, judicial interpretation of federal legislative powers has been more restrictive in Australia than in the United States. In both countries, the manner of the division of power has led naturally to a gradual expansion of federal power, in the absence of express limitations. Similar questions also have arisen about the extent to which laws made by one can bind the institutions of the other, and there have been similar instances of wavering. Nevertheless in Australia it is, and always has been, possible to say that there are limits on federal power that are recognised by the courts and will judicially be enforced. Thus, for example, and not without criticism, the High Court so far has maintained a sphere for 'intrastate' trade and commerce when interpreting the federal power over overseas and inter-State trade and commerce,[22] precluding its emergence as the broad base for action that the commerce clause now offers in the United States.[23]

A further major difference between the federal systems of the two countries concerns fiscal arrangements. From the outset, there was an imbalance in the taxation resources available to the Australian States, thanks to the constitutional conferral on the Commonwealth of exclusive power to impose duties of customs and excise.[24] The imbalance was entrenched by the effective Commonwealth monopoly over income tax from 1942. In consequence, the States have relied on the redistribution of revenue by the Commonwealth for almost 100 years.[25] Revenue redistribution, through general or specific purpose grants, has given the Commonwealth substantial influence over aspects of government within the State sphere and over State

20 *Re Wakim; ex parte McNally* (1999) 73 ALJR 839.

21 *Kable v Director of Public Prosecutions for New South Wales* (1996) 189 CLR 51 at 112 per McHugh J.

22 *Minister for Justice (WA) ex rel Ansett Transport Industries (Operations) Pty Ltd v National Airlines Commission* (1976) 138 CLR 492.

23 *Wickard v Filburn* 317 US 111 (1942).

24 Australian Constitution s 90.

25 It remains to be seen whether the diversion of the revenue from the Goods and Services Tax (GST) to the States, after coming into effect in mid-2000, will change the dynamics of Australian fiscal federalism.

budget policy generally. This influence was reinforced by the centralised borrowing arrangements that operated from 1927[26] to 1994 and which, whilst since relaxed, remain in place in another guise.

The fiscal aspects of the Australian federal system, in turn, deepened Australian economic union by, for example, ensuring that the main taxation regimes were uniform throughout Australia.[27] The union was extended further in the 1990s, through co-operation, with the introduction of mutual recognition arrangements under which each Australian jurisdiction recognises each other's standards for goods and occupations.[28] Mutual recognition, loosely patterned on similar arrangements in the European Union, is a mechanism for positive enlargement of the national market while enabling the States to retain regulatory competence, at least in law. It thus goes further than the negative protection for the market provided, respectively, by the negative commerce clause in the United States and the express protection for freedom of inter-State trade in Australia.[29] The mutual recognition arrangements were subsequently extended to include New Zealand as well, in a manifestation of the closer constitutional relationship between the two countries.[30]

Context

More important for present purposes than the differences between the federal systems of the United States and Australia are differences in the wider constitutional context within which each operates. The following are particularly significant.

The first concerns the relationship between the legislature and the executive. While Australian doctrine claims a three-way separation of powers, both the Commonwealth and the State spheres have a parliamentary system of government, in which the executive relies on the confidence of Parliament for authority to govern. In the Australian version of parliamentary government, legislative power also trumps executive power,[31] although not judicial power.[32] The boundaries and content of executive power are not clearly defined, other than as the residue of all public power that is neither legislative nor judicial.

---

26 Financial Agreement, 1927; Australian Constitution s 105A.

27 Section 51(ii) of the Australian Constitution effectively requires the Commonwealth to impose taxation uniformly.

28 *Mutual Recognition Act* 1992 (Cth) and complementary State legislation.

29 Australian Constitution s 92.

30 *Trans-Tasman Mutual Recognition Act* 1997 (Cth) and complementary State and New Zealand legislation.

31 *Bradley v Commonwealth* (1973) 128 CLR 557.

32 *R v Kirby; ex parte Boilermakers' Society of Australia* (1956) 94 CLR 254.

The present significance of the Australian adoption of parliamentary government is threefold. It means that Australian constitutional arrangements lack the in-built checks on power provided by the formal three-way separation of powers in the United States. It also means that, with the potentially important exceptions of Upper Houses and hung Parliaments, Australian governments generally can rely on their Parliaments to implement their policies, relatively quickly. This fact in turn facilitates co-operation between the Commonwealth and the States. Finally, the porous border between legislative and executive power and the undefined character of the latter offers the executive branch of government greater flexibility of action in Australia than in the United States – a point taken up again below.

A second distinguishing feature of the context of Australian federalism is the virtual absence of constitutional protection of rights. Its immediate significance for the federal division of powers is that rights principally are a State responsibility. Its broader significance lies in the absence of yet another check on power in the Australian constitutional system, by contrast with the Constitution of the United States. Conceptually, this point of distinction may be coupled with the explicit reliance of the Constitution of the United States on popular sovereignty. While the Australian Constitution has been said to rest on popular sovereignty,[33] and while the manner in which it was framed may justify that claim, in law the Australian Constitution originally derived its force from the authority of the United Kingdom Parliament. Formally, that remains its setting. Whatever the subsequent shifts in judicial doctrine, neither the political nor the legal culture of Australia has fully adapted itself to the notion that the Constitution draws its authority from the people.

The third contextual distinction is the manner in which the two systems deal with entry into and implementation of international arrangements. In the United States this involves both the executive branch and the Senate. Once ratified, treaties may take direct effect, if accepted as self-executing. In Australia, entry into treaties is the responsibility of the executive branch alone, but treaties take effect in domestic law only if implemented by a parliament with the power to do so. Australian thus more easily undertakes commitments in international law than does the United States. Once undertaken, however, questions of implementation inevitably arise and there are no circumstances in which a treaty of a legislative character takes direct effect.[34] The potential for this to impede Australian compliance with its international obligations is undercut by the course of judicial decisions accepting that the Commonwealth Parliament may legislate to implement any international treaty to which Australia is a party, if it chooses to do so.[35]

---

33 *Australian Capital Television v Commonwealth* (1992) 177 CLR 106.

34 *Minister for Immigration and Ethnic Affairs v Teoh* (1995) 183 CLR 273.

35 *Commonwealth v Tasmania* (1983) 158 CLR 1.

Judicial decisions

The previous part considered the principal differences between federal arrangements in the United States and Australia as they have emerged over time. This part asks whether there is any Australian parallel to the patently pro-State trend in decisions of the United States Supreme Court over the decade of the 1990s. It shows that there have been isolated recent instances in Australia in which the High Court has given effect to limits on federal power with corresponding implications for the scope of State power. At the time, these cases gave rise to some speculation about a new direction for Australian constitutional law. So far, however, there has been no sustained trend against federal power in favour of the States. On the other hand, the High Court has shown a new willingness to recognise limitations on federal power that have the effect of protecting individual rights. It is possible that, in time, more critical judicial scrutiny of the validity of co-operative schemes[36] will also have implications for Australian federalism.

Since the early 1980s, Australian cases involving the border between Commonwealth and State legislative power have dealt principally with the powers with respect to corporations;[37] industrial relations;[38] taxation;[39] races;[40] and external affairs.[41] With the exception of the first of these categories, disputes generally have been decided by the High Court in the Commonwealth's favour. Two cases on the corporations power, however, went against the Commonwealth, giving rise to the speculation to which reference has been made.

In the first of these, the court held that the Commonwealth's power under s 51(xx) of the Constitution to legislate for 'foreign trading or financial corporations formed within the limits of the Commonwealth' did not extend to legislation for the incorporation of companies.[42] It followed that the Commonwealth Parliament was unable, unilaterally, to enact a national corporations law. A corporations law with national effect had been assumed to be necessary for the convenience of Australian business since the early 1960s at the latest.

In the second case,[43] the issue was whether Commonwealth industrial relations legislation could validly extend to the conditions of a subcontract. Neither party to this contract was a 'constitutional' corporation. The sub-

---

36 C Saunders, 'In the Shadow of *Wakim*' (1999) 17 *Companies and Securities Law Journal* 507–17.

37 Australian Constitution s 51(xx).

38 Ibid, s 51(xxxv).

39 Ibid, s 51(ii).

40 Ibid, s 51(xxvi).

41 Ibid, s 51(xxix).

42 *New South Wales v Commonwealth* (1990) 169 CLR 482.

43 *Re Dingjan; ex parte Wagner* (1995) 183 CLR 323.

contract contributed to the performance of a further contract, however, between one of the parties and a constitutional corporation. The majority Justices adopted different formulations to decide that this was not, in fact, a law 'with respect to' constitutional corporations and therefore did not fall with Commonwealth power. In neither of these cases was the outcome clearly dictated by the text of the Constitution. Rather, in each case, the text left room for judicial discretion and individual justices referred to a range of factors in reaching their final decision.

In a further two decisions, in 1988 and 1992, the High Court recognised limits on federal legislative power in a context that protected the rights of individuals rather than the rights of States. In both, the question was whether the relevant head of power authorised particular limits on freedom of speech or whether the use of the power was, in the circumstances, disproportionate.[44] In both cases, the Commonwealth law was held invalid in part, at least, on this basis. This line of cases ultimately was diverted by others recognising that some limits on Commonwealth power might be implied from those parts of the Constitution dealing with democratic, representative and responsible government.[45] Both lines of development recently have been slowed. In the case of the first, this is the result of decisions limiting the range of powers in relation to which notions of proportionality are likely to have some effect.[46] The second is due to the decision in *Lange*, requiring any implied limitation on federal power to be attributable more directly to the text or structure of the Constitution.[47] Individually and collectively, however, both constitute new and significant doctrines linked, directly or indirectly, with the federal division of powers. Unlike the cases described earlier, their effect is to restrict Commonwealth action without corresponding consequences for States.

The Commonwealth decisively won another important and long-running struggle over power between the Commonwealth and the States during this period. The issue was the scope of the exclusive power to impose duties of excise in s 90 of the Constitution. At stake was the ability of the States to impose non-discriminatory taxes on the sale of goods. A more narrow definition of excise would, in large part, have resolved the vertical fiscal imbalance and removed a source of effective Commonwealth influence over State power. After more than a decade of speculation, *Ha* finally settled that s 90 indeed precludes any State tax on goods up to the point of consumption and including, at least, retail sales taxation.[48] Rather than re-

44 *Davis v Commonwealth* (1988) 166 CLR 79; *Nationwide News Pty Ltd v Wills* (1992) 177 CLR 1.

45 *Australian Capital Television Pty Ltd v Commonwealth* (1992) 177 CLR 106 and subsequent cases.

46 *Cunliffe v Commonwealth* (1994) 182 CLR 272; *Leask v Commonwealth* (1996) 187 CLR 579.

47 *Lange v Australian Broadcasting Corporation* (1997) 189 CLR 520.

48 *Ha v New South Wales* (1997) 189 CLR 465.

solving the fiscal imbalance, the consequence was to worsen it, through the invalidation of cumbersome but lucrative business franchise licence fees under which States effectively had taxed liquor, tobacco and petrol.

A final group of cases might collectively be described as dealing with the autonomy and integrity of the institutions of government of the jurisdictions that make up the Australian federation. While the story is a complex one, three generalisations can gingerly be made.

The first is that the scope of immunity of each sphere of government from general laws made by the other has progressively been narrowed. In each case, the court has left a core of continuing immunity the scope of which is not entirely clear but which is intended to reflect federal proprieties. In the case of the States the core is small, centred on the key institutions of government themselves.[49] The immunity of the Commonwealth is more extensive, but recently has been shown to be more limited than previously had been thought.[50] The diminution of immunities is significant for federalism, but also is consistent with a tendency otherwise evident in the court to limit the outmoded prerogatives of government.[51]

Secondly, on balance, court decisions have allowed minor inroads into the institutional autonomy of the States. Commonwealth power has been interpreted to override the somewhat ambiguous preservation of State Constitutions in s 106.[52] And at the high water mark of the implied rights cases, the protection afforded representative democracy by the Australian Constitution was held to provide some protection for freedom of political communication at the State level as well.[53] While the specific reasoning in *Stephens* has since been doubted,[54] it apparently remains the law that the Australian Constitution imposes some constraint on State action limiting political speech, if only because it is impracticable to segment speech along federal lines.[55] The tentative extension of the Australian Constitution into the State constitutional sphere has not been carried through to electoral rules. In *McGinty*,[56] the High Court refused to accept that whatever implications might be drawn for Commonwealth electoral boundaries from provisions of the Commonwealth Constitution dealing with representative democracy affected the powers of the States. In *Kable*,[57] on the other hand, the Court pointed to the role that State courts perform in the exercise of

49 *Victoria v Commonwealth* (1996) 187 CLR 416.

50 *Re Residential Tenancies Tribunal of New South Wales v Henderson; ex parte Defence Force Housing Authority* (1997) 190 CLR 410.

51 *Bropho v Western Australia* (1990) 171 CLR 1. See also Churches, Chapter 14.

52 *Port McDonnell Professional Fishermen's Association v South Australia* (1989) 168 CLR 340.

53 *Stephens v West Australian Newspapers Ltd* (1994) 182 CLR 211.

54 *Lange v Australian Broadcasting Corporation* (1997) 189 CLR 520.

55 *Levy v Victoria* (1997) 189 CLR 579.

56 *McGinty v Commonwealth* (1996) 186 CLR 140.

57 *Kable v Director of Public Prosecutions New South Wales* (1996) 189 CLR 51.

federal jurisdiction to reach the conclusion that State Parliaments could not confer functions on their courts that would be 'incompatible' with their responsibilities in this regard.

Thirdly, *Kable* aside, the effect of decisions of the court has been to maintain the existence of dual court structures. In *Wakim*,[58] a majority of the court overturned the decision of the previous technical majority in *Gould v Brown*[59] to hold that State jurisdiction could not be conferred on federal courts. The decision may have some effect on the role and significance of State court systems, by preventing a progressive loss of State jurisdiction to the federal sphere.[60] It has systemic implications for the Federal Court as well, by preserving it as a court of specialist federal jurisdiction.

Australian federalism and globalisation

Bright lines

There are bright lines, in Aman's sense, circumscribing federal legislative power in Australia. These are recognised by and enforced through the courts. The lines have changed position over time, generally but not exclusively in a manner that has favoured federal power. Nevertheless, there are clear limits on what the Commonwealth Parliament constitutionally may do in relation to, for example, trade and commerce, corporations, industrial relations and external affairs.

Leaving aside for a moment the demands of globalisation, in the Australian context there are some advantages of a federal division of power, enforced through the courts.

In the first place, Australian federalism receives even less institutional support from the political context than does federalism in the United States. Points of difference include a strong two-party system (the legacy of responsible government) and habits of mind born of inherited notions of parliamentary sovereignty, both antithetical to limitations on power. In this respect the Australian Senate is a point of difference as well. Whatever significance the Senate may have for federalism in terms of the proportionate representation of States, it does not restrain the exercise of Commonwealth power in a way that has substantial implications for the federal system or for the autonomy of the States.

Secondly and more importantly, the federal division of power represents one of the few constitutional limitations on public power in Australia. The only significant exception is the separation of judicial power itself,

58 *Re Wakim; ex parte McNally* (1999) 73 ALJR 839.

59 (1998) 193 CLR 346.

60 Although query the effect of the likely growth of the concept of 'accrued' jurisdiction, as discussed and applied in *Re Wakim*.

originally a derivative of federalism.[61] The other checks and balances incorporated in the Constitution of the United States, including the separation of legislative and executive power and the Bill of Rights, are not present here. This enhances Australia's capacity to respond to globalisation, as will be seen below. But it also invests the federal division of power with additional significance. To the extent that the federal division of power can be used positively to further individual liberty,[62] its significance is greater still. Examples of the use of the division of power for this purpose include the cases dealing with freedom of political communication[63] and, in earlier times, the invalidation of legislation outlawing the Communist party of Australia.[64]

Implications for globalisation

From the standpoint of the complications presented by federalism in a globalising world, many of Aman's observations are applicable to Australia as well. The special advantages of federalism in terms of diversity, experimentation and democracy are often theoretical rather than real. The tendency towards homogeneity and the weakening of citizenship bonds between individual States and citizens may be even greater in Australia than in the United States.

And the boundaries between the powers of the Commonwealth and the States are artificial and increasingly so. The logic of a division between overseas and inter-State on the one hand and intra-State trade on the other, or of an industrial relations power limited to disputes extending beyond the borders of any one State, has long been the subject of criticism. Uncertainty about the scope of the corporations power has been a source of frustration as well. Arbitrarily defined and overlapping spheres within the fields of health and social services are costly and inefficient. The circuitous devices through which the Commonwealth influences education and training complicate policy development and blur accountability.

In Australia's case, however, there are considerations that mitigate the significance of the federal division of power from the standpoint of globalisation.

One is the Australian constitutional regime for international relations. The reliance on executive power, only lightly affected by recent changes allowing greater participation for the Parliament and the States, gives the executive of the Commonwealth virtually complete constitutional flexibility in relation to external affairs. This flexibility now is matched by a Com-

---

61 *R v Kirby; ex parte Boilermakers' Society of Australia* (1956) 94 CLR 254.

62 In some cases, inevitably, its effect on individual liberty is negative. The imposition of mandatory sentencing requirements by Western Australia and the Northern Territory were examples that attracted world attention in 2000.

63 *Lange v Australian Broadcasting Corporation* (1997) 189 CLR 520, and the cases that preceded it.

64 *Australian Communist Party v Commonwealth* (1951) 83 CLR 1.

monwealth legislative power that extends to all matters physically external to Australia as well as to the implementation of all treaties and other international agreements. The greater the forces of globalisation and internationalisation, the more extensive the Commonwealth's power. In these circumstances, arguably, globalisation confronts Australia with a problem of a different nature. The idea that for historical or other reasons the Australia States lack capacity to conduct external affairs is outmoded in a world that increasingly recognises the activities of actors other than sovereign nation-states.[65] The time may have come for the rhetoric of Australian doctrine to be adapted accordingly.

The second, and equally important, is the ability of Australia to overcome the problems of limited federal power through intergovernmental co-operation. The absence of substantial separation of legislative from executive power, coupled with the small number of States, makes co-operation far more practicable in Australia than in the United States and limits the need for the Commonwealth to commandeer the States in the manner of either *New York v United States* or *Printz*. The capacity of State Parliaments to refer matters to the Commonwealth offers further flexibility as well.[66] Thus, through co-operation, national corporations legislation was established in the aftermath of *New South Wales v Commonwealth*. The artificiality of the divided power with respect to industrial relations has been ameliorated in part by references of power and could be completely resolved in this way. The national market has been deepened by co-operation, through mutual recognition and other devices. Government borrowing is co-ordinated and controlled through a co-operative, voluntary regime. The consequences of excessive centralisation are occasionally met through co-operation as well, with the pending experiment of the assignment of the GST revenue to the States as a recent example, with far-reaching consequences. There is little in the Constitution itself to provide support for what has become an extensive and complex network of intergovernmental agreements. Co-operation nevertheless has been facilitated by judicial acceptance of the constitutionality of pooled power.[67] Admittedly the implications of the reasoning of the majority justices in *Re Wakim* are not yet entirely clear. Even if the effects of decision spread beyond the judicial sphere, however, they will inhibit only a small, if important selection of the techniques available for co-operative purposes.

A third mitigating factor also flows from the relationship of legislative and executive power in Australia. To the extent that globalisation calls for a more flexible approach to the division of public and private power, the Australian constitutional framework is a convenient host. If anything, it may

65 The World Trade Organisation is an example.

66 Australian Constitution s 51(xxxvii).

67 *R v Duncan; ex parte Australian Iron and Steel Pty Ltd* (1983) 158 CLR 535.

be argued that the degree of flexibility is excessive. Actions that fall within the traditional definition of legislative power must of course be dealt with by or under legislative authority. But globalisation is typically accompanied by a substantial increase in non-regulatory action of a kind akin to private power, and this falls within the sphere of executive power. Within that sphere, apart from federal limitations, executive power is virtually unconstrained under the Australian Constitution.

Issues and problems

Some tentative conclusions may be drawn. Firstly, Australian federalism does not necessarily impose major impediments to a creative Australian response to globalisation. Secondly, while the advantages of federalism in a globalising world can be exaggerated in Australia as elsewhere, nevertheless they exist and should be given weight. Thirdly, Australian federalism performs a wider role in the Australian constitutional system and has additional significance for that reason. This broader dimension should not be overlooked in any evaluation of it. This is not to say, however, that everything in the Australian constitutional garden is rosy. The following issues, at least, arise. Each is a topic in its own right and can be mentioned only briefly here.

Firstly, in practice, intergovernmental co-operation is notoriously cumbersome. To the extent that Australia's capacity to respond flexibly to globalisation depends on co-operation, it is desirable for processes and results to be improved. A prerequisite, verified by a brief summer of improved co-operation in the early 1990s, is greater commitment to co-operation on the part of all Australian governments.

A spur would be recognition by Australians themselves that it is both desirable and proper for governments to act in the collective interest, while keeping an eye out for their own. This is, after all, the approach that increasingly is required in the international sphere.

Secondly, government through co-operation is dogged by problems of openness and accountability. These will be magnified if, to overcome the artificiality of divided power, Australia relies on these techniques more. Again, there is no secret about what needs to be done. This issue also repeats itself in the international sphere.

Thirdly, there is a real question about whether Australia should continue to rely on federalism as the main check and balance in the constitutional system. From the standpoint of rights protection it is erratic. If globalisation continues to force centralisation, undermining the federal division of power, the issue may become more pressing still. On the other hand, if the power of the nation-state and government dwindles significantly, national checks and balances will become less relevant, and possibly even counterproductive.

The final issue concerns the shifting boundary between the public and the private, nationally and globally. This is an issue of the moment for constitutional law. Even where nations have the flexibility to deal with it in a principled way, they lack the conceptual capacity to do so, because the problem is novel. Nor is there incentive for governments, unprompted, to seek new mechanisms to extend participation and to improve accountability for the exercise of public power in new, essentially private ways. These problems are not confined to a single jurisdiction. On the contrary, thanks to globalisation, they affect all developed states in the Western political and economic tradition. For this reason, amongst others, comparative constitutional projects are likely to be particularly productive in the years that lie ahead.

11

A Federation amid Global Imperatives?

Glyn Davis and Naomi Sunderland[1]

Should boundaries and borders dissolve, what future for federation? How can we protect citizens by balancing power between levels of government, if significant choices are no longer constrained by the original constitutional settlement? And how can decision-making be made local and immediate when national and international agreements define the possible?

To explore these questions, this chapter offers three related discussions. The first asks whether globalisation contributes to greater centralism in Australian government. Perhaps the apparent accumulation of constitutional power by Canberra is illusory, hiding a fundamental 'hollowing out' of the state by forces external and domestic. Our second section uses two contemporary case studies to show how international aspirations and obligations reshape Australian federalism. International agreements on greenhouse issues, and the recently adopted *Environment, Protection and Biodiversity Conservation Act* 1999 (Cth) (*EPBC Act*), both illustrate how neither States nor local governments can control the policy agenda should the Commonwealth elect to intervene. This leads to the final discussion, focusing on the difficulties for promoting democratic citizen participation amid centralised, and globalised, policy processes. What are the implications for a healthy local polity in a federation amid global imperatives?

Hollowing out the state?

Since at least the 1970s, the literature on Australian federation has emphasised the growing power of Canberra. Despite the 'new federalisms' of Malcolm Fraser and Bob Hawke, it is easy to cite examples of Canberra now settling matters that were once the prerogative of State Government. Indeed, in 1998 former Chief Justice Sir Anthony Mason argued that States have become largely regulators, abandoning their traditional role of providing services to local communities. In a break from conventional accounts of

1 Both authors speak personally rather than for the Queensland Government.

centralisation, Mason detects two sources of this change – national and international. The 'steady accretion in the exercise of Commonwealth power', he suggests, 'has been matched, if not surpassed, at the international level by the exercise of power and influence by international and transnational bodies'.[2] In doing so, Mason raises a new and perhaps unexpected possibility: that Canberra, in turn, will have no choice but to cede power to international institutions. An increasing amount of decision-making already occurs at the international level, particularly in the areas of trade and competition policy.[3] A steady erosion of the national state has implications for the polity. As Mason suggests, the '[r]atification of international and regional conventions (treaties) by Australia establishing regulatory regimes or standards can result in a so-called contraction of national sovereignty and a democratic deficit'.[4]

How do sub-national governments, both state and local, respond to this apparent transfer of responsibility to Canberra? In part, they respond by fostering their own global links, creating international cultural and trade relationships outside the national diplomatic framework. The Queensland Government, for example, maintains offices in Indonesia to pursue a business and tourism presence for the State whatever the current standing of the Australian National Government with Indonesian authorities.

Such activity contributes to the complexity of globalisation, the layers of connection between individuals, regions and non-government organisations that build an emerging international order of public and private institutions. Thus while constitutional developments have already tipped the balance between the Commonwealth and the States, globalisation has more profound implications. The Commonwealth's domestic ascendancy may not be the only influential trend for the long-term shape of Australian governance. International pressures can accelerate the centralisation of power within Australia's national borders yet also challenge the sovereignty of the nation-state. With globalisation, the constitutional equation is no longer just a zero-sum tussle between the States and Canberra.

As the distribution of power shifts, States, the Commonwealth and citizens may all lose a sense of control or experience what Mason referred to as a 'democratic deficit'. Such a situation obviously undermines the intended benefits of federalism. Although the Australian Constitution does not clearly articulate the original motivations behind the federal system, these may include accommodating State differences, the capacity for States to respond to

2 A Mason (1998) 'The Constitution in a Contemporary Context' in *Selected Proceedings of the Federation into the Future: Government in a Global Era Convention*, Committee for Economic Development Australia, p 2.

3 A Fels (1998) 'Economic Globalisation: Creative Government Responses' 46(11) *Growth*.

4 Mason (1998), p 4.

local needs, and the possibilities for democratic participation.[5] A transfer of influence from States to Canberra, and then from the Commonwealth to international bodies calls into doubt the continued efficacy of Australia's political settlement. As Mason notes, Australia's involvement in international treaties is particularly significant, for while the Commonwealth has committed the nation to international obligations it is yet to identify and implement consultation structures that maintain the original values of federation.[6]

But how credible is Mason's assertion that national power is being ceded to global pressures? The evidence divides commentators. A recent symposium of Australian policy analysts[7] epitomises the inconclusive debate. Writing on international relations, Wesley and Gyngell find a clear diminution of policy power, lost to the new world of electronic commerce and global markets.[8] Craik et al trace the difficulty of Australian Governments imposing traditional controls on new media content and ownership.[9] Yet papers on economic, industry, social and labour market policies all find that government policy capacity has both expanded and contracted in line with a number of complex and interrelated factors including: the area of policy-making and its usefulness in advancing the Commonwealth's foreign-policy goals; cohesion between national and international imperatives; the influence of both national and international interest groups; and the role of the new media. Although globalisation changes the way governments operate, and the policy arenas in which they can make a difference, it does not necessarily reduce the influence or scope of public policy. That is, governments often retain the capacity – albeit if not the inclination – to act using both traditional and novel approaches amid global imperatives.

Similar disputes mark the theoretical literature on globalisation. For example, an influential article by Rhodes argues that Britain is being 'hollowed out' by pressures from above and below.[10] Rhodes identifies four interrelated trends he believes have shifted power simultaneously to the top and the bottom rungs of national governance: privatisation and limitations to the scope and forms of public intervention; the loss of functions by central and local government departments to alternative service delivery systems

---

5 J Nieuwenhuysen (1998) 'Commonwealth–State Cooperation: A Fresh Approach' in *Selected Proceedings of the Federation into the Future: Government in a Global Era Convention*, Committee for Economic Development Australia, pp 18–19.

6 Mason (1998).

7 G Davis and M Keating (eds) (2000) *The Future of Australian Governance: Policy Choices*, Allen & Unwin.

8 A Gyngell and M Wesley (2000) 'Interweaving of Foreign and Domestic Policy: International Policy' in G Davis and M Keating (eds), *The Future of Australian Governance: Policy Choices*, Allen & Unwin.

9 J Craik, G Davis and N Sunderland (2000) 'Cultural Policy and National Identity' in Davis and Keating (2000).

10 RAW Rhodes (1994) 'The Hollowing Out of the State: The Changing Nature of the Public Service in Britain' 65(2) *Political Quarterly* 138.

(such as agencies); the loss of functions by British Government to European Union institutions; and limiting the discretion of public servants through the new public management.[11]

Although he clearly does not limit his analysis to external international pressures on the nation-state, Rhodes' conclusions align him to a growing body of literature that is pessimistic about the effects of internationalisation on the traditional distribution of power within nation-states.

Like Rhodes, Cleaver believes the primacy of the nation-state is being challenged from above and below.[12] He attributes blame to the usual suspects: globalisation, supranational institutions, multinational companies and free trade, which challenges the nation-state from above. Yet Cleaver notes that, from below, 'the increasingly active role of regional and city governments in foreign trade, immigration and political issues has challenged national governments' constitutional monopoly over foreign affairs'.[13] They do so in part by interacting with the growing number of international non-government organisations (NGOs). Cleaver argues that NGOs actively exploit cross-border international networks to 'outflank' national government policy-makers and, often, work directly against national policies.[14] Similarly, Smith refers to the 'the rapid expansion of transnational social movement organisations (TSMOs)', which lobby against international arrangements and treaties such as the Multilateral Agreement on Investment.[15] Recent protests against global free trade by groups ranging from anti-biotechnology activists to radical lesbians at meetings of the World Trade Organisation in Seattle are another prominent example.

Yet not all are persuaded. Saward has substantial reservations about the 'hollowing out' thesis.[16] Like the Australian policy analysts, Saward detects government officials who are redefining their roles and operations to 'underscore what remains of their distinctive capabilities . . . to foster new forms of selective and flexible policy intervention, and . . . ultimately, to reinforce sources and forms of legitimacy'.[17]

Similarly, Weiss stresses that nation-states have the capacity to exploit the opportunities of international economic change rather than merely succumb to its pressures:

> rather than counterposing nation-state and global market as antinomies, in certain important respects we find that 'globalisation' is often the by-product of

11 Ibid, p 138.

12 HM Cleaver 'The Zapatista Effect: The Internet and the Rise of an Alternative Political Fabric' (1998) 51(2) *Journal of International Affairs* 621.

13 Ibid, p 621.

14 Ibid.

15 J Smith (1998) 'Global Civil Society?' 42(1) *The American Behavioral Scientist* 93.

16 M Saward (1997) 'In Search of the Hollow Crown' in P Weller, H Bavkis and RAW Rhodes (eds), *The Hollow Crown: Countervailing Trends in Core Executives*, Macmillan.

17 Ibid, pp 32–3.

> States promoting the internationalisation strategies of their corporations, and sometimes in the process 'internationalising' state capacity. However, because state capacities differ, so the ability to exploit the opportunities of international economic change – rather than simply succumb to its pressures – appears much more marked in some countries than others.[18]

Weiss understands globalisation as a by-product of international policy choices made by nation-states. This offers an interesting juxtaposition of both the 'top-down' and the 'bottom up' interpretations. While Weiss acknowledges that further 'globalisation' is occurring, her empirical data supports the case that nation-states determine their own sovereignty by their capacity successfully to carry out international policy objectives. In the picture offered by Weiss, nation-states can respond to external pressures without being captured by their imperatives.

In short, while the weight of literature supports the argument advanced by Sir Anthony Mason that international obligations erode national sovereignty, there are also doubting voices. These argue that governments can find new and different ways to maintain policy influence within national borders. A government that can no longer impose currency controls nonetheless maintains important central bank, labour market and social security policy instruments that help steer the economy. A government that no longer restricts foreign entrants to media markets can nonetheless extend public funding to support local arts, indigenous film and television production and other forms of cultural expression. Globalisation creates a new world, but with many familiar features. Regional governments must cede power to the centre, but they, like the centre, can find new ways to retain and maintain policy capacity.

Global imperatives

To explore the interplay between a federal nation and its international context, we now turn to two case studies. While both examples are complex and unresolved, they illustrate patterns of centralisation, the implications for the States, and the question of whether ascending power may work eventually against the interests of the Commonwealth. Each examines the way international obligations enforced by the Commonwealth influence the policy capacity of State governments. In the case of greenhouse agreements, an international agreement has been used by Canberra to centralise power. The *Environment Protection and Biodiversity Conservation Act* 1999 (*EPBC Act*) presents a more complex interplay between global imperatives and federalism. The Act essentially provides leverage for the Commonwealth to assume power from the States in areas such as land planning. It does so by redefining some resources as 'national treasures' and so outside the sovereignty of a particular

18 L Weiss (1998) *The Myth of the Powerless State: Governing the Economy in a Global Era*, Polity Press.

State. Given that powers over the environment are not conferred on the Commonwealth by the federal Constitution, this is an important development.

Greenhouse

Global warning is an international issue, requiring a co-ordinated response from many nations. A series of international conferences sponsored by the United Nations has led to a Framework Convention on Climate Change (UNFCCC). As a signatory to the Convention, Australia must report annual greenhouse gas emissions according to guidelines developed by the Intergovernmental Panel on Climate Change. These provide a basis for international agreements about reduction of greenhouse gas.[19] Australia's commitments were defined and documented when it joined 55 other nations in signing the Kyoto Protocol in April 1998. This agreement requires Australia and its States to limit greenhouse gas emissions to no more than eight per cent above 1990 levels by 2008–12.

The Kyoto Protocol reflects a larger debate on the nature of international treaties and the power of the nation-state. Procedures introduced in May 1996 require any international treaty to be tabled in Parliament before it becomes binding on Australia.[20] The tabling of the treaty is accompanied by a 'National Interest Analysis' to identify the impact of the proposed treaty on Australia. A Joint Standing Committee on Treaties then considers the treaty, takes public submissions and analyses both the treaty and the National Interest Analysis before the treaty is given final consideration by Parliament. Once ratified, though, a treaty binds the Commonwealth; Parliament must legislate in accordance with the treaty.[21] For Mason, as for many critics of Australia's international obligations, ratification contributes to a democratic deficit, since meaningful opportunities for individuals or interest groups to influence the detail of treaties are limited.

Although the Kyoto Protocol has not yet commenced, Australia is already under international political and diplomatic pressure to exhibit progress towards limiting greenhouse gas emissions. The Commonwealth Government announced a National Greenhouse Strategy in 1998, supported by a National Greenhouse Office. These provide a framework and vehicle for meeting Australia's Kyoto Protocol commitments.

In theory, the Australian Commonwealth Government is pursuing an incentives-driven, rather than punishment-avoidance, model for the Strategy. Yet the politics of intergovernmental relations ensure there are more subtle pressures on the States to 'come to the party' on greenhouse issues. For example, the Commonwealth's Australian Greenhouse office is establishing the National Carbon Accounting System (NCAS) of land-based sources and

---

19 Australian Greenhouse Office (1999) *National Carbon Accounting for Land Based Sources and Sinks* (available at http://www.greenhouse.gov.au/ncas/).

20 Mason (1998), pp 4–5.

21 Ibid, p 5.

sinks to provide the framework and services necessary to account for greenhouse gas emissions reduction and sink enhancement programs. The NCAS will underpin future reporting of Australia's greenhouse gas emission for the National Greenhouse Gas Inventory and Kyoto Protocol requirements, support an internationally credible emissions trading scheme and provide a basis for emissions projections to assess progress towards meeting international emissions reduction commitments.[22]

The States are still developing a formal position with regard to NCAS. Yet there is an expectation the NCAS will emerge as a primary bargaining chip for the Commonwealth in fulfilling its Kyoto commitments. Clearly those States disadvantaged by NCAS conditions will object. Yet while the Commonwealth has not announced any sanctions for failing to conform with its National Greenhouse Strategy, the *EPBC Act* described below will give Canberra new power to override State decisions about development projects. In the name of an international commitment to reduce greenhouse gas emissions, the Commonwealth is assuming significant power over resource and planning decisions.

Are these changes the inevitable outcome of international pressures? Gyngell and Wesley suggest not, arguing the Commonwealth has used an international opportunity to achieve domestic objectives.[23] As they observe, the nature and distribution of economic and environmental interests expressed at the international level were 'remarkably similar' to those expressed in Australian domestic politics. They emphasise, as does Weiss,[24] that nation-states retain the capacity to carry out their objectives through international fora, and are not simply captive to external pressures. Indeed, the greenhouse example indicates how the Commonwealth can use international arrangements to limit State autonomy within the federation. Though various State officials have been present at international meetings on greenhouse issues, only the Commonwealth can sign for Australia. In doing so, the Commonwealth can listen to State concerns – or not. In this example, Canberra can use an international agreement to shift the balance of federalism. It does so, however, by making commitments that may prove onerous and costly in future years.

The *Environment Protection and Biodiversity Conservation Act* 1999 (Cth) (*EPBC Act*)

The *EPBC Act* received royal assent on 16 July 1999 and takes effect from 16 July 2000. The Act provides that a person must not take an action 'which has, will have or is likely to have a significant impact' on:

- a matter of national environmental significance;

22 Australian Greenhouse Office (1999).

23 Gyngell and Wesley (2000).

24 Weiss (1998).

- the world heritage values of a declared World Heritage property;
- listed threatened species and ecological communities;
- listed migratory species; and
- the Commonwealth marine environment leading to significant effect on the environment.

The Act further specifies that a person must not take a nuclear action that has, will have, or is likely to have a significant impact on the environment. The authority claimed by the Commonwealth rests, in part, on international agreements about World Heritage properties. Indeed the *EPBC Act* shores up Commonwealth power not just within World Heritage areas, but outside their boundaries should an action have possible implications for the area. Thus the Commonwealth has signalled an intention to regulate some Queensland inland waterways to prevent nutrient run-off from aquaculture projects into the Great Barrier Reef Marine Park.

Although the supporting regulations of the *EPBC Act* remain the subject of intergovernmental negotiation, the Act will comprehensively affect current State development approvals processes. The Commonwealth will be able to define those applications that automatically trigger the Act. This power extends to activities that, under current State laws, do not require planning applications. To manage the workflow, the Commonwealth is now offering to reach bilateral agreements for assessments and approvals – in effect, creating Commonwealth accreditation for decision processes once the exclusive prerogative of States.

Some political parties, notably the Australian Democrats, have long argued for a referendum to provide the Commonwealth with constitutional authority over environmental matters. In practice, the national greenhouse commitment and the *EPBC Act* provide much of this power. The Commonwealth has used international treaties to significantly extend its domestic reach, without apparent devolution of power to the international community. The effect is to 'hollow out' the States, leaving them with 'dignified' constitutional coverage – but little effective influence – over environmental outcomes.

The difficulty of participation

While some interest groups support strongly the Commonwealth's greenhouse strategy and environmental legislation, they were not players in its development. On the contrary, neither greenhouse initiatives nor the *EPBC Act* included much scope for participation by citizens in decision-making. The centralisation of power in national government raises difficult questions about how the voice of citizens will be included in the policy process. One virtue claimed for federalism is subsidiarity, the devolution of choice to the lowest possible level. Yet as domestic and international trends challenge the federal principle, so they undermine opportunities for consultation and participation.

As with most discussion about globalisation and its consequences, there is disagreement about the implications for citizen involvement in policy choices. Some suggest a new political process will emerge, with transnational social movement organisations (TSMOs) as significant new influences on policy outcomes. Smith argues that transnational social movements have influenced the formation and functioning of international institutions; in doing so, 'they have helped to democratise the international polity, which formally limits participation to national governments'.[25] Smith develops this optimistic analysis at some length:

> First, TSMOs signal the presence of much broader transnational social networks . . . Second, as the population of TSMOs develop (both quantitatively and qualitatively), they will provide new and ongoing opportunities for marginalised groups to seek to influence global political change. Third, TSMOs help bring together constituencies – such as unskilled migrant laborers in varied national contexts – that lack natural ties or that have 'thin infrastructures' at the national level that frustrate collective action . . . Fourth, and perhaps most important, is the fact that TSMOs help generate and guide a transnational public discourse and debate around global problems.[26]

In the case of greenhouse response and greater environmental protection by governments, there can be little doubting the influence of TSMOs. Organisations such as the World Wide Fund for Nature and Greenpeace worked successfully to place their issues on a global political agenda. Yet despite a catalytic role, the influence of TSMOs has not extended to policy detail. Decisions have been taken, as always, in fora limited to nation-states. International treaties do not allow for deliberative decision-making within a federation, let alone a distribution of power between governments and citizens. TSMOs may welcome environmental controls such as those embodied in the *EPBC Act*, but like the Australian States, transnational social movement organisations remain observers rather than participants when choices are taken.

Perhaps, following Smith, TSMOs will eventually find a place at the table. But this does not equate *necessary* with *greater* participation in decision-making. The global distribution of TSMOs is unequal. They tend to operate in the Northern Hemisphere with a disproportionate number based in London and New York.[27] The reach of TSMOs relies to a significant degree on First-World communications, democratic processes and an affluent domestic constituency. As Bauman states:

> If for the first world, the world of the rich and the affluent . . . space has lost its constraining quality and is easily traversed in both its 'real' and 'virtual' renditions, for the second world, the world of the poor, the 'structurally redundant', real space is fast closing up – the deprivation made yet more painful by the

25 Smith (1998), p 94.

26 Ibid, p 95.

27 Ibid, pp 95–6.

> obtrusive media display of space conquest and 'virtual accessibility' of distances unreachable in the non-virtual reality.[28]

The growth of a global political response is uneven and uncertain. Current international institutions emphasise the continuing importance of national governments, arguably at the expense of both sub-national representatives and individual participation. Bauman predicts stratification around two populations: the 'globalised and the localised'.[29] Citizens may be able to exert more choice within communities, yet have little say in global debate. Such trends exacerbate the democratic deficit identified by Mason,[30] given that individual Australians have few mechanisms to influence an already centralised Commonwealth Government.

Mason concludes that 'international treaty-making procedures should be structured to allow a proper place for national democratic decision-making processes'.[31] He is right to caution about the consequences of global agreements: beyond issues of sovereignty, the limited nature of participation in such choices raises seemingly intractable dilemmas for government at all levels. As the discussion of greenhouse policy and the *EPBC Act* suggest, despite growing international activities by NGOs and TSMOs, globalisation tips the balance of *federalism* towards the centre. In this sense there is a growing gap between informal participation and consultation via NGOs and TSMOs and formal participation and consultation via structures embedded in the Australian federal system. Because of this, even traditional (theoretical) forms of participation and consultation encased in federalism are in some cases rendered largely obsolete due to a combination of internal and external pressures. The sum total of pressures linked to globalisation 'hollow out' regional government, allowing Canberra to assert power amid constitutional silence. Yet, as empirical evidence increasingly shows there is risk too for the Commonwealth, in exacerbating a widening sense of powerlessness among some Australians.[32] Governments cannot legislate for legitimacy; they can only create the conditions in which legitimacy might be acknowledged. Yet these conditions increasingly require that governments maintain a space for both formal and informal participation and consultation within and beyond the Australian federation.

---

28 Z Bauman (1998) *Globalisation: The Human Consequences*, Polity Press, p 45.

29 Ibid, p 45.

30 Mason (1998).

31 Ibid, p 5.

32 See E Papadakis (1999) 'Constituents of Confidence and Mistrust in Australian Institutions' 34 *Australian Journal of Political Science* 1 at 75–93.

12

The Role of Upper Houses

Is Washminster Washed Up?

Senator Helen Coonan

Government in the global village

As Australia enters its second decade of globalisation in an uncertain geo-political environment, many crucial challenges face the governance system that will take us into the new millennium.[1] Globalisation has so transformed the environment in which our political institutions operate that, inevitably, we must ask whether Westminster-style Upper Houses still have any useful role in 'Cyberworld'. After examining the Australian Senate as an example of an unusually powerful Upper House, I conclude that, paradoxically, globalisation offers an important – even an expanded – role for that chamber.

A number of related changes – privatisation, competition policy, labour market and economic reforms, and rapid technological advances – have accelerated in speed, diminishing the traditional importance of geography to political representation. Other powerful economic and political forces have emerged with profound implications for established ideas of governance. One trend is the growing impact on the individuals' lives of decisions made by such international agencies as the United Nations, World Trade Organisation, World Bank and International Monetary Fund – described by Daniel Bradlow, Director of International Legal Studies at Washington's American University, as a 'select group making rules for the whole world'. Secondly, capital mobility, price transfers, and the opportunity to choose favourable tax environments with the click of a mouse, all weaken national governments' power. Australia's future requires international and regional co-operation on matters as diverse as trade, environmental protection standards, and Internet intellectual property rights. Our prosperity depends on our global competitive advantages to make Australia an attrac-

1 This chapter expands on my paper 'Survival of the Fittest', delivered at the Conference Marking Fifty Years of Proportional Representation for the Senate (Canberra, 6 August 1999).

tive place to invest, and provide jobs and security for our citizens. A third trend is the rapid emergence of cyber-democracy, offering individuals direct democratic participation. Indeed, some envisage an 'electronic republic' with citizens voting directly on decisions.[2]

What are the implications of these developments, in a fast-changing world, for our particular version of the Westminster system, now a century old? Is our bicameral Parliament, with both Houses having equal veto powers and a double majority necessary to pass all legislation, capable of meeting the changes of the new global environment? Will it be sufficiently responsive to the need to manage change and ensure its benefits are distributed equitably – or will it succumb to demands by many to retreat from Australia's strategic opportunities to be a leader in international affairs and global governance?

A proper answer to these questions must go beyond Australia's past constitutional debates about Upper Houses and their merits. Instead, any constructive discussion of checks and balances must recognise and respond to these broader global trends if our domestic legislature is not to become increasingly irrelevant, or even bypassed completely.

Senate static

Despite theoretical problems with reconciling responsible parliamentary government with a strong Senate, Australia's hybrid Washminster model has so far delivered stable government and a relatively robust representative democracy. That is not to downplay the constitutional crisis surrounding the 1975 Whitlam Dismissal, nor to minimise the Senate's ability to act more like an obstructionist rival to the government than a constructive house of review. The Senate's role is important for our future governance because Australia's ability to meet new challenges depends in no small measure on the flexibility and responsiveness of our political system, including the ability of our two Federal Parliamentary Houses to resolve their disagreements in timely and effective ways.

For all but five years since 1948, minor parties[3] have held the Senate balance of power. With the use of a proportional representation voting method, to fill even numbers of seats,[4] no government is likely to win a Senate majority in the foreseeable future. The reality is that governing Australia now requires the support of minor parties to pass laws. What does this mean in practice?

---

2 LK Grossman (1995) *The Electronic Republic: Reshaping Democracy in the Information Age*, Penguin.

3 'Minor parties' here includes Independents, but not the National/Country Party.

4 Two per Territory; six per State at a half-Senate election, 12 per State at a double dissolution.

At the very least, it means delay – and sometimes reluctance by governments to give necessary and effective attention to problems demanding national or even international attention. At its worst, it means policy gridlock, even deadlock, with no effective constitutional procedure for resolving the disagreement short of a double dissolution and general election. Even then, this cumbersome, time-consuming and uncertain procedure is futile if a solution is needed urgently. Most often, prudence prevails: if minor-party Senators are prepared to negotiate with the government, compromises are reached allowing contentious Bills to pass in some form.

But this deal-making is not without consequences. Eleventh-hour deals on major policy issues like native title, privatisation and taxation raise fundamental issues of principle, quite apart from political expediency. Many argue that such compromises represent harmonisation of diverse views and demonstrate representative democracy at work; or that consensus-building produces better legislation even if, on occasion, the compromise may reflect highly idiosyncratic personal agendas. But were these the best outcomes available in the national interest – or do such compromises represent special-interest pay-offs, and deliver third best outcomes?

And importantly, what message do they give an already disillusioned and disenchanted electorate? Do voters accept that 'politics is the art of the possible' and the Senate should play a pivotal role in finding a political solution – or is the electorate's will frustrated by their government's inability to deliver the policies it promised?

Faced with an impasse, a government may be tempted simply to give up its promises rather than put the country through another general election. Worse, my experience in the Senate suggests that necessary reforms may be rejected if they are temporarily unpopular, regardless of their merits. Hard but necessary decisions in the national interest are vulnerable to being sacrificed for the sake of political opportunism and populism, whatever spin is put on it.

With the realignment (at time of writing) of minor-party voting in the Senate, I would not say that the Senate is presently unworkable. Of course this could change quickly. Although both Labor and Democrats are in negotiating mode on business-tax reform, the so-called 'second wave' of workplace relations reforms may meet a different fate. The government recently abandoned its petrol-reform package which would have benefited consumers and narrowed the gap between urban and rural prices because of entrenched Labor and Democrat opposition to repealing the *Petroleum Retail Marketing Sites Act* 1980. This is a clear example of sectional interests using the Senate to shoot down economic reforms that would have served the broader community interest.

However, given the constitutional constraints under which it operates, the Senate has shown in recent months that it *can* act responsibly and deliver acceptable outcomes on domestic legislation, when it wants to. We may even see coalitions of interests being negotiated between major and minor parties *before* elections, rather than emerging piecemeal long after polls close.

An obsolete model?

When pared down to basics, the most fundamental problem with the Senate (and more broadly with the Australian political system) is that both were designed to meet the needs of a different era. The fledgling Federation, with slow communications across a sparsely populated continent, required (and could afford) gradualism and compromise to take account of distance and regional differences. But these obstacles no longer determine how and when Australia does business, the speed of communications, or how effectively States and Territories can be represented. As Paul Kelly, the *Australian*'s International Editor, recently told the *Australia Unlimited* Conference: 'Compared to the speed of decision-making in the market place, parliamentary democracy is hopelessly old-fashioned.'[5]

The Senate's processes – particularly the need to stitch together a negotiated coalition for every contested Bill – are simply not able to meet the requirements of the information age. Legislation can be near obsolete before it is even passed, with technological advances outstripping the legislative timeframe.

Business has been understandably annoyed at long delays in the government's financial reform timetable. Key measures like relaxing off-shore banking regulations, tightening thin capitalisation rules, and changes to withholding tax arrangements were stalled in the Senate for just over two years, and passed on the last day of the winter sittings under the guillotine! Many of these measures were not even controversial when eventually debated. But legislative traffic through the Senate is so slow, its static and posturing so loud, and its delaying tactics so time-consuming that sensible, necessary reforms get pushed into the background.

Australia cannot afford such a leisurely and haphazard approach to decision-making. To quote Paul Kelly again: 'We need to ensure that parliamentary democracy survives globalisation. It may be a close-run thing.'[6] Without exaggerating, we must ask whether our parliamentary system, based the traditional adversarial role of political parties, is equipped to respond to the information age?

5 P Kelly (1999) 'The New Social Glue', Australia Unlimited Conference, 4 May.

6 Ibid.

Winners and losers

Our parliamentary system will be challenged as never before what Thomas Friedman calls the 'FastWorld'.[7] Unfortunately, global progress leaves economic, social and political casualties. Friedman identifies those least likely to survive the transition:

> entrepreneurs and cronies who were anointed with . . . monopolies by the Government, industrialists . . . protected by the Government through high import tariffs . . . big labour unions who got used to . . . fewer work hours with more pay . . . workers in state-owned factories who got paid whether the factory made a profit or not, the unemployed . . . who enjoyed relatively generous benefits and health-care no matter what, and all those who depended on the largesse of the State to protect them from the market.[8]

If correct, Friedman has identified an emerging socio-economic phenomenon – the division in society between those who benefit from globalisation and those who see themselves as missing out. To have large sections of the populace so disaffected has serious political implications. One reflex action is to try either to shut the 'FastWorld' out or to have the rules of the system changed. Over the past two years Australia has seen the anger of rural and regional Australia expressed at the ballot box – the success of One Nation, the unexpected defeat of Jeff Kennett and the loss of the Republic referendum. This anger is caused at least partly by long-term economic trends beyond any government's control; it reflects expectations that government can solve these difficulties and restore confidence, when plainly it cannot. But the political temptation remains to 'buy off' those single-issue groups that can marshal votes for their own causes, to the detriment of other priorities for the entire community. Here the Westminster system, particularly the Senate, is vulnerable in today's political climate to hijack by special pleaders and populist causes. Minor-party Senators have seen their role as promoting minority interests. Diversity of viewpoints is important to democracy, but to see localised interests promoted over shared community values only alienates voters from politics.

Upper Houses revisited

A survey of other Westminster systems shows that only 15 Commonwealth member nations have any Upper House at all. Many of these, including the UK's 'Mother of Parliaments', are considering reforms to give their second chambers popular legitimacy and relevance, and avoid redundancy.

This problem is not faced by the Australian Senate, which has enjoyed strong popular legitimacy and entrenched constitutional power since

7 T Friedman (1999) *The Lexus and the Olive Tree*, HarperCollins.

8 Ibid.

its creation. Given the history of failed amendments (only eight carried since Federation), constitutional reform of the Senate is unlikely and the broader quest to modernise our Constitution seems forlorn. Galligan and Walsh pointedly observe that there is 'no realistic possibility of radical restructuring creating a new regime, and we would argue, no need'.[9]

Although I have previously advocated a robust public debate on the Senate's role today, proposing several reform options,[10] there are some contextual matters worth noting.

The Senate's role

The first is that the Senate performs a range of essential functions not carried out as comprehensively, or at all, by the House of Representatives: for example, providing the only parliamentary scrutiny for volumes of delegated legislation. Of course the Senate's Committee system needs an overhaul. It has been hijacked by party politics (with reports reflecting little more than entrenched positions), or used as a delaying tactic. Professor Ian Marsh proposes a revised Committee system that would offer opportunities for consensus-building at a much earlier stage.[11] Either way, the Senate's role is ultimately justified by the distinctive role it occupies in our federal system.

The Senate's evolution

The second point is that despite the rigidities of the constitutional framework within which Parliament operates, the Senate has shown an ability to adjust its procedures and practices to meet emerging needs. For example, it has established processes to safeguard against retrospectivity, administrative decisions without review, and infringement of human rights. From 16 July 1997 to 6 August 1999, the Senate Standing Committee on Regulations and Ordinances scrutinised 3559 disallowable instruments of delegated legislation and detected 502 apparent defects and matters worthy of mention.[12]

The Senate's future

Globalisation will open up an expanded and even more important role for the Senate as a deliberative and investigative body that safeguards our local

9 B Galligan and C Walsh (1992) 'Federation: Yes or No?' in G Craven (ed), *Australian Federation: Towards the Second Century*, Melbourne University Press.

10 H Coonan (1999) 'The Senate: Safeguard or Handbrake on Democracy?' Address to the Sydney Institute, 3 February.

11 I Marsh (1999) 'The Senate, Policy-Making and Community Consultations', Senate Occasional Lecture, Canberra, 23 April.

12 Regulations and Ordinances Committee (1998) *Annual Report 1996–1997*, June; (1999) *Annual Report, 1997–1998*, March; (1998) 'Statement of Work of the Committee during the Spring Sittings 1998', *Hansard*, 9 December, p 1588; (1999) 'Statement of Work of the Committee during the Autumn and Winter Sittings', *Hansard*, 30 June, p 6942.

and national interests. One sign of this is Parliament's new role in scrutinising proposed treaties before these become binding: they are tabled in Parliament and reviewed by a Treaties Committee. Introducing these reforms in 1996, the Hon Alexander Downer, Minister for Foreign Affairs, stated that these new arrangements would apply 'to all treaties, bilateral as well as multi-lateral. They will also apply to all actions which amend a treaty if the amendment would alter obligations with a legally binding impact on Australia'.[13]

Parliamentary oversight of treaty-making (albeit via by a joint committee of both Houses) responded to concerns that Australia's sovereignty was being undermined not only by global forces, but by Australia's willing participation in a number of treaties that subjected our legal and constitutional system to unrepresentative committees of the United Nations.[14] To quote Downer again:

> We believe that . . . Australia's national interests are most effectively upheld by Australians throughout our parliaments, our courts and other bodies, and not through UN or other international committees that are ill-suited to playing any direct role in the Australian legal system and many of which are themselves widely recognised as being in need of reform.[15]

Of particular concern to many Australians is the effect of international agreements on Australian law. The High Court's recent decision that existing Australian film-content standards were unlawful, under bilateral obligations requiring Australia and New Zealand to give each other market access on equal terms, came as a shock;[16] as did the *Teoh* judgment requiring administrative decision-makers to take account of treaty obligations.[17] Small wonder that the Treaties Committee was inundated with submissions opposing the very suggestion that Australia might enter the proposed Multilateral Agreement on Investment (MAI).[18] Parliamentary inquiries provide an excellent opportunity for voters to express their concerns about such international obligations.

Paradoxically, economic internationalisation and the rise of powerful global trade, currency and security groupings have helped restore the legitimacy of individual nation-states. Many argue that these 'global guardians' must be made more transparent and accountable to the countries and in-

---

13 A Downer MP (1996) House of Representatives, *Hansard*, 2 May, p 232.

14 Senator R Kemp (1994) 'International Tribunals and the Attack on Australian Democracy', in *Upholding the Australian Constitution, Volume 4*, Samuel Griffith Society.

15 A Downer MP (1994) Speech to National Press Club, 8 June.

16 *Project Blue Sky Inc v Australian Broadcasting Authority* (1998) 194 CLR 355.

17 *Minister for Immigration and Ethnic Affairs v Teoh* (1995) 183 CLR 273.

18 Joint Standing Committee on Treaties (1999) *Report No 18: Multilateral Agreement on Investment*, March.

dividuals their decisions affect.[19] If their process is not inclusive, their decisions will be politically unacceptable to domestic electorates.

Because Senators represent large (State- and Territory-wide) electorates, the Senate will become increasingly important as guardian of our national interests in a globalised world. It is not hard to imagine the Senate playing a deliberative role in expressing the community's concerns over such complex issues as whether we should supply arms and military training to our near neighbours, or attach more stringent prescriptions to foreign aid.

As we embark on the most confronting foreign policy challenge Australia has ever faced, we should give our Senate a defining role in articulating and protecting democratic values and respect for human rights. In a timely recent article, Professor Anthony Milner, Dean of Asian Studies at the Australian National University, notes that Australia's political culture still makes it an outsider in this region: 'The forces of globalisation do not extend to the globalisation of moral values. Rather, there are ethical codes (Asian values) that conflict with those dominant in Western liberal democracies'.[20] If we simply reject opposing values that emphasise order, community over individual needs, and a formidable work ethic, that will be dismissed as cultural aggrandisement. Instead we must seek to persuade, rather than imposing our values on the region or assuming Asian values will simply converge with ours in the ongoing struggle for democracy.

Our national interest requires that statesmanship prevail over brinkmanship: this could well be the catalyst that redefines the Senate relates to the Lower House, and how our national Parliament is viewed internationally. It is uncertain whether the Senate (more accurately, the political parties that Senators represent) will recognise the need to 'change their game' in a global world. But the old saying '*Always back self-interest – at least you know it's trying*' should offer the necessary motivation for change.

It is inconceivable to think the Senate will be operating the same way in 50 years' time. Global forces will have rewritten the rules of representative democracy. Political power will have been redistributed, international and national interests re-balanced. It will require a very different style of politician and party politics to be effective in such a constantly changing environment. Self-preservation should be a strong enough motive for change, because only those institutions that adapt will survive.

---

19 J Gray (1999) 'The Rise of Global Guardians', *Australian Financial Review*, 18–19 September, p 22.

20 A Milner (1999) 'Why We Should Not Swagger in Asia' *Quadrant* (September) 21, 24.

13

Washminster Revisited

The Role of the Upper House

Senator Andrew Bartlett

What do we mean by 'Government', and do we spell it with a big or little 'G'?

When frontbenchers talk about 'Government', they usually mean the Prime Minister and Ministers and themselves having all power, and making all decisions, irrespective of the Parliament. However, the founders of the Constitution talked of government as something completely different.

The Constitution establishes a government consisting of three branches – legislative, executive and judicial – and provides that the legislative, executive and judicial powers are to be exercised by these three branches. Section 51 of the Constitution states, 'The *Parliament* shall, subject to the Constitution, have power to *make laws* for the peace, order, and good government of the Commonwealth' (my emphasis) and lists the range of commonwealth responsibilities.

What the party in power calls 'the Government' is, usually, the executive. The Prime Minister and his senior Ministers – very big G. The House of Representatives currently operates simply as an arm of the executive, an echo chamber for the Prime Minister. It is left to the Senate to perform the function of the Parliament; that is, to make laws, as set out in the Constitution.

There are plenty of supporters of big-G government – that is, all power to the executive – both inside and outside the Parliament, who criticise perceived challenges to that power, including the Senate, the judiciary, international treaties, and the United Nations.

Just as the distinction between big-L and small-l liberals leads to confusion within the general community, so does the distinction between big-G and small-g governments. This confusion serves the executive well in its quest for absolute power.

The Clerk of the Senate, Harry Evans, made this point recently in an article by journalist Laurie Oakes who writes often on the age-old battle between the executive and Parliament as it is played out in contemporary

Australia. In Evans's view, the talk of Senate reform emanating from the Coalition Government at present is easily explained:

> Governments always want to remove any obstacles to their power, and the more power they've got, the more they try to remove the residual obstacles... Governments just naturally drive for absolute power, and people just have to be awake to that and resist it, because unless you have checks on power then you go down the slippery slope.[1]

It has been claimed that of all Upper Houses in the world, the Australian Senate is one of the most powerful, most other second chambers being relatively unimportant.[2] The Senate's power to reject Supply and some of its other legislative powers are not shared by most Upper Houses operating in the parliamentary executive system. The Australian Constitution makes it clear that, apart from initiating money bills, the Senate has powers equal to the House of Representatives. Our most fundamental law simply does not back up the view that the Senate is somehow the poor relation of the Lower House.

In the current federal sphere, the executive has already captured the House of Representatives. The executive, however, can't 'capture' the current Senate, so instead they seek to discredit it before attempting to dismantle its powers.

What 'hostile Senate'?

Former Liberal Senate Leader, Fred Chaney said, 'By the time I left Parliament in 1993, it was my firm conviction that good government was served by the government of the day not having control of the Senate'.[3]

Most politicians from the major parties will defend the role of the Senate until they hold a majority in the House of Representatives. Prime Minister John Howard, when in opposition in 1987, lauded the Senate as 'one of the most democratically elected chambers in the world – a body which at present more faithfully represents the popular will of the total Australian people at the last election than does the House of Representatives'.[4]

Despite these views, over the last few years the Coalition has been very successful in building a strong public perception that the Senate is 'hostile'. They have done this through highly disciplined repetition and they

---

1 L Oakes (1999) 'Century-old Idea May Help Resolve Modern Problem', *The Bulletin*, 23 February, p 25.

2 S Bennett (1999) *Should the Australian Electoral System be Changed?*, Current Issues Brief No 10, April, Politics and Public Administration Group, Department of the Parliamentary Library, Information and Research Services; AR Ball (1993) *Modern Politics and Government* (5th edn), Macmillan, p 160; (1987) *Report of the Advisory Committee on Executive Government*, Canberra Publishing and Printing, p 22.

3 'No Majority Best, Says Chaney' (1999) *Melbourne Age*, 7 August.

4 House of Representatives (1987) *Hansard*, 8 October.

started on day one of John Howard's administration. Even senior political journalists, who should know better, pepper their articles with the adjective 'hostile' without stopping to think if it is accurate.

Notwithstanding Government claims, the Senate is not 'hostile' and it could not realistically be called 'hostile' at any time since the Whitlam Government. For example, from May 1996 to 11 July 1998, 427 Bills were passed and only two remained negatived – the Workplace Relations Amendment Bill and the Telstra Privatisation Bill. The others were either passed after recommitting or laid aside by the Reps. Two Bills negatived and 427 passed means 99.54 per cent of Bills were passed.

The introduction of proportional representation in the Senate made the Senate more powerful and gave a voice to the many who vote away from the two major parties, but ultimately it only legitimises the use of powers the Senate is granted by the Constitution.

Does the Senate need reform?

Any party would be likely to gain a majority of seats in the Senate under the current system if they got a majority of primary votes from the public over two elections. Many people regularly vote differently in the Senate than the Lower House specifically to ensure the government does not face a tame Parliament that will lamely acquiesce to the Prime Minister's every wish.

The proposal put forward in 1999 by Liberal Deputy Whip, Senator Helen Coonan, to introduce arbitrary primary vote thresholds in the Senate electoral system is just the latest in a long and inglorious line of attempts by the major parties to suggest they should be granted total power and not have to deal with a supposedly hostile Senate.

The bottom line is that, without completely removing the proportional nature of the Senate voting system, a party is unlikely to be able to hold a majority of Senate seats unless they receive a majority of the primary vote. This is how it should be.

Even if we accept the straw man argument put up by proponents of Senate 'reform', most of the proposed solutions would not work in any case. The threshold quotas proposed by Senator Coonan – which are more properly known as exclusion quotas – would not deliver a majority in the Senate to the Government of the day. In almost every case the seats won by minor parties would go to the Opposition instead.

Similarly proposals to reduce the Senate back from 12 to 10 Senators per State also would not have delivered control to the government of the day. If the 1983 legislation to increase the Senate never passed, and there had been 10 Senators per State for the last 15 years, the Democrats would probably have held the balance of power outright throughout the entire period.

There is a legitimate concern that if the balance of power were to fall to Senators elected on a tiny vote, the political legitimacy of the Senate would be seriously undermined. However if ever there was an opportunity for the public to express their concern at Upper Houses acting in an excessive and inappropriate way and impeding effective government, it was the 1999 New South Wales State election. This election saw widespread publicity about a plethora of 'micro-parties', with unknown candidates and unknown policies, generating a 'tablecloth' ballot paper. There was little secret that at least some of these micro-party candidates had deliberately negotiated a series of cascading 'preference swaps' to help them win seats on a minuscule vote.

The ALP was widely expected to win, so when people cast their votes for the NSW Legislative Council they did so knowing which government they were likely to have. Surely if an electorate ever had a chance to say 'We want the Upper House to get out of the way and allow the government to govern', it was this election.

Despite this, there was an unprecedented level of support for non-major party candidates in the Upper House. Around 35 per cent voted for a candidate other than ALP or Coalition. Indeed the 'minor/micro party' vote exceeded that for the Coalition. While both major parties paint the Upper Houses (and particularly smaller or 'micro' parties holding the balance of power) as obstructionist, the latter's vote is still rising.

Some argue for removing the Senate's power to reject the budget. In 1988 the Constitutional Commission recommended a constitutional amendment to this effect,[5] but there is unlikely to be inter-party agreement over this change, even though it would probable suit both major parties' long-term interests.[6]

There are real constraints in place, some practical and some – importantly – self-imposed. For instance, over 22 years, every generation of Democrat Senators has pledged not to block Supply. The important difference between Supply Bills and other legislation is that blocking the former can force a government from office.

The power to block Supply legislation – a matter of great controversy in 1974–5 – is central to the question of Senate power. Many commentators argue it was public opposition to the Senate's behaviour in 1975 that underpinned the initial success of the Democrats in 1977 and 1980. However, there has been a balance of power situation in the Senate only since 1981 – Fraser had majorities in 1977 and 1975. The Democrats have enjoyed enduring voter appeal ever since the late 70s on the basis of our own performance.

---

5 Constitutional Commission (1988) *Final Report*, AGPS, Vol 1, pp 218–47.

6 S Bennett (1999).

Another proposal to reduce Senate power would be to amend the Constitution to strip back all Senate power to a position where the Upper House had little more than a delaying power, much like the House of Lords since the *Parliaments Acts* of 1911 and 1949. In Britain a Royal Commission is investigating options for the House of Lords after the removal of the hereditary peers. There is a basic dilemma because too much pruning of an Upper House's power it leaves it largely redundant.[7]

Mandate, negotiation, public discussion and compromise

Similar to discussions of a so-called 'hostile' Senate are executive claims of a mandate to govern unhindered. Despite receiving less than half the vote and having repudiated the notion of 'mandate' when in opposition, the Howard Government laid claim to a multi-purpose mandate arising out of the 1998 election.

As Dr Campbell Sharman recently said, from one perspective:

> no one has a mandate to do anything except enter into negotiations. The present situation in the Commonwealth Parliament requires governments to compromise so that a larger group than the governing party, perhaps even a body of parliamentarians representing a real majority, supports a proposed measure. This mean that . . . legislation is closely scrutinised, and the government of the day and its supporting bureaucracy must publicly justify every proposed law to a legislative body whose support cannot be taken for granted.[8]

On the theme of compromise, Sharman points out that the creation of legislation is a process of compromise before and after it is introduced into Parliament:

> The views of the relevant interest groups, competing concerns of Ministers and government departments, not to mention the considerations of the cost, constitutional validity, legal effect and partisan impact of the proposed law, all have to be accommodated. . . . It is a case of the Senate being criticised for doing in public what the government has been doing in private.[9]

That decisions are made publicly is an important point. Because the major parties' policies coincide in a range of areas, all sorts of legislative decisions would go through unquestioned, barely even appearing in *Hansard* if it were not for the voices of smaller parties and independents who, when they cannot amend legislation, can at least ask questions, getting the answers on the public record.

---

7 Ibid.

8 C Sharman (1998) 'The Senate and Good Government', Senate Occasional Lecture Series, 11 December.

9 Ibid.

Senate inquiries, which the Australian Democrats often initiate to examine in more detail the implications of legislation, take that backroom compromising and negotiating, puts it into a more public sphere and makes it more accessible for anyone to comment through submissions.

As Sharman notes:

> There is no question that the scrutiny of bills that occurs in the Senate can improve their technical coherence – all kinds of unforeseen issues are raised once legislation is open to the full glare of public scrutiny – but the main virtue of the process that is so painful to the government is that it permits the views of large constituencies outside the charmed circle of executive and its advisers to have a say in shaping legislation. When a few Senators are criticised for 'holding the government to ransom' the reason for this impasse is that these few Senators are voicing the concerns of a large section of the community.[10]

Sharman points out that strong Upper Houses, the courts and the Constitution, work on the assumption that:

> government action requires a process of weighing up a number of arguments and harmonising a number of views. In this respect, the Australian tradition has more in common with that of the United States than it does with the United Kingdom . . . and is] labelled 'consensus democracy' by the American political scientist Arend Lijphart, in contrast to majoritarian democracy.[11]

Reform of the House of Representatives

The Senate performs the functions of the Parliament as set out in the Constitution, while the House of Representatives currently operates simply as an arm of the executive.

This was illustrated in the 1999 tax debate. Firstly, the House of Representatives was allowed a paltry 20 hours to debate 17 tax Bills, described by the Government as the biggest change in taxation law since Federation. Secondly, it was left up to the Democrats in the Senate to force a public parliamentary inquiry to examine how the package would affect different groups in Australia and as an opportunity for the community to have open input into the tax debate.

With the passing of the tax package, with considerable amendments, the attacks on the so-called 'hostile' Senate stopped temporarily and instead the Opposition and sections of the media accused the Democrats of being 'in bed with the Coalition'. This also occurred with the passing of the Environment Protection and Biodiversity Conservation Bill, despite the fact the Democrats had negotiated 500 changes to that legislation and produced a strong environment protection tool for the Commonwealth.

---

10 Ibid.

11 Ibid.

The major parties continue to frequently vote together – for instance in the passing of the Regional Forests Agreement Bill. The Democrats continue to pass, reject or seek to amend legislation based on its individual merits – not on perceptions of whether we are being obstructionist or overly close to the Party in power.

The need for proportional representation in the House of Representatives electoral system

It is my view that the overriding objective of any electoral reform should be swinging the pendulum back towards vesting power in the Parliament. In discussing the merits of major electoral reform, there is a good case for reform of the House of Representatives' voting system.

If democracy can be defined as a situation wherein the will of the majority prevails, Labor leader Mr Beazley should have formed government after the October 1999 election. Mr Howard enjoys a 12-seat majority in the House of Representatives having attracted only 48.7 per cent of the two-party preferred vote. Worse still, this outcome was not exceptional. In one in four Australian elections, the electoral system delivers government to the 'wrong' party in two-party-preferred terms. In less politically stable countries, similar outcomes could lead to civil unrest.

There are five main problems with the current House electoral system, which could be ameliorated, with more democracy:

- The current electoral system denies representation to over one in five Australians who do not vote for the major parties.
- It provides a huge electoral advantage to incumbent Governments who are able to use their power to hold marginal seats in very tight elections despite not attracting the majority of the vote. Major parties focus on the 20 to 30 marginal seats which will decide the fate of Government, producing pork-barrelling such as the 'Sports Rorts' affair and the Centenary of Federation Grants. In power, governments largely ignore the other 120 or 130 electorates, particularly the 30 or 40 safe Opposition seats.
- It reduces the role of the House of Representatives to that of an echo chamber for the Government of the day.
- It limits voters' effective choice to only two similar major parties, even though 20 to 25 per cent would prefer another party to represent them. Indeed, 93 of the 148 members chosen at the last election were not the first preference choice of the majority of voters in their electorates.
- It creates political 'ghettos', with large areas not having representation from both major parties. Sydney's North Shore, with eight safe Liberal electorates of 80,000 voters, each denies representation to

> 120,000 Labor voters. Sydney's west has 10 safe Labor seats and 200,000 unrepresented Liberal supporters. And with a two-party-preferred vote of around 43 per cent, Labor won only one of the 16 non-metropolitan seats in Queensland, and the Liberals none of the five seats in Tasmania.

These facts and figures suggest our current electoral system does not deliver a representative House of Representatives.

A Royal Commission, headed by Lord Roy Jenkins, tackled the issue of the unrepresentative nature of Britain's House of Commons and recommended a new electoral system. The Australian Democrats have looked to the Jenkins Commission's report to inform our own proposals for the reform of Australia's electoral system.

The Jenkins model offers a practical compromise between the competing principles of local representation and fair representation, recommending a mix of local seats being 'topped up' from a party-based vote. Under the proposal, 80 to 85 per cent of members of the Lower House would continue to be elected based on single-member constituencies and preferential voting. A further 15 to 20 per cent of members would be elected based on a second vote by electors for the party of their choice. These seats would be allocated in each region (or in Australia, each State) to the most under-represented parties. This second category of members would provide the pool to 'top up' the representation of that Party until the numbers of MPs accurately reflected voter support in each State. This would ensure that a party with a minority of the two-party vote never accidentally 'wins' an election again – as the Howard Government did in October 1999.

It could lead to a rejuvenation of the House Committee system – as has occurred in the Senate over the last two decades since the Democrats arrived. It could also lead to all seats being, in effect, marginal, placing real power back into the hands of the voters at election time, rather than only those in a handful of swinging seats.

As a Party, the Democrats have long supported the introduction of proportional representation in all Houses of Parliament in Australia; however the major parties are unlikely to accept such a change in the face of their own declining support from voters.

The debate about electoral reform will only be productive if Australians realise the motive of the major parties in this debate is the drive of the executive to secure for itself greater power.

The main area we could do with reform is in the political culture in Australia. Given that the public repeatedly refuses to give one party control of both houses of Parliament, perhaps it is time for politicians to take a less combative approach. If a party does not have the numbers, maybe they should put more energy into co-operation, negotiation and consensus rather than simply plotting to disenfranchise their rivals?

If we want to remain a real democracy, our Parliament should be expected to perform its traditional democratic role, a significant part of which includes legislating. In the United States they call their politicians 'legislators'. That is a major part of what Members of Parliament are supposed to do – examine proposed laws and, where appropriate, pass them in a form which they believe will make good and fair law.

Unfortunately, due to the capturing of the Lower House by the executive, the Senate is often the only chamber that effectively carries out this important responsibility.

14

Government as a Public Trust

Crown Mystique, Unequal Laws, and Modern Democracy

Steven C Churches

Introduction

Two recent but disparate publications show the various ways in which law is unevenly applied in Australia:

> (1) . . . if you did business in West Australia [*sic*], or for that matter Australia, it was important to know politicians. . . . Today, so much of industry and finance is controlled by regulations. Politicians can enforce or relax them, invent new ones or abolish old ones just as they please, without going anywhere near the parliaments to which they have been elected.[1]

> (2) THE LAW SOCIETY OF WESTERN AUSTRALIA'S QUALITY PRACTICE STANDARD [PHOTOGRAPH: beaming practitioner receives Approved Quality Practice certificate] Quality Practice Standard coordinator [X] and Law Society president [Y] congratulate [Z] of [Z] and Co.[2]

From these we glean that the British Conservative Party's former Treasurer believes the process of modern governmental regulation consists of deals done in private (where presumably the public interest is an optional accessory) and that WA lawyers like to give each other certificates attesting to their good qualities.

---

1 A McAlpine (1997) *Once a Jolly Bagman*, Weidenfeld & Nicolson, p 171.

2 *Brief* (organ of the WA Law Society) (1999) August, p 32.

Two issues of accountability

The issues raised by the opening quotations are those of accountability. McAlpine focuses us (apparently unwittingly) on the need for constant scrutiny of, and a process of accountability for, the actions of executive government. In the situation conjured by McAlpine the government action requiring scrutiny was that most palpable display of power: the 'relaxation' of regulatory law in favour of identified individuals.[3]

The (presently obscure, but shortly to be explained) extract from the WA Law Society relates to the non-accountability of the jurisprudence in that area of public law in which governments may claim medieval immunities from obedience to the law, and share that advantage with their friends. Scientifically based professions (eg, medicine) are ultimately confronted with objective standards based on empirical observation. Persuasive as Galen's medical doctrines were for 1500 years, five centuries ago doctors like Andreas Vesalius began dissecting bodies to find out how they worked. Theory could be tested against a benchmark. It is that possible external reference which is missing for lawyers, particularly in the more antique portions of public common law.

Administrative accountability

A recent advance

> The high constitutional functions of the Legislative Council encompass both legislating, and the enforcement of the accountability of the Executive.[4]

The New South Wales Court of Appeal's recent decision in *Egan v Chadwick* provides a useful compendium of issues concerning the machinery of accountability in the context of responsible government. It leads in turn to an analysis of a matter not litigated before that time, but with great importance to a House of Parliament set on performing its accounting function: the right to demand government documents, in respect of which public interest immunity (the 'Crown Privilege' of yesteryear) and/or legal professional privilege is claimed.

3 McAlpine and WA are hardly unique. See B Cohen (1997) *Whitlam to Winston*, Allen & Unwin, pp 193–4 for a similar example involving Queensland Government Minister, Russ Hinze, in the 1980s.

4 *Egan v Chadwick* (1999) 46 NSWLR 563 per Spigelman CJ at [54].

'Reasonable necessity': its reach and limits

Spigelman CJ (with whom Meagher JA agreed) found that Cabinet documents, not themselves the record of the actual deliberations in Cabinet, must be produced on demand to either House of Parliament. The Chief Justice reasoned by reference to the 'common law rule – that the Legislative Council has such powers as are reasonably necessary for the proper exercise of its functions'.[5] That customary usage and political reality tempered his Honour's reasoning appears in the exemption afforded Cabinet's deliberative papers:

> In order to avoid inconsistency between the power to call for documents and one of the bases on which it has been determined that the power is reasonably necessary (namely executive accountability derived from responsible government) the power should, at least, be restricted to documents which do not, directly or indirectly, reveal the deliberations of Cabinet.[6]

The discrimen was whether demanding a document would undermine responsible government. Priestley JA went further and noted that under the modern law of public interest immunity, the courts (not the Executive) now assessed whether government documents were privileged. Priestley JA could not see why the legislature was any less trustworthy with this power than the courts considered themselves.

Parliamentarians' duty to ensure accountability

But *Chadwick* is not merely a statement of the transcending power of Parliament to, in effect, override public interest immunity and legal professional privilege in respect of all but deliberative papers, it contains reminders of the fundamental bases on which accountability of government rests in an elective democracy. Thus Spigelman CJ quoted Isaacs J that:

> One of the duties [of an MP] is that of watching on behalf of the general community the conduct of the executive, of criticising it, and, if necessary, of calling it to account in the constitutional way by . . . censure, which if sufficiently supported, means removal from office. That . . . is the main constitutional safeguard the community possesses.[7]

Western Australia: errors and responses

Isaac J's stark reminder of the duty of accountability was, of course, framed in a remote past when Ministers fell on their swords upon revelation of departmental wrongdoing. My State of acquired domicile over the last decade

5 *Chadwick* at [15]. The rule regarding 'reasonable necessity' in a parliamentary context was analysed in preceding High Court litigation: *Egan v Willis* (1998) 195 CLR 424.

6 *Chadwick* at [70].

7 *Horne v Barber* (1920) 27 CLR 494 at 500.

has shown inadequate attention to the duty of accountability in the past, but more recently a determination, in at least some quarters, to ensure that accountability be an imperative, with machinery to make it effective.

Parliamentary Committees, particularly of the Upper House, were seen as the appropriate mechanism, and accountability was to extend to executive officials below the level of Ministers. The reports of the Royal Commission into the Commercial Activities of Government (1992) and the Commission on Government Report (1995) both dealt with these issues.

The WA Inc Royal Commission and parliamentary committees

The 1992 Report set three factors as an acceptable foundation for public trust in government. The first and third were open government and integrity of the conduct of officials, but the second required that 'public officials and agencies must be made accountable for their actions'.[8] As the Report noted:

> the practice of open government requires the good faith commitment of the officials who are at the heart of the action. . . . To be a reality, open government must be a habit, . . . an attitude which must be encouraged at all times. Importantly, it requires a willingness to expose miscalculation and failure as well as to publicise innovation and achievement.[9]

As for Parliamentary Committees, the Report stated:

> it is of the first importance that a more realistic approach be taken to the obligation of the various arms of government to satisfy Parliament's information needs. Parliamentary committees in particular must be entitled as of right to exact, from responsible officers of government, information falling within their spheres of actual responsibility.[10]

Information to parliamentary committees

As to the actual content and nature of information to be provided by public officials to Parliamentary committees, the 1995 Report quoted Mr Les Scott MHR, then Chairman of the Commonwealth Parliament Joint Committee of Public Accounts, that:

> parliamentarians . . . want information (1) that is easily and quickly grasped; (2) that presents the bottom line; (3) that focuses on performance rather than administrative details; (4) and that highlights exceptions.[11]

It is no surprise that Professor (now Justice) Finn had a hand in drafting these WA reports, and the concept of government as a trust with the public

8 1992 Report, Part II, para 1.2.8.

9 Ibid, para 2.1.7.

10 Ibid, para 2.4.11.

11 1995 Report, p 211, enumeration added.

as beneficiary is drawn directly from his recent writings.[12] In *Hughes Aircraft Systems International v Airservices Australia*, Finn J drew these threads together: a statutory authority had to keep the responsible Minister informed because it 'was accountable in some measure to the public'.[13]

The fight is never-ending

That McAlpine published his thoughts on getting preferential treatment from governments *after* the publication of the two Commission reports testifies to the enduring attraction of governmental power. It is the honey pot around which flies perpetually gather. In December 1999, the Ecologically Sustainable Development (ESD) Committee of the WA Legislative Council tabled a lengthy report on *Sustainability of Current Logging Practices in the State's Forests*. The saga of interlocking activities between the Department of Conservation and Land Management (CALM) and private industry, and the apparent wilful denial by the Department and its industry allies of accountability either to the legal system or the State Parliament makes sobering reading, coming as it does after two extensive (and expensive) reports on State administration in the same decade.[14]

Dispensing with statutes: the need for Parliamentary supervision

As the ESD Committee Report noted,[15] CALM had wide powers to license exemptions from the strict requirements of conservation laws. This power of exemption from the operation of statutes ('dispensing', in the language of the Bill of Rights 1689) is, since the overthrow of James II, not available to the Executive except with Parliamentary approval. (Yet McAlpine proposes pursuing the same course in relation to subordinate legislation that James II's friends had him adopt, with disastrous consequences, in relation to statutes. *Plus ça change . . .*) But as the Westminster tradition of Parliamentary scrutiny makes clear, it is not enough that the Bill of Rights enunciate the principle that statutes should apply evenly throughout the community. If the British Parliament does allow for exemptions by the Executive, each exemption must be tabled in, and is disallowable by, either House. Australian Parliaments appear never to have adopted this necessary accountability measure.

---

12 (1995) '"The Forgotten Trust": The People and the State' in M Cope (ed), *Equity: Issues and Trends*, Federation Press; and (1995) 'A Sovereign People, A Public Trust' in PD Finn (ed) *Essays on Law and Government*, Vol 1, Law Book Company.

13 (1997) 146 ALR 1 at 88.

14 See ESD Committee Report (1999) *The Sustainability of Current Logging Practices*, December, pp 174–81.

15 ESD Committee Report (1999), pp 167–9.

If the Executive may dispense with the application of regulatory statutes in favour of private entities, giving them potentially huge and unfair advantages, this power must be reviewed, and where appropriate, invalidated by Parliament. In this area all Australian polities appear seriously deficient; to compensate for the lack of Parliamentary tradition, all need clearly expressed supervisory legislation, requiring tabling and possible disallowance of dispensing instruments.[16]

Professional paradigms and change

Thomas Kuhn, in language of poignant relevance to common lawyers, noted the scientific community's tendency to become set in its ways until confronted with a new paradigm:

> As in political revolutions, so in paradigm choice – there is no standard higher than the assent of the relevant community. . . . Just because it is a transition between incommensurables, the transition between competing paradigms cannot be made a step at a time[:] . . . it must occur all at once . . . or not at all.[17]

But the problem for common lawyers (or at least the reason for their insularity) is that law, unlike science, has no immediately compelling objective basis for testing propositions empirically.[18] In the face of the dictates of common sense, governmental policy, or even public outrage, courts will remain hang-dog in their adherence to propositions with a shelf life that expired, on any fair analysis, in another century.

Case study: the presumption that statutes do not bind the Crown

An example to justify such a harsh verdict is the WA Supreme Court's apparently religious adherence to a full-blown presumption that statutes do not bind the Crown in the absence of clear legislative indication. This presumption in full flight of course tilts the playing field in favour of government (and its friends),[19] mocks the equal application of the law, and advances the cause of arbitrary governmental power, unfettered by statutory considerations.[20] In practice the presumption allows for de facto dispensing with

16 See my letter (1993) 67 *ALJ* 239 on dispensations, but noting the propensity of Australian Parliaments to act as rubber stamps for the Executive in these areas.

17 T Kuhn (1970) *The Structure of Scientific Revolutions* (2nd edn), pp 94, 149, 150.

18 Contrast Blackstone's claim that the common law was based in scientific verities: D Boorstin (1941) *The Mysterious Science of the Law*, pp 11–31.

19 *Bradken v BHP* (1979) 145 CLR 107.

20 This presumption is not, however, part of the Crown's 'prerogative', merely a tool of statutory interpretation. In *Byrne v Ireland* [1972] IR 241 at 272–5 per Walsh J (O'Dalaigh CJ agreeing), Ireland's Supreme Court indicated that when a written constitution declares all governmental authority derived from the people, Crown prerogatives have no function.

statutes, contrary to the Bill of Rights and to the reasonably inferred intention of Parliament.

In 1990, in litigation concerning the *Aboriginal Heritage Act* 1972 (WA), the High Court determined (7–0) that the presumption of Crown immunity from the operation of statutes was not an inflexible rule, and that a legislative intent to bind the Crown could 'be found in the provisions of the statute – including its subject matter and disclosed purpose and policy'.[21] In 1993 the High Court followed up those views:

> Whatever . . . the situation in earlier times, it is clear from *Bropho* that the presumption that general words do not bind the Crown . . . must now yield to 'the circumstances, including the content and purpose of the particular provision and the identity of the entity in respect of which the question of the applicability of the provision arises.'[22]

With these admonitions from Australia's highest court as wind in his sails, Bill Atyeo, health officer for the Kimberley shire of Halls Creek, approached the WA Supreme Court for a declaration that the *Health Act* 1911 applied to the Crown as landlord. This Act required owners of houses to provide sanitary conveniences; if they did not, the local council could do so and bill the owner.

The vast majority of the inhabitants of Halls Creek Shire are Aboriginal, most living as tenants of the Aboriginal Lands Trust, a Crown body under the *Aboriginal Affairs Planning Authority Act* 1972 (WA). The Aboriginal tenants' plight, and their desire to be part of mainstream society, is summarised in the words of Mr Allan McDonald who said he 'was fed-up with his family being forced to go to the toilet in the scrub, and attend school without a shower or clean clothes'.[23] On reading those words I assumed it would be bluebell time in the Kimberley, and that Mr McDonald would join the ranks of the blessed with old Peter Beswick,[24] and Charles Bundy of Yew Tree Farm,[25] but it was not to be: Templeman J was no Denning-come-to-court.

Relying on a number of construction devices, not the least being (in presumably unintended irony) that 'the *Aboriginal Affairs Planning Authority Act* represents an attempt by the legislature to advance the interests of persons of Aboriginal descent',[26] and that the Act was administered by a Minister whose discretion should remain untrammelled, Templeman J came 'firmly to the view'[27] that the Crown was not bound by the relevant provi-

---

21 *Bropho v WA* (1990) 171 CLR 1 at 21–2.

22 *Registrar of the Accident Compensation Tribunal v FCT* (1993) 178 CLR 145 at 171.

23 *Atyeo v Aboriginal Lands Trust* (1996) 136 FLR 47 at 48.

24 *Beswick v Beswick* [1966] Ch 538.

25 *Lloyds Bank Ltd v Bundy* [1975] QB 326.

26 *Atyeo* at 53.

27 Ibid, p 56.

sions. I contemplate this judgment while reading in the report on *Aboriginal People in the Economy of the Kimberley Region*[28] that 994 Aboriginal people, in 22 WA communities, lacked a sewerage disposal system.[29]

A failure of governmental theory

Templeman J's concern that the Crown's discretionary power not be subordinated to an inferior tier of government (a local shire) reminds us how little the law has moved in 50 years: *Bombay*[30] in 1946 reflected the same concern for 'Crown' government at the expense of a subordinate council vested by statute with extraordinarily important responsibilities for public health.

At the other end of the century from *Atyeo*, Greave CJ in Barbados had no difficulty in finding the Bajan prison authorities (Crown employees) subject to health regulations prohibiting release of human waste in a manner offensive to a neighbourhood.[31] How then, a century later, when every Australian politician (bar one) with views on Aboriginal affairs is preaching the importance of Aboriginal health, can the WA Supreme Court reach a decision like *Atyeo*? Of course judges must not be swept away on transitory tides of policy, and to be fair to Templeman J, *Atyeo* was not a one-off: his Honour relied on that decision when he led the Full Court the following year to a determination that the *Wildlife Conservation Act* 1950 (WA) did not bind the Crown either.[32] But clinging to a concept first given a flutter by Crown counsel in 1311 (to the rather more limited effect that 'statute does not affect the king's prerogative')[33] does seem anomalous, at the least, when public health is at stake.

The failure of feedback on legislation

The problem is that Parliaments and courts, as manufacturers and processors of the law, are not subject to constant feedback about their product, particularly in the field of public law. Only losers complain – and they would, wouldn't they? Only powerful and well-placed losers get anywhere with their complaints (not everyone can be the Deputy Prime Minister receiving a *Wik* rebuff) and those who construct the response to the

28 G Crough and C Christophersen (1993) *Aboriginal People in the Economy of the Kimberley Region*, ANU.

29 Ibid, pp 31, 111.

30 *Province of Bombay v Municipal Corporation of Bombay* [1947] AC 58.

31 *Brewster v Lash* (1903) 2 Cases in the Court of Error, Barbados 72.

32 *Bridgetown/Greenbushes Friends of the Forest Inc v CALM* (1997) 18 WAR 126.

33 *Courtenay v the King* (1311) YB 5 Ed II, 31 Selden Society 130 at 131.

decision in any case are lawyers, who bring no external or objective judgment to bear.

Doctors and scientists cannot escape feedback

Medicine is a parallel example of an introverted profession with established paradigms, challenge to which brings ruin or at the least estrangement from the hierarchy of the profession.

In 1847, Ignaz Semmelweiss, after observing doctors proceeding directly from the post-mortem room to the maternity wards of the Vienna Public Hospital, ordered that all entering the wards must wash their hands with calcium chloride. Over two years the mortality rate of women in the ward worst affected dropped from 12 per cent to zero. Semmelweiss's colleagues attacked his theory of conveyed disease (contradicting the long-held nostrum of poisonous invisible vapour): dismissed from his post, he returned embittered to Budapest. Hand-washing ceased at the Vienna *Krankenhaus*, and the death rate among newly delivered women soared to its former level. The only solace in this miserable tale of public interest sacrificed to professional unity[34] is that 20 years later Lister's work on antiseptic surgery led to the acceptance of hygiene in maternity wards.

In medicine, however, public interest and demand for a better product, backed by opportunities to test theory against observation of 'the real world', eventually led the profession to accept a new paradigm. Common lawyers merely remain impervious to changes around them, while contentedly congratulating each other on their prowess. That is the point of the second quotation with which I began. The lawyer [Z] receiving his Approved Quality Practice certificate was the unsuccessful counsel for Atyeo. This is in no way intended as a criticism of the lawyer or his performance: the report shows that he ran all the possible arguments. Rather, it is a comment on the law and the legal profession. What use would a certificate of quality be to a doctor (or more importantly, the doctor's patients), if her or his profession rejected a paradigm of antisepsis?

Legislation as a possible answer: antagonism between courts and legislators

We should not underestimate the yawning chasm of 'professional mystery' between lawyers and legislators. Legislators must be introduced to the signs and symbols, the major arcana of the lawyers' mysteries: after all, legislators are drawn from the same lay stock as the Wiltshire justices who decided half a century ago that Crown land fell under rent restriction legislation. Of those justices Goddard LCJ was moved to say: 'it must be a surprise for anyone to

---

34 The lesson that novelist Kurt Vonnegut drew was that 'vanity rather than wisdom determines how the world is run', (1982) *Palm Sunday*, Cape, p 276.

learn that . . . the *Rent Restriction Acts* do not apply to the cottage or house so long as the property remains Crown property'.[35]

The law reveals its majesty even (or perhaps particularly) when humble legislators show insight into what goes on in the inner sanctum. In 1962, in debate in the New South Wales Legislative Assembly on a work-place safety Bill, a backbencher asked that the Crown be expressly included, which elicited this plaintive exchange with the responsible Minister:

> The hon. member is not suggesting that the Crown will not be bound to comply with the provisions of the measure?
>
> No, but I think it would be of assistance to provide specifically to that effect.[36]

Needless to say, the Crown was not specifically included, and in 1971, in a case involving work-place injuries to a teenage boy, the High Court held the Crown was not bound, despite a lengthy, entertaining and erudite dissent from Windeyer J.[37]

Similarly, in 1947 at Westminster, in debate on the Crown Proceedings Bill, a Mr Foster cited a concrete example:

> The *Housing Act*, 1936, imposes on landlords the duty of seeing that houses are reasonably fit for human habitation. . . . It does not affect the Crown. Therefore, if the Crown is the landlord of some property and has broken this very salutary proposition by letting the house while it is not fit for human habitation and as a result the tenant is injured, it will be impossible under the Bill . . . to bring an action against the Crown. I would like the Attorney General to look at that point, and if I am right, I am sure that he will admit that justice demands that the Crown should be affected by that.[38]

The Attorney General admitted no such thing, and in 1986 the Court of Appeal found the Crown exempt from such requirements.[39] Well may the English tenants, like the Aborigines in *Atyeo*, echo Starke J's quotation from *Macbeth* in reflection on the Commonwealth's exemption from the *Re-establishment and Employment Act* 1945, that the relevant sections:

> keep the word of promise to our ear,
> and break it to our hope.[40]

The law-making and law-deciding functions are plainly dysfunctional when this degree of dissonance affects both.

---

35 *Rudler v Franks* [1947] 1 KB 430.

36 NSW Hansard (1962), Vol 43, p 2038.

37 *Downs v Williams* (1971) 125 CLR 61.

38 *Parliamentary Debates*, House of Commons, Vol 439, cols 1730–1.

39 *Department of Transport v Egoroff* [1986] TLR 226.

40 *Cain v Doyle* (1946) 72 CLR 409 at 421.

Conclusion

When this chapter was written (as a rather longer paper) in October 1999, the author still believed that Parliamentary scrutiny of the Executive was feasible, and that legislation might alleviate the backwardness of public law. Amongst other examples, the debate in the WA Legislative Council on the State Forests Report in May 2000[41] has reversed this view. This debate, which raised important questions about Executive accountability, and during which CALM's long-serving Departmental head moved on, was reduced to a slanging match agitated by the 'pro-loggers', when the issue was always accountability. Clearly, the more remote the Parliament, the more provincial its behaviour.

The author sees very little hope of WA achieving responsible and accountable government in the foreseeable future; party politics and short-term gain obscure the wider public interest.

41 See fn 14 above, and WA *Parliamentary Debates*, 11 May 2000, pp 6839ff and 25 May 2000, pp 7222–7.

Part III: Individuals, Minorities and Their Rights

15

Recognising Rights

Alice ES Tay

It so happened that the 50th Annual Fulbright Symposium marked exactly 18 months after I left the hallowed sanctuary of the academic world and entered the realm of the bureaucracy in the form of the Human Rights and Equal Opportunity Commission (HREOC). HREOC is of course charged with important work, in Australia and also internationally and I find myself learning a great deal. Only a week before the Symposium, I was in China where, as part of the Australia/China Human Rights Technical Assistance Program, I took part in a joint seminar on civil society. One of the things which we spoke about in China was the re-emergence of the concept of civil society as evidenced in Eastern Europe after the fall of Communism there.

The abuse of human rights by the former Communist bloc countries in Eastern Europe was one of many contributing factors to the events of 1989 and 1990. Most obvious was the failure of these countries to provide for the economic and social rights of their citizens. As a result of this, many of the new nations which emerged were concerned to make genuine efforts to reshape governments, redraft their constitutions and reform their societies in ways which would offer real protection for the rights of citizens and for the future of liberal democracy. This meant more than simple legal protection. For years many of the Communist countries, including the Soviet Union itself, had constitutional guarantees of human rights which, on their face, offered admirable pledges of personal rights and liberties but which bore no relation to the harsh realities for many ordinary citizens during the years of Socialist rule. This was because these constitutions had no direct legal effect: they could not be relied upon in court and offered no direct protection of rights without implementing legislation. Stalin's 1936 Soviet Constitution is the best known. And yet in countries like Britain and Australia we had no such guarantees but, for the most part, enjoyed far greater protection of human rights.

So while the 1990s constitution-makers of Eastern Europe were certainly greatly concerned with the enumeration of individual rights in the basic legal documents of their new constitutions, they also recognised that respect for human rights, and values such as tolerance necessary for the adequate enjoyment of these rights, have to be instilled into the institutional structures of society and the mechanisms responsible for rights enforcement. The uncertainty of the long and in many instances still continuing transitional period is reflected in the time it took for the new constitutions to be formalised. In the meantime the various nations made preliminary attempts to protect rights by establishing ombudsmen, rights charters and by expressing concern for rights in various other ways, not necessarily constitutional ones. Many of these constitutions incorporated statements conducive to social, economic and cultural concerns and conceptions of social democracy and welfare.

The goal of the new elites across East and Central Europe was to democratise political life thoroughly and, as part of this, reconstitute civil society as a necessary condition for democratic government. Democratic institutions and recognition of human rights represent the very first constitutive conditions of modern civil society. Rights are necessary to civil society: the 'glue' that holds civil society together is made up of trust, co-operation and networks of engagement founded on shared values, human rights values.

Human rights have provided a set of overarching ethical principles to both motivate and guide civil society: principles that have resonance across cultures, principles that have united diverse groups, principles that form a blueprint for a just society of peace and human dignity. But in order to continue to fulfil this role rights must be real and not merely words. One of the best ways to ensure the place of rights and proper recognition of them is to encourage a culture and build up a practice of human rights. The events of the 1980s and 1990s in Eastern Europe show the necessary relationship between human rights and civil society. Recognition of rights is one of the basic elements necessary for it to operate. And it is clear that the norms of civil society are essentially human rights norms.

Human rights have long been implicit within the theory and action of civil society. That the vision of a modern civil society is driven by the same set of ethical principles set out in the Universal Declaration of Human Rights is no coincidence. It is a shared vision based on a set of shared values: freedom, justice and the peaceful resolution of disputes; social progress and better standards of living; equality, tolerance and dignity.

And the ingredients of civil society are also necessary for the adequate practical recognition of rights. Constitutionalising rights is not enough: the words alone, even fortified by legal mechanisms, can easily be ignored or bypassed or renounced. No society can truly talk of human rights unless and until it understands what rights are and what we are talking about when we use the words. Human rights talk should not continue to pin its hopes on legal solutions. Liberty and pluralism enumerated in law do not solve the ills of society, as the peoples of Eastern Europe discovered. Instead they are the first conditions essential for building a community which recognises and respects individual rights.

Although all of the Eastern European countries have constitutional provisions guaranteeing, for example, the rights of ethnic minorities, the force of the protection varies enormously. Social and economic rights also have a strong presence in the new constitutions, but they range from the potentially useful through to the empty and absurd. By introducing rights that are obviously unenforceable, there is a devaluation of other rights in the constitution.

Human rights may only flourish when they exist in a society which also practices tolerance and has respect for the notion of individual rights and the political equality of its citizens. All of the new post-Communist constitutions include clauses guaranteeing basic human rights, including free speech, association, press, but the crime rates in many of these countries and more obviously events such as those which have recently taken place in Serbia and Kosovo are examples of a failure to assure respect for the rights enumerated in the law. In Romania the authorities have tolerated and sometimes allegedly encouraged organised violence against Gypsy communities, and in the former East Germany they have turned a blind eye to attacks on foreigners by skinheads. The basic right to freedom of religion has become highly politicised in the Balkans and also affected by intolerance in the Catholic Church in Poland and the Orthodox Church in Romania. Class inequality has increased enormously in the region in the decade since the collapse of the Communist monopoly.

In Australia we too must do more to instil a culture of rights in society. The week before the Fulbright Symposium, Zita Antonios, the Commonwealth Race Discrimination Commissioner, finished her five-year term – a term that has seen a volatile period of rights debate in modern Australian society. Words such as 'equality' and 'fairness' have been at the centre of national debate – in newspapers, television and talkback radio. The real problem in many societies active in the promotion of human rights – including Australia – lies in the lack of a commonly understood meaning for these words. If the opposite of racism is equality and the One Nation Party constructs its platform on an appeal to equality, then you know you have a problem of understanding. Without a shred of irony, the most dispossessed and chronically disadvantaged people in Australia, Aboriginal and Torres Strait Islander people, are attacked as privileged and the recipients of preferential treatment. Ethnic minorities, because of their desire to maintain their distinct cultural traditions and identity, are stigmatised as a threat to national unity and cohesion. Yet the assertion that 'it is never immoral to want to retain one's own independence and identity' is a core principle of the One Nation immigration, population and social cohesion policy.

Recognising human rights is not about moralising, indoctrination or providing simplistic remedies, in which I include simple legal recognition. What is important is to provide individuals, groups, organisations and communities with relevant information and resources that will help them make informed and sensitive decisions. Through effective education, discrimination and abuse of human rights can be countered and prevented from occurring in the first place. Broad community education programs and developing a culture of respect and tolerance is of the utmost importance. Institutions such as non-governmental organisations are of great importance here. I have some practical experience of this. The Asia Pacific Forum of National Human Rights Institutions was established in 1996 and each year members of the Forum meet to discuss issues of regional concern.

The last annual meeting was in Manila, October 1999. The previous meeting (Jakarta, 1998) took as its theme the relationship between human rights and the economic crisis in the Asia-Pacific region. At that time there was deep concern expressed at the effect of the economic crisis on the observance of economic, social and cultural rights and at the possible misuse of the crisis to further restrict the civil and political rights in the region. The Forum requested the UN High Commissioner for Human Rights to work with intergovernmental organisations and the international financial institutions to raise their awareness of the human rights impacts of their work.

The 1998 meeting produced a range of practical outcomes and initiatives and drew heavily on the input of a range of non-government organisations that attended in an 'observer' capacity. Community organisations, businesses as well as governmental institutions are all of importance in ensuring proper recognition of rights. Following the October 1999 meeting in Manila, the representative of the UN High Commissioner emphasised the importance of national institutions and their role in working with NGOs to improve the position of human rights in the region.

Educating citizens, institutions and non-governmental organisations is the primary way of promoting human rights recognition and leads to a society where the values are embedded in the foundations of every legal institution, every part of the public sector and every community-based organisation. Newer democracies like those in Eastern Europe and in the former Soviet republics, and in South Africa, must still push forward with the promotion of human rights in ways that are not related to legal recognition. Law itself can be too mechanised, can become a tool of social engineering, a matter of form and not of content, a distraction from the real business of recognising and acting on human needs.

By concentrating too much on law instead of thinking clearly about what we think rights are, rights become muddled and endangered. It is true that many moral rights have become legal rights. This can be attributed to the strength of popular outrage against morally repugnant behaviour coupled with the politicisation of law in contemporary Australian society. It is true that the legal protection of human rights is a distinguishing achievement of the 20th century. Yet our confidence in the prominence we give to legally supported rights carries with it grave specific dangers.

In recent years, as the powers of the state and the demands made upon it increase, many see law more and more as an instrument for social control and social change. They want to substitute social policies and administrative direction for law and legal values and procedures. They elevate purposes over tradition, the forward-looking over the backward-looking, the dynamic over the static.

Ten years ago the dangers of this trend had already been identified – particularly in relation to asserting the existence of new generation rights in law long before societies had the capacity to accommodate them. Ian Brownlie noted the risks involved in attempting to approach human rights aspirations through an inappropriately legal discourse:

> As policy goals, as standards of morality, the so-called new generation of human rights would be acceptable and one could sit round a table with non-lawyers and agree on practical programs for attaining these good ends. What concerns me as a lawyer is the casual introduction of serious confusions of thought, and this in the course of seeking to give the new rights an actual legal context. The type of law invention about which I have reservations involves a tendency to cut out the real pioneering – the process of persuasion and diplomacy – and put in its place the premature announcement that the new settlement is built.[1]

Some human rights are weak without enforcement procedures. Assertion of rights in law is essential to build a political culture in which human rights claims can be contested either domestically or internationally. Rights can be validated only through this process, but they must also be recognised in society, by those who claim them and those who must respect them.

But turning our attention from law to education, thought and practice will clarify our own perceptions of what rights are and will lead to a deeper understanding in society of what rights mean. Whether Australia needs a Bill of Rights is not, I think, the primary question. As I have moved from academia to a statutory rights-protection agency, my experience has been that what matters is the mindset of ordinary people – it is with them that work must be done to promote the recognition of human rights.

I see this as a primary function of HREOC: to draw attention to the issues of rights which confront Australian society. Law may have a role in this: the political debate surrounding an attempt to introduce a Bill of Rights may indeed arouse public interest in an unexpected way. But this has not been the experience in Britain, where the lengthy passage and debate of the *Human Rights Act* 1998 has been mostly met with magnanimous indifference. Public debate on rights generally occurs in Britain when sensational and sometimes salacious cases from the United Kingdom are sent to the European Court of Human Rights in Strasbourg.

Despite the apparent disinterest, however, in Britain and Australia we are lucky to have public awareness of the concept of rights inherent in the

1 I Brownlie (1988) 'The Rights of Peoples in International Law', in J Crawford (ed), *The Rights of Peoples*, Clarendon Press, p 14.

common law. Indeed before the trend of implying rights into the Australian Constitution the common law was the only domestic remedy for individuals to enforce their rights. The problem is that there are many rights which are not enforceable using the common law, and we can look only to our other domestic law as, unlike the United Kingdom, Australia is not subject to a developed international system like the European Convention on Human Rights. In the promotion of rights recognition we do not have the powerful effects that membership of the Council of Europe has on the Eastern European democracies.

Our legal and social traditions in Australia make it easy for us to be relaxed about rights recognition. But globalisation means that we must be more aware of rights, particularly in our own region. We must be clear about what they are and of the values we treasure in order to develop our own society and to lead the way for other countries. So much of what we hear about rights is meaningless. Milan Kundera notes the emptiness of much human rights talk. He writes:

> I don't know a single politician who doesn't mention ten times a day the fight for human rights or violation of human rights. But because people in the West are not threatened by concentration camps and are free to say and write what they want, the more the fight for human rights gains in popularity, the more it loses any concrete content, becoming a kind of universal stance of everyone toward everything, a kind of energy that turns all human desires into rights. The world has become man's rights and everything in it has become a right; the desire for love the right to love; the desire for rest the right to rest; the desire for friendship the right to friendship; the desire to exceed the speed limit the right to exceed the speed limit; the desire for happiness the right to happiness.[2]

I believe that confusion over the nature of human rights has led to an inappropriate use of rights terminology. Such confusion, combined with the growing popularity of rights talk, will continue to cause a proliferation of rights claims, an ad hoc expansion of human rights agendas that will ultimately devalue the very thing which we set out to protect – human dignity. When we find ourselves in a situation where human rights has become a kind of universal stance of everyone towards everything, a kind of energy that turns all human desires into rights, it is time for a backwards glance to establish exactly how we arrived at this spot and precisely what is needed to remain true to our original, our best, goals.

How we talk about human rights, the language that we choose, is very powerful and the impact that it has in the daily lives of individuals and communities can be profound. Placing rights in a purely legal context is not the best way to promote recognition and practice. For example the achievement of economic and social rights can be managed by a multifaceted policy, social and educational program. There is a particular danger in proclaiming these kinds of rights in law as it narrows their content and places

2 M Kundera (1991) *Immortality*, Faber and Faber, p 153.

the attendant duties and strategies for their realisation in a purely legal context. Formal legal texts and judicial decisions can have only a limited capacity to realise these rights and there is a paucity of organisations with a developed and sophisticated interest in pursuing these rights as such.

The full promotion of economic, social and cultural rights will demand a deep cultural change in many societies and across humanity as a whole. The accommodation of these rights clashes with powerful and established interests, particularly economic and property-holding interests. Some of these interests have legal rights and/or moral rights attached to them, thus we are faced with an ideological warfare. Tensions between traditional customs and the common law within Australia itself, and between economic development and cultural autonomy in various parts of Papua New Guinea, provide suitable examples.

I have for many years been thinking about rights and in my present position I find myself facing, on a daily basis, the real stories of ordinary citizens whose rights have been abused or ignored in one way or another. Bolstering the *legal* rights and providing clear and specific claims for these people in an American fashion may be one way for Australia to proceed. But I wonder if having a Bill of Rights will, even if provided with legal teeth, put an end to the stories of racism, discrimination and abuse that occur everyday or will even affect the larger human rights issues concerning Australia's Indigenous population.

Legal measures must be taken in tandem with educational and political and social measures to promote a culture of rights and an understanding of what we mean when we talk about rights.

Familiarity within society with the concept of rights will not breed contempt, it will instead lead to comprehension and true recognition and will further the cause of all human rights and of human dignity.

16

Constitutional Transformations

Universal Values and the Politics of Constitutional Understanding

Heinz Klug

In the first half of the 1990s well over a billion dollars was spent on Rule of Law projects in every conceivable corner of the globe. A host of different institutions, from private and non-government organisations through to state agencies and the UN are engaged in this new 'Rule of Law' movement.[1] While legal reform has not been restricted to the dramatic developments in public law accompanying the enormous political reconstructions of the post-Cold War era, the adoption of new, justiciable constitutions, has been a major product of this movement.

Although the magnitude of this late 20th century wave of legal renewal is extraordinary – with approximately 104 of the 188 members of the United Nations Organisation making major amendments to their constitutions in the decade between 1989 and 1999 – the most remarkable feature of this development is that of these states, approximately 78 per cent (81 countries) adopted completely new constitutions.[2] While the fate of each state's process of reconstruction cannot be predicted, the common features that

1 Programs range from that of the Ford Foundation, which has historically supported social movements struggling for democratic rights; through to the United States Agency for International Development's programs 'designed to support the creation of legal and political environments that will promote processes of democratisation and market-based reform' [Rule of Law Consortium: ARD/Checchi Joint Venture, Program Circular, 18 November 1994, p 1] in the former Soviet Union; to the World Bank's 1994 Economic Law Reform Project, assisting China in the reform of its legal framework. The World Bank noted that the 'key to any market system is the reliance on a fair and credible legal framework: legal norms and procedures are needed to substitute for government control of economic decisions and to demarcate government's regulatory role in many areas of economic activity' (World Bank press release, Washington, DC, 18 October 1994, p 1).

2 Thus approximately 40 per cent of the 185 member states of the UN adopted completely new constitutions between 1989 and 1999. All figures used were calculated from a survey of constitutions using Blaustein, *Constitutions of the World* and the web site http://www.uni-wuerzburg.de/law/index.html.

characterise a high proportion of the resulting constitutions provide adequate testimony to the hegemonic normative trends in this post-Cold War period. At least one-quarter of all of the member states of the UN introduced Bills of Rights and some form of constitutional review into their constitutional orders during this period. As a result at least 92 countries (approximately 50 per cent of member states) have incorporated Bills of Rights, Fundamental Rights, or some form of individual and/or collective rights into their constitutional orders. While the content of these rights varies dramatically in form as well as application, nevertheless, it may be argued that the notion of rights, whether individual or collective, became a central aspect of constitutionalism in the late 20th century.

Despite this apparent contradiction between the adoption of 'universal norms' and the particularism of each country's institutional arrangements, and even differing understandings of these universal commitments, it is the way in which the particular has been bounded by the universal that marks this process. Unlike the debate between law and justice, or 'positive law' and 'natural law' or 'universal human rights', this globalisation of constitutionalism has introduced a dynamic process in which the idealism of universal principals serves to both limit the range of local variation while being simultaneously enhanced by incorporating the specific attributes that come from viewing the universal though the prism of local conditions. Although this leaves open the possibility of seemingly opposite outcomes – such as the acceptance or rejection of affirmative action as a necessary attribute of equality – it is precisely the dynamic character of this process that precludes an absolute answer to the problem of equality, but instead introduces a dynamic and continuing debate about both the nature of equality and the degree of acceptable action in seeking a more equitable distribution of resources in a democratic society.

The legalisation of political conflict inherent in this implicit, if not explicit, turn to the courts marks a central shift in the structure of constitutionalism around the globe. Before 1989 approximately 10 countries around the globe had effective systems of constitutional review in which a constitutional court or the courts in general *regularly*[3] struck down proposed or validly enacted legislation as contrary to the state's constitution. Only 10 years later, at least 70 states (approximately 38 per cent of all member states

3 This is an extremely important qualification because although many constitutions have incorporated some form of constitutional review, the application of the power by the judiciaries has been so limited in many jurisdictions that it is extremely difficult to argue that an effective system of constitutional review exists despite its formal constitutional status. So, for example, while the Malaysian Constitution of 1957 explicitly provided for judicial review, during the first 30 years the Constitution was in force 'no single legislative enactment . . . has been held to be void for being unconstitutional'. A Ibrahim and MP Jain (1992) 'The Constitution of Malaysia and the American Constitutional Influence', LW Beer (ed) *Constitutional Systems in Late Twentieth-Century Asia*, University of Washington Press, p 528.

of the UN) had adopted some form of constitutional review. A much larger percentage have legislative guarantees of individual rights, Bills of Rights or Chapters of Fundamental Rights in their constitutions but limit their enforcement to the reversal of particular acts of government in individual cases with limited or no impact on the validity of the implicated legislation.

While this embrace of rights and constitutionalisation of politics has been heralded by some as the rise of "World Constitutionalism",[4] the jury is still out when it comes to judging either the meaningful implementation or effectiveness of these new institutions. In some cases, the decisions of Constitutional Courts have already been explicitly rejected by executive authorities, or the courts themselves disbanded. In other cases, despite the explicit inclusion of a power of constitutional review in the Constitution, the judiciary has declined or very rarely exercised this power to strike down a legislative act. In more extreme cases, the constitutional developments so heralded in the first half of the 1990s have already been swept aside by military coups or have been ignored in the face of protracted civil wars. However, for those states where there is an attempt to consolidate the process of political reconstruction which swept through so dramatically in the early 1990s, the balance between adherence to a globally defined constitutionalism and the imperatives of local political dynamics remains a central legacy of this latest wave of state reconstruction.

It is in this context that longstanding assumptions about traditional constitutional values must be rethought in order to understand their role in the construction and maintenance of different constitutional orders. In my view there are three sets of values which frame traditional notions of constitutionalism: (1) federalism, or the spatial division of power; (2) the separation of powers between different branches of government; and (3) the notion of constitutional rights. Each of these sets of values address different aspects of the 'problem' of power – its allocation, application and restriction – within the nation-state. While these constitutional values with their diverse historical origins have become increasingly 'universalised', their application in increasingly varied historical, cultural, and political contexts has produced a diversity of approaches and understandings which provide a diverse 'global text' for political actors, constitution-makers, constitutional interpreters and litigants.

So, for example, the classic understandings of the allocation of legislative power between a Federal Government and states or provinces has been transformed from a list of designated subject-matter competencies and theories of pre-emption, via notions of concurrent powers, into an idea of co-operative governance in which the regions participate in the creation of central legislation and the allocation of authority may be constantly

4 See B Ackerman (1997) 'The Rise of World Constitutionalism' 83 *Virginia Law Review* 771.

rearranged according to a set of designated constitutional principles. In South Africa's new constitution the notion of 'co-operative government' is based, according to Professor Nicholas Haysom, legal advisor to President Mandela and a former member of the ANC Constitutional Committee, on a break with the 19th century approach to federalism which allocated 'areas of responsibility to one particular area of government only'.[5] What the new South African approach does, argues Haysom, is to:

> give the different areas of government the right to legislate on the same topic or area but only in respect of their appropriate responsibilities. Responsibility, in turn, is decided relative to appropriate interest, capacity and effective delivery but the apportionment of it is more complex than merely isolating an area of social life and parcelling it out to a single sphere of government.[6]

While this new understanding of the division of powers does not preclude continuing jurisdictional conflict and constitutional adjudication, it does provide an opportunity for achieving constitutionalism's promise – the taming and reshaping of irreconcilable political goals. Here the indeterminate nature of constitutional formulations and subsequent shaping of constitutional imaginations through constitutional discourse provides the key to overcoming or managing potentially destructive social forces.

Similarly, with respect to the separation of powers between different branches of government and in the content and application of Bills of rights, there have been significant shifts. While the separation of powers between executive, legislature and judiciary has been premised on the unity of lawful jurisdiction within the nation-state, its strict construction, as in the United States, has given way on the one hand to the realities of the administrative state, while on the other hand, a globalised world has brought forth both a dispersal of jurisdictional authority beyond the state, as well as a fragmentation of power within the state. Whole realms of authority have migrated from exercises of strictly national sovereignty – through the resurgence of a privatised legal pluralism, such as the *lex mercatoria*;[7] through treaties and developing transnational regimes to international and transnational authorities such as the regionally authoritative European Courts[8] and the decision-making panels under NAFTA or at the WTO. At the same time, new national constitutional dispensations are replete with a fragmentation of authority through the creation of constitutionally independent institutions that conduct democratic elections; uphold human rights; promote gender equality; protect cultural, language and religious minorities; or simply to ensure clean government.

---

5 P Bell (ed) (1997) *The Making of the Constitution*, Churchill Murray, p 72.

6 Ibid.

7 See G Teubner (ed) (1997) *Global Law Without a State*, Dartmouth.

8 European Court of Justice and the European Court on Human Rights. See A-M Slaughter, A Sweet and J Weiler (eds) (1997) *The European Courts* and *National Courts: Doctrine and Jurisprudence*, Hart.

In the realm of constitutional rights, the classic focus on political and civil rights, while in may respects still dominant, has been infiltrated by claims for socio-economic and other even more aspirational rights. Likewise, the understanding of the purpose of constitutional rights – to protect the individual or distinct minorities against state or majoritarian power – has also been broadened through attempts to expand the application of rights into arenas of power beyond the state. While earlier recognition of socio-economic rights was implicit in constitutional definitions of the state as a social state,[9] more explicit recognition occurred in the constitutionalisation of policy goals in the form of directives of social or state policy.[10] Unlike the effervescence of the declaratory statement of socio-economic rights which characterised the former state–Socialist constitutions (eg, the USSR), these directives of state policy have developed into interpretative guides,[11] giving socio-economic rights a jurisprudential reality that provided a basis for their inclusion in more recent Bills of Rights as enforceable constitutional rights.[12] Significantly, there has been a similar trend in the expanded application of rights. From the interpretative expansion of the state action requirement by the United States Supreme Court, to include privately formulated, racially discriminatory contracts to the notion of *Drittwirkung* (effect on private individuals) in the jurisprudence of the German Constitutional Court, there has been a constant struggle over the impact of constitutional rights on the private exercise of power. While the requirement of state action has remained largely constrictive in the United States, the German Constitutional Court has long recognised the radiating effect constitutional rights have on private actions impugning the rights of other private parties. Although this horizontal application of the Bill of Rights was at first rejected by the South African Constitutional Court in its interpretation of the 1993 Constitution, the reaction of the Constitutional Assembly was to rewrite the application clause in the 'final' 1996 Constitution to explicitly apply the Bill of Rights to relevant private action.

In order to understand the ways in which constitutional values are being rethought and the role different formulations of these values play in the 'globalised' constitutionalism of the late 20th century, it is useful to focus on one particular process. Given the intense and irreconcilable conflicts over property, and land in particular, that marked the South African policy of apartheid and hence the democratic transition that brought about its demise, the adoption of a property clause in South Africa's post-apartheid, constitutional order provides an important context in which to explore these issues. The constitutional treatment of property rights is also

9 See Basic Law of the Federal Republic of Germany (1949).

10 See Constitution of India (1950).

11 See Namibian Constitution (1990).

12 See, for example, the South African (1996) and Columbian (1991) Constitutions.

significant as it is a central part of the post-Socialist notion of 'universal human rights' that provided the backdrop to the transformation of constitutional values in the post-Cold War era.

'At the core is property'

The conflicts, debates and final compromise on the inclusion of a property rights clause in the South African Constitution provides a process from which to view the globalised interactions through which constitutional values are being adopted, re-imagined and hybridised. While the internationally endorsed process for the transition from apartheid included a commitment to the Rule of Law and the inclusion of a justiciable Bill of Rights, there was no clarity on the contents of this commitment. As a result, the different political parties and interest groups entered into a process in which they sought to shape the meaning of these commitments so as to achieve their particular goals. While this 'debate' over the content of particular commitments or rights reflected the political goals and assumptions of the different parties, it was also substantially framed by the available intellectual resources. These included primarily the historical 'text' of local experience as well as the 'text' of international and foreign jurisdictions, which served simultaneously as exemplary resources in the pursuit of particular goals and as the bounded universe constraining the choices and options of the parties.

At the onset the ANC's draft Bill of Rights only protected limited rights to personal property, yet it became clear at the May 1991 conference convened by the ANC Constitutional Committee, that the ANC was under a great deal of pressure to grant greater recognition to property rights. Attempts at that conference to question whether there should be any constitutionally protected property rights at all elicited a highly charged response from one member of the Constitutional Committee who warned that the rejection of property rights would directly endanger the democratic transition. In response, participants at the conference called for a reworking of the draft, for the recognition of land as a specific form of property and land to be treated separately from property in general. In addition, concern was expressed about the recognition of property rights before the implementation of the necessary process of redistribution. Furthermore, participants made a commitment to include positive rights to land for the landless.[13]

While this internal ANC debate sought simultaneously to limit the reach of existing property rights and to secure a more equitable distribution of property in the future, the response of the old regime and the existing economic interests was expressed most clearly by the South African Law

---

13 See Centre for Development Studies (1991) *A Bill of Rights for a Democratic South Africa: Papers and Report of a Conference Convened by the ANC Constitutional Committee*, May, pp 129–32.

Commission – a nominally independent statutory body. In its August 1991 'Interim Report on Group and Human Rights', the Law Commission launched a sustained attack against the ANC Draft, charging that the 'ANC's Bill . . . provides, in a manner which hardly disguises the aim, for nationalisation of private property without objectively testable norms for compensation', and that what the ANC intended was 'in fact nothing but nationalisation under the cloak of expropriation . . . designed to secure state control over property'.[14]

Instead, the Law Commission called for the protection of private property and for the payment of just compensation in the event of expropriation in the public interest. Likewise, the Democratic Party, traditionally the party of big capital, proposed a comprehensive right to property which could only be derogated by lawful expropriation in the public interest, and only then, with 'proper payment of equitable compensation, which in the event of dispute, shall be determined by an ordinary court of law'.[15] Neither of these proposals provided for the restitution of property taken under apartheid and as such failed to comprehend the threat to property rights, and even the very notion of constitutional rights, that any attempt to legally entrench apartheid's spoils entailed.

Meanwhile the ANC itself adopted a set of policy guidelines in the form of a 'Land Manifesto' at its national conference in June 1991. The most important features of the Land Manifesto were: its simultaneous commitment to both land restitution and land redistribution; its recognition of a diversity of land tenure forms; and the advancement of a policy of affirmative action as the main device to achieve specific policy goals.[16] With these guidelines the ANC effectively endorsed a strategy against the simple constitutional recognition of private property as recognised by the apartheid state. Firstly, by demanding both restitution and land reform, it questioned and threatened the legitimacy of existing property rights. Secondly, the recognition of different forms of tenure de-centred private land ownership and provided a basis for the recognition of communal and other forms of land tenure. Finally, the manifesto recognised that affirmative action-type policies would provide a structure in which the multitude of specific policy goals and claims of different constituencies within the ANC could be accommodated and targeted to address land issues and the interests of the rural poor.

Also, the struggle over land and property rights continued. Firstly, in actual land occupations and attempts to return to land, from which communities had been forcibly removed – whether by occupation or legal and

---

14 South African Law Commission (1991) *Interim Report on Group and Human Rights* (August), pp 359–65.

15 See Article 9, Democratic Party (1993) *Freedom Under the Rule of Law: Advancing Liberty in the New South Africa*, Draft Bill of Rights, May.

16 ANC Land Commission (1991) *Land Manifesto for ANC National Conference*, July.

administrative negotiations with ACLA[17] and the de Klerk Government. Secondly, at the level of ideas, with debates over different policy options continuing at a series of conferences and meetings, either organised by the ANC Constitutional Committee together with various University-based institutes or directly by the academy. One of the most important of these was organised by long-time land activist Aninka Claassens through the Centre for Applied Legal Studies (CALS) at the University of the Witwatersrand, to discuss 'the effect that a constitutionally entrenched right to property might have on future land reform legislation and programmes'.[18]

The opening of a discussion on particular options for the recognition of land rights and the consequences a property clause might have on land claims was, at this stage, a vital intervention, making it clear that the issue of land rights could not be divorced from the wider question of property. At this conference new substantive ideas were introduced into the public debate while simultaneously being framed through their presentation in the context of different international histories and examples. Among the important substantive interventions was the public floating of the suggestion for a land claims court – in the form of a report to the conference from a group of lawyers and activists from the 'land claims movement' who were working on this option at the behest of the ANC Land Commission.[19] Others included Geoff Budlender's construction of a legal right to land for the landless,[20] as well as the work of Catherine Cross, who demonstrated the continued vitality and existence of an alternative understanding of land rights in opposition to the prevailing legal notions of individual private property rights.[21] Presentation of the Canadian decision to preclude the

---

17 For a critique of the government's Advisory Commission on Land Allocations (ACLA) See H Klug (1996) 'Bedevilling Agrarian Reform: The Impact of Past, Present and Future Legal Frameworks' in J Van Zyl, J Kirsten and HP Binswanger (eds), *Agricultural Land Reform in South Africa: Policies, Markets and Mechanisms*, Oxford University Press, pp 166–71.

18 See A Claassens (1992) 'Editorial' 8 *South African Journal on Human Rights* v.

19 E Swanson (1992) 'A Land Claims Court for South Africa: Report on Work in Progress' 8 *South African Journal on Human Rights* 332. While I participated erratically in the meetings of this group, I did submit a memorandum on the experience of the Indian Claims Commission in the United States as both an example of a land claims process and as a warning against limiting the claimants' remedies to monetary compensation instead of the return of land which was the basic demand of claimants. In the debates that followed we were able to use the experience of the ICC to argue that cash settlements could never satisfy demands for the return of land, pointing to the fact that despite thirty years and millions of dollars Native American claims remained unsatisfied.

20 G Budlender (1992) 'The Right to Equitable Access to Land' 8 *South African Journal on Human Rights* 295. Budlender is now Director-General of the Department of Land Affairs, the highest-ranking civil servant in the Department.

21 C Cross (1992) 'An Alternative Legality: The Property Rights Question in Relation to South African Land Reform' 8 *South African Journal on Human Rights* 305.

explicit recognition of property rights from their 1982 Charter of Rights[22] and the history of constitutional conflict over land reform in India in the post-independence years[23] both introduced substantive examples of alternative approaches and provided grist for debate over the dangers of, and alternatives to, the constitutional enshrinement of property rights.

It was these interventions that forced the ANC to re-evaluate its own proposed 'Draft Bill of Rights'. After several meetings with land activists and members of the Land Commission, Albie Sachs proposed new sections on Land and the Environment as well as a separate Property clause for the revised text of the ANC draft Bill of Rights. These new sections essentially expanded the ANC's proposals making it clear that land rights would remain a central claim of the anti-apartheid movement and that the protection of property would remain subject to these claims. While property rights were given separate recognition for the first time in the new text, the text also suggested that these references to property, along with all other 'principles governing economic life' might be better placed outside the Bill of Rights in a non-justiciable section of the Constitution defined as 'Directive Principles of State Policy' – which is the case with similar sections of the Irish and Indian Constitutions.

Thus, when substantive constitutional negotiations began in early 1993, the ANC and government presented dramatically alternative notions of how property should be constitutionally protected. While the ANC was willing to protect the undisturbed enjoyment of personal possessions, property entitlements were to be determined by legislation and provision was to be made for the restoration of land to people dispossessed under Apartheid. The National Party Government's proposals aimed at protecting all property rights and would only allow expropriation for public purposes and subject to cash compensation determined by a court of law according to the market value of the property. In response the ANC suggested that no property clause was necessary.

As the negotiations progressed the conflict over the property clause became focused on specific issues. The apartheid government insisted that property rights be included in the Constitution and that the measure of compensation include specific reference to the market value of the property. In response the ANC insisted that the property clause not frustrate efforts to address land claims and that the state must have the power to regulate property without obligations to pay compensation unless there was a clear expropriation of the property. The conflict soon focused on whether provisions for land restitution should be included within the property clause or whether they should be limited to the corrective action provisions of the

22 RW Bauman (1992) 'Property Rights in the Canadian Constitutional Context' 8 *South African Journal on Human Rights* 344.

23 J Murphy (1992) 'Insulating Land Reform from Constitutional Impugnment: An Indian Case Study', reprinted in 8 *South African Journal on Human Rights* 362.

equality clause. The interim 1993 Constitution resolved these conflicts by providing a separate institutional basis for land restitution, which was guaranteed in the corrective action provisions of the equality clause and compromising on the question of compensation by including a range of factors the courts would have to consider in determining just and equitable compensation.

Despite predictions that there would be very little change in the Constitution during the second phase of the constitution-making process, particularly on such sensitive issues as the property clause and the Bill of Rights, the property issue, in fact, once again became one of the unresolvable lightning rods in the Constitutional Assembly. Although the committee charged with reviewing the Bill of Rights was at first reluctant to change the formulation of the 1993 compromise, challenges centred on the question of land restitution and reform once again forced open the process.[24] In this case the impetus came from a Workshop on Land Rights and the Constitution organised by the Constitutional Assembly's subcommittee, Theme Committee 6.3, whose task it was to resolve issues related to specialised structures of government such as the Land Claims Commission and Court provided for in the 1993 Constitution. Focusing on the land issue this meeting once again raised the problem of property rights in the Constitution. While some participants once again raised the question whether there should be any property protection within the final Constitution, the major change from the period in which the 1993 Constitution was negotiated was that the participants in this workshop, even those representing long established interests like the National Party and the South African Agricultural Union, now agreed on the need 'to rectify past wrongs' and for land reform. Disagreement here was over the means. The South African Agricultural Union, for example continued to assert that 'it should be done in a way without jeopardising the protection of private ownership', while the National Party now embraced the World Bank's proposals, arguing that land reform should 'be accomplished within the parameters of the market and should be demand-driven'.

The outcome of this workshop and the submissions made to Theme Committee 6.3 was a report to the Constitutional Assembly which both challenged the existing 1993 formulation of property rights and called for a specific land clause to provide a 'constitutional framework and protection for all land reform measures'.[25] While Theme Committee 4, which was re-

24 See Constitutional Assembly, Constitutional Committee Sub-Committee: Documentation: Land Rights, 9 October 1995; Theme Committee 6.3: Specialised Structures of Government: Land Rights, Documentation 11 September 1995; and, Constitutional Assembly, Theme Committee 6.3: Specialised Structures of Government: Documentation Volume 2A: Land Rights, 15 September 1995.

25 See Constitutional Assembly (1995) Constitutional Committee Subcommittee, Documentation: Land Rights, 9 October.

sponsible for the Bill of Rights, had thus far uncontroversially adopted a property clause that merely incorporated the 1993 Constitution's restitution provisions into the property clause itself, the report on Land Rights threw the proverbial cat among the pigeons. Some objected to Theme Committee 6.3's very discussion of property rights, while others sensed an opportunity to reopen the debate on property rights and to question once again their very inclusion in the Bill of Rights. As a result the Draft Bill of Rights published by the Constitutional Assembly on 9 October 1995 included an option that there be 'no property clause at all'.

It was in this context that an alternative option, a property clause including specific land rights as well as a sub-clause insulating land reform from constitutional attack began to gain momentum. While a strategy to insulate land restitution and land reform from constitutional attack had been implicit from early on in the debate, it was now suggested in a submission to Theme Committee 6.3 that the property clause include a specific sub-clause insulating state action aimed at redressing past discrimination in the ownership and distribution of land rights. The negotiators were able to rely on this formulation as a compromise between those demanding the removal of the property clause and those, like the Democratic Party, who remained opposed to even the social democratic formulation modelled on the German Constitution.[26] Still the debate raged on and the draft formulations of the property clause continued to evolve.[27] Political agreement on the property clause was only finally reached at midnight on 18 April 1996, when s 28(8), the 'affirmative action' or insulation sub-clause of the property clause was modified so as to make it subject to s 36(1), the general limitations clause of the Constitution.[28]

Despite agreement in the Constitutional Assembly the property clause was presented to the Constitutional Court as violating the Constitutional Principles and therefore grounds for denying certification of the Constitution.[29] Two major objections were raised: firstly, that unlike the interim Constitution the new clause did not expressly protect the right to acquire,

---

26 See Constitutional Assembly (1995) Constitutional Committee, Documentation: Volume 2A Land Rights, 15 September, pp 13–41.

27 New versions were published in the 30 October 1995 Refined Working Draft (2nd edn) of the Constitution; and another ANC proposal was published in the 9–16 February 1996 edition of *Constitutional Talk* – the official newsletter of the Constitutional Assembly – and yet another was published in the 22 April – 8 May 1996 edition of *Constitutional Talk*.

28 See P Bell (ed) (1997) *The Making of the Constitution*, Churchill Murray.

29 Under the original political compromise, the Constitutional Assembly was to be constrained by the Constitutional Principles negotiated between the parties and appended to the 1993 interim Constitution. The Constitutional Court was empowered to certify whether a draft Constitution prepared by the Constitutional Assembly met the requirements of the Constitutional Principles. The Constitutional Court in 1996 first declined to certify the draft and then certified the new text adopted in response to the Court's first certification judgment.

hold and dispose of property; secondly, that the provisions governing expropriation and the payment of compensation were inadequate.[30] The Constitutional Court rejected both of these arguments. Firstly, the Court noted that the test to be applied was whether the formulation of the right met the standard of a 'universally accepted fundamental right' as required by Constitutional Principle II. Secondly, the Court surveyed international and foreign sources and observed that:

> [i]f one looks to international conventions and foreign constitutions, one is immediately struck by the wide variety of formulations adopted to protect the right to property, as well as by the fact that significant conventions and constitutions contain no protection of property at all.[31]

In conclusion the Court argued that it could not 'uphold the argument that, because the formulation adopted is expressed in a negative and not a positive form and because it does not contain an express recognition of the right to acquire and dispose of property, it fails to meet the prescription of CPII'.[32] The second objection met the same fate with the Court concluding that an 'examination of international conventions and foreign constitutions suggests that a wide range of criteria for expropriation and the payment of compensation exists', and thus the 'approach taken in NT 25 [new text s 25] cannot be said to flout any universally accepted approach to the question'.[33]

The final property clause reflects the democratic origins of the Constitutional Assembly. It guarantees not only the restitution of land taken after 1913[34] and a right to legally secure tenure for those whose tenure is insecure as a result of racially discriminatory laws or practices,[35] but also an obligation on the state to enable citizens to gain access to land on an equitable basis.[36] Furthermore, the state is granted a limited exemption from the protective provisions of the property clause so as to empower it to take 'legislative and other measures to achieve land, water and related reform, in order to redress the results of past racial discrimination'.[37] The substance of this outcome reflects both the general contours of the political conflict over the property clause and the bounded alternatives available to the parties – from the recognition of existing property rights on the one hand to the recognition of land claims on the other. Significantly, the factors to be considered in the determination of just compensation reflect this outcome.

---

30 *Ex parte Chairperson of the Constitutional Assembly: In Re Certification of the Constitution of the Republic of South Africa*, 1996 (4) SA 744 (hereinafter *First Certification Case*), para 70.

31 *First Certification Case* para 71.

32 *First Certification Case* para 72.

33 *First Certification Case* para 73.

34 Constitution of the Republic of South Africa 1996 s 25(7).

35 Constitution 1996 s 25(6).

36 Constitution 1996 s 25(5).

37 Constitution 1996 s 25(8).

On the one hand they were directed at the problem of land claims and included: 'the use to which the property is being put, the history of its acquisition, the value of the investments in it by those affected and the interest of those affected',[38] while on the other hand, at the insistence of the *ancien régime* and making possible the inclusion of other factors, it enshrined 'market value'. It was under this constitutional regime that Mandela's Government and South Africa's first democratic Parliament began to address land claims. Acting in terms of the specific clauses of the 1993 Constitution which provided for the establishment of a land claims process, Parliament passed the *Restitution of Land Rights Act* in 1994 setting up regional Land Claims Commissions and the new Land Claims Court.[39]

Although it may be argued that the property clause in the final Constitution is unique to South Africa and is the product of South Africa's particular history of dispossession, it is also important to note how resolution of the property question was framed by international options. While the Constitutional Court could argue that the particular formulation of the clause was compatible with global standards – given the variety of formulations in existence – it is also true that those who advocated that there should be no property clause in the Constitution were compelled by the politics of recognition of property rights to accept its inclusion. At the same time, the acceptability of the property clause – in the sense that the opposing parties were prepared to live with the compromise – was still premised on the inherent complexity and vagueness of the final clause. Although it clearly does not protect all property rights unconditionally it also provides for market-value compensation in the case of an outright expropriation outside of the land restitution or land reform context. By leaving the specific conflicts to the future, and to the process of piece-meal constitutional litigation rather than once-off political settlement, the process of constitutionalisation has allowed the parties to continue to imagine and even work towards their preferred outcomes. As circumstances change and political and economic power and interests shift, so the constitutional vagueness of the clause will enable new compromises or even presently politically unpalatable outcomes to become possible.

The politics of constitution-making in this instance were thus bounded on both sides. Both the option of widespread nationalisation initially advocated by the African National Congress, which may have been facilitated by the exclusion of a property clause, and the demands for a strict protection of property guaranteeing market-value compensation for any interference were silenced. Instead the parties were able to use the international and foreign lexicon of treaties, constitutions and case law to formulate a specifically South African compromise. This resolution both enabled the political

38 Constitution of the Republic of South Africa, Act 200 of 1993 s 28(3).

39 See H Klug (1996) 'Historical Claims and the Right to Restitution' in Van Zyl et al.

transition and left open, for future fact-specific confrontations, the exact interpretation to be given to the new Constitution's property clauses.

Conclusion

Reflecting on this outcome – which enables South Africa to address the legacy of forced removals under apartheid while protecting significant existing property rights – allows us to understand the changing roles constitutional values are playing in processes of constitutional transformation. Firstly, by contextualising the 'universal' right to property, the notion of a fundamental right to property has been transformed so as to address both past injustice and to revitalise the very notion of property rights. At the same time, the open-ended character of constitutional values has allowed the competing interests to re-imagine their own demands and to accept the result as an adequate protection of their non-negotiable requirements. Secondly, this rethinking or reformulation of the universal claim of property rights provides the beginning of a new hybridised text through which other peoples, struggling to resolve conflicting claims to property, may turn. Thirdly, to the extent that this ongoing text provides a alternative narrative of cases and experiences, it will be available to others who will draw on it in their attempts to reinvigorate their own understandings or interpretations of the dominant understanding of the constitutional role of property rights. Thus, instead of seeing property rights as simply the 'guardian of every other right',[40] protecting individuals against the might of the state, we may begin to see property rights as inhabiting a constitutional realm in which the balance between public and private exercises of power may be mediated. This however is only one alternative, and the very nature of the global constitutional transformation we have been witnessing reminds us that there is no single outcome, but rather that constitutional values are in continual flux – both bounding the possible alternatives and being constantly reshaped through their application and hybridisation in different historical and cultural contexts.

40 See JW Ely Jr (1992) *The Guardian of Every Other Right: A Constitutional History of Property Rights*, Oxford.

17

Globalisation – the Bane of Popular Sovereignty?

John Pyke

This book's theme – challenges to the sovereignty of nation-states from the pressure of globalisation – has special piquancy for me. I have long advocated[1] that the constitutional law of our sovereign nation[2] should expressly recognise the sovereignty *of the people*, and provide mechanisms through which the people can enact enforceable legal rules specifying that their legislators *must not* make certain laws, or *must* advance certain objectives. Yet now it is suggested this notion is anachronistic, or futile, in view of nations' increasing subjection to international law and international markets.

In response, I first describe the different ways in which a people may be said to be sovereign; discuss examples of constitutions that put these different ways into effect; criticise Australia's feebler manifestations of popular sovereignty; and suggest we emulate those systems where *real* sovereignty of the people is most developed. Finally, I address two globalisation-based objections to popular sovereignty, demonstrating that reports of its demise are greatly exaggerated.

The sovereignty of the people: fiction and various levels of reality

In a democracy, we hear frequent references to the 'sovereignty of the people'. However, this can have a variety of meanings in reality. Edmund

1 Primarily through submissions to public inquiries into constitutional reform. See Electoral and Administrative Review Commission (Queensland), *Review of the Preservation and Enhancement of Individuals' Rights and Freedoms, Public Submissions*, Vol 3, Submission 130; and my submission to the Queensland Constitutional Review Commission (at http://www.constitution.qld.gov.au/subs/sub_pyke.html). These focus on State constitutional issues, but my arguments readily apply to the Commonwealth Constitution.

2 Only recently, ironically, has Australia's independent sovereignty been recognised: *New South Wales v Commonwealth* (*Seas and Submerged Lands Case*) (1975) 135 CLR 337; *Sue v Hill* (1999) 73 ALJR 1016). Now it seems (if we believe the globalisation rhetoric) it might be nugatory anyway: *Sic transit imperium Australiae*!

Morgan persuasively suggests[3] that the concept was first used as a fiction, by people fighting for power against rivals who invoked another then-powerful fiction: the divine right of kings. Although (as Morgan agrees) the fiction was eventually given more and more reality, it has varying *degrees* of reality when English, Australian and American constitutional law are compared.

Merely political sovereignty

In the 19th century even Dicey, famous for insisting that in England the Parliament was legally sovereign,[4] accepted that the word also had a political sense[5] – and that this 'political sovereign', the authority whose will was *ultimately* obeyed, was the electorate.[6] Now that every adult citizen (with a few reasonable disqualifications) is represented, the fiction is even more credible: in a sense that we can all believe, 'the people' exercise their 'sovereignty' at every election.

But, where Diceyan theory remains unmodified, there is a basic problem with this notion. Under this model, the people's political sovereignty depends, in law, absolutely on the grace of the legally sovereign Parliament. Parliament enacted the laws that gave everyone the vote, and that limit its term – and as a matter of law Parliament could repeal them. A system which says Parliament is legally sovereign, but which relies on politicians' decency (or fear of the electorate) to ensure the people *remain* the political sovereign, is curious indeed. Anyone but the English would expect *at least* universal franchise and regular fair elections to be guaranteed in a document of higher legal status than ordinary legislation.

Legal sovereignty of a reactive kind

In Australia, of course, no parliament has an unfettered legal sovereignty. The powers of the Commonwealth and State parliaments are limited by the Commonwealth Constitution. In the free speech cases,[7] and again in *McGinty's Case*,[8] three Justices of the High Court have expressly recognised that the sovereign power over this Constitution is vested in the people. The rules protected by this sovereignty seem to satisfy the criteria above for

---

3 E Morgan (1988) *Inventing the People*, WW Norton.

4 AV Dicey (1885) *Introduction to the Study of the Law of the Constitution* (7th edn, 1915), p 39.

5 Compare Gummow J's reference in *McGinty v WA* (1996) 186 CLR 140 at 275 to a 'popular or political meaning' of sovereignty.

6 Dicey (1885); 7th edn, (1915), p 73.

7 *Nationwide News Pty Ltd v Wills* (1992) 177 CLR 1 and *Australian Capital Television Pty Ltd v Commonwealth* ('ACTV') (1992) 177 CLR 106 per Mason CJ at 138 and Deane and Toohey JJ at 70.

8 *McGinty v WA* (1996) 186 CLR 140 per Toohey J at 199, McHugh J at 230 and Gummow J at 274–5.

constitutionally guaranteeing the people's *political* sovereignty. As to the Federal Parliament, the Constitution guarantees a term limit[9] and, although on its face it leaves electoral qualifications up to parliament,[10] the implications drawn from the words 'directly chosen by the people' in the free speech cases certainly guarantee the universal franchise as well as 'freedom of communication in relation to public affairs and political discussion'.[11] As the latter guarantee extends to laws affecting State political affairs,[12] it may be speculated that some guarantees as to State electoral processes may be implied as well – though no guarantee of equal electoral districts, at least for the moment.[13]

However, even as their Honours recognised the sovereignty of the people, one of them[14] noted accurately that they (we!) are 'sovereign' in a very qualified way, because we cannot initiate Constitutional amendments ourselves. The Parliament proposes and we the electors merely dispose. Indeed the reality is somewhat worse. Although s 128 *does* allow for a referendum if one House passes an Alteration Bill twice, only proposals favoured by the executive have any chance; it is generally agreed that because the Governor-General will follow Ministerial advice on whether to hold a referendum, an Alteration Bill sponsored by Opposition or Independent Senators will get nowhere. So in reality, the *executive* proposes and we the electors dispose.[15] If we are the sovereign, we are merely a *reactive* sovereign, not a 'proactive' one.

Problems with either of the above two models

The fact that our reactive legal sovereignty guarantees our political sovereignty is certainly a source of some comfort – at the end of a parliamentary term, we can throw the scoundrels out. But, especially given that in our Parliaments the executive generally has the loyalty of the majority of members, there is *no* guarantee even of rights closely connected with the preservation of our sovereignty. Consider three recent examples from Australian States:

- If the executive has first drafted a liberal *Freedom of Information Act* that it later finds irksome, it can push through Parliament an amendment

---

9 Section 28.

10 Sections 8 and 30.

11 The phrase is from *ACTV* per Mason CJ at 138.

12 *Stephens v West Australian Newspapers Ltd* (1994) 182 CLR 211; *Lange v Australian Broadcasting Corp* (1997) 189 CLR 520.

13 *McGinty v WA* (1996) 186 CLR 140

14 Gummow J in *McGinty* at 275–6

15 And the situation is the same in those States where some provisions of the *Constitution Act* are 'entrenched' by 'manner and form' provisions. In each case only the parliament can initiate change, and except in times of minority government only proposals from the government benches will be passed by parliament.

that broadens the exemptions so that any papers taken to a Cabinet meeting, whether or not considered by the meeting or even relevant to it, are exempt. Then *both* major political parties can play the game of promising to repeal the amendments in opposition, and neglecting to do so in government.[16]

- If the Premier is about to be subpoenaed to give evidence of a meeting with leading businessmen, the executive can have Parliament amend the *Evidence Act* so as to reverse the decision in *Conway v Rimmer*[17] by restoring the conclusive status of a certificate by the Attorney-General claiming Crown privilege.[18]
- If the Auditor-General is embarrassing the executive (a sign that he is doing his job!), the executive can tell Parliament to 'privatise' some of the Auditor's functions,[19] and reduce his budget to inhibit his carrying out the remaining ones.

Instead of mere political sovereignty, exercised only on polling day, we need rules that limit the powers of Parliaments and executive governments throughout the other three (in many jurisdictions, four) years between elections, and we need to be able to initiate the entrenchment of such rules in constitutions ourselves.

Real ('proactive') legal sovereignty, and mechanisms for implementing it

We hear less about America's State Constitutions than about its federal document,[20] but the former offer interesting precedents for truly implementing of the sovereignty of the people. As Edmund Morgan has noted,[21] the fiction of popular sovereignty eventually gave birth, in the United States, to the notion that the many could construct safeguards against the few. It is pleasing to be able to note, in a book sponsored by the Fulbright Commission, that we find two safeguard mechanisms used widely in the United

16 *Freedom of Information Act* 1992 (Qld) s 36(1) as progressively amended in 1993 and 1995. See WB Lane, 'Reform of Administrative Law in Queensland' (1996) 79 *Canberra Bulletin of Public Administration* 174 at 180–1.

17 [1968] AC 910.

18 *Evidence (Amendment) Act* 1979 (NSW). The new sections were repealed, after a change of government, by the *Evidence (Crown Privilege) Amendment Act* 1988.

19 *Audit (Amendment) Act* 1997 (Vic). See W Funnell (1997) 'The Curse of Sisyphus: Public Sector Audit Independence in an Age of Economic Rationalism' 56 *AJPA* 87; M Rayner, (1997) 'Watchdog on a Leash', *Eureka Street*, December, 24–5; R Manne (1999) 'Victoria's State of Silence', *Sydney Morning Herald*, 13 September.

20 'Public law scholarship and professional literature are overwhelmingly occupied with the single national government'. HA Linde (1999) 'Structures and Terms of Consent: Delegation, Discretion, Separation of Powers, Representation, Participation, Accountability?' 20 *Cardozo Law Review* 823 at 824.

21 E Morgan (1988) *Inventing the People*, WW Norton, pp 282–5.

States at State level. One is Citizen-Initiated Referendum (CIR); the other, a requirement that an elected Constitutional Convention be held (or at least that a referendum decide if one shall be held) at regular intervals, or if a certain number of voters demand. If I count right, 14 State Constitutions allow constitutional amendment by CIR; another 14 require that if no Constitutional Convention has been held in the last nine, 10, 16, or 20 years, a referendum is to be held giving the electors the power to demand such a Convention; and 14 enable a Convention to be called via CIR.[22] Four States have two of these mechanisms, and one (Montana) has all three, so 24 States have at least one.[23] Australia has copied many important ideas from America's federal Constitution; as we emerge from the shadow of colonialism and the legacy of Professor Dicey, we could do worse than to copy from American State Constitutions also.[24]

If mechanisms like these were available, they could be used to introduce Bills of Rights (and other controls on legislative and executive power) into our State and federal constitutions – and make them rather more like American constitutions. Despite the fears of gloomy liberals,[25] I suspect a majority of Australians would support entrenchment of the traditional 'Bill of Rights rights', including guarantees of fair criminal process – but exactly what is enacted will be up to the majority to decide, and they may prefer more or fewer restrictions from time to time. If at any time the people feel confident that the Parliament or executive is unlikely to misuse its powers, they *might* even take restrictions away, but they would retain power to re-impose them. The actual list of rights and restrictions selected is less important than the overriding principle that the people have authority to specify the limits of legislative power and to vary these limits from time to time.

The United States experience also shows that entrenched, justiciable Constitutions are *not* used solely to mandate 'right-wing' classical liberal ideas of *laissez-faire* and limited government. They can, and do, also direct governments to take positive action for the collective good. In what is generally seen as the world's least 'Socialist' democracy, almost all State Constitutions command that there shall be State-funded education. Many require it to be 'uniform', 'thorough' or 'efficient'; hence in 1971 California's Supreme Court could rule that distributing funds among school districts

22 I propose to post a complete table of these details on my website at http://ozconstinfo.freehomepage.com/US_States.html.

23 I am not saying that the people of 26 US States are 'not sovereign'. Remember, I distinguish *forms* of sovereignty. The people of those States, like the people of the United States as a whole, indeed enjoy *political* sovereignty and *reactive legal* sovereignty – but they do not have *proactive legal* sovereignty, and in my opinion they are the poorer for that.

24 See P O'Brien and M Webb (eds) (1991) *The Executive State: WA Inc and the Constitution*, Constitutional Press, for similar proposals.

25 See particularly C Puplick (1996) 'Citizen-Initiated Referendums: The Case Against' in K Wiltshire (ed), *Direct Democracy: Citizens-Initiated Referendums*, Constitutional Centenary Foundation.

proportional to the property taxes raised in each (creating richer schools in affluent districts) was unconstitutional. Over the next 20 years, about half the States saw lawsuits challenging their school funding systems, about half of which succeeded.[26] This is the kind of policy that (assuming that a majority wanted) we voters could impose on our governments if Australians, too, enjoyed proactive popular sovereignty.

CIR is controversial in Australia; often advocated, but vigorously opposed. The literature on CIR[27] contains the standard arguments, which need not be repeated here, for and against a system that involves proactive popular sovereignty ('direct democracy'). Of course, to realise popular sovereignty it is not strictly necessary to allow the making of ordinary laws by CIR, as long as constitutional amendments can be initiated.[28] But if even that form of CIR is thought to give the uneducated People too much of a say, there is the other alternative – that if there has been no Constitutional Convention for some years, the people *must* be asked if they want one, and if so, they *must* be permitted to elect one directly. After all, Constitutional Conventions are an established Australian tradition,[29] although more in connection with the federal than the State constitutions. What I must answer here, however, is an objection not much addressed in the CIR debate cited above, and never, to my knowledge, raised in respect of Constitutional Conventions – that to put such sovereignty into effect (at State *or* national level) by either mechanism would conflict with, or be rendered futile by, the forces of globalisation.

Does proactive popular sovereignty clash with globalisation?

The sovereignty of nations (whoever exercises it *within* each nation) is now said to be under threat from two different, but overlapping, sources. Firstly,

26 See JD Leshy (1990) 'The State of Constitutional Law in the States of the United States: Are There Any Lessons for Australia?' 20 *UWA Law Review* 373.

27 The best recent arguments against CIR are found in DA Bell Jr (1978) 'The Referendum: Democracy's Barrier to Racial Equality' 54 *Washington Law Review* 1; G Brennan (1997) 'Direct Democracy: The Case Against' *Policy* (Autumn) 32–4; JN Eule (1990) 'Judicial Review of Direct Democracy' 90 *Yale Law Journal* 1503; NE Franklin (1992) 'Initiative and Referendum: Participatory Democracy or Rolling Back the State?' in M Munro-Clark (ed), *Citizen Participation in Government*, Hale & Iremonger; C Puplick (1996). Arguments in favour are presented in G Walker (1987) *Initiative and Referendum: The People's Law*, Centre for Independent Studies.

28 In practice, however, limiting CIR to 'constitutional' matters tends to invite the 'constitutionalisation' of policy matters otherwise left to ordinary statute – eg, the Swiss Constitution's Art 25 *bis* which bans slaughter of animals without first stunning them – so, in practice, popular sovereignty may require 'legislative' as well as 'constitutional' CIR.

29 Conventions whose proposals succeeded at referenda were held in 1891, 1897–8, and the mid-1970s. Although the 1999 republic model was rejected, many praised the participatory process of the 1999 Canberra 'ConCon'.

the growth of international customary law and treaties affects domestic legal systems more and more, precluding legislators and voters from selecting certain policies for fear of trans-national disruption. Secondly, the hard facts of competition in globalised markets make it futile for nations or States to attempt to regulate industries and workplaces. Does either of these forces limit what the people of a State or nation might want to enact in the exercise of their proactive sovereignty; and if so, which should prevail? My answer is that in some cases the conflict is illusory, and in other cases the people are perfectly entitled at least to *try* to make a free choice rather than passively wait for the globalisation juggernaut to roll over them.

Popular sovereignty and 'redneck' populism

Under the Westphalian tradition, nations were supposedly immune from external interference in their internal affairs, even if those involved discrimination against minorities or the general tyrannisation of the whole populace. Today – when most countries at least pay lip service to the *International Covenant on Civil and Political Rights* (ICCPR), and many have signed the protocol allowing citizens to seek declarations against their own nation – this extreme sovereignty is no doubt qualified. So if a people, exercising their proactive sovereignty, sought to enact a Constitution amendment discriminating against a minority, there would indeed be conflict between international norms and this particular attempt to assert their sovereignty.

However, there would be no such conflict between international norms and the *principles that justify* the sovereignty of the people. I am assuming that, under either of the mechanisms advocated, a majority vote is sufficient to enact new constitutional provisions. But 'majority rule' is not *in itself* an axiom of democracy.[30] The reason *why* we follow majority decisions in a democracy is more fundamental: because everyone counts, and equally.[31] To say that democracy requires not only majority rule but also respect for minorities is not contradictory; instead, *both* principles are derived from the same idea.[32] In a democracy, any move to strip one group of its fundamental right of political participation can be opposed with the argument 'If them today, why not you tomorrow?' If that democracy is truly healthy, that argument will sway most people's votes – and if the majority still makes a decision that violates some international norm, then international law is only reminding the majority of a principle it forgets at its peril.

30 I know of no attempts to justify majority rule as an end in itself, except for an offhanded analogy with the vector addition of forces in Locke's *Second Treatise*.

31 Thus a commitment to 'equal concern and respect' entails equal votes for all: RM Dworkin (1977) *Taking Rights Seriously*, Harvard University Press, p 273.

32 See LG Sager (1981) 'Rights Scepticism and Process-Based Responses' 56 *New York University Law Review* 417 at 445.

Moreover, recourse to international law helps overcome the fears of the 'gloomy liberals' mentioned above. James Madison first realised, and many elections have confirmed, that irrational 'populist' candidates or proposals are less likely to reach majority support in a large than a small population.[33] So federations can have two possible safeguards against the people of a small community exercising what they might think of as their local sovereignty to, say, forbid sale of land to people of Asian birth or descent. By voluntarily joining a federation, each State and its people agree to submit their local sovereignty to the overall sovereignty of the federated people. If, as in America, the federal Constitution contains a Bill of Rights, it will override anything inconsistent in the State's laws – or even its Constitution.[34] Alternatively, as in Australia, the power over external affairs in a federation will almost certainly belong to the national government: therefore a federal law implementing the *ICCPR* and other treaties will also override the offensive provision. If the federal Constitution provides mechanisms for proactive sovereignty, supporters of the offensive policy can try to 'constitutionalise' it at the national level, but they would have the large population principle working against them.

A more specific fear in the area of discrimination is that the people may use proactive sovereignty mechanisms to discriminate against recent immigrants; Switzerland is currently debating a proposal to limit the number of non-Swiss residents,[35] and California adopted a proposition[36] banning non-naturalised migrants from welfare entitlements. Though these worry me, as showing a disregard for the notions of the 'siblinghood' and interrelatedness of all humanity, it has to be said that whilst no people, under principles of international law or general decency, has a right to be actually brutal to guests, each people does have a right to regulate entry into itself. The fact that such measures may be proposed is not a strong reason for a liberal democrat to oppose CIR or other proactive sovereignty measures; if the anti-migrant measures are proposed, she or he will still be free to campaign against their adoption. Once a migrant has been naturalised, or once children have been born in the new country, of course things are different – someone who is a member of a nation is entitled not to be discriminated against, under both the rules of international law and the principles underlying popular sovereignty.

---

33 '[A]s each representative will be chosen by a greater number of citizens . . . it will be more difficult for unworthy candidates to practice with success the vicious arts by which elections are too often carried': J Madison, A Hamilton and J Jay (1987) *The Federalist Papers*, Penguin Books, No 10. It is tempting to contrast the success of Pauline Hanson's One Nation Party in Queensland's 1998 State election (11 of 89 seats) with its failure to win any seats in the federal poll later that year.

34 Even if the State provision is enacted via referendum. Cf *Lucas v Colorado* 377 US 713 (1964); *Reitman v Mulkey* 387 US 369 (1967); *James v Valtierra* 402 US 137 (1971).

35 'Swiss Beauty Proud of her Maori Roots' (2000) *Courier-Mail*, 19 September, p 11.

36 Proposition, 187, approved by referendum on 8 November 1994.

Popular sovereignty and international market forces

The other main objection to stronger implementation of popular sovereignty is that a populace, not comprehending the full import of economic and political factors, might attempt in vain to prevent or reverse some inevitable or necessary change. Now of course a people can no more legislate for the *factually* impossible than King Canute could stop the incoming tide, or the apocryphal American legislature could legislate that *pi* should equal three. But globalisation – as even *The Economist* admitted after the 1999 anti-WTO protests – is not such a foregone conclusion.[37] Unless and until it cedes its autonomy to a larger union, a society is entitled to *try* to insulate itself from external market or political influences *if* its voters see any benefit in trying. So if Switzerland refuses to join the European Union, or even the United Nations, that is its right.[38] So Denmark votes against the Maastricht Treaty at its first referendum? Those in favour campaign harder, and the second time the majority votes 'yes'. After all, joining a federation, or a quasi-federation like the European currency union, is probably irrevocable;[39] a society is entitled to think carefully before signing up. The argument 'You are only delaying the inevitable' may turn out to have been true; but even so, your state can still join the union later, like Denmark (or South Carolina and Rhode Island in 1779, or Newfoundland in 1948). A people has a perfect right to resist even the 'inevitable' while it can.

If the pressures are market forces rather than moves towards political union, the argument becomes more complex. Resistance to globalisation usually takes the form of calls to restore quotas or tariff protections, but the problem is that protecting one domestic industry may disadvantage another. If they had the legislative power, the people of Orange, NSW (where Email Ltd's main factory is located) may well decide to protect whitegoods against import competition, and the people of Kingaroy might vote to protect peanuts, to the disadvantage of importers and consumers. But no jurisdiction so small ever has power to make laws about overseas trade. The point above concerning federations applies here also: the people of each State have transferred their power over those matters to the people at the federal level. Even if CIR were available at the federal level, the national populace has such a variety of economic interests that a voter- (or Convention-)initiated referendum proposing higher or lower tariffs would likely be rejected on the prudent ground that such fine-tuning is best left to our parliamentarians –

---

37 J Smith and TP Moran (2000) 'WTO 101: Myths about the World Trade Organisation' 47 *Dissent* (Spring) 70.

38 Although some criticise this decision (KW Kobach (1993) *The Referendum: Direct Democracy in Switzerland*, Dartmouth, pp 201–2), it is hard to call Switzerland a worse 'international citizen' than many UN members (even some permanent sinecurists on its Security Council)!

39 As the US South found in 1861–5, although contrast the (relatively) peaceful secessions of Singapore in 1965 and Slovakia in 1992.

just as, at the 1891 Convention, the delegates from the high- and low-tariff Colonies avoided the 'lion in the path' by agreeing to leave tariff levels to the majority in the new Parliament. And even if the sovereign people did enact something that turned out unworkable, they would retain the right and power to revoke the decision later.[40]

Conclusion

The idea of the 'sovereignty of the people' emerged in 17th century English revolutionary tracts, but was first given real effect in 18th century America. The idea that globalisation is inevitable is more 'modern' – but that does not mean that, in succumbing to this greater modernity, we Australians cannot also do some belated catching-up on an older wave of modernity. As we take our place in this brave new globalised world, we should do so as a nation which recognises that – insofar as *any* nation preserves the old concept of sovereignty – that sovereignty should be exercised directly by its people.

40 For examples see KN Vines and H Jacob (eds) (1976) *Politics in the American States: A Comparative Analysis*, Little, Brown.

18

Constitutional Cants

Gerald N Rosenberg

Introduction

From Canada to South Africa to the recently created countries of the former Soviet Union, the world is awash with new constitutions, usually drafted to protect human rights. Australia's Human Rights Commissioner Brian Burdekin noted a 'growing acceptance that such a development is necessary to protect certain fundamental human rights'.[1]

The belief that Burdekin and others share is that the adoption of constitutional language declaring human rights will protect those rights. This belief was colourfully illustrated in 1992 when Canadian Chief Justice Lamer likened the introduction of the Canadian Charter to 'a revolution on the scale of the introduction of the metric system, the great medical discoveries of Louis Pasteur, and the invention of penicillin and the laser'.[2]

Constitution-writers in other countries have often focused on the US Bill of Rights,[3] and the 'idea of constitutional review and the protection it provides for fundamental rights'.[4] As Australia enters the 21st century, the adoption of a US-like Bill of Rights may seem an obvious and easy choice. But little critical thought has been given to the efficacy of US-like Bills of Rights. Rather than providing inspiration, the US experience should signal caution.

Initial problems

There are several problems with adopting a US-type Bill of Rights. The first is that the US model offers only one conception of rights: protecting individuals from abusive governmental action. This is often a good thing,

1 B Burdekin, 'Foreword', in P Alston (ed) (1994) *Towards an Australian Bill of Rights*, ANU Centre for International and Public Law/Human Rights and Equal Opportunity Commission, p v.

2 Quoted in WA Bogart (1994) *Courts and Country: The Limits of Litigation and the Social and Political Life of Canada*, Oxford University Press, p 257.

3 L Henkin (1990) 'Introduction', in L Henkin and AJ Rosenthal (eds) *Constitutionalism and Rights: The Influence of the United States Constitution Abroad*, Columbia University Press, p 2.

4 L Favoreu (1990) 'Constitutional Review in Europe', in Henkin and Rosenthal, p 38.

but it is a narrow conception. Threats to individual liberty also arise from concentrations of capital; insufficient individual resources; other citizens; and psychological obstacles that prevent individuals from making a 'real choice'.[5] Bills of Rights based on the US model 'do not serve to secure these multi-dimensional rights'.[6]

A second problem is the uncritical assumption that constitutional provisions are transferable across political systems and cultures. This is problematic because constitutions exist, are interpreted, and influence behaviour within an existing culture and social structure.

A third problem with adopting a US-type Bill of Rights to protect human rights is that it assumes that the United States Constitution has a done a good job in protecting those rights. This is dubious. The US Constitution allowed slavery for a century and then tolerated apartheid for another. It turned a blind eye to the genocide of Native Americans and permitted the jailing of over 70,000 US citizens, without any due process whatsoever, solely because of their Japanese ancestry.[7] More recently (and in contrast to virtually every other Western democracy, including Australia), the US Constitution has failed to protect political dissidents.

The problem is not lack of a textual commitment, for surely the majestic language of the Bill of Rights and the Fourteenth Amendment promise all the protection disadvantaged minorities could want. Rather, the problem is that constitutional language is invariably understood in ways that reflect the interests of powerful groups. This suggests that constitution and a Bill of Rights are neither necessary nor sufficient for protecting and furthering human rights.

Constitutions, Bills of Rights, and the courts that enforce them do not exist in a vacuum but are embedded in a broader political, economic and cultural system which determines their efficacy. A society's core beliefs, cultural understandings, political and economic system, and social organisation are more important than pious parchment pronouncements. Adding or changing constitutional provisions will make a difference only if the key institutions of the society have already embraced those changes, or are moving to do so. Protecting human rights is a noble undertaking; but relying solely (or mainly) on constitutions may be misguided.

The assumption of judicial independence

For a constitution or a Bill of Rights to protect and further human rights, it needs an institution independent of the legislature and executive that can invalidate their acts on constitutional grounds. Following the US example, the

---

5 C Sampford (1997) 'The Four Dimensions of Rights and Their Means of Protection' in B Galligan and C Sampford (eds), *Rethinking Human Rights*, Federation Press, p 56.

6 Ibid, p 52.

7 *Korematsu v US* 323 US 214 (1944).

'independent' judiciary is invariably the institution of choice. But pronouncing, or even designing, an institution to be independent does not guarantee that it will be so. It is important to examine practice. In the United States, there is considerable evidence which suggests that the Supreme Court, far from acting independently, generally defers to government preferences as well as business interests and majority opinion.[8]

The Court's role as defender of the status quo should be no surprise. The appointment process limits judicial independence because political elites select judges who they think share their views. Similarly, the United States Solicitor General, who litigates on behalf of the Federal Government, is accorded a special role. Often called the 'Tenth Justice', the Solicitor General has unusual access to the Court, is often asked by the Court to intervene to present the government's position, and historically, wins about 70 per cent of the time.[9] Congress, too, can constrain courts through tools such as court-packing and jurisdiction removal.[10] Further, business interests have historically been successful in the Supreme Court.[11] Finally, while protecting human rights is often unpopular, Supreme Court decisions have seldom strayed far from what was politically acceptable.[12] United States history and practice suggest, then, that the Court's role is to further the views of the ruling coalition, not to protect rights unsupported by that coalition.[13] These findings are generalisable. As Shapiro notes: 'No regime is likely to allow significant political power to be wielded by an isolated judicial corps free of political restraints'.[14]

Penetrating the impenetrable: human rights and public opinion

One of the most prevalent claims is that a Bill of Rights can raise the consciousness of the public at large about rights. Rights pronouncements by

---

8 See, for example, RG McCloskey (1994) *The American Supreme Court* (2nd edn), University of Chicago Press; D Kairys (ed) (1998) *The Politics of Law: A Progressive Critique* (3rd edn), Basic Books; AM Paul (1960) *Conservative Crisis and the Rule of Law*, Cornell University Press; AS Miller (1968) *The Supreme Court and American Capitalism*, Free Press.

9 L Epstein, JA Segal, HJ Spaeth and TG Walker (1994) *The Supreme Court Compendium: Data, Decisions and Developments*, Congressional Quarterly, pp 66–71, 569–72.

10 On the judiciary's historic deference to Congress, see GN Rosenberg (1992) 'Judicial Independence and the Reality of Political Power' 54 *Review of Politics* 369.

11 See, MJ Horwitz (1977) *The Transformation of American Law 1780–1860*, Harvard University Press.

12 McCloskey (1994), pp 208–9. More specifically, comparing the Court's opinions with those of the public on issues in 146 decisions over the years 1935–86, Marshall found consistency nearly two-thirds of the time: TR Marshall (1989) *Public Opinion and the Supreme Court*, Unwin Hyman, ch 4.

13 RA Dahl (1957) 'Decision-Making in a Democracy: The Role of the Supreme Court as a National Policy-Maker' 6 *Journal of Public Law* 279.

14 M Shapiro (1981) *Courts: A Comparative and Political Analysis*, University of Chicago Press, p 34.

courts, it is claimed, can remind citizens of their highest aspirations and chide them for their failings. As former Australian Chief Justice Sir Anthony Mason put it, rights pronouncements can serve a 'major educative role in promoting greater awareness of, and respect for, human rights'.[15] By bringing conditions to light, and showing how far from aspirations practice has fallen, court cases can provide a 'cheap method of pricking powerful consciences'.[16]

If constitutional rights did carry such persuasive weight, people would become more supportive of judicially determined rights. But the data do not confirm this. In the areas of civil rights,[17] abortion,[18] school prayer and religion, and criminal defendants' rights, even authoritative Supreme Court pronouncements appear to have negligible effect on public opinion.[19]

The negligible 'educative effect' of constitutional rights on the public was dramatically illustrated by a major 1989 study which found that American young people are committed not to human rights but rather, in one respondent's words, to 'freedom to do as we please when we please'.[20] When asked 'what makes America special', the responses suggested lifestyle and cultural issues – not democratic rights or civil liberties. One focus group, 'asked to name qualities that make this country special, . . . sat in silence until one young man offered, "Cable TV"'.[21]

Protecting political dissent: the First Amendment in cultural context

Compared to most other countries, the United States has done exceedingly well in protecting political dissent. The reason, it is generally believed, is the formal constitutional guarantee: 'Congress shall make no law . . . abridging the freedom of speech'. And the First Amendment is among the most well-known and copied rights-guarantees outside of the United States. As one British scholar notes, 'exporting the First Amendment may well be the most significant contribution the United States makes to international legal culture towards the end of the twentieth century'.[22]

---

15 A Mason (1989) 'A Bill of Rights for Australia?' 5 *Australian Bar Review* 79.

16 Note (1977) 'Implementation Problems in Institutional Reform Litigation' 91 *Harvard Law Review* 428, 463.

17 See GN Rosenberg (1991) *The Hollow Hope: Can Courts Bring about Social Change?*, University of Chicago Press, ch 4.

18 See ibid, chs 6, 8.

19 See GN Rosenberg (1998) 'The Irrelevant Court: The Supreme Court's Inability to Influence Popular Beliefs about Equality (or Anything Else)', in N Devins and D Douglas (eds), *Redefining Equality*, Oxford, pp 172–90.

20 People for the American Way (1989) *Democracy's Next Generation: A Study of Youth and Teachers*, People for the American Way, p 14.

21 Ibid, pp 9, 28, 67.

22 E Barendt (1994) 'Free Speech in Australia: A Comparative Perspective' 16 *Sydney Law Review* 149.

The historical record, however, does not support this understanding. Until the late 20th century – from the Alien and Sedition Acts to the Civil War to the repression of the First World War and the silencing of labour and left-wing activists in subsequent decades – the First Amendment gave little protection to political dissent.[23] The great free speech opinions of Justices Holmes and Brandeis, for example, in cases like *Abrams v US*,[24] *Gitlow v NY*,[25] and *Whitney v California*,[26] were either concurrences or dissents in which convictions for speeches critical of the government were upheld. Not until 1965 did the Supreme Court invalidate a Congressional Act on free speech grounds.[27] And, of course, the First Amendment was entirely useless in protecting the speech rights of African-Americans. If the United States is offered as an example of how constitutional provisions protect the right to criticise government, then almost all US history must be ignored.

This point is well illustrated by the treatment of political dissent during the Cold War. In 1940, the federal *Smith Act* (passed with only four votes against) made it a crime to advocate the forceful overthrow of the US Government, or to be a member of a group advocating such action.[28] In July 1948, the American Communist Party (CPUSA)'s national leaders were indicted under the Act. The Supreme Court upheld their convictions.[29] The government then indicted nearly 150 secondary CPUSA leaders, convicting more than 100.[30] Party leaders who served their terms and were released from prison were then re-arrested and charged with violating the Act's 'membership' clause. Again, the Court upheld this.[31]

This attack on political dissent also can be seen in a host of other Bills. The *Taft-Hartley Act* of 1947[32] denied the protection of the *National Labor Relations Act* to any union unless its officers filed affidavits swearing that they did not believe in, or belong to any organisation that believed in, the

---

23 RJ Goldstein (1978) *Political Repression in Modern America from 1870 to the Present*, Shenkman; PL Murphy (1979) *World War I and the Origins of Civil Liberties in the United States*, WW Norton; RB Nye (1963) *Fettered Freedom*, Michigan State University Press (on the 1830–60 period); W Preston Jr (1963) *Aliens and Dissenters*, Harper & Row (on the 1903–33 period); DM Rabban (1981) 'The First Amendment in its Forgotten Years' 90 *Yale Law Journal* 514; L Whipple (1927) *The Story of Civil Liberty in the United States*, Vanguard.

24 250 US 616 (1919).

25 268 US 45 (1925).

26 274 US 357 (1927).

27 *Lamont v Postmaster General* 381 US 301 (1965).

28 *Aliens Registration Act* 54 Stat 670 (1940).

29 *Dennis v US* 341 US 494 (1951). Only Justices Black and Douglas dissented.

30 JW Peltason (1954) 'Constitutional Liberty and the Communist Problem' in AH Kelly (ed), *Foundations of Freedom in the American Constitution*, Harpers, p 119; R Mollan (1965) 'Smith Act Prosecutions: The Effect of the *Dennis* and *Yates* Decisions' 26 *University of Pittsburgh Law Review* 705 at 708–10. In *Yates v US* 354 US 298 (1957), the Supreme Court reversed the convictions of five defendants (and remanded nine for new trials).

31 *Scales v US* 367 US 203 (1961).

32 *National Labor Relations Act* 61 Stat 136 (1947).

forcible overthrow of the US Government. The Supreme Court upheld this in 1950,[33] and the National Labor Relations Board estimated that 1947 to 1957 saw 'at least 1,500,000 individual affidavits filed'.[34] There was also, of course, the famous House Un-American Activities Committee. Relying on the spotlight of exposure, and supported Congress's contempt powers, it probed the political beliefs of Americans, their colleagues and friends. Repeated First Amendment challenges were unsuccessful.[35]

Efforts were also made at all levels of government to purge political dissidents from employment.[36] Executive orders and Congressional legislation required investigations into the loyalty of every person seeking or holding federal employment. Basic procedural safeguards, including the right to cross-examine witnesses, were not respected. By 1955, at least nine million Americans were covered by federal programs and about half the States required them for their employees, including teachers.[37] By the end of 1956, approximately 11,500 Americans had lost their jobs under loyalty-security programs.[38]

By 1958, 35 States had prohibited parties or individuals advocating violent overthrow of government from running for office.[39] As late as 1968 Minnesota denied the Communist Party a place on the ballot,[40] and not until 1974 did the courts invalidate Indiana's exclusion of the Communist Party from the ballot.[41] Other State governmental action prevented dissidents 'becoming lawyers, jurors, or accountants and (in Indiana) . . . professional boxers'.[42]

---

33 *American Communications Association v Douds* 339 US 382 (1950).

34 Cited in N Dorsen, P Bender and B Neuborne (1976) *Emerson, Haber, and Dorsen's Political and Civil Rights in the United States* (4th edn), Little, Brown, Vol 1, p 110.

35 See, for example, *Barenblatt v US* 360 US 109 (1959), and *Uphaus v Wyman* 360 US 72 (1959).

36 In general, see E Bontecou (1953) *The Federal Loyalty-Security Program*, Cornell University Press; RS Brown Jr (1958) *Loyalty and Security: Employment Tests in the United States*, Yale University Press; E Latham (1966) *The Communist Controversy in Washington*, Harvard University Press; *Report of the Special Committee on the Federal Loyalty-Security Program of the Association of the Bar of the City of New York* (1956) Dodd, Mead. For a brief history with special emphasis on court cases, see Dorsen et al (1976), pp 13–53.

37 HH Hyman (1964) 'England and America: Climates of Tolerance and Intolerance' in D Bell (ed), *The Radical Right*, Anchor, pp 289 (n 35), 290. New York City, for example, even required a loyalty oath for subway conductors (upheld in *Lerner v Casey* 357 US 468 (1958)).

38 AF Westin (1954) 'Constitutional Liberty and Loyalty Programs', in Kelly, pp 208, 211; Brown (1958), Appendix A, pp 487–8.

39 K Barber (1966) 'The Legal Status of the American Communist Party: 1965' 15 *Journal of Public Law* 94 at 103 n 92.

40 Dorsen et al (1976), p 89.

41 *Communist Party of Indiana v Whitcomb* 414 US 441 (1974).

42 DC Kramer (1982) *Comparative Civil Rights and Liberties*, University Press of America, p 49.

Professional organisations also stifled dissent. Led by the American Bar Association which voted in 1951 to expel any member who 'advocates Marxism-Leninism',[43] many States excluded lawyers and bar candidates they considered subversive. The Supreme Court upheld most such exclusions.[44] The motion picture industry, with its infamous Hollywood Blacklist, acted in similar fashion

In the 1960s and 1970s, government at all levels took steps to harass civil rights and anti-Vietnam War activists, viewing their activities through a Cold War lens. The FBI put Dr Martin Luther King Jr under surveillance[45] and the Black Panthers were harassed, with numerous arrests, although few convictions.[46] In 1968 a group of anti-war leaders including Dr Benjamin Spock and Rev William Sloane Coffin were convicted of conspiracy to counsel, aid and abet draft resistance.[47] The Federal Government's massive surveillance of the lawful political actions of countless Americans was upheld by the Supreme Court.[48] United States Senator Charles Goodell, a Republican critic of the war, discovered that his phone was tapped.[49] And the FBI kept a 'confidential file on the United States Supreme Court from 1932 until at least 1985'.[50]

While most Americans retained the right to participate in political debate during the Cold War, that right was protected only so long as they communicated 'acceptable' ideas. When they did not, neither the First Amendment nor the courts protected their rights. As Mark Twain put it: 'in our country we have those three unspeakably precious things: freedom of speech, freedom of conscience, and the prudence never to practice either of them'.[51] By ignoring US experience, and by ignoring the broader societal context of unequal wealth, status, and power, proponents of Bills of Rights overlook the reality of political practice.

This point is strengthened by comparing the treatment accorded political dissidents by the United Kingdom and France during the same period.

---

43 (1951) 37 *ABA Journal* 312–13.

44 See, for example, *Konigsberg v California* 366 US 36 (1961); *In re Anastaplo* 366 US 82 (1961); *Law Students Civil Rights Research Council v Wadmond* 401 US 154 (1971). In general, see Dorsen et al (1976), pp 114–31; J Auerbach (1976) *Unequal Justice*, Oxford University Press, ch 8.

45 DJ Garrow (1981) *The FBI and Martin Luther King Jr*, Penguin.

46 C Goodell (1978) *Political Prisoners in America*, Random House, pp 110–25.

47 On appeal, the conviction was overturned. *United States v Spock* 416 F 2d 165 (1st Cir 1969). For brief discussion of other conspiracy indictments for anti-Vietnam war activities, see C Goodell (1978) *Political Prisoners in America*, Random House, ch 9.

48 *Laird v Tatum* 408 US 1 (1972). On the extent of government surveillance, see Note (1972) 'The National Security Interest and Civil Liberties' 85 *Harvard Law Review* 1130.

49 C Goodell (1978) *Political Prisoners in America*, Random House, p 261.

50 'FBI Kept Secret Files on the Supreme Court' (1988) *New York Times*, Nat Ed, 21 August, sec 1-13.

51 Quoted in LC Bollinger (1986) *The Tolerant Society*, Oxford University Press, p 7.

Neither had a full-fledged First Amendment or a tradition of judicial review. Both Britain and France were 'weaker militarily and economically' than the United States, and nearer to the Soviet Union.[52] While the United States suffered some espionage, the 'English had their Fuchs, their Pontecorvo, their Burgess and MacLean, and still others',[53] and the French a Communist Party polling roughly 20 per cent of the vote. Shapiro notes that the United States, by contrast, had only the 'whole pitifully ineffective record of the Communist movement'[54] and points out that despite massive FBI work, the best case the government could bring against American Communists was 'conspiracy to advocate', not any actual espionage or violence.[55]

Britain and France both did a substantially better job of protecting political dissent than the United States. While there were some dismissals from government employment for security reasons in Britain, they were minimal. Employees were accorded many due process rights and, where charges were upheld, were allowed transfers to non-sensitive posts where possible.[56] No action was taken against unions, teachers, or other professionals. France acted in much the way Britain did, making use of administrative transfers.[57] The French Assembly did not enact anti-dissent laws like its American counterpart.

This comparison shows that in protecting Cold War political dissidents, the British, although lacking formal constitutional protection, did an excellent job while the French, with some constitutional protection, also did well. The United States, however, with the strongest constitutional protection, did the least well. Indeed, Cold-War US treatment of political dissent stands out among Western democracies, characterised by Dahl as a 'deviant case',[58] and by Shapiro as 'pathological'.[59] This leaves a puzzle. Why did the United States do so poorly?

The First Amendment in cultural context

Constitutions are interpreted and enforced within a given political culture. Many students of the United States see in its political culture rigid pressures

---

52 Hyman (1964), p 274. Hyman was writing about Britain but his statements fit France as well.

53 Hyman (1964), p 276.

54 M Shapiro (1966) *Freedom of Speech: The Supreme Court and Judicial Review*, Prentice-Hall, p 134.

55 Ibid, p 125.

56 MR Joelson (1963) 'The Dismissal of Civil Servants in the Interests of National Security' *Public Law* 51 pp 54–6; Hyman (1964).

57 MR Joelson (1963) 'Legal Problems in the Dismissal of Civil Servants in the United States, Britain, and France' 12 *American Journal of Comparative Law* 149 at 168.

58 RA Dahl (1966) 'Epilogue' in RA Dahl (ed), *Political Oppositions in Western Democracies*, Yale University Press, p 391.

59 Shapiro (1966), p 109.

for conformity alongside important beliefs in freedom. Tocqueville famously worried about the uniformity of American culture and the 'tyranny of the majority'. Once the majority makes up its mind, 'everyone is silent, and friends and enemies alike seem to make for its bandwagon'. The price for dissenting, Tocqueville wrote, in language chillingly similar to the 1950s blacklists, was to be cast out of the social fabric: 'even those who believe in your innocence will abandon you too, lest they in turn be shunned'.[60]

This suggests that the protection afforded dissent is governed less by written documents than by general notions of acceptable behaviour. Tocqueville, like others, 'insisted that America was held together not by its political institutions but by its widely shared values and *mœurs*'.[61] It is these beliefs that provide the framework in which political institutions operate and legal documents are interpreted.

Survey research sheds light on these beliefs. For the last 50 years, pollsters have asked Americans their views on political dissent and fundamental democratic freedoms. Overall, responses clearly show that Americans are both deeply committed to free speech in the abstract *and* strongly opposed to free speech for unpopular groups[62] – such as 'radicals' or 'Fascists and Communists'.[63] In 1954 Samuel Stouffer employed 537 interviewers to interview a cross-section of 4900 Americans and 1500 selected community leaders. Ninety-one per cent supported firing a Communist high school teacher, 89 per cent a Communist professor, and 68 per cent a Communist store-clerk;[64] 77 per cent would take away a Communist's American citizenship.[65] In no other survey from 1953 to 1964 did more than 20 per cent of respondents agree that Communists should be allowed to speak on the radio.[66]

These responses were not based on fear of Communist espionage and sabotage. When asked what aspects of Communism were most troubling, only eight per cent mentioned sabotage while 28 per cent cited '*the danger of Americans today becoming converts to . . . Communist ideas*'.[67] The contrast was even more striking among community leaders. As Stouffer concluded,

---

60 A de Tocqueville [1835] in JP Mayer (ed) (1969) *Democracy in America*, Anchor, pp 252, 254, 256.

61 JP Diggins (1988) 'Class, Classical, and Consensus Views of the Constitution' 55 *University of Chicago Law Review* 570.

62 OPR and Gallup polls, cited in H Erskine (1970) 'The Polls: Freedom of Speech' 34 *Public Opinion Quarterly* 483 at 485–6. H McClosky and J Zaller (1984) *The American Ethos: Public Attitudes toward Capitalism and Democracy*, Harvard University Press, p 17.

63 Cited in Erskine (1970), p 489.

64 In contrast, in Britain after the John Lewis department stores began to require signed statements from employees as to their political beliefs in 1949, a nationwide poll found that 78 per cent disapproved. HH Wilson and H Glickman (1954) *The Problem of Internal Security in Great Britain 1948–1953*, Doubleday, p 66.

65 SA Stouffer (1963) *Communism, Conformity, and Civil Liberties: A Cross-Section of the Nation Speaks Its Mind*, Peter Smith, pp 40, 43.

66 Erskine (1970), p 488.

67 Stouffer (1963), p 158, 160 (emphasis in original).

'substantial proportions of the American population are intolerant *in spite of the fact* that they perceive relatively little internal Communist threat'.[68]

As noted above, the Cold War stifling of dissent is not unique in United States history. Further, majority opposition to protecting the rights of political dissidents remains strong. In surveys in 1976 and 1978, Sullivan et al asked respondents a series of questions about those groups they most disliked. In 1978 they found, for example, that only 16 per cent would *not* ban a member of the group they most disliked from being President, only 19 per cent would allow a member to teach in public schools, and only 29 per cent would *not* outlaw the group.[69]

There is also evidence that younger Americans are not committed to basic democratic rights. In the survey of over 1,000 young Americans noted above, when asked which rights they would fight hardest to keep, barely one-third chose freedom of speech, barely one in 10 the right to vote, and almost nobody (one in 100!) a free press.

What then explains why the United States has unequivocal constitutional guarantees, an independent and active judiciary – but, at the same time, a history of repressing political dissent? It is, I suggest, the political culture. It is not the Constitution as a document distinct and removed from it, nor a judicial system independent and apart. The 'central norms of the constitutional regime', Blasi writes, 'depend for their effectiveness on the attitudes of the political community'.[70] As Peltason puts it, 'the amount of free expression we get is in large measure the amount of free expression we want'.[71]

This is the pattern in other countries. In a comparative study of Communist parties and high courts, Sheldon found that the 'decisive factor' in explaining why 'Communist parties are treated differently in similar constitutional systems' is 'the content of the political climate'.[72] Cole, too, in his comparison of three constitutional courts, finds that their functioning 'depends heavily upon the nature of the social structures within which they operate'.[73]

Is it really sensible to expect 'parchment barriers' to preserve freedom? The United States Framers didn't think so. Hamilton, in *Federalist 84*, argued that 'liberty of the press . . . whatever fine declarations may be in-

---

68 Ibid, p 208.

69 JL Sullivan, J Pierson and GE Marcus (1979) 'An Alternate Conceptualisation of Political Tolerance: Illusory Increases 1950s–1970s' 73 *American Political Science Review* 781 at 787.

70 V Blasi (1985) 'The Pathological Perspective and the First Amendment' 85 *Columbia Law Review* 449 at 462.

71 Peltason (1954), p 109. See also Z Chafee Jr (1942) *Free Speech in the United States*, Harvard University Press, p 564; Z Chafee Jr (1947) *Government and Mass Communications: A Report from the Commission on Freedom of the Press*, University of Chicago Press, p 35.

72 CH Sheldon (1965) 'Constitutionalism: A Comparative Study of Communist Parties and High Courts', dissertation, University of Oregon, pp 16–17, 301–2.

73 T Cole (1959) 'Three Constitutional Courts: A Comparison' 53 *American Political Science Review* 963 at 970.

serted in any constitution . . . must altogether depend on . . . the general spirit of the people and of the government'.[74] Madison, too, distrusted 'parchment barriers'[75] which 'will never be regarded when opposed to the decided sense of the public'.[76] Our focus needs to be on culture and structure, not constitutions.

The downside

As shown, the United States Constitution has not done a good job in protecting human rights. But has it harmed them? If not, then its potential for positive results may still make a Bill of Rights worth the effort. United States experience suggests, however, it presents dangers to human rights.

Bills of Rights give added protection and power to concentrations of wealth. When corporations are considered individuals for constitutional purposes, they can invoke constitutional protections. In the United States, historically, business interests made use of the Due Process Clause to block government regulation for nearly half a century. More recently, in campaign finance, the United States, virtually alone among Western democracies, allows corporations and the wealthy to spend without limit, distorting the political process.[77]

A Bill of Rights can derail governmental attempts to improve the treatment of minorities and the relatively disadvantaged, the very groups such constitutional provisions are often designed to help. When rights are defined as individual, as they are understood to be in the United States Constitution, it becomes easy to ignore the fact that individuals live and act in a broader society. So the 'right' of an individual to spew forth hateful words about minorities and the disadvantaged is protected: there can be no inquiry into the broader harm it may do. Similarly, pornography is protected and arguments that it may harm women are derided as 'thought control'[78] because they interfere with the rights of an individual to produce pornography. In the area of race relations, affirmative action in employment and education are seen as no different from the race-based segregation the United States officially practised for so long.[79] Since both use race as a

74 *The Federalist Papers*, Mentor edn (1961), p 514.

75 Ibid, p 308.

76 Letter of 17 October 1788.

77 *Buckley v Valeo* 424 US 1 (1976); *National Bank of Boston v Bellotti*, 435 US 765 (1978). See, GN Rosenberg and JM Williams, 'Do Not Go Gently into That Good Right: The First Amendment in the High Court of Australia' (1998) *1997 Supreme Court Review* 439.

78 *American Booksellers Association v Hudnut* 771 F 2d 323 (7th Cir 1985), *affirmed* without opinion, 475 US 1001 (1986).

79 In *Adarand Constructors Inc v Peña* 515 US 200 (1995), Justice Thomas, concurring, wrote, 'there is a 'moral [and] constitutional equivalence' between laws designed to subjugate a race and those that distribute benefits on the basis of race in order to foster some current notion of equality'.

factor, they are understood in the abstract as denying individual rights, without any consideration of social context.

The broader point is that rights-based talk can turn public debate away from concerns with justice and fairness towards a more limited focus on abstract rights.[80] While Dworkin is right in stressing the importance of individual rights in any just society,[81] no individual is an island. Guaranteeing equal opportunity may mean limiting individual choice. Creating a civil society that respects everyone may mean denying individuals the right to discriminate. Reducing deadly violence may mean limiting an individual's right to own firearms. In the late 20th century version of the abortion debate in the United States, the rhetorical issue is a clash between the 'right' of a woman to choose and the 'right' of the foetus to life. There are, however, many other issues involved in abortion policy – including the danger of illegal abortions; battered and abandoned children; the cost of caring for children with horrendous genetic abnormalities; and so forth. These issues are not discussed in the United States because they are not relevant to the rights issue. The focus on individual rights created by a Bill of Rights effectively precludes policy debates where various factors can be weighed in favour of a clash of abstract rights, where such factors are seen as unprincipled and irrelevant.

Democratic demobilisation and the politics of irresponsibility

A Bill of Rights can actually make rights harder to obtain. This is because protecting and furthering human rights requires democratic engagement by the population at large. With constitutional Bills of Rights, however, the temptation is to leave their interpretation and enforcement to the courts. James Bradley Thayer, writing in 1901, was concerned that reliance on litigation would sap the democratic process of its vitality. He warned that the 'tendency of a common and easy resort' to the courts, especially in asking them to invalidate acts of the democratically accountable branches, would 'dwarf the political capacity of the people'.[82] Reliance on the Court seriously weakened the political efficacy of US pro-choice forces. After the 1973 Supreme Court decisions finding a constitutional right to abortion, many pro-choice activists simply assumed they had won and stopped their political activity. The political organisation and momentum that had changed laws nationwide dissipated in celebration of Court victory. In practice, that victory has proved hollow, with abortion services difficult to obtain in many

80 MA Glendon (1991) *Rights Talk: The Impoverishment of Political Discourse*, Free Press.

81 See RM Dworkin (1977) *Taking Rights Seriously*, Harvard University Press.

82 JB Thayer (1901) *John Marshall*, Houghton, Mifflin, p 107. See also MV Tushnet (1999) *Taking the Constitution Away from the Courts*, Princeton University Press.

parts of the United States.[83] By winning a Court case 'without the organisation needed to cope with a powerful opposition',[84] pro-choice forces vastly overestimated the Court's power.

Reliance on courts also allows politicians to act in irresponsible ways, which makes creating a supportive political culture more difficult. It frees them to grandstand to satisfy extreme groups knowing full well that the courts will invalidate their actions. Father Frank Brennan, SJ, who after returning from a study tour in the United States declared himself an 'Australian Convert from a Constitutional Bill of Rights',[85] noted this:

> The bill of rights has probably given politicians greater licence over time to pass the buck to the judges. . . . Politicians can pass laws for the display of the Ten Commandments knowing they will be struck down. They can wildly promise to ban abortion – even in cases of rape – knowing that the courts will not permit it. Meanwhile, they satisfy their more fundamentalist constituents.[86]

Symbolism and legitimacy

A further danger of litigation as a strategy for furthering human rights is that symbolic victories may be mistaken for substantive ones, covering a reality that is distasteful. Rather than working to change that reality, reformers relying on constitutional rights may be misled (or content?) to celebrate the illusion of change. There is a danger that symbolic gains cover for actual failings.

A final danger is that a Bill of Rights may convince people that any governmental practice that is upheld by the courts must be fine. That is, if an independent judiciary upholds governmental action against a charge that it violates human rights, then people may uncritically accept that decision. This danger is nicely illustrated by the editorial reaction of a major Texas paper, the *Fort Worth Star-Telegram*, to the US Supreme Court's decision in the *Dennis Case*, upholding the jailing of the leadership of the CPUSA for its speeches: 'We cannot feel that the Supreme Court's decision endangers any of the fundamental American rights'.[87] Repressive governmental action is thus bestowed with constitutional legitimacy.

What is to be done?

If the clamour for a Bill of Rights to protect human rights is little more than constitutional cant, and if the protection of human rights is something

83 GN Rosenberg (1995) 'The Real World of Constitutional Rights: The Supreme Court and the Implementation of the Abortion Decisions' in L Epstein (ed), *Contemplating Courts*, Congressional Quarterly Press, pp 390–419.

84 ER Rubin (1982) *Abortion, Politics, and the Courts*, Greenwood, p 169.

85 (1996) 7 *Public Law Review* 132.

86 'One Vote No' (1996) 6 *Eureka Street* 21.

87 Quoted in J Lofton (1980) *The Press as Guardians of the First Amendment*, University of South Carolina Press, p 241.

constitutions can't do without a broad-based societal commitment, how can such a commitment be created? An accurate understanding of the United States experience suggests that adopting constitutional protections for human rights is neither necessary nor sufficient for creating such a commitment. What can make a difference is the legislative enactment of rights that are, absolutely crucially, enforced and funded by governments to induce implementation.

There are several reasons why this can make a difference to the protection of human rights. Firstly, in order to enact legislation a majority of democratically elected officials must be willing to support it. Legislators tend not to take actions lacking support among large segments of the population. This is particularly the case when the expenditure of money is involved. While the public rarely follows legislative debate, when money is at stake interest groups do. They, in turn, can mobilise members and involve the population in large in the issue. This mobilisation can help create the commitment necessary for human rights to be protected.

The provision of resources to induce implementation is key. If legislation is enacted furthering human rights, and if those whose actions are essential to implementation are given an incentive to implement, change can occur. Once change occurs, and is institutionalised, everyday behaviour will start to change. The force of these two factors, legislation and the provision of resources, can be seen in the US experience with public school desegregation.[88]

Although the Supreme Court outlawed racial segregation in public schools in 1954,[89] a decade later barely one in 100 (1.2 per cent) African-American children living in the 11 States of the former Confederacy that required race-based school segregation by law was in a non-segregated school. For nearly 99 of every 100 African-American children in the South a decade after *Brown*, the finding of a constitutional right changed nothing. In the mid-1960s, however, the United States political system, responding to the civil rights movement, enacted legislation prohibiting race-based discrimination in any program receiving federal funds and provided large sums of federal money to generally poor Southern school districts. This combination of federal funding and the prohibition of racial discrimination gave the executive branch a tool to induce desegregation when it chose to do so. By the 1972–3 school year, over 91 per cent of African-American school children in the 11 Southern States were in integrated schools, up from 1.2 per cent in the 1963–4 school year. School desegregation occurred in the years 1968–72, then, not because of the Bill of Rights but because legislation provided incentives to desegregate and imposed costs for failing to do so.

It is sometimes suggested that there is an alternative between the stark choice of adopting or not adopting a Bill of Rights. Perhaps, for exam-

---

88 The material that follows is based on Rosenberg (1991), ch 3.

89 *Brown v Board of Education*, 347 US 483 (1954).

ple, Australia might adopt a Bill of Rights as an aid to statutory construction (as in New Zealand) or, if constitutionally entrenched, with a legislative override (as in Canada).[90] The difficulty these alternatives present is that the rights they protect will inevitably become the province of the judiciary, with all the problems for the protection of human rights that I have outlined. In Canada, for example, the legislative override quickly became seen as illegitimate, further empowering the courts. The legislative provision of rights and resources remains the best hope for protecting and furthering human rights.

Conclusion: constitutional cants

Constitutions exist in cultural context. Changing constitutions without first changing the culture in which they will operate is unlikely to further human rights. Problems that are unsolvable in the political context can rarely be solved by courts. As Scheingold puts it, the 'law can hardly transcend the conflicts of the political system in which it is embedded'.[91] Turning to courts to protect and enhance human rights substitutes the myth of constitutional change for the reality of political practice. It credits courts, constitutions, and judicial decisions with a power that they do not have.

Proposals to constitutionalise human rights without first creating broad societal support for such rights are examples of the 'lawyers' vision of change without pain'.[92] It is so much easier to write flowery language than to organise political movements. It is much easier for lawyers and academics to deal with each other than to organise less educated working-class citizens. Thus, it is understandable that so many dedicated proponents of human rights succumb to the 'lure of litigation' as a way of enhancing human rights protections. But while principled arguments are cleaner than partisan, precinct, politics, they are less likely to make a difference. The challenge for those who wish to enhance human rights is to learn how to change societal understandings. The United States experience suggests that constitutionalising rights is not likely the way to go.

90 As recommended for Australia by JL Hiebert (1999) 'Why Must a Bill of Rights be a Contest of Political and Judicial Wills? The Canadian Alternative' 10 *Public Law Review* 22.

91 SA Scheingold (1974) *The Politics of Rights*, Yale University Press, p 145.

92 Ibid.

19

Law's Laws

The Demand and Supply of Rights

Neil Komesar

When United States lawyers and legal scholars use the term 'constitutional law', they generally mean court-made law. When they use the term 'constitutional rights', they mean court-based constraints on the political process. This emphasis on courts and rights is by no means exclusively associated with the United States. It has been developed in various forms by many Western democracies. In fact, this vision of law and rights is exported globally under labels like the Rule of Law and constitutionalism. A strong judicial presence and strong legal rights are seen as providing the protection of property and the individual that allows markets and democracies to flourish.[1]

But these hopes for courts, rights and law are bound to be frustrated by systemic forces operating through supply and demand. The same forces that produce the call for law and rights cause a deterioration in their functioning. The same forces that increase the demand for law and rights diminish their supply. These forces are increasing in intensity as globalisation increases the complexity of societal issues. The impact of these forces requires us to re-examine the role of law and rights and the associated role of courts. There may be an important role for law, rights and courts, but it cannot be facilely defined.

Court-made law and rights are the product of a process – the adjudicative process – filled with limitations and trade-offs. This process relies on a dynamics of litigation in which skewed patterns of participation can distort results. Its elaborate procedures raise the cost of participation and reduce access to information. It has limited physical resources and its growth is constrained by the bottleneck of an appellate system installed to

1 CR Sunstein, 'On Property and Constitutionalism' (1993) 14 *Cardozo Law Review* 907; BA Ackerman, 'The Rise of World Constitutionalism' (1997) 83 *Virginia Law Review* 771; TM Franck, 'The Emerging Right to Democratic Governance' (1992) 86 *American Journal of International Law* 46.

produce consistency and oversight but which also restricts the range of issues capable of judicial action. This is the supply side of law.

But if we want to allocate these limited judicial resources appropriately, we must consider more than the courts. Law and the courts are most needed where alternative decision-makers like political processes, markets and informal communities severely malfunction. If we focus solely on questions of supply and, therefore, solely on the characteristics and imperfections of the courts, we will waste law by using it where it is least needed. In order to understand what law is or ought to be, we must consider demand as well as supply; we must consider the character of political processes, markets and communities as well as the character of the courts.

Analysing constitutional law, rights and judicial review by joining supply and demand means facing a fundamental quandary: *The greatest need for judicial protection and legal rights is likely to occur in those settings in which it is most difficult to deliver this protection.* Institutions like courts, markets and political processes tend to move together. They all deteriorate as the number of people affected by societal decisions and the complexity of these decisions increase. Because numbers and complexity are increasing, this fundamental quandary is growing in significance. This quandary is structural and it cannot be avoided by distinctions between principle and policy or by imagining courts as promoting deliberation or reinforcing democracy or by any of the romantic imagery common to constitutional inquiry.

In order to explore these themes in this limited space, I will focus on United States constitutional law and on one case in particular.[2] The lessons drawn from this context should help to understand the broader problems facing the globalisation of constitutionalism and the Rule of Law. Factors like numbers and complexity are important in understanding all institutions and all legal systems. The need to see law in terms of systemic factors and difficult institutional choices rather than simply in terms of values, goals and disembodied principles is universal. This essay proposes a fundamental change in the way we think about constitutional rights and about law and rights in general.

The challenge presented by these systemic factors and difficult choices is exhibited in a peculiar but poignant way in a 1985 decision of then Supreme Court of the United States, *City of Cleburne v Cleburne Living Center Inc.*[3] *Cleburne* shows the United States Supreme Court struggling with the role of the federal courts under the Equal Protection Clause – for at least 50 years, one of the major sources of United States judicial activism. In *Cleburne*, this struggle produces a clouded, shaky and strange decision. Yet, if we do not come to better understand the forces of supply and demand, institutional

2 The themes are more extensively developed in my new book, *Law's Limits: The Role of Courts, the Rule of Law and the Supply and Demand of Rights* (2001, Cambridge University Press).

3 473 US 432 (1985).

choice and the implications of increased numbers and complexity, this curious decision represents the future of constitutional jurisprudence.

The main plaintiff in the case, Cleburne Living Center Inc (CLC), wanted to operate a group home for the mentally retarded in Cleburne, Texas.[4] But local zoning regulations prohibited such homes unless specially permitted. CLC applied for such a special permit, but the city council denied its request. CLC sued, alleging that the Cleburne zoning ordinance discriminated against the mentally retarded in violation of the Equal Protection Clause of the United States Constitution.

Under standard equal protection analysis, the fate of such a claim depends on the level of judicial scrutiny applied. Employing this analysis, the District Court, not finding 'mental retardation' on the list of suspect or quasi-suspect classifications, applied minimal scrutiny to the government's actions. Minimal scrutiny generally means no scrutiny and, predictably, the Cleburne ordinance easily passed this highly deferential standard. The Circuit Court of Appeals for the Fifth Circuit, however, decided that the mentally retarded should be considered a quasi-suspect class and, therefore, applied heightened scrutiny. Under this more serious judicial scrutiny, the Circuit Court invalidated the Cleburne ordinance.

Although the District and Circuit Courts differed in their perceptions of the correct scrutiny, each attached the predictable result to its chosen level of scrutiny. The Supreme Court of the United States, however, mixed and matched results from the two courts below. Like the District Court, the Supreme Court applied – or claimed to be applying – minimal scrutiny. Like the Circuit Court, however, the Supreme Court found the provision as applied to the plaintiffs in the case unconstitutional. Something made the justices uncomfortable and it showed. Although all the justices concurred in the conclusion of unconstitutionality, there was wide disagreement about the basis and coverage of the decision.

The majority in *Cleburne* insisted it was only applying minimal scrutiny. The dissenting and concurring opinions showed convincingly that the majority was doing more. Even if the dissenting and concurring judges had not blown the whistle, however, powerful supply side realities tell us the majority justices were either fooling themselves or us. In theory, the language of the Equal Protection Clause and the concept of equal protection can accommodate judicial review of all governmental action. Every law involves non-uniform treatment of citizens. If minimal scrutiny meant serious examination of all issues of equality, then every law is subject to serious judicial review. But the size and competence of the judiciary can accommodate at most only a tiny fraction of that potential. The remainder must be left to the neglect of real minimal (meaning, zero) judicial scrutiny.

---

4 I recognise that the term 'mentally retarded' is not the most contemporary or thoughtful. Since the term was used in the case, however, I use it here to avoid confusion.

For at least the last 50 years, the United States courts have struggled to define the tiny fraction of legislation that is subject to serious judicial review. When courts or commentators have given thought to the institutional factors that define this judicial role, they have turned to demand-side notions: courts should review those instances of government action in which there is serious political malfunction and, therefore, serious reason to distrust the political process. This demand-side approach has surfaced often in constitutional law and is reflected throughout the *Cleburne* opinions.[5]

But demand without supply – like supply without demand – provides an inadequate analysis. We can see the problems in this one-sided approach by exploring a basic bromide of United States equal protection theories raised in *Cleburne*. Since the mid-1930s, most so-called 'economic classifications' have received virtually no judicial scrutiny. The conventional explanation is that legislation involving 'economic classifications' is not subject to serious and systemic political malfunction or, as put in *Cleburne*, because this legislation does not adversely impact a class with a 'tradition of disfavour'.[6] With all due respect, this conventional wisdom is simply wrong.

The two classes most frequently and systematically disfavoured by legislation are consumers and taxpayers. These dormant majorities are systematically underrepresented in favour of concentrated special interests. Moreover, the impacts of this political malfunction are serious and fall disproportionately on those with lower income. The legislation produced by this minoritarian bias commonly employs economic classifications. If this sort of legislation is presumed constitutional, the reason lies not in the absence of problems in the political process but in the presence of problems in the adjudicative process. Supply side problems accompany increasing demand-side needs.

Before turning to these supply side problems, however, I need to clarify the demand side. I just described a political malfunction where concentrated minorities are over-represented to the detriment of dispersed majorities. This form of political malfunction is the backbone of the interest group theory of politics. I call it minoritarian bias. But the political malfunction at issue in *Cleburne* is not minoritarian bias. It is its polar opposite, majoritarian bias – the overrepresentation of a majority (the local homeowners) to the detriment of a concentrated minority (the mentally retarded).

As I have shown elsewhere, the interaction and choice between these two polar opposite forms of political malfunction is crucial to understanding

5 This approach traces back at least to the famous *Carolene Products* Footnote 4 and has been articulated by many commentators, most prominently, John Hart Ely. For my critique of Ely's theory, see NK Komesar (1994) *Imperfect Alternatives: Choosing Institutions in Law, Economics, and Public Policy*, University of Chicago Press, pp 198–215.

6 This reasoning appears most explicitly in Justice Stevens's concurring opinion in *Cleburne* at 935–6.

the demand side of law and rights.[7] This 'two-force' model of politics includes both the power of the few and the power of the many in one analytical framework. Political malfunction is conceived in terms of skewed patterns of participation and, therefore, of skewed patterns of representation in the political process. The 'two-force' model exposes the conditions under which one or the other version of political malfunction is more likely and, therefore, it informs an essential element in defining the role of the courts, especially constitutional courts.

Minoritarian bias, captured in the interest group theory of politics, depends on a skewed distribution of the benefits of political action.[8] In the extreme but not uncommon case, the per capita impact on each member of the dispersed majority is so low that it does not even justify the expenditure of resources necessary to recognise the issue involved. Even if members of the dispersed majority recognise the impact of the legislation, there is an incentive to refuse to contribute and allow others to bear the costs of political participation – an incentive to free ride. If free riding is pervasive, the dispersed majority will have no political influence and everyone in the group will lose. On the other hand, the concentrated few with their substantial per capita stakes have the incentive to understand their interests, organise for political activity and determine the correct channels of influence in a complex political process. Their small numbers make organisation and collective action easier. Once they have overcome threshold or start-up costs, subsequent activity becomes less expensive. From this vantage, it is easy to see why the dominant image of the political process and its biases is minoritarian.

There is, however, a significant range of variation for each of these factors which can produce significant variation in the dormancy of the many and, therefore, the dominance of the few. As the *absolute* per capita stakes for the majority increase (even holding constant the ratio between majoritarian and minoritarian per capita stakes), members of the majority will more likely spend the resources and effort necessary to understand an issue and recognise their interests. In turn, variation within the distribution of the per capita benefits of political action – the degree of heterogeneity – affects the probability of collective action on behalf of the majority by subgroups of higher stakes individuals. Those with higher stakes can operate as a catalytic subgroup, activating the more dormant members.

On the cost side, the probability of majoritarian response varies as the costs of political action vary. These costs depend, in part, on characteristics of the political process such as the size and population of the jurisdiction, the size of the legislature, frequency of election, size and scope

7 See Komesar (1994), ch 3 for an extensive consideration of political malfunction and the advantages of the two-force model relative to the interest group theory of politics.

8 I explore the intellectual underpinnings of the interest group theory of politics in Komesar (1994), pp 55–8.

of the legislative agenda, and the rules of the political process. Smaller numbers of voters are easier to organise and it is easier to prevent free riding and, therefore, the probability of majoritarian activity increases. Smaller legislatures with fewer legislators mean that it is easier to understand the position of any legislator and, therefore, it is easier to discipline unwanted action at the ballot-box and to make the threat of such voting power known and credible.

Complexity and, therefore, the cost of information vary with the subject matter of the social issue in question. The degree to which someone understands any issue often depends on that person's endowment of general information. This endowment is determined by culture, formal education, and the coverage of the press and media. Each culture or subculture has symbols such as religion or ethnicity that are central to its members' common identity. This stock of 'simple symbols' provides certain issues with easy recognition. Because the press and the media provide cheap and accessible information, press and media response is central in determining the degree of majoritarian activity.

Taken to its logical conclusion, this analysis suggests not just that the relative advantage of the concentrated group will vary, but that there may be instances in which the larger group can dominate and even be overrepresented. This potential for domination stems from the simplest dimension of the difference between larger and smaller groups – the number of members in the two groups. In the most straightforward sense, larger numbers translate to political power via voting. The fear of majority influence has a long history and its imprint can be found in present day politics in many ways – most obviously in the tremendous effort public figures expend on public and press relations.

We can see these demand-side factors at play in *Cleburne*. Majoritarian bias is likely in *Cleburne* because the local homeowner majority will be active and, therefore, control the political process. The homeowners will be active because their stakes are large and the cost of political participation is relatively low.

Since, for most people, a house is the largest investment that they will ever make, homeowners are aware of and sensitive to risks or dangers to their property. Mental retardation provides a simple symbol to which these homeowners can react. The mentally retarded are also safe targets for mistreatment. Local homeowners are unlikely to be mentally retarded or need group homes. They can exclude these group homes with little need to count the significant cost to those they exclude. In turn, low costs of political participation allow homeowners to translate their fears into political action. Small local governments have simple agendas allowing easy monitoring by homeowners who can then sanction unpopular government actions at the ballot-box. The resulting majoritarian bias provides a demand-side reason for judicial review of the *Cleburne* ordinance.

Having explored the demand side, we can now return to the supply side. The supply side provides an explanation for the judicial treatment of 'economic classifications'. Judicial review of 'economic classifications' is negligible not because the possibility of harm to traditionally disfavoured groups is small and unimportant, but because, if anything, that possibility is so pervasive. There is too much to review and that amount will grow in the future. More importantly, it is difficult to separate valid from invalid uses of economic classifications. Serious political malfunction does not mean that all the resulting legislation is bad. It only means that there is a bias in a given direction. Some of the legislation passed by a biased political process would have been passed by an unbiased process. The presence of the good among the bad makes the task of the reviewer difficult and sensitive. Even courts distrustful of the political process would and should fear throwing out babies with bathwater, especially given the decreasing ability to discern babies from bathwater. The issue is not the absence of serious political malfunction. It is whether the adjudicative process can do better.

These sorts of supply side concerns can be found throughout the majority opinion in *Cleburne*. The Court is uncomfortable with the fact that mental retardation is a category that has many legitimate uses in legislation – both to aid the mentally retarded and, in some instances, to legitimately restrict them. That the category can often be used for legitimate purposes means that sweeping denunciations or simple rules are dangerous strategies of judicial review and, therefore, in order to review laws affecting the mentally retarded, courts must handle difficult and sensitive public policy determinations case by case. The *Cleburne* majority struggles with the possibility that heightened scrutiny by imperfect courts may negate good legislation. The majority is also concerned that designating the mentally retarded as a quasi-suspect classification would invite other similarly situated groups – such as 'the aging, the disabled, the mentally ill, and the infirm'[9] – to apply for judicial protection. Here lie concerns about both judicial competence and limited physical capacity – the fear that the courts will be swamped with difficult calls.

The *Cleburne* Court was confronted with the basic quandary with which we began: serious need for judicial protection arises in settings in which it is difficult to deliver this protection. Supply meets demand, resulting in difficult institutional choices. The Court's response to these difficult choices is at once understandable and disturbing. Although the majority's attempt to avoid characterising the mentally retarded as 'quasi-suspect' and its scrutiny as 'heightened' is unlikely to fool observers, the Court's attempt to hide the higher scrutiny – successful or not – signals the uncertain character of the judicial protection accorded in the case and the uncertain character of judicial protection in general. This uncertainty is enhanced by the narrow and

9 Ibid, p 932.

peculiar holding in the case. The result is a tortured, narrow application of a purposely confusing doctrine. *Cleburne* seems designed to have little or no prospective effect.

That only a fraction of government action is seriously reviewed or reviewable by courts and that this fraction can only decrease in the future does not negate an important role for constitutional judicial review. Even given their limited resources, United States courts have made their influence felt. The increasing deterioration of alternative decision-makers increases the need to use these scarce judicial resources carefully. But, if the pattern of judicial decisions and articulation of the relevant doctrines grow increasingly opaque, the chance of wasting these resources increases. Equal protection law has long been confusing and difficult and cases like *Cleburne* add to the confusion. All areas of constitutional law are, in reality, defined by tough compromises between supply and demand that are inconsistent with the grand rhetoric that accompanies them.[10] It is time to bring rhetoric, reasoning and analysis into line with reality.

Such a change would not require wholesale abandonment of precedent. Quite the opposite it would serve to clarify existing doctrine. Systemic and institutional issues already pervade legal outcomes and lie at the basis of established legal doctrine. One only needs to look carefully at the relationship between legal doctrine and institutional choice. At first blush, institutional choice seems to follow from legal doctrine. The role of the courts seems to be defined by a series of well-established legal constructs. Suspect classifications and fundamental rights determine the role of courts in United States equal protection law. The takings of private property triggers judicial review of just compensation. Perhaps most broadly, the construct of legitimacy determines the judicial role in general. Every area of law has a series of doctrinal constructs that seem to define the role of the courts without recourse to the comparison of institutions.

As one examines these constructs, however, a peculiar pattern appears. These constructs defy a straightforward construction based on the common meaning of their terminology. 'Fundamental rights' do not cover all or even most of what is fundamental. The 'taking of private property' falls far short of the full conceptual meaning of that term.[11] As we have just seen, the term 'suspect classification' omits many suspicious classifications. All these terms seem distorted and strained.

10 Because the same factors can impede both political and judicial decision-making, simply noting that politicians cannot be trusted with particular decisions is not enough to justify judicial activism. Too often, the areas where legislators' good faith is suspect are the same areas where judges lack institutional competence. Here institutional choice will be a close call and the advantage of one institution over another may be quite marginal. See the discussion of the *Pentagon Papers* case, *Korematsu* and *Hampton* in Komesar (1994), pp 44–9, 210–13.

11 See discussion of Richard Epstein's program for takings in Komesar (1994), pp 235–7.

There is, however, a straightforward way to understand these terms. Reverse the causality. Although, in theory, these constructs define an institutional choice (judicial intervention), in reality, they are defined by it. As *Cleburne* shows, these constructs are defined by considerations of institutional characteristics and by rough and sometimes unarticulated senses of the relative merits of judicial versus market or governmental decision-making. The various *Cleburne* judges, like the proverbial blind investigators of the elephant, each recognised bits and pieces of the systemic concerns that underlie institutional choice – suspectness here and the strains on judicial capacity there. Unfortunately, this piecemeal investigation is confused by the trappings of equal protection doctrines that are themselves piecemeal and unarticulated reactions to systemic forces and by an articulated jurisprudence preoccupied with goals, values and ideology.

Judges and scholars must bring systemic considerations to the surface and integrate them into a sensible analytical framework. A deeper understanding of existing doctrine would occur if courts eliminated the dead wood of false doctrinal causality. Courts must not mislead themselves or the legal community into believing that some neat doctrine will determine difficult institutional choices like the role of the courts when, in fact, it is the other way around. The courts must also abandon the notion that constitutional judicial review can be defined by sweeping commitments to values and goals that cannot be met. Actions of the political and market processes will regularly mangle these values and goals without judicial response because courts cannot handle these issues any better.

There is no avoiding the role of systemic forces and the difficulties of institutional choice and institutional comparison inherent in doctrines like equal protection and cases like *Cleburne*. Limited judicial resources and competence will be factors even if courts and commentators try to ignore them. That is the character of budget constraints. As other institutions – such as the market and the political process – come under greater strain, calls for judicial intervention will increase on fronts from unconscionability to unconstitutionality. The resulting strain between supply and demand will shape law and legal doctrine whether or not the courts or the legal academy recognise its existence. These strains and difficulties can only increase in the future. The legal community could make progress in dealing with this challenge only by recognising and confronting the tough issues of institutional choice that lie at the core of law and rights.

These crucial structural and institutional issues should become the focus of both legal analysis and legal education. Focusing on institutional choice and institutional comparison provides an ability to understand law at all levels and for all purposes. All law can be seen as a request to the courts to do something or to refrain from doing something – to substitute themselves for other decision-makers or to be substituted for. Strategies for advocacy can be potently understood and stated in these terms. If you are asking courts to expand their role, emphasise the demand side: show how badly the alternative system is doing. Sophisticated advocates must know and understand both political malfunction and market malfunction. If you want courts to back off, emphasise the supply side: stress the dire implications of their decisions – the flood of cases, the substantive difficulty of the decisions and the dangers of adjudicative mistakes.[12] Sophisticated advocates must understand the implications of the dynamics of litigation and the scale of the adjudicative process as well as the competence of judges and juries. Anyone seeking court intervention must be prepared to show courts that there is a way to control the strain on judicial competence and resources. Because able advocates must understand and be able to address both the strengths and weaknesses in their cases, they must understand the pros and cons of the institutional alternatives in each relevant context.

A focus on institutional choice and the use of comparative institutional analysis clarifies. It helps us understand legal doctrine and sharpens both advocacy and planning. Once one understands that institutional choice issues lie at the core of every major legal doctrine, it becomes easier to understand and to evaluate the legal decisions we see. Focusing legal education on institutional choice and institutional comparison provides an analytical

---

12 These considerations can be seen in Australian jurisprudence. In *State Government Insurance Commission v Trigwell* (1979) 142 CLR 617, Sir Anthony Mason noted at 633 that:

> 'The court is neither a legislature nor a law reform agency. Its responsibility is to decide cases by applying the law to the facts as found. The court's facilities, techniques and procedures are adapted to that responsibility; they are not adapted to legislative functions or to law reform activities. The court does not, and cannot, carry out investigations or inquiries with a view to ascertaining whether particular common law rules are working well, whether they are adjusted to the needs of the community and whether they command popular assent. Nor can the court call for, and examine, submissions from groups and individuals who may be vitally interested in the making of changes to the law. In short, the court cannot, and does not, engage in the wide-ranging inquiries and assessments which are made by governments and law reform agencies as a desirable, if not essential, preliminary to the enactment of legislation by an elected legislature. These considerations must deter a court from departing too readily from a settled rule of the common law and from replacing it with a new rule'.

Likewise *Minister for Immigration and Ethnic Affairs v Teoh* (1995) 183 CLR 273, Justice Michael McHugh, dissenting, at 316–17:

> 'If the result of ratifying an international convention was to give rise to a legitimate expectation that that convention would be applied in Australia, the . . . consequences for administrative decision-making in this country would be enormous . . . the Minister informed the Court that Australia is a party to about 900 treaties . . . Administrative decision-makers would have to ensure that their decision-making complied with every relevant convention, or inform a person affected . . . Total compliance with the terms of a convention may require many years of effort, education and expenditure of resources. For these and similar reasons, the parties to a convention will often regard its provisions as goals to be implemented over a period of time rather than mandates calling for immediate compliance'.

framework that prepares students to represent private clients, governments and the public interest.

The message of cases like *Cleburne* is that courts must consider and enunciate the real bases of their decisions. The existence of concerns about judicial resources and competence require courts to carefully consider where those resources will be used. Judges must speak openly and sophisticatedly about the institutional choices that are the core of constitutional law and of law in general. Legal academics who are blessed with the time to study these issues must turn their full efforts to aiding judges with a deeper understanding of institutional realities. Neither judges nor commentators will agree among themselves on a single picture of institutional choice. But they must begin to consistently speak and think in these terms.

I recognise the risks for the courts in opening a dialogue that reveals the conditional and incomplete nature of constitutional judicial review and, therefore, constitutional rights. The existing culture of legal discourse depends on a rhetoric of rights phrased in terms of broad principles and important-sounding values. But this is not the true character of law and rights. The systemic forces that underlie the demand for and supply of law and rights will not go away. Their power grows. The role of courts and the realities of legal rights will be dictated by these forces whether we like it or not.

Institutional choices are being made everywhere and continuously. The only issue is how well they will be made. That depends on how willing we are to confront the task of institutional comparison. Its exploration will require the patience to struggle with the unknown and the willingness to forego the facade of easy answers. Much depends on the extent and quality of this exploration. To a significant degree, our willingness to examine and creatively study the limits of the law will determine what those limits will be.

20

Recognition of Indigenous Rights

American Law, Australian Law and International Law

Garth Nettheim

> Take care . . . that what you call murder and robbery may not *really* be war and conquest, those sacred foundations of empires, those sources of all human virtues and all human greatness. . . . [A]s regards ownership the right of the first occupier is uncertain and badly founded. The right of conquest, on the other hand, rests on more solid foundations. It is the only right that receives respect since it is the only one that makes itself respected. The sole and proud origin of property is force. It is born and preserved by force.[1]

Recognition of rights before the 19th century

The United States and Australia present remarkable contrasts in terms of the historical recognition of the rights of Indigenous peoples. In part this reflects the differing histories of contact in the two continents in the period up until the late 18th century.

In 1996, Canada's Royal Commission on Aboriginal Peoples provided a useful summary of the experience of British North America (before the United States' independence).[2] First contacts were traced back 1000 years, to visits by Norsemen from Iceland and Greenland.

> Further intermittent commercial contacts ensued with other Europeans, as sailors of Basque, English, French and other nationalities came in search of natural resources such as timber, fish, furs, whale, walrus and polar bear. . . .
>
> Relations were established in a context in which Aboriginal peoples initially had the upper hand in population and in terms of their knowledge of the land and how to survive in it. These factors contributed to early patterns of co-operation

1 A France (1933) *Penguin Island*, Random House.

2 Volume 1, *Looking Forward, Looking Back*, ch 5.

> and helped to overcome the colonial attitudes and pretensions the first European arrivals may originally have possessed....
>
> The links between Aboriginal and non-Aboriginal societies in this initial period of contact were primarily commercial and only secondarily political and military.[3]

Politically, each side tended to treat the other 'as a political equal in most important respects'.[4] Even until the late 18th century, Europeans did not outnumber the Indigenous peoples. During the 18th century, wars between the French and the British, in particular, placed a premium on securing military alliances with Indian nations.

The year 1763 was critical. In that year, New France fell to the British and was ceded to the Crown. The Crown issued a Royal Proclamation setting out what had become the basic tenets of British policy towards the Indian nations. What were those tenets? The Canadian Royal Commission writes that:

> Aboriginal/English relations had stabilised to the point where they could be seen to be grounded in two fundamental principles.
>
> Under the first principle, Aboriginal peoples were generally recognised as autonomous political units capable of having treaty relations with the Crown....
>
> A second principle emerged from British practice. This acknowledged that Aboriginal nations were entitled to the territories in their possession unless, or until, they ceded them away.[5]

Much of these two basic tenets were retained after the United States won their independence from Britain, and they were to receive some judicial recognition in the Supreme Court. But the immediate point is this: if British colonial policy had developed in this way in regard to North America, why did it not follow a similar development in Australia?

The critical times were close. The Royal Proclamation was issued in 1763. It was only five years later, in 1768, that the Admiralty issued its instructions to Lt James Cook for his first great voyage into the Pacific. A primary task was to observe the transit of Venus from Tahiti, and there were a number of other scientific dimensions to the voyage. The search for the great south land was almost an afterthought. If he should find it, his instructions offered two alternatives:

> You are also *with the consent of the natives* to take possession of convenient situations in the country in the name of the King of Great Britain, or, if you find the country uninhabited take possession for His Majesty by setting up proper marks and inscriptions as first discoverers and possessors.[6]

---

3 Ibid, pp 100–1.

4 Ibid, p 102.

5 Ibid, p 114.

6 JM Bennett and AC Castles (1982) *A Source Book of Australian Legal History*, LBC, pp 253–4 (emphasis added).

This instruction is entirely consonant with the policy developed in relation to North America. However, when Cook sailed up the eastern coast of Australia in 1770, having some encounters with 'natives', he neither sought nor obtained their consent before proclaiming possession of 'New South Wales', then amounting to about half of the Australian continent, in the name of the Crown.

And when the First Fleet set sail for Botany Bay, the commission issued to Governor Arthur Phillip said nothing about the rights of the natives, and authorised him to grant land to those who would 'improve it', without any reference to Aboriginal consent.[7]

Had policy changed so drastically in such a short period of time? When one refers to events after the 1770s it is clear that it had not. Historian Henry Reynolds referred to the North American experience and to British practice in Africa and the Pacific. He placed the instructions issued to Cook in the context of consideration, by the House of Commons Committee on Transportation, of possible locations for a penal settlement, including Das Voltas Bay on the African coast as well as Botany Bay. The Committee took for granted that it would be necessary to have the agreement of the inhabitants. Britain wrote the principle into the Anglo-Spanish Convention of 1790 in relation to a possible settlement at Nootka Sound on the American northwest coast.[8] Later still, the principle was applied firmly in relation to New Zealand, culminating in the Treaty of Waitangi in 1840.

As Helen Irving points out in Chapter 3, 'The Empire Strikes Back: The Constitution, Sovereignty and Nineteenth Century Globalisation', the British Empire at its height represented a form of globalisation within which one might expect to find some degree of consistency at the level of broad principle, if not in matters of detail.

So why did the British settlement (invasion?) of the Australian colonies represent such an aberration from established policy and practice? Again, Reynolds casts illumination on the critical factors:

- Firstly, when the House of Commons Committee on Transportation examined Sir Joseph Banks, who had travelled with Cook in 1770, he was asked whether the Aborigines would be willing to bargain for their consent to settlement. He thought not, as Reynolds notes:

> The real problem wasn't that the Aborigines had nothing to sell. They were unwilling to sell because the Europeans had nothing to tender which would be considered of value, apart from provisions which in 1770 had been too valuable to part with.[9]

---

7 G Barton (1889) *History of New South Wales from the Records, Vol 1 (Governor Phillip)*, Charles Potter, pp 481, 483, 485, 486.

8 H Reynolds (1987) *The Law of the Land*, Penguin, pp 51–2.

9 Ibid, p 54. See also Christine Morris, Chapter 24, p 296.

- Secondly, there was a belief that Australia was *literally* uninhabited (*terra nullius*), apart from a few scattered groups along the coast. This, too, appears to have derived from Banks's testimony. He reported that the people that he had encountered seemed to derive their sustenance from the sea, and lacked the arts of cultivation; it would follow that the interior could provide no food and would, therefore, be uninhabited. Reynolds comments: 'It all would have been so easy if Banks had been right. . . . But he wasn't.'[10]
- A third factor may have arisen from perceptions that the Aborigines were less 'advanced' than other native peoples. In the hierarchy of land use, hunter-gatherers were regarded as being at a lower level than nomadic herders who were themselves regarded as more 'backward' than cultivators, let alone those peoples (such as Europeans) who had developed commercial societies. There was a tradition among European scholars such as Henry Home, John Locke, Sir William Blackstone and Emerich de Vattel, denying that the use of land by hunter-gatherers and herders merited recognition as property interests.

Whatever the reasons, the fact was that the colonisation of Australia proceeded on the basis of non-recognition of the rights of Aboriginal peoples and Torres Strait Islanders. There was no Indigenous consent to the assertion of British sovereignty over the several colonies, and there was no recognition of territorial rights.

Developments in the 19th century

In the United States, 'the Marshall cases' in the 1820s and 1830s seemed to provide judicial underpinning to the principles that had emerged after some two centuries of settlement from Britain. Indeed, the political status of the Indian nations appears to have been recognised in the Constitution. Among the legislative powers conferred on Congress is the power, in Art 1, s 8: '3. To regulate Commerce with foreign nations, and among the several States, and with the Indian tribes'.

The issue of territorial rights was judicially considered by Chief Justice Marshall of the Supreme Court in *Johnson v M'Intosh*.[11] After discussing the claims of European 'discoverers' of North America among each other, he drew on the international law principle that, while 'discovery' gave title as against other governments,

> [T]he rights of the original inhabitants were, in no instance, entirely disregarded; but were necessarily, to a considerable extent, impaired. They were admitted to be the rightful occupants of the soil, with a legal as well as just claim to retain

10 Ibid, p 32.

11 *Johnson and Graham's Lessee v M'Intosh* 8 Wheat 543, 21 US 543 (1823).

> possession of it, and to use it according to their own discretion; but their rights to complete sovereignty, as independent nations, were necessarily diminished, and their power to dispose of the soil at their own will, to whomsoever they pleased, was denied by the original fundamental principle, that discovery gave exclusive title to those who made it.[12]

The juridical character of Indian nations was further considered in *Cherokee Nation v Georgia*.[13] Marshall held that the Indian tribes 'may . . . be denominated domestic dependent nations . . . [Indians] are in a state of pupillage; their relation to the United States resembles that of a ward to his guardian.[14] These themes were reiterated in Marshall's opinion in *Worcester v State of Georgia*.[15] While Indian nations retained a residual sovereignty, this was subject to the overriding sovereignty of Congress.

Indeed, as the 19th century progressed, the rights of Indian nations underwent steady erosion. For example, in the *Indian Appropriations Act* 1871, Congress exercised its sovereignty by forbidding any future treaty arrangements with Native Americans. United States law still recognises a right of internal self-government and a degree of sovereign immunity in Indian nations, especially with regard to matters arising on Indian lands. However, court decisions since the 1840s have served to legitimate Congressional encroachments on Indian sovereignty and Indian territory.

Evidently, these 19th century shifts related to changes in the power balance between settlers and the Indigenous peoples. The great expansion of population in the United States in the second part of the century coincided with immense pressure on Indian lands. United States policy also went through a series of policy shifts even more numerous than the successive policies which Australian governments adopted.[16]

In contrast to the United States, Australia never recognised Aboriginal political rights or territorial rights. The best that the British Government and colonial governments were able to achieve as the 19th century progressed, was the establishment of a number of reserves, and some provision that the vast pastoral leases granted for running cattle and sheep should not displace Aboriginal uses of the land.[17]

Australian law did not follow United States interpretations of common law as to 'native title' until the 1992 landmark decision of the High

12 Ibid, pp 572–4.

13 30 US (5 Pet) 1 (1831).

14 Ibid, p 17.

15 31 US 530; 6 Pet 515 (1832).

16 For a guide to US law (and Canadian and New Zealand law) in relation to Australia, see S Dorsett and L Godden (1998) *A Guide to Overseas Precedents of Relevance to Native Title*, Native Title Research Unit, Australian Institute of Aboriginal and Torres Strait Islander Studies.

17 *Wik Peoples v Queensland* (1996) 187 CLR 1; *Hayes v Northern Territory* [1999] FCA 1248 (9 September 1999, Federal Court of Australia).

Court of Australia in *Mabo v Queensland (No 2)*.[18] Some Australian commentators at the time described the *Mabo* decision as a 'judicial revolution'.[19] However, in the context of the law in other lands settled by the British, it is better characterised as a cautious correction to Australian law.[20]

Reasserting Indigenous rights, globally and in Australia

Experience since the first meeting in 1982 of the United Nations Working Group on Indigenous Populations shows that Indigenous peoples share a remarkably similar agenda worldwide. This represents a form of globalisation. They seek recognition of their right to *equality* with the dominant non-Indigenous peoples. They also insist on recognition of their *distinctive and collective rights* as the first peoples of their respective nations.

Equality rights

The tendency over the centuries has been for the coloniser to justify colonisation by denigrating the colonised. The adverse impacts of colonisation on them also served to reinforce the colonisers' prejudice that they are inferior people. Even when discriminatory laws have been repealed, Indigenous people have experienced *de facto* discrimination. Australian constitutionalism has not, to date, extended to guarantees of equal protection. But there is a network of anti-discrimination legislation at both Commonwealth, and State and Territory levels. Proportionately the largest volume of complaints to anti-discrimination bodies has come from Indigenous Australians.

Past patterns of discrimination are evident in the socio-economic indicators for Indigenous peoples. The Council for Aboriginal Reconciliation, reporting in 1995 on its consultations for the then-mooted 'social justice package', distinguished between what it called 'citizenship rights' and 'Indigenous rights':

> 'Citizenship rights' comprise such matters as a right to the socially accepted standards of housing, community environmental health services, personal health services, education, empowerment in the political system, equality under the law – in short, the range of rights which most members of the wider Australian community not only enjoy in their lives and take for granted for themselves, but assume are enjoyed by all others.

---

18 (1992) 175 CLR 1.

19 H McRae, G Nettheim and L Beacroft (1997) *Indigenous Legal Issues: Cases and Commentary* (2nd edn), LBC, pp 213–18; M Goot and T Rowse (eds) (1994) *Make a Better Offer: The Politics of Mabo*, Pluto Press; MA Stephenson and S Ratnapala (eds) (1993) *Mabo: A Judicial Revolution*, University of Queensland Press.

20 G Nettheim (1993) 'Judicial Revolution or Cautious Correction? *Mabo v Queensland*' 16 *University of New South Wales Law Journal* 1.

> By virtually every test on the range of usually accepted social indicators such as rates of unemployment, rates of custody, rates of infant mortality, life expectancy, household income and other indicators, Aboriginal and Torres Strait Islander individuals and communities are now, and have been in the past, at a serious disadvantage. This disadvantage arises because of long-term failures by Commonwealth, State, Territory or local governments to ensure that Indigenous individuals and communities have access to their citizenship rights.[21]

Indigenous rights

The Council for Aboriginal Reconciliation went on to contrast 'Indigenous rights' which 'are only partly acknowledged within the legal framework of the wider Australian society'. The term is used to refer to the distinctive and collective rights of Indigenous peoples deriving from their status as the first peoples of the land in such matters as self-government, territory, and culture.

- ***Autonomy:*** The right of Indigenous peoples to govern their own affairs may be termed sovereignty, even in the residual sense of the word as applied in the United States. Use of the term is less accepted in Australia, and even Canada took some time to achieve widespread acceptance of the same notion under the rubric of an 'inherent right of self-government'.

  Australian Government policy since 1972 has been to recognise the right of Indigenous Australians to self-determination, but this has seldom resulted, in practice, in any full-blooded recognition of the right of communities to formulate and operate their own systems of government.[22] Queensland is probably more advanced than other Australian jurisdictions.[23]

- ***Territory:*** On matters of territory – land and waters – however, Aboriginal campaigns in the 1960s led to the development of statutory land rights regimes in most States and Territories, commencing with the landmark *Aboriginal Land Rights (Northern Territory) Act* 1976 (Cth). A further degree of recognition was achieved in 1992 with the High Court of Australia's decision recognising the possible survival of unextinguished 'native title' in Australia. The subsequent *Native Title Act* 1993 (Cth), as amended, and supplemented by State and

---

21 Council for Aboriginal Reconciliation (1995) *Going Forward: Social Justice for the First Australians – A Submission to the Commonwealth Government*, AGPS, pp 26–7.

22 McRae et al (1997), pp 151–7.

23 Alternative Governing Structure Program: Program Description and Funding Guidelines (1996) 1 *Australian Indigenous Law Reporter* 675. That program was, in 1997, merged with other programs into a broader Community Development Program; see G Nettheim (1999) *Governance Bodies and Australian Legislative Provision for Corporations and Councils*, Discussion Paper 7 for project *Governance Structures for Indigenous Australians, on and Off Native Title Lands*, University of New South Wales, pp 41–3.

Territory legislation, reinforces (and limits) the scope of such native title.

As a result, and also as a result of publicly funded land purchase schemes, numbers of Indigenous Australians now hold land in terms recognised by Australian law. Various Acts also give Indigenous Australians some control over development on their lands. Other legislation provides levels of protection for sacred and significant sites.

As at February 1994, some 9.46 per cent of Australia was held by Indigenous peoples under freehold title, with a further 4.79 per cent held under lease or occupied as reserves.[24]

- ***Culture:*** Indigenous peoples also seek recognition of their rights in such matters as culture, language and law. In Australia, recognition is relatively limited, and even the cautious proposals of the Australian Law Reform Commission for recognition of Aboriginal law remain largely unimplemented.[25]

Developments in international law

The agenda of the world's Indigenous peoples can be set against a broader form of globalisation. Increasingly, and especially since the 1960s, modern International Law has developed human rights standards which are capable of accommodating the demands of Indigenous peoples.[26]

In the Charter of the United Nations itself, Article 1 sets out the purposes of the UN as including 'the principle of equal rights and self-determination of peoples' and 'promoting and encouraging respect for human rights and for fundamental freedoms for all without distinction as to race, sex, language or religion'. The terms 'human rights' and 'fundamental freedoms' are not defined, but the two particular principles of self-determination and of equality pervade the Charter.

The task of fleshing out the content of the term 'human rights' was completed by the UN's Commission on Human Rights (UNCHR) in 1948 when the Universal Declaration of Human Rights was proclaimed by the General Assembly. The Declaration was translated into terms legally binding on States ratifying the two 1966 Covenants – the International Covenant on Civil and Political Rights (ICCPR) and the International Covenant on Economic, Social and Cultural Rights (ICESCR). Article 1 of the two Covenants use identical language:

24 McRae et al (1997), p 163 and generally chs 4–6; *The Laws of Australia*, Title 1, *Aborigines and Torres Strait Islanders*, 1.3, Land Law, LBC Information Services.

25 Australian Law Reform Commission (1986) *Report No 31: The Recognition of Aboriginal Customary Laws*, AGPS.

26 S Pritchard and C Heindow-Dolman (1998) 'Indigenous Peoples and International Law: A Critical Overview' 3 *Australian Indigenous Law Reporter* 473.

> 1. All peoples have the right of self-determination. By virtue of that right they freely determine their political status and freely pursue their economic, social and cultural development.

There has been some debate as to whether Indigenous peoples are 'peoples' for the purpose of this provision. Indigenous peoples argue that they are, and they also point out that exercise of a right to self-determination does not necessarily lead to secession, but can be exercised within the encompassing State. To reassure nervous governments, they cite the influential 'Friendly Relations Declaration' of 1970[27] as limiting the circumstances in which the 'territorial integrity' of a State may be overridden.

In developing the Draft Declaration on the Rights of Indigenous Peoples, the UN Working Group on Indigenous Populations, with the active participation of Indigenous peoples from around the world, insisted that Article 3 of the Draft Declaration replicate the language of Article 1(1) of the Covenants, so as to read 'Indigenous peoples have the right of self-determination '.[28] In the sessions to date of the UNCHR Working Group considering the Draft Declaration, it is apparent that a number of governments are wary about use of the language of self-determination.[29] The Australian Government, formerly supportive, is now not supportive.[30]

The Universal Declaration of Human Rights deals with property rights in Article 17:

> 1. Everyone has the right to own property alone as well as in association with others.
>
> 2. No one shall be arbitrarily deprived of his property.

This principle was not incorporated in the two Covenants. It did however find a place in the International Convention on the Elimination of All Forms of Racial Discrimination (ICERD), Article 5, as one of a number of rights in respect to which discrimination on the basis of race, etc, is prohibited. The Convention was implemented in Australian law by the *Racial Discrimination Act* 1975 (Cth), and was influential in the decision of the High Court of Australia to overturn previous understandings of Australian common law and to recognise native title.[31]

---

27 UN, GA Res 2625 (XXV).

28 S Pritchard, 'The Right of Indigenous Peoples to Self-Determination', in *The Laws of Australia*, Title 1, *Aborigines and Torres Strait Islanders*, 1.7 International Law, LBC Information Services.

29 S Pritchard (1998) 'Commission on Human Rights Working Group (CHRWG) Third Session 27 October–7 November 1997' 4 *Indigenous Law Bulletin* 4.

30 M Dodson and S Pritchard (1998) 'Recent Developments in Indigenous Policy: The Abandonment of Self-determination?' 4 *Indigenous Law Bulletin* 4.

31 G Nettheim (1999) '"Retreat from Injustice": The High Court of Australia and Native Title' in M Gibney and S Frankowski (eds), *Judicial Protection of Human Rights. Myth or Reality?*, Praeger, p 163.

The centrality of territory to Indigenous peoples world-wide has led to the development of strong provisions in two international instruments developed specifically for Indigenous peoples: the International Labour Organisation Convention No 169 (1989) concerning Indigenous and Tribal Peoples in Independent Countries (ILO 169); and the Draft Declaration on the Rights of Indigenous Peoples (1993 draft still under consideration).

It has been argued that Indigenous rights to territory may be implicit in Article 27 of the ICCPR, because of the close connection for Indigenous peoples of land and culture:

> In those States in which ethnic, religious or linguistic minorities exist, persons belonging to such minorities shall not be denied the right, in community with the other members of their group, to enjoy their own culture, to profess and practice their own religion, or to use their own language.

Similar language, for Indigenous children, appears in the Convention on the Rights of the Child. Strong provisions in regard to both territory and culture are included in ILO 169 and the Draft Declaration.

As to the 'equality rights', specific provisions relating to social and economic standards appear in ICESCR and in ICERD. Specific provisions relating to justice appear in the ICCPR and ICERD. As is to be expected, both ILO 169 and the Draft Declaration address such matters in detail. The broader principle of equality/non-discrimination is deeply entrenched in the Charter, both Covenants and the Convention.

There is now probably sufficient in the way of international law standards of general application to support the particular rights of Indigenous peoples. There will be fuller coverage if there is wider ratification of ILO 169, and more again if the Draft Declaration is adopted with not too many changes.

A Declaration is not binding in international law. Nor are treaties except to the extent that they are ratified by States. Australia has ratified the major human rights Covenants and Conventions, though not ILO 169. The United States has been more cautious about engaging in the treaty system.

Even ratification of a treaty does not necessarily mean that its terms will be fully implemented within the State. That is why the monitoring procedures under the treaties are so important. They involve periodic reports to the Committee established by the Convention and, in some cases, a right of individual communication to the Committee.[32]

These developments over the past 50 years represent a remarkable example of globalisation. The primary focus for action, however, has to be within the nation.

---

32 S Pritchard (ed) (1998) *Indigenous Peoples, the United Nations and Human Rights*, Zed Books/Federation Press.

Current Australian developments

Land rights, Native Title and heritage

The development of statutory land rights regimes, and the recognition of native title at common law have represented substantial moves to the overdue recognition of the territorial rights of Indigenous Australians. So, too, has legislation at Commonwealth, State and Territory level for the protection of sacred and significant sites, and legislation giving Indigenous peoples some control over resource development projects on (or affecting) their territories.

When underpinned by valid Commonwealth legislation, as in the case of native title and heritage protection, such Indigenous interests may be protected by the Constitution (s 109) against encroachment by States and Territories.

A major goal of Aboriginal and Torres Strait Islander political activism into the 1960s was to enhance the power of the Commonwealth Parliament to pass laws with respect to Indigenous Australians, as against the express exclusion of Commonwealth power in Constitution s 51(xxvi). This was achieved with the success of the 1967 Referendum to amend the Constitution.

Native title is protected against State and Territory legislation by the *Racial Discrimination Act* 1975 (Cth) and by the *Native Title Act* 1993 (Cth).[33]

But the Commonwealth Parliament retains power to amend or repeal its own legislation, expressly or impliedly. Three recent examples can be mentioned:

- The High Court has upheld the validity of legislation which removed, from the Hindmarsh Bridge area in South Australia, the protections available under the *Aboriginal and Torres Strait Islander Heritage Protection Act* 1984 (Cth).[34]
- The *Native Title Act* 1993 (Cth) was amended in 1998 in ways which many commentators consider to be inconsistent with Australia's obligations under CERD. The monitoring body under that Convention, the Committee on the Elimination of Racial Discrimination, reached the same conclusion.[35]

---

33 *Mabo v Queensland (No 1)* (1988) 166 CLR 186; *Western Australia v Commonwealth* (1995) 183 CLR 373.

34 *Kartinyeri v Commonwealth* (1998) 152 ALR 540; 72 ALJR 722.

35 ATSIC (1999) *Aboriginal and Torres Strait Islander Peoples and Australia's Obligations under the United Nations Convention on the Elimination of all Forms of Racial Discrimination: A Report Submitted by the Aboriginal and Torres Strait Islander Commission to the United Nations Committee on the Elimination of Racial Discrimination*, February; extracts reproduced in (1999) 4 *Australian Indigenous Law Reporter* 134; Committee on the Elimination of Racial Discrimination *Decision on Australia*, CERD/C/54/Misc 40/Rev 2, 18 March 1999, reproduced in (1999) 4 *Australian Indigenous Law Reporter* 140.

- The Commonwealth Government commissioned a review of its *Aboriginal Land Rights (Northern Territory) Act* 1976 (Cth). The Reeves Report recommended a range of measures including the break-up of the major Aboriginal land councils in the Northern Territory, the transfer of the ownership of Aboriginal land and Aboriginal revenues to new bodies, and reduced Aboriginal control over who enters Aboriginal land.[36] The Reeves Report was considered by the House of Representatives Standing Committee on Aboriginal and Torres Strait Islander Affairs, which was critical of many of the proposed changes and recommended, amongst other things, that the Act not be amended without the informed consent of traditional Aboriginal owners and adequate consultation with Aboriginal communities or groups that may be affected.[37]

Such developments have heightened the desire of Indigenous Australians to achieve stronger protection for rights. Reliance on Commonwealth legislation is no longer seen as adequate, and there is a growing demand for the constitutionalisation of the rights of Indigenous Australians.

The 'Social Justice Package' proposals

In 1994, the Keating Government requested ATSIC and the Council for Aboriginal Reconciliation to consult widely and develop proposals to address outstanding issues (apart from land issues, which the government had addressed through the *Native Title Act* 1993, and the establishment of the Indigenous Land Fund). Both organisations, and others, notably the Aboriginal and Torres Strait Islander Social Justice Commissioner, reported in 1995, with a number of proposals.[38] Since then, most of the proposals have been ignored.

---

36 J Reeves QC (1998) *Building on Land Rights for the Next Generation: The Review of the Aboriginal Land Rights (Northern Territory) Act 1976* (2nd edn), ATSIC. For a critical review of the report, see JC Altman, F Morphy and T Rowse (eds) (1999) *Land Rights at Risk? Evaluations of the Reeves Report*, CAEPR Research Monograph No 14, ANU Centre for Aboriginal Economic Policy Research.

37 House of Representatives Standing Committee on Aboriginal and Torres Strait Islander Affairs (1999) *Unlocking the Future: The Report of the Inquiry into the Reeves Review of the Aboriginal Land Rights (Northern Territory) Act 1976*, AGPS.

38 ATSIC (1995) *Recognition, Rights and Reform. Report to Government on Native Title Social Justice Measures*, ATSIC; Council for Aboriginal Reconciliation (1995) *Going Forward: Social Justice for the First Australians – A Submission to the Commonwealth Government*; Aboriginal and Torres Strait Islander Social Justice Commissioner (1995) *Indigenous Social Justice: Strategies and Recommendations – A Submission to the Parliament of the Commonwealth of Australia on the Social Justice Package*, ATSICJC; P Jull (1996) 'An Aboriginal Policy for the Millennium: The Three Social Justice Reports' 1 *Australian Indigenous Law Reporter* 1; McRae (1997), ch 10.

One development, which did produce a Commonwealth Government response, was the work of the Constitutional Convention, which generated two proposals to be put to the electors on 6 November 1999. One proposal was for an Australian Head of State, in place of the Queen. The other proposal was for a Preamble to the Commonwealth Constitution which, among other things, would offer some recognition to Indigenous Australians. Both proposals failed to achieve the necessary support at the Referendum to amend the Constitution.

There are however, much more significant agendas among Aborigines and Torres Strait Islanders for Constitutional recognition. At the most fundamental level, Michael Detmold has raised the question whether Aborigines and Torres Strait Islanders have ever entered the polity that is now represented by the Commonwealth of Australia.[39]

Indigenous Australians have posed the same question. In August 1998, the Combined Aboriginal Nations of Central Australia met to consider a draft constitution which had been put forward as a basis for the Northern Territory to be admitted as a State. In their Kalkaringi Statement, they affirmed that they had, and still have, their own constitutions, their own laws and their own authority structures, and that they would withhold their consent to the draft constitution until there was adequate recognition for essential Aboriginal rights. This position was endorsed in November 1998 at a Territory-wide Aboriginal Constitutional Convention held at Batchelor. The draft constitution failed to win sufficient support from the territory electorate when put to referendum.[40]

Turning to the specifics of the Commonwealth Constitution, a number of proposals were put forward in the 'social justice package' proposals.[41]

- ***The Races Power:*** Constitution s 51(xxvi) originally conferred power on the Commonwealth Parliament to make laws with respect to 'The people of any race, *other than the Aboriginal race in any State,* for whom it is deemed necessary to make special laws'. The italicised words were deleted as a result of the successful referendum in 1967.

  The power has been given a broad interpretation.[42] The argument that it should be read as a power which may be exercised only

39 M Detmold (1985) *The Australian Commonwealth: A Fundamental Analysis of its Constitution,* LBC, pp 62–6.

40 S Pritchard (1998) 'Recent Constitutional Developments in the Northern Territory: The Kalkaringi Convention' and 'The Kalkaringi Statement' 4 *Indigenous Law Bulletin* 12; A Heatley and P McNab (1999) 'The Northern Territory Statehood Referendum 1998' 10 *Public Law Review* 3; G Nettheim (1999) 'Aboriginal Constitutional Conventions in the Northern Territory' 10 *Public Law Review* 8.

41 G Nettheim (1999) 'Indigenous Australians and the Constitution' 74 *Reform: A Journal of National and International Law Reform* 29.

42 For example, *Western Australia v Commonwealth* (1995) 183 CLR 373 at 460–2.

for the *benefit* of Aborigines was rejected by a majority in the Hindmarsh Island Bridge Case – at least to the extent that it might limit the power of Parliament to repeal or amend prior legislation.[43]

In 1988 the Constitutional Commission recommended that s 51(xxvi) be deleted as a generalised race power and replaced by a specific power to pass laws with respect to 'Aborigines and Torres Strait Islanders'.[44] This might serve to free it from the historical origins of the provision and to emphasise Commonwealth responsibility to maintain national standards as against State and Territory governments.

- ***Racial Discrimination:*** One strong proposal among Indigenous Australians is for a new Constitutional prohibition of racial discrimination, given the power of the Commonwealth Parliament to displace the operation of the *Racial Discrimination Act* 1975. The Council for Aboriginal Reconciliation has proposed such a provision.

  In 1988 the Constitutional Commission recommended a general guarantee of freedom from discrimination on the basis of race, colour, ethnic or national origin, sex, marital status, or political, religious or ethical belief, with an exception for measures taken to overcome disadvantage. A broader, generalised guarantee of non-discrimination along these lines would probably suit Indigenous Australians as well as a provision confined to racial discrimination, and might attract wider community support. Such a provision might provide a Constitutional basis for the 'equality' or 'citizenship' rights.

- ***Indigenous Rights:*** ATSIC in its 'social justice package' report urged acceptance by the Commonwealth of fundamental rights of Aborigines and Torres Strait Islanders to:

  (a) recognition of Indigenous peoples as the original owners of this land, and of the particular rights that are associated with that status;
  (b) the enjoyment of, and protection for the unique, rich and diverse Indigenous cultures;
  (c) self-determination to decide within the broad context of Australian society the priorities and the directions of their own lives, and to freely determine their own affairs.

  These territorial rights, cultural rights and political rights find significant support in international law standards, as noted.

Agenda for reconciliation

The Council for Aboriginal Reconciliation published in 1999 its Draft Document for Reconciliation, to be finalised, on the basis of community

43 *Kartinyeri v Commonwealth* (1998) 152 ALR 540; 72 ALJR 722.

44 Constitutional Commission (1988) *Final Report*, AGPS.

consultations, in May 2000. The Council also recommended that the Document should be supported by four National Strategies:

- a National Strategy for Economic Independence;
- a National Strategy to Address Aboriginal and Torres Strait Islander Disadvantage;
- a National Strategy to Promote Recognition of Aboriginal and Torres Strait Islander Rights;
- a National Strategy to Sustain the Reconciliation Process.

The scope of the third of these four National Strategies is suggested by the following paragraphs from the Draft Document publication:

> A National Strategy to Promote Recognition of Aboriginal and Torres Strait Islander Rights will be based on the principles that all Australians should share equal rights and responsibilities as citizens; should be able to participate, as they choose, in all levels of decision-making on matters which affect them and their communities; and should enjoy equal social and economic conditions, according to their aspirations.
>
> The strategy will recognise the unique status of Aboriginal and Torres Strait Islander peoples as the original custodians of Australia, their continuing cultures and heritage, and their rights under the common law. It will recognise the unique relationships of Aboriginal and Torres Strait Islander peoples with their traditional lands and waters and the importance of traditional land management knowledge in sustaining the natural environment. The strategy will also recognise Aboriginal and Torres Strait Islander peoples' continuing aspirations for greater recognition and self-determination within the framework of the Australian Constitution, and will propose strategies for increased representation in Australian parliaments.

Former Chairman of the Council for Aboriginal Reconciliation, Patrick Dodson, delivered the fourth Vincent Lingiari Memorial Lecture in Darwin on 20 September 1999.[45] He stated that 'a comprehensive framework agreement is needed' to deal with 'Unfinished Business' in a time-scale which will necessarily extend beyond the 'current Olympian and millennium sunset clauses'. He offered an indicative list of the matters to be negotiated under such an agreement which reflects a draft agenda put together at a meeting of Australian Indigenous leaders for discussion at community level. It also echoes substantive provisions of the UN Draft Declaration on the Rights of Indigenous Peoples.

It seems evident that if true and lasting reconciliation is to be achieved, an essential element will have to be the constitutional recognition of Indigenous rights.

---

45 Patrick Dodson 'Lingiari: Until the Chains are Broken' (available at http://www.austlii.edu.au/au/special/rs.ct/rsjlibrary/car/lingiari/4dodson.html).

Summary

There are marked contrasts between the United States and Australia. The United States was heir to a long tradition of recognising the political and territorial rights of the Native Americans. Treaties were an established means of dealing with them. Within the federation, Congress had the primary legislative power from the outset. Australia has lacked these important constitutional elements.

While it is true that the rights of Native Americans have been eroded over the years, the constitutional base remains to support such recovery as has been experienced in recent times. (Similarly, in New Zealand, the Treaty of Waitangi has made a remarkable comeback as a basis for relations between Maori and Pakeha since 1975.)

Indigenous peoples, world-wide, have formulated their rights both as citizens and as the Indigenous peoples of their lands. Those claims have substantial support in international law. There is a globalisation in relation to human rights generally, and Indigenous peoples' rights in particular.

Aboriginal peoples and Torres Strait Islanders assert the same rights in the particular context of Australia. Until recently, they placed primary reliance for protection of their rights on securing overriding Commonwealth legislation. This was the goal of the campaign that led to the referendum of 1967. The experience of recent years has shown that this can be a fickle basis for rights: the Parliament giveth, and the Parliament taketh away. Accordingly, there is a growing demand that fundamental matters be dealt with at the constitutional level – the 'equality/citizenship rights' and the distinctive 'Indigenous rights'.

Sufficient knowledge is available of experience in a number of other First-World nations as to the advantages and disadvantages of particular approaches to the recognition of Indigenous rights. Peter Jull has pointed out on a number of occasions, that it is unwise simply to borrow other models 'off the shelf' – it is necessary to craft solutions to fit the particular history and character of the society in question.

Forms of recognition could be crafted for Australia quite simply, as a matter of drafting. Indigenous people have been working on the issues for some considerable time, as have other bodies such as Commissions and parliamentary committees. The larger difficulty is at the level of politics – in persuading political parties, and the electorate at large, to support such measures.

21

First Peoples, Late Admissions

Recognising Indigenous Rights

Peter Jull and Helena Kajlich

Background

A basic international consensus on Indigenous political economy has been growing in recent decades.[1] This has resulted from advocacy and court-decreed or negotiated practices of Indigenous peoples and governments – some very reluctant governments becoming among the most enthusiastic advocates once they have been won over. Change has resulted largely from social, educational, political, and attitudinal changes following the Second World War among both Indigenous and non-Indigenous peoples. The United Nations framework and ideals, and court decisions in various countries, may be seen as cause or effect, or both. But the move to more enlightened politics *vis-à-vis* ethno-cultural and racial diversity is complex, and the precise role of any factor hard to isolate. Australians, meanwhile, tend to under-rate the relevance of North American Indigenous experience on the grounds that wonderful constitutional, legal, and treaty frameworks there make that situation utterly remote from Australia. That view is incorrect. The complex of changes on both continents is similar.

The vehement debates within parts of the Indigenous world on some issues and, more precisely, on their remedies, may also obscure trends. Indigenous peoples everywhere have a common basic agenda. Apart from reasserting their former status as self-sufficient and recognised 'nations', in particular they want respect by outsiders for their traditional territories of land, sea, and freshwater; continued access to their resources and livelihoods

1 International Work Group for Indigenous Affairs (1999) Special Issue for 50th Anniversary of the Universal Declaration of Human Rights, *Indigenous Affairs*, No 1/1999 (January–March), IWGIA, Copenhagen; F Wilmer (1993) *The Indigenous Voice in World Politics: Since Time Immemorial*, Sage. See also Nettheim, Chapter 20, p 246.

based on those; respect as distinct cultural and political communities; and freedom to take significant decisions and choices for their future and the future of their descendants. Ideally this translates into governance and ownership or control of territory, or some such arrangement to the extent achievable in contemporary terms where non-Indigenous settlement and industry have impinged on or overwhelmed traditional territories. The large and increasingly educated portions of Indigenous communities relocated to urban areas in recent decades are working through other complex questions. Mixing both views may be the Sami, or 'Lapps', who retain strong local and regional roots in remote hinterlands with high living standards, while representing themselves through highly educated professionals, artists, and educators stressing a cultural more than a 'land claims' agenda.

Initially isolated in their failed Indigenous policies (when not trying to blame these on the 'apathy' or recalcitrance of 'the natives'!) developed European-peopled countries have come a long way in the post-1945 period. Some countries have worked through significant portions of the Indigenous political agenda, including constitutional recognition and affirmation of rights, recognition of new or renewed self-governing institutions, both ownership and use rights for land and waters, acceptance of cultural autonomy, etc. They have even come to share ideas and problems internationally in seeking solutions, for example, through the Arctic Council. While this has incidentally broadened non-Indigenous national political cultures, it may not yet have overcome grim Indigenous realities, for example, bitterness and socio-economic ravages. Collective pride and restored identity are essential ingredients, not fragmenting forces.[2] Indigenous needs are generations long while non-Indigenous attention span in the TV era is very short.

The legal and political status of Aborigines and Torres Strait Islanders is widely and increasingly recognised as a touchstone for the identity and future of Australia. The dismal social and economic conditions in which so many Indigenous people live are often seen as a national failure and a matter of international shame. Nevertheless, there is little consensus within or among governments, the public, universities, or other commentators on what should be done. In the past several years, populist politicians including some in the federal Liberal–National Coalition Government have widened those differences of opinion and attacked what progress had been made. 'Recognition, rights and reform', in the title phrase of one important report, is needed in the Australian constitutional system in respect of Indigenous people.[3]

---

2 M Boldt (1993) *Surviving as Indians: The Challenge of Self-Government*, University of Toronto Press; T Alfred (1999) *Peace, Power, Righteousness: An Indigenous Manifesto*, Oxford University Press.

3 Aboriginal and Torres Strait Islander Commission (1995) *Recognition, Rights and Reform: A Report to Government on Native Title Social Justice Measures*, ATSIC.

In other chapters the South African transformation is insightfully considered, notably the expansion and renewal of political culture and society resulting from the 'reconciliation' processes underway there after many decades of the deepest and most painful division.[4] Canada, too, has been transforming its political culture through accommodation or reconciliation with Indigenous peoples since the 1960s. It is important to move beyond the frequent assumption by public figures in Australia that reconciliation diminishes and takes away something from the majority and transfers it to a needy group. Rather, reconciliation enlarges prospects and perspectives, identity and nationhood.

Northern Territories

The constitutional politics of their 'northern territories', Alaska and the Northern Territory, has been a striking parallel between the United States and Australia. Both enjoy iconic status as national hinterlands, and both enjoy communicating their eccentric charm to awed fellow citizens in more temperate climates. But those facts obscure the basic political dynamic: that in each of those regions a highly transient non-Indigenous population and more permanent settlers are in collision with the cultures, claims, political values, and economic imperatives of the resident Indigenous peoples.[5]

In Alaska the basic rights and imperatives of Indigenous peoples have been protected up to a point by national institutions, notably Congress, courts, and the executive branch. Although Alaska was granted Statehood in 1958, the national government did not abandon Alaska's Natives or their land rights, and the *Alaska Native Claims Settlement Act* 1971 – or ANCSA as it is known – was negotiated by Indigenous leaders with Congress. It was sped along by American desire for access to the supplies of oil of the Beaufort Sea region of the Arctic Ocean, supplies which would be immune to the international politics or wars of non-Americans. The *circa* 200 villages of Native Alaska and the dozen or so Indigenous regions are the cultural matrix of this old and persistent Alaska, while Anchorage, Fairbanks, and Juneau account for most of the non-Indigenous population. Although several times larger than the Northern Territory, Alaska has a similar proportion of largely transient non-Indigenous to permanent Indigenous people, about four or five to one. There are two Alaskas with two ways of life.[6]

The Northern Territory since 1978 has been self-governing with one-party rule and that party not receptive to Aboriginal rights, imperatives, or

4 See Heinz Klug, Chapter 17; Bede Harris, Chapter 23; Bertus de Villiers, Chapter 24.

5 J Downing (1988) *Ngurra Walytia: Country of My Spirit*, ANU North Australia Research Unit, Darwin; T Berger (1985) *Village Journey: The Report of the Alaska Native Review Commission*, Hill and Wang.

6 Berger (1985); GA McBeath and TA Morehouse (1994) *Alaska: Politics and Government*, University of Nebraska Press.

aspirations. The Northern Territory Government wants to take over the federal Northern Territory land rights legislation and have full control of Aboriginal lives on the same model as Australia's 1901 constitutional settlement.[7] Under that 1901 framework Australia's Indigenous peoples continued to be marginalised, abused, and sometimes massacred. The lack of constitutional and legal protection for Indigenous peoples was a departure from British Empire practice – United States, Canada, and New Zealand all inherited a different approach from Britain, although the British sometimes had similar good intentions for Australia.[8] Northern Territory Aboriginal leaders and peoples want to work out their constitutional status at local, regional, and Territory-wide level rather than be marginalised in a system designed by white settlers eager to exploit Aboriginal land. To the amazement of many people, a supposedly safe win for the Northern Territory Government's preferred Statehood constitution was defeated in a 1998 referendum, thanks in no small part to Aboriginal organisation of 'anti' forces.

In the post-1945 world the 'First World' has tried to do things in a new spirit – one might almost say a post-colonial spirit. Old habits die hard, and Indigenous people in Australia, United States, or anywhere else would laugh at the notion that 'the White Man' had really reformed.[9] However, Alaska, like Northern Canada, Northern Scandinavia, Greenland, and New Zealand in the post-war years, saw Indigenous peoples treated in a new way – paternalistic at first but tending towards a new respect and equality. That is, those countries departed significantly from their 19th century style of frontier Indigenous policy.

The Second World War was no less important for Australia's Torres Strait Islanders and Aborigines in its social and political impacts.[10] However, the constitutional arrangement whereby the States had exclusive power in Indigenous affairs persisted until a massive national referendum vote in 1967 saw the Federal Government given paramountcy in the field. Nevertheless, the mindset of State control has largely persisted despite some brave federal steps by some Prime Ministers at some times. The current Federal Government believes land issues are appropriately a State or Territory matter. United States and Canadian experience accords, but with the exception that Indigenous land rights are a particular federal and national responsibility

---

7 J Chesterman and B Galligan (1997) *Citizens Without Rights: Aborigines and Australian Citizenship*, Cambridge University Press; P Jull (1996) *Constitution-Making in Northern Territories: Legitimacy and Governance in Australia*, Central Land Council, Alice Springs, NT, pp 44.

8 H Reynolds (1987) *The Law of the Land*, Penguin; H Reynolds (1995) *Fate of a Free People*, Penguin. See Nettheim, Chapter 20, pp 242–4.

9 'White Man' here is not a politically incorrect slip, but a term much used among Indigenous (and many other) peoples for the historical fact of past and present European dominance.

10 D Ball (ed) (1991) *Aborigines in the Defence of Australia*, ANU Press; J Beckett (1987) *Torres Strait Islanders: Custom and Colonialism*, Cambridge University Press.

there. The Australian experience of leaving Indigenous rights to settler and development interests who control State and Territory capitals has been disastrous, of course.

Australia and the Northern Territory have the opportunity to 'do it right'. Section 121 of the Australian Constitution invites Federal Parliament to 'make or impose such terms and conditions . . . as it thinks fit' when admitting States to the federation. The 20th century has taught the world, including Australia, many things about race relations and ethno-cultural accommodation.

Recent decades have also set new standards of practice and ideals in the accommodation, or *reconciliation* in the Australian term, of Indigenous peoples and territories within contemporary nation-states. These latter lessons have not been learned by some politicians in Australia. The future of the Northern Territory provides a critical test. If Aborigines and their lands and seas are handed over to a Darwin-based government they distrust, and without a system or systems of local and regional government under their control, it will be very wrong. Australia will be deservedly criticised abroad and face ructions at home.

Northern Territory Aboriginal peoples have taken their own constitutional initiatives. Workshop-style conferences in 1989, 1992 and 1993, as well as the successful Kalkaringi and Batchelor constitutional conventions of 1998 have shaped, restated and updated constitutional outlooks at sub-national Northern Territory as well as national levels.[11] Many other discussions of related self-government and native title issues, and problems of community governance, occur all the time. Outsiders have also paid attention to the constitutional situation of Northern Territory Indigenous peoples, to the annoyance of the Northern Territory Government who have wanted attention focused instead on white 'grievances'.[12]

Unlike Alaska or Northern Canada, however, Indigenous peoples have not been anything like real partners in the negotiation of new structures. In Canada's Northwest Territories a frank multi-ethnic legislative committee report found Indigenous peoples disaffected from a government they did not consider their own, a valuable prelude to serious constitutional

---

11 H Brown and D Pearce (1994) 'National Aboriginal Constitutional Convention Report' in C Fletcher (ed), *Aboriginal Self-Determination in Australia*, Report Series, Australian Institute of Aboriginal and Torres Strait Islander Studies, Aboriginal Studies Press, pp 107–12; S Pritchard (1998) 'Constitutional Developments in the Northern Territory: The Kalkaringi Convention' 4 *Indigenous Law Bulletin* 12–13; Northern Land Council (1998) *Resolutions of the Northern Territory Aboriginal Nations Convention on Standards for Constitutional Development*, Batchelor, NT. See Nettheim, Chapter 20, p 253.

12 R Gray, D Lea and S Roberts (eds) (1994) *Constitutional Change in the 1990s*, Northern Territory Legislative Assembly Sessional Committee on Constitutional Development and the ANU North Australia Research Unit, Darwin.

reform.[13] It is not hard to imagine what such authentic soundings would find in the Northern Territory.

In Alaska, as in other northern hinterlands – Northern Canada, the Scandinavian North (or *Sapmi*, 'Lapland') – national authorities and political parties have had to encourage their northern friends to fall into line with modern values of racial tolerance and cultural diversity. In Australia, however, Australian federal and State political leaders – not all of them from the Right wing of politics – have gone to the Northern Territory seeking advice over the years on dealing with Aborigines, a dubious sort of advice about electoral advantage to be gained from stirring racial fears. It would have been better for the country if that particular genie had not been let out of the bottle.

Backsliding is not unique to Australia. In Norwegian areas of Sapmi (Lapland), a burst of nasty populism has entangled recent local government elections. After a Sami notable suggested that some Sami language and culture should be elements of curriculum for all schoolchildren, an uproar ensued – over and above the simmering tensions over Sami territorial rights of land, freshwater and sea. Prime Minister KM Bondevik recently opened the Sami Parliament session in Karasjok with many fine words about strengthening Parliament's role and powers. However, when the Parliament's president Sven-Roald Nystø said they looked forward to negotiating land and water rights with the government, Prime Minister Bondevik was abrupt and dismissive.[14] In a political system when every group from fishers to herders to model plane clubs negotiates agreements with Oslo, this appears to make Sami third-class citizens. It also undermines the role and purpose of the Sami Parliaments that now exist in Finland, Sweden and Norway, as Ole Henrik Magga, the founding president of Norway's Sami Parliament, commented.[15] The Sami Rights Committee, an expert commission working since 1980, has made a total mess of the Sami rights issue in North Norway in recent years despite the fine work it did earlier under its first chair, so positive outcomes and calm are urgently needed.[16] Like Aboriginal leaders in Australia (see below), Sami leaders are looking for a sort of political accord to produce a workable and satisfactory outcome for all sides. We may hope that Prime Minister Bondevik's mixed messages in Karasjok,

13 R MacQuarrie (1980) *Report of the Special Committee on Unity to the 3rd Session of the 9th Assembly at Frobisher Bay*, Tabled Document No 16-80, Legislative Assembly of the Northwest Territories, Yellowknife, 22 October.

14 *Nordlys* (1999) Tromsø, 29 September; *Finnmark Dagblad* (1999) Vadsø, 29 September; and personal communications.

15 *Nordlys* (1999) 30 September.

16 OT Brantenberg (1993) 'The End of 13 Years of Silence: The Sami Land Rights Issue in Norway', *IWGIA Newsletter*, No 4/1993 (October–December) pp 26–40; OT Brantenberg (1995) 'Murky Agenda in the Mørketid: Norwegian Policy, Sami Politics and the Tromsø Conference' in *Becoming Visible: Indigenous Politics and Self-Government*, Centre for Sami Studies, University of Tromsø.

Sami persistence, and the Nordic reputation for progressive and rational policy will yet produce a good outcome. There are ugly forces loose in the world, but ethno-cultural relations are not a matter on which our civilisation can be allowed to unravel.

National recognition and rights

Some Australians seeking constitutional reform since the 1960s have been interested in Canadian experience from the late 1970s onward and Norwegian reform of the 1980s, both involving national constitutional amendments and careful wording.[17] At the Constitutional Centenary Conference of 2–5 April 1991, the beginning of serious national constitutional work towards the centenary of federation in 2001, Australian notables and constitutional specialists delivered to the Prime Minister, Premiers, Chief Ministers, and Opposition leaders, their *Statement* after a week's work. It recommended among other items for action that the Reconciliation process should 'seek to identify what rights the Aboriginal and Torres Strait Islander peoples have, and should have, as the Indigenous peoples of Australia, and how best to secure those rights including through constitutional changes'.[18] This was very much how similar Canadian work had begun in 1978.[19]

In the first days of June 1993, exactly a year after the *Mabo* decision, the then Prime Minister issued a formal response to prepare the way for national native title legislation. In those same days, and with its participants avidly reading that formal response while they waited for the next speaker, a conference on 'the position of Indigenous peoples in national constitutions' was also taking place in Canberra.[20] The United States, New Zealand, and Canada had Indigenous experts present to tell of their recent national experience. Despite the extremely heterogeneous invitation list and the novelty of the subject, there was a startling degree of consensus bubbling up through the workshops and plenary sessions that:

---

17 Human Rights and Equal Opportunity Commission (1995) *Indigenous Social Justice, Vol 1, Strategies and Recommendations*, Submission to the Parliament of the Commonwealth of Australia on the Social Justice Package by Michael Dodson, Aboriginal and Torres Strait Islander Social Justice Commissioner, HREOC (Vol 2, *Regional Agreements*, and Vol 3, *Resource Materials*); P Jull (1998) 'Constitutional Work in Progress: Reconciliation and Renewal in Indigenous Australia and the World' (background paper for Indigenous Law Centre, University of New South Wales), Centre for Democracy, University of Queensland, Brisbane, pp 62, including 'executive summary'.

18 Centre for Comparative Constitutional Studies (CCC) (1991) *Statement: Constitutional Centenary Conference* (Sydney) 5 April, University of Melbourne.

19 P Jull (1981) 'Aboriginal Peoples and Political Change in the North Atlantic Area' 16 *Journal of Canadian Studies* 41.

20 Council for Aboriginal Reconciliation (CAR) (1993) *The Position of Indigenous Peoples in National Constitutions: Conference Report* (4–5 June), CAR and CCF; Council for Aboriginal Reconciliation (CAR) (1993) *The Position of Indigenous Peoples in National Constitutions: Speeches from the Conference* (4–5 June), CAR and CCF.

- indigenous peoples are distinct political communities in Australia with unique needs; and
- processes should be established as soon as possible for them to work out the nature and details of their constitutional place in Australia.

At the conference dinner Professor Daes of the United Nations thanked Australia for its support in advancing work for the world's Indigenous peoples by substantially unveiling the *Draft Declaration on the Rights of Indigenous Peoples.*

Then, in 1994–5, an extraordinary Indigenous policy process took place in Australia, one not attempted in any other country. Three national Indigenous organisations at more or less arm's length from the Commonwealth executive government, drawing on various other Indigenous leaders, and holding two rounds of Indigenous community hearings around Australia, worked together, debated (often heatedly) together, and summoned experts in many fields to workshop tough questions before issuing three distinct but overlapping and essentially consensual reports.[21] The main proposals were constitutional and process-oriented. That is, it was recognised that issues of constitutional recognition of Indigenous peoples, self-government, sea rights, 'regional agreements' (as the claims settlements in northern North America from Alaska to Greenland are called in Australia), ownership, Indigenous sovereignty, etc, required processes for dialogue, research, understanding, and negotiation rather than quick or glib replies by uncomprehending white politicians and officials. During these years there were various other major reports and inquiries which also noted the need for resolution of Indigenous political status.

From 11 to 13 February 1996, the Indigenous Constitutional Reform Conference met in Adelaide, sponsored by ATSIC, and identified the need for more information and discussion of constitutional issues in the Indigenous community. One of the resource papers available, ombudsman Mick Dodson's constitutional chapter, found particular favour with delegates.[22] Professor Cheryl Saunders, head of the Constitutional Centenary Foundation, noted that there were many pressures for constitutional work in

---

21 Council for Aboriginal Reconciliation (CAR) (1995) *Going Forward: Social Justice for the First Australians*, CAR – a submission to the Commonwealth Government from CAR, Canberra; Aboriginal and Torres Strait Islander Commission (ATSIC) (1995) *Recognition, Rights and Reform: Report to Government on Native Title Social Justice Measures*, ATSIC; Human Rights and Equal Opportunity Commission (HREOC) (1995) *Indigenous Social Justice, Vol 1, Strategies and Recommendations*, HREOC (Vol 2, *Regional Agreements*, and Vol 3, *Resource Materials*) – as submission to the Parliament of the Commonwealth of Australia on the Social Justice Package by Michael Dodson, Aboriginal and Torres Strait Islander Social Justice Commissioner. For a summary, see Australians for Native Title and Reconciliation (ANTaR) (1999) *Indigenous Social Justice: What it Means and How to Achieve It*, ANTaR Occasional Paper No 2.

22 M Dodson (1995) 'Constitutional Reform', in HREOC (1995), pp 9–18.

Australia, and that despite the political earthquake looming, that work would continue.

The federal election campaign of February–March 1996 brought out Aboriginal issues as a negative issue. Afterwards the new government, backed by new populist forces which later coalesced as Pauline Hanson's One Nation Party, belaboured what it called the 'Aboriginal industry'. However, the High Court decision in *Wik* at the end of 1996 became the focal point for Indigenous policy debate, leading to toughened laws on native title passed in mid-1998 amid fears of a national 'race election' tearing the country apart.[23] Following the May 1997 release of a national report on Indigenous 'Stolen Children' systematically removed from generations of black mothers, another powerful issue, and demands for a formal national apology, made the Federal Government seem heartless.[24] The Federal Government, meanwhile, has maintained the position that Indigenous policy 'progress' achieved during the 13 years of Labor Government was elite whimsy rather than real or valid social or political change.

On the night of his re-election, 3 October 1998, Prime Minister Howard, who keeps Indigenous affairs in his own portfolio of responsibilities, said, to the surprise of many,

> I also want to commit myself very genuinely to the cause of true reconciliation with the Aboriginal people of Australia by the centenary of Federation [January 2001]. We may differ and debate about the best way of achieving reconciliation, but I think all Australians are united in a determination to achieve it.

Unfortunately a conceptual gulf rather than noble sentiments have appeared to prevail since. However, the Prime Minister again surprised Australia by mooting and later unveiling a draft constitutional preamble, and a much revised further draft later again (ie, 23 March and 11 August 1999), while the Council for Aboriginal Reconciliation released its long-awaited draft 'document of reconciliation', also in two successive drafts, 5 March and 3 June 1999.[25] Both documents involved the Prime Minister in heated public exchanges, and both involved the missing word, *custodianship*, in reference to Indigenous links to territory. The February 1998 national Constitutional Convention had recommended in its Communiqué that 'the original occupancy and custodianship of Australia by Aboriginal peoples and Torres Strait Islanders' be acknowledged in such a preamble.[26] The Prime Minister's

23 G Hiley (ed) (1997) *The Wik Case: Issues and Implications*, Butterworths.

24 R Wilson and M Dodson (1997) *Bringing Them Home: Report of the National Inquiry into the Separation of Aboriginal and Torres Strait Islander Children from Their Families*, Human Rights and Equal Opportunity Commission.

25 Prime Minister of Australia (PMA) (1999) Media Releases, Prime Minister of Australia, Canberra (available at http://www.pm.gov.au/media/pressrel/index.htm); Council for Aboriginal Reconciliation (CAR) (1999) *Documents of Reconciliation*, CAR (available at http://www.austlii.edu.au/au/orgs/car/).

26 Constitutional Convention, *Communiqué*, 13 February 1998.

revised draft preamble, put to referendum on 6 November 1999 but rejected, said: 'We the Australian people commit ourselves to this Constitution' while, among other things, 'honouring Aborigines and Torres Strait Islanders, the nation's first people, for their deep kinship with their lands and for their ancient and continuing cultures which enrich the life of our country'. Its words are excluded from any role in judicial interpretation, a let-out clause that Aborigines viewed as taking away with one hand anything gained with the other (while experts foresaw further and more basic problems with this attempted exemption).[27]

The Federal Government faces real pressure, despite its official view that social, education, and health programs, not a political or rights agenda, are what is needed.[28] Mere welfare-state programming of this type has not undercut Indigenous political and constitutional demands anywhere else, it may be noted. There is strong public support for Indigenous constitutional progress among Coalition voters as well as among Labor, Democrat and Green voters, while foreign attention and reports[29] and some diplomatic rebuffs have provided another sort of measuring stick. A reliable insider had warned beforehand that a Howard Government would be uncomfortable with social and cultural diversity and with discussions of ideas, and he was right.[30] Nevertheless, there are great problems accumulated in this country and plenty of years' work for plenty of hands and minds to remedy.[31]

Getting to there from here

Now Australia's most widely respected Aboriginal leader, Pat Dodson, formerly the founding head of the Council for Aboriginal Reconciliation, has issued a call for a framework agreement – that is, a formalised political accord – and negotiation process through which to build a new relationship between Indigenous and non-Indigenous Australians secured in constitutional arrangements and law.[32] There is a new or renewed consensus among

27 Constitutional Centenary Foundation (CCF) (1999) *1999 Referendum: A New Preamble*, CCF.

28 J Herron (1999) *Speech to the United Nations*, Minister of Aboriginal and Torres Strait Islander Affairs, Geneva, 29 July 1999.

29 M Dodson (1999) 'The Human Rights Situation of Indigenous Peoples in Australia' 1 *Indigenous Affairs* 32.

30 G Henderson (1995) *A Howard Government? Inside the Coalition*, HarperCollins.

31 R Kidd (1997) *The Way We Civilise: Aboriginal Affairs: The Untold Story*, University of Queensland Press; Human Rights and Equal Opportunity Commission (HREOC) (1991) *Racist Violence: Report of the National Inquiry into Racist Violence in Australia*, Race Discrimination Commissioner, HREOC.

32 P Dodson (1999) *Until the Chains Are Broken*, 4th Annual Vincent Lingiari Memorial Lectures, Northern Territory University, 27 August (available at http://www. ntu.edu.au/cincrm/events/lectures/lectures/dodsonht.htm and http://www.austlii.edu.au/au/special/rs.ct/rsjlibrary/car/lingiari/4dodson.html, and Appendix below for excerpted agenda items).

Australia's Indigenous leaders for such a moderate and directed approach to overcome the lack of progress or understanding in recent Indigenous relations with the Federal Government.[33] Indeed, Aboriginal leaders explicitly endorsed the political accord and negotiation approach at a special conference in mid-September 1999.[34] Some federal, State and Territory politicians affect to believe that Indigenous aspirations are outrageous, but despite public scare-mongering by them and others, the Indigenous Australian agenda is modest and practicable by international standards. What is more, it is well-precedented abroad where its elements have not caused national fragmentation, *mirabile dictu*, or the other woes typically predicted there and here. Indeed, the inclusion of alienated and marginal groups and regions within the socio-economic and political mainstream can only benefit national cohesion and strength. Australians have taken bemused note of the recent media attention paid to the establishment in 1999 of the Inuit-run territory, Nunavut, which makes up one-fifth of Canada's expanse, although other achievements in Indigenous self-government and resource and territory management in the United States, Canada, Greenland, and elsewhere are too little known here.[35] Pat Dodson says of a proposed framework agreement that it:

> should define, and set out a path, to resolve all the matters of unfinished business between the Parliament and the Aboriginal peoples. It will also need to extend the period of time beyond the current Olympian and millennium sunset clauses [in 2000 and 2001 AD respectively] and establish an independent body to facilitate and mediate the issues towards resolution.[36]

Certainly the regions where basic discussion is going on between the Indigenous and non-Indigenous societies are rethinking their own history and broadening their own assumptions about society – for example, Alaska or

33 For example, G Djerrkura (1999) 'No Secret in Unfinished Indigenous Business' *Sydney Morning Herald*, 29 September; and M Kingston (1999) 'Unfinished Business. . .', *Sydney Morning Herald*, 16 September; see also Aboriginal and Torres Strait Islander Commission (ATSIC) (1999) *Indigenous Peoples, Constitution and Treaties: A Paper for Presentation at a Dialogue on Indigenous Rights in the Commonwealth Institute of Commonwealth Studies (London)* ATSIC; and G Djerrkura (1999) 'Indigenous Peoples, Constitutions and Treaties' Speech, Chair of Aboriginal and Torres Strait Islander Commission (ATSIC) Dialogue on Indigenous Rights in the Commonwealth Institute of Commonwealth Studies (London) Canberra (available at http://www.atsic.gov.au/).

34 Aboriginal and Torres Strait Islander Commission (ATSIC) (1999) 'Indigenous Leaders Summitt [*sic*] Urges Federal Government Talks on Rights' *Media Release*, ATSIC, 15 September.

35 M Soublière and G Coleman (eds) (1999) *Nunavut '99: Changing the Map of Canada*, Nortext Multimedia and Nunavut Tunngavik; P Jull (1999) 'Constitutional Ambles and Preambles: With or Without the Country's Indigenous Peoples!?' Note, Department of Government, University of Queensland, Brisbane, 11 February.

36 Dodson (1999) *Until the Chains Are Broken*.

Northern Canada, or whole countries like New Zealand or Canada. That requires some national openness and goodwill, but produces new confidence and even pride. Australia seemed to have that spirit before the populist backlash of recent years. Progress also requires structured processes or forums to achieve tangible results, and intellectual and moral leadership from some on each side. The use of political accords to mark progress made, to note consensus, and to define or refine further agendas is helpful, as Canada's Indigenous constitutional processes in national and several regional contexts in recent decades have shown.[37] Such processes and accords allow the slower and faster, the more and less informed, the more aggrieved and less convinced to remain part of a moving consensus without breakdown, recrimination, or failure. Maintaining Indigenous hope and willingness to give the White Man's system another chance, and official willingness to keep talking, are critical.

Norway has not been the only relevant news offstage. Canada's Atlantic fisheries were in turmoil after a court decision that belatedly recognised the marine rights of Micmac (Mi'kmaq) and Maliseets promised in a 1760 British treaty.[38] While some white fishers have treated themselves to tantrums against the Indians to relieve decades-old anxiety about an industry that governments, non-Indigenous fishers and industry have all mishandled – and with no Indian input! – Indian leaders and the Federal Government are calling for a political accord to guide a process for accommodation of interests and needs. The federal minister is providing firm and calm leadership, as are Mi'kmaq organisations, despite free-lances both Indigenous and non-Indigenous stirring the pot.[39] In such sudden emergencies, no less than in working through ancient and entrenched injustice, the *political accord* is useful.

We may note that Indigenous leaders and their non-Indigenous supporters have consistently called for processes through which Aborigines, Torres Strait Islanders, and other Australians[40] may work to explore and understand each other's views and negotiate practical outcomes. Process, dialogue, accommodation and mutual respect are the keys to all other hard political issues, so why not Indigenous status?[41] In a country that prides itself on the vehemence and vividness of its public rhetoric, it would be disingenuous to fall in a faint when Indigenous peoples strongly outline their

---

37 P Jull and H Kajlich (1999) 'A Reconciled Constitution and Reconciled Queensland: Opportunity for a Political Accord?', Brief to the Constitutional Reform Commission (Queensland), Department of Government, University of Queensland, Brisbane, 16 September, pp 15 and appendices.

38 For example, *Globe and Mail* and *Ottawa Citizen* daily.

39 'Dhaliwal to Propose Fish Accord' (1999) *Ottawa Citizen*, 1 October.

40 The word 'Australian', like the word 'Tasmanian', originally referred to Aborigines only!

41 Jull and Kajlich (1999); J Tully (1995) *Strange Multiplicity: Constitutionalism in an Age of Diversity*, Cambridge University Press.

view of rights, a view which has been under negotiation and implementation recently in more earnest 'First World' countries. As for the United States, it did its hard thinking *per* the Marshall court decisions early in the 19th century.

Australia's failure to deal justly with Indigenous peoples or to accept them as political communities, and the failure of the British authorities before there were self-governing Australian colonies from the mid-19th century, provide a major constitutional challenge for the 21st century. While Indigenous leaders are ready, willing, and able for the task, and large numbers of that mythical and much-patronised species, 'ordinary Australians', are also ready (as support for Australians for Native Title and Reconciliation (ANTaR) has shown), current political elites are not.

22

Recognising Indigenous Law in Australia

Drawing on the African Experience

Bede Harris

Globalisation and sub-national groups

While one might expect development of an international culture and forging of transnational links to attenuate national allegiances, its strengthening of group identities is more common; it seems to herald the fracturing, not the coalescence, of the global population.

On the other hand, in an era of increasing awareness of international law as a source of rights, the usefulness of global values to groups for whom the nation-state is an artificial, and perhaps malign, construct, is understandable. Globalisation thus has strong potential for furthering the interests of such groups. International law recognises Indigenous rights to self-determination.[1] In addition, Article 27 of the ICCPR protects cultural rights of minorities.

The specific focus of this chapter is the status of Indigenous law, an important aspect of Indigenous cultural rights. The United Nations' draft Declaration on the Rights of Indigenous Peoples[2] is particularly relevant: Paragraphs 28 and 33 expressly recognise the right of Indigenous peoples to retain and develop their customary laws and legal systems. This chapter therefore takes as its starting point the legitimacy of Indigenous claims to have their law recognised by the Australians legal system.

The Law Reform Commission's 1986 report on *The Recognition of Aboriginal Customary Laws* recommended such recognition for Aboriginal law,[3]

---

1 *International Covenant on Civil and Political Rights 1966* (GA Res 2200 A (XXI); *International Covenant on Economic, Social and Cultural Rights 1966* (GA Res 2200 A (XXI)).

2 This is available at http://www.unhchr.ch/html/menu4/subres/9445.htm#draft.

3 Australian Law Reform Commission (1986) *Report No 31: The Recognition of Aboriginal Customary Laws*, AGPS, para 194.

but little has been done to implement this.[4] Such promise of general recognition of Aboriginal law as was held out by *Mabo v Queensland (No 2)*[5] has not been realised. In *Coe v Commonwealth (No 2)*[6] and *Walker v New South Wales*,[7] the High Court made it clear that, native title aside, all other aspects of Indigenous law had been extinguished by the received legal system. Since in these and other cases[8] it was also affirmed that Indigenous sovereignty no longer survives, it is clear that recognition of Indigenous law would require statutory enactment.

South Africa's re-admission to the international community (and the Commonwealth of Nations in particular) provides an opportunity to assess the solutions that country has found to two important issues which would have to be addressed were recognition to be given to Indigenous law in Australia: (1) how to choose whether Indigenous or received law is applicable to any given case, and (2) how to reconcile conflicts between Indigenous law and human rights.

Indigenous law in South Africa

In South Africa Indigenous law (or customary law, as usually referred to) has long been recognised as a source of law, and courts have developed internal conflict of law rules to determine which legal system should govern any particular case. Furthermore, a substantial body of case law has accumulated as courts of the general legal system have heard appeals from tribal courts.

Indigenous law in South Africa is recognised not as a manifestation of vestigial sovereignty surviving colonisation (as in the United States, for example), but rather as a body of rules deriving their authority from the received legal system, which is paramount. (Its subordinate status is starkly illustrated by the *Black Administration Act* 1927, which vests the President of South Africa with the title of 'Supreme Chief', and with power to depose chiefs, unconstrained by customary laws of succession.)[9] Customary law was first recognised under the *Native Administration Act* 1927 (now titled the *Black Administration Act*). The currently applicable provision is s 1 of the *Law of Evidence Amendment Act* 1988:

4 See the report on implementation of the Commission's recommendations: Office of Indigenous Affairs, Department of the Prime Minister and Cabinet (1994) *Aboriginal Customary Law: Report on Commonwealth Implementation of the Recommendations of the Australian Law Reform Commission*, AGPS.

5 (1992) 175 CLR 1.

6 (1993) 118 ALR 193 at 199–200.

7 (1994) 182 CLR 45 at 47–50.

8 *Coe v Commonwealth* (1979) 53 ALJR 403 at 408–9; *Thorpe v Commonwealth (No 3)* (1997) 71 ALJR 767.

9 Sections 1, 2(7) *bis*. See *Minister of Native Affairs v Buthelezi* 1961(1) SA 766 (D).

> (1) Any court may take notice of the law of a foreign state and of indigenous law in so far as such law can be ascertained readily and with sufficient certainty.
>
> (2) The provisions of subsection (1) shall not preclude any party from adducing evidence of the substance of a legal rule contemplated in that subsection which is in issue in the proceedings concerned.

Note that the application of customary law is a matter of discretion, and that customary law 'is to be applied in so far as [it] can be ascertained'. Given the unwritten, diverse and variable nature of customary law,[10] it was necessary that the statute address the situation where a rule of customary law not already known to the formal legal system is relied upon by a litigant. Customary law not already incorporated into formal sources (that is, into statutes or case reports) has to be proved as a question of fact, by expert evidence from anthropologists and tribal elders.[11]

Lessons from the South African experience: the choice of law problem

A pluralist legal system requires conflict of law rules. Little attention was paid to this issue in the LRC Report, yet it would be a fundamental practical issue to be resolved should recognition be accorded to Indigenous law.

The choice of law regime in South Africa

In South Africa choice of law rules are found in s 1 of the *Law of Evidence Amendment Act* and in case law under the almost identical s 11(1) of the *Black Administration Act* 1927. In *Ex parte Minister of Native Affairs: In re Yako v Beyi*,[12] it was held that s 11(1) did not require a *prima facie* presumption in favour of either common law or customary law, but rather left the court an open discretion to determine which system would be fairest to apply, bearing in mind the dominant objective of reaching a just decision between the parties. Unfortunately, the court offered no guidelines as to what 'fairness' and 'justice' meant, although Shreiner JA commented that it would not be inconsistent with the Act to take into account the extent to which the litigants were 'urbanised or detribalised'[13] and that justice might require that a court take into account 'the whole personality of the person . . . including his or her social standards'.[14]

How should the choice of law issue be tackled? Such problems are of course common when the legal implications of 'multiple citizenships' are addressed in the private international law arena between states, and in the

---

10 TW Bennett (1985) *The Application of Customary Law in Southern Africa*, Juta, p 17.

11 Ibid, p 19.

12 1948(1) SA 388 (A).

13 1948(1) SA 388 (A) at 398.

14 1948(1) SA 388 (A) at 399.

domestic law arena within federal states.[15] However, these experiences are of limited usefulness in relation to legal pluralism of the type discussed here: private international law and federal constitutional law techniques are employed in making choices of law between *jurisdictions* whereas the issue at customary law is which of a number of *personal law systems within a jurisdiction* is applicable.[16] Furthermore, private international law involves characterisation of a legal issue followed by the use of the relevant connecting factor – for example, if the validity of a marriage is the issue, the connecting factor is the *lex loci celebrationis*, which will lead to identification of the *lex causa*. By contrast, in choosing between customary and the received law, the appropriate legal system is indicated by factors associated with the parties rather than by reference to the branch of substantive law involved, and so a contractual dispute, for example, might be decided under customary law between litigants A and B, but under common law between litigants C and D because of their differing personal circumstances.[17]

Bennett suggests that the discretion should be guided by the fundamental principle underlying legal pluralism that the members of each community are entitled to have their own law applied to them, and that 'their expectations must be accommodated by application of the system of law which they could reasonably have anticipated [would apply] in the circumstances of the case'.[18]

According primacy to the intention of the parties is unproblematic where there is an express choice of law agreement. In the absence of agreement, their expectations should be discovered by taking into account as many connecting factors as are relevant,[19] with the courts basing their decisions on the aggregate impression thus created.[20] This is what occurred after *Yako v Beyi*, and it is instructive to survey the factors – none of them conclusive – which have been taken into account by the courts:

- The broadest is that of 'lifestyle',[21] meaning the litigants' cultural orientation, indicated by factors such as whether the person resides with the tribal community in a rural area (or has left to pursue an independent life in an urban area), his or her occupation, religion, mode of habitation, dress, *et cetera*.[22] This very broad criterion does however have its limitations, primarily that it is rarely possible to conclude that

15 See, for example, *Goryl v Greyhound Australia* (1994) 179 CLR 463; *Erie Railroad Co v Tompkins* 304 US 64 (1938).

16 AJGM Sanders (1990) 'The Role of Comparative Law in the Internal Conflict of Laws' in AJGM Sanders (ed), *The Internal Conflict of Laws in South Africa*, Butterworths, p 58.

17 Bennett (1985), pp 106–8.

18 Ibid, p 105.

19 Ibid.

20 Ibid.

21 Ibid, pp 74–75, 109–10.

22 See, for example, *Mvubu v Chilisa* 1972 BAC 66 (NE).

a person's lifestyle is wholly 'tribal' or wholly 'Western'. Furthermore, this criterion is no use if opposing litigants have different lifestyles.[23]

- The nature of the transaction may help if the transaction is known only to one system of law.[24] Thus a court would have no difficulty in concluding that a *lobolo* (bride-wealth) agreement will be governed by customary law,[25] while a contract of insurance would be subject to common and statute law.[26]
- The form a transaction takes may well signal which system of law the parties expected to apply.[27] Customary law will govern a marriage entered into by performance of Indigenous rites, while the execution of a will according to the formalities of the received law indicates that received law is applicable.
- Finally, the location of some event occurs or property may indicate the applicable law.[28]

A proposed choice of law regime for Australia

The South African experience offers a useful precedent for devising a set of conflict of law rules were Indigenous law to be accorded general recognition in Australia. In light of the foregoing, the following principles are suggested:

- As a primary rule, persons would be governed by whichever legal system (either the received system or an Indigenous system) they intend to apply to them.
- There would be a rebuttable presumption that Aborigines intend Indigenous law to apply in cases arising between Aborigines on Aboriginal lands. Choice of law questions arising between different Indigenous legal systems would be settled by referring to connecting factors of the type discussed above.
- Indigenous law would not apply between Aborigines on Aboriginal land if the parties' intention displaces the operation of Indigenous law. This may be express, or may be implied from the lifestyle of the parties or the form or subject matter of the transaction.
- Indigenous law would not apply in cases involving Aborigines arising outside Aboriginal land, or between non-Aborigines and Aborigines wherever arising. Exceptions would be where there is an express or implied intention that Indigenous law would apply, such intention

---

23 Bennett (1985), pp 75, 110.

24 Ibid.

25 *Fuzile v Ntloko* 1944 NAC (C&O) 2.

26 *Nhlanhla v Mokweno* 1952 NAC 286 (NE).

27 Bennett (1985), p 110.

28 *Mokoba v Langa* 1952 NAC (S) 76.

again being inferred from the lifestyle of the parties or the form or subject matter of the transaction.

- So far as criminal law is concerned, Indigenous law should govern cases involving Aboriginal complainants and defendants, except where crimes cannot be characterised as ones 'between Aborigines' – licensing and taxation being obvious examples.

Lessons from the South African experience: the human rights issue

The debate in Australia

Among the most contentious issues relating to the recognition of Indigenous law is conflict between some rules of Indigenous law and human rights. Most controversial has been the issue of corporal punishment. International human rights documents to which Australia is a signatory prohibit torture and cruel or inhuman punishment.[29] Academic comment is divided on the question of whether recognition of Indigenous law should extend to such practices. Zdenkowski tentatively suggests that customary law punishments be granted statutory recognition, and acknowledges, but does not resolve, the potential conflict with international human rights standards.[30] McLaughlin adopts a universalist approach: 'it is unconscionable to place Indigenous rights under the banner of human rights, but then to exclude the operation of those human rights within customary law'.[31] By contrast, Blay argues that while the prohibition of torture and cruel, inhuman or degrading treatment is universal, what amounts to such treatment may be culturally specific; for example, an Aborigine may consider imprisonment more cruel than spearing in the thigh.[32]

Debates of this type are simply a manifestation of a broader engagement between universalists and cultural relativists, which is not restricted to Indigenous law. One's view thus ultimately depends upon one's stance in relation to the broader question. As we shall see, indications are that the courts in South Africa are likely to adopt a universalist approach, but by means of an interesting home-grown development of natural law jurisprudence which underlies the concept of human rights.

---

29 ICCPR, Article 7; see also *Convention Against Torture and Other Inhuman or Degrading Treatment or Punishment* 1984 (GA Res 39/46), Article 1.

30 G Zdenkowski (1994) 'Customary Punishment and Pragmatism: Some Unresolved Dilemmas' 68 *Aboriginal Law Bulletin* 26.

31 R McLaughlin (1996) 'Some Problems and Issues in the Recognition of Indigenous Customary Law' 86 *Aboriginal Law Bulletin* 4 at 9.

32 S Blay (1986) 'The International Covenant on Civil and Political Rights and the Recognition of Customary Law Practices of Indigenous Tribes: The Case of Australian Aborigines' 19 *Comparative and International Law Journal of Southern Africa* 199 at 207–8.

Customary law and the Bill of Rights in South Africa

The drafting of the 1996 South African Constitution saw Indigenous rights constitutionalised for the first time. However, although customary law was explicitly recognised as a source of law in s 211, and the institutions of tribal governance were recognised in s 212, the express subjection of s 211 to the rest of the Constitution represented a defeat for customary law traditionalists, who had lobbied strongly for customary law to be exempt from the Bill of Rights,[33] on the ground that subjecting Indigenous law to a Western-style Bill of Rights would be ethnocentric. Female representatives at the constitutional negotiations, including those representing Black women, successfully resisted this stance.

The result is that s 8(1) of the Constitution provides that the Bill of Rights binds all three branches of government (ie, has both 'vertical' and 'horizontal' application), and that therefore the courts must act consistently with those rights when applying private customary law. Whether a rule of customary law will survive judicial review depends upon whether it satisfies the general test laid down in s 36(1) for valid limitations of rights – it must be 'reasonable and justifiable in an open and democratic society based on human dignity, equality and freedom'.

There is potential for significant conflict between customary law and the Bill of Rights. Equality is protected by s 9; by contrast, customary society is patriarchal,[34] with inheritance to both chieftaincy[35] and property[36] passing only to male heirs under primogeniture.[37] Under customary law women are regarded as lacking the intellectual judgment of males and have the status of perpetual minors, without contractual capacity or *locus standi*.[38] A woman passes from the legal guardianship of her father or nearest male relative to that of her husband upon marriage. Furthermore, customary law marriages are polygynous.[39]

Key factors in determining constitutional challenges will be whether discriminatory rules of customary law fall within the exceptions clause con-

---

33 As one of the chiefs said: 'My son can be successfully challenged for my throne by my daughter, because the Bill says that all forms of discrimination – and it is emphatic on gender – should not be permitted'. C Albertyn (1994) 'Women and the Transition to Democracy in South Africa' *Acta Juridica* 39 at 58 n 76.

34 TW Bennett (1991) *A Sourcebook of African Customary Law for South Africa*, Butterworths, p 301.

35 NJJ Olivier (1995) *Indigenous Law*, Butterworths, p 162.

36 *Mbekushe v Dumiso* 1941 NAC (C&O) 57. See also Olivier (1995), pp 147–52; and M Chanock (1991) 'A Peculiar Sharpness: An Essay on Property in the History of Customary Law in Colonial Africa' 32 *Journal of African History* 65.

37 *Sonti v Sonti* 1929 NAC (C&O) 23. For a general discussion see AJ Kerr (1990) *The Customary Law of Immovable Property and of Succession*, Grocott & Sherry, p 99.

38 Olivier (1995), pp 4–5.

39 Bennett (1991), pp 224–8.

tained in s 9 which permits discrimination if shown to be 'fair' or, even if discriminatory under s 9, if found to constitute a reasonable limitation of rights under s 36(1). It is safe to predict that discriminatory law will survive only if the distinction is based on some factual circumstance which, on an objective basis, can be shown to justify the differential treatment. Subordination of women under customary law is based on a presumption of intellectual inferiority for which there is obviously no rational foundation,[40] and so rules founded on that view are vulnerable to invalidation.

Thus far, no rules of customary private law have been challenged. However, in two cases the courts have considered challenges to structures of traditional government: recognition of chiefly authority inherited through the male line appears *prima facie* inconsistent both with democratic principles,[41] and gender equality, but in *Minister of Local Government and Housing, Kwa-Zulu Natal*,[42] the Constitutional Court upheld the statutory entitlement of chiefs to be *ex officio* members of elected local authorities, recognising that the importance of chieftaincy to a large section of the population meant that the institution could not be rejected out of hand, notwithstanding its undemocratic nature. In *Bangindawo v Head of the Nyanda Regional Authority*,[43] the Court rejected the appellant's claim that Indigenous courts were invalid under s 96(2) of the Interim Constitution, which required an independent judiciary. Although these Indigenous courts were presided over by chiefs who wielded legislative, executive and judicial powers, the Court held that to impose the Western concept of separation of powers on such courts would erode customary law in the face of the Constitution's clear intention that it be preserved. The court did, however, invalidate statutory provisions denying legal representation to litigants in Indigenous courts, holding that this infringed the rights to access to court and to a fair trial (ss 22 and 25(3)).

The search for a universal value

I would like to end on an optimistic note by suggesting that a clash between Indigenous law and human rights is not inevitable. I am fortified in this by the recognition in South African jurisprudence of the African concept of *ubuntu*, which the statement on National Unity and Reconciliation appended to South Africa's 1993 Constitution referred to as a fundamental value underling the Constitution.[44] In *S v Makwanyane*,[45] Mokgoro J stated that 'one

40 TW Bennett (1995) *Human Rights and African Customary Law*, Juta, pp 80–1, 92–3.

41 KB Motshabi and SG Volks (1991) 'Towards Democratic Chieftaincy: Principles and Procedures' *Acta Juridica* 104.

42 1998(4) BCLR 399 (CC).

43 1998(3) BCLR 314 (Tk).

44 For a critical discussion of the concept of *ubuntu*, see R English (1996) 'Ubuntu: The Quest for an Indigenous Jurisprudence' 12 *South African Journal on Human Rights* 641.

45 1995(6) BCLR 665 (CC).

shared value and ideal that runs like a golden thread across cultural lines is *ubuntu*. . . . Generally *ubuntu* translates as *humaneness*. . . . Its spirit emphasises respect for human dignity, marking a shift from confrontation to conciliation'.[46] In the same case Langa J stated that 'The dominant theme of the culture is that the life of another person is at least as valuable as one's own'.[47] Clearly Indigenous society in South Africa recognises the universal value of human dignity. The key to conflicts between rights thus lies in recognising that the problem is not whether there is a universal value, but rather in discovering the content of that value, and that whereas Western society may speak of 'natural law' and South African society may speak of *ubuntu*, both refer to a similar concept.

Might such a concept exist within Indigenous societies in Australia? Firstly, it is important to realise that there are at least some points of similarity between Western human rights jurisprudence and the way Indigenous societies in Australia view law. Just as a natural lawyer would argue that while natural law is immutable, human *understanding* of that law is progressive, it is clear that while Indigenous law is not positivist, being rather understood as a body of rules forming part of an established moral order,[48] neither is it static, as is shown by the fact that while the death penalty was imposed by some Indigenous communities in the 19th century and even into this century,[49] nowadays such is rarely, if ever, the case.[50] Thus, evolution in Indigenous law can be explained as a new understanding of the rules ordained by the natural order, in terms familiar to the adherent of natural rights theories. A possible candidate meeting the criteria of a universal concept is *djugaruru*, identified by Meggitt in his study of Walbiri society as meaning a holistic morally right order.[51]

The search for points of contact between Western and Indigenous concepts of human dignity requires at least as much attention as more mundane issues such as choice of law rules. Arguing over whether human dignity is recognised by our differing cultures is redundant. The challenge lies in recognising that no culture can claim infallibility in determining what precise rules are mandated by human dignity, and that the chances of ascertaining those rules increase in proportion to the effort members of various cultures invest in the process of finding common philosophical positions and learning from each other.

---

46 1995(6) BCLR 665 (CC) at 771 I-J.

47 1995(6) BCLR 665 (CC) at 752 C-D.

48 K Maddock (1984) 'Aboriginal Customary Law' in P Hanks and B Keon-Cohen (eds), *Aborigines and the Law*, George Allen & Unwin, pp 212–13.

49 Ibid, p 224.

50 B Debelle (1983) 'Aboriginal Customary Law: Progress Report' in G Nettheim (ed), *Human Rights for Aboriginal People in the 80s*, Legal Books, pp 63, 68.

51 M J Meggitt (1962) *Desert Peoples*, Angus & Robertson, pp 251–2.

23

Rights of Indigenous People and Conservation

Joint Management of National Parks in South Africa and Australia

Bertus de Villiers[1]

Introduction

The restoration of land rights is a key facet in the transformation and reconciliation processes taking place in South Africa and Australia. In both countries it is complex, uncertain, and politically sensitive. The need to balance competing interests can make the process lengthy and emotive.[2] In South Africa the majority party is committed to land reform after an 80-year liberation struggle; but in Australia, the national government is reluctant in its support of native title, and some State governments are openly hostile.

Potential for conflict is high when land claims affect national parks and other conservation areas held dear by a nation. More is at stake than mere tourism. Access for cultural purposes; hunting; commercial tourism; heritage protection; and mining, are often divisive issues. Parks are also seen as 'soft targets' for redistributing land easily, unlike freehold, pastoral and other public land.

While conservation areas have a valuable role in economic development, any historical wrongs committed while establishing such areas (eg, taking land from Indigenous people through discriminatory means) should be rectified. Unless this is addressed, and Indigenous involvement in management is established, the future of such areas is doubtful – especially in Southern Africa where demands for grazing, hunting, and plant collection are placing conservation areas under severe strain. The Makuleke region in

---

1 The views expressed here are entirely my own and do not necessarily represent those of my current or previous employers (Goldfields Land Council and South African National Parks).

2 Consider Zimbabwe's recent civil unrest due to frustration at the slow pace of land reform.

the north of South Africa's Kruger National Park (KNP), and Australia's Kakadu and Uluru-Kata Tjuta National Parks, offer promising solutions, which others are copying.[3] While basic consultation with neighbouring Indigenous communities is increasingly part of best management practice,[4] 'joint management' by contrast means Indigenous people are involved in policy-making and management as *owners* of land.

Joint management in Australia

Australia is considered an international leader in joint management of national parks.[5] The main elements of the Kakadu and Uluru-Kata Tjuta arrangements are:

(1) Ownership of the Uluru land was transferred to the community in 1986, *subject* to a 99-year agreement to lease back the land to the Australian Nature Conservation Agency (ANCA) to manage it.[6] A similar agreement was entered in relation to Kakadu. Both leases are to be reviewed over time.[7] The long-term, mandatory nature of the lease has been criticised as 'merely a token gesture as long as the hand-back means a perpetual lease-back'.[8]Although it is assumed that the Aboriginal communities will remain willing to lease the land, it is unclear what would happen if any refused.

(2) The joint management boards have Aboriginal majorities (although the federal Minister can override them).[9] However, the technical

---

3 T de Lacy and B Lawson (1997) 'The Uluru-Kakadu Model: Joint Management of Aboriginal-owned National Parks in Australia' in S Stevens (ed), *Conservation through Cultural Survival: Indigenous Peoples and Protected Areas*, Island Press.

4 The key objective of 'joint management' is 'to develop strategies to ensure the collaboration of park managers and local peoples'. K Rao and C Geisler (1990) 'The Social Consequences of Protected Areas Development for Resident Populations' 3(1) *Society and Natural Resources* 21.

5 J Davies (1999) 'Of Caribou and Kangaroos: Agreements about Wildlife' 4 *Indigenous Law Bulletin* 27–9. See also B de Villiers (1999) *Land Claims and National Parks: The Makuleke Experience*, HSRC.

6 '[A] 'non-park' option was not available . . . and . . . none of the titles would have been granted had each Aboriginal group not agreed . . . that the land would remain a national park': S Woenne-Green, R Johnston, R Sultan and A Wallis (1992) *Competing Interests: Aboriginal Participation in National Parks and Conservation Reserves in Australia – A Review*, Australian Conservation Foundation, p 273.

7 MA Hill and AJ Press (1993) *Kakadu National Park: An Australian Experience in Joint Management*, prepared for the Claiborne Art Ortenberg Foundation Community-Based Conservation Workshop, p 14. Compared to the initial lease for Kakadu, concluded in 1978, the 1991 lease review 'reflected a maturation of the relationship' between owners and conservation authorities. Ibid, p 9.

8 New South Wales Aboriginal Land Council (1992) *Annual Report*, NSWALC.

9 *National Parks Act* 1976 (SA) s 14c(5). 'Early criticism was made of the lack of real input by traditional owners, despite their nominal majority': P Toyne and R Johnston (1991)

nature of issues, and the boards' bureaucratic procedures, may have 'diluted' or 'weakened' Aboriginal influence. As one staff member remarked: 'basically, you can say that the Aboriginal people got the title but we kept the park'.[10] But Aboriginal owners and conservation authorities are both still learning to work together.

(3) A comprehensive management plan (covering zoning,[11] infrastructure, tourism, sacred sites, employment, plant and wildlife protection, and natural resources) is drafted after consultation with Aboriginal and other stakeholders. This process is cumbersome, requiring extensive public input and ratification by Federal Parliament.[12] If the Board cannot agree on a plan, the matter is referred to the Minister.[13]

(4) Day-to-day management is the responsibility of ANCA,[14] on the understanding that, where possible, staff are recruited from the Aboriginal communities.[15] Opinions differ as to whether sufficient progress has been made. In both parks about one-third of employees are Indigenous.[16]

(5) The communities receive an annual rent for use of their land, and derive income from contracting out certain activities (eg, weed and wildlife control, creation of interpretative material, and infrastructure maintenance) to Aboriginal businesses, and selling artefacts. Each also has a non-exclusive right to undertake tourism activities in the park.

(cont)

'Reconciliation or the New Dispossession? Aboriginal Land Rights and Nature Conservation' 18 (June) *Habitat* 8–10 at 10. But according to one Aboriginal member 'since hand-back the rangers . . . pay attention to us': T Tjamiwa (1991) 'We're Working Well Together' 19 (June) *Habitat Australia* 4–7 at 5.

10 Quoted in Woenne-Green et al (1992), p 273.

11 Four primary zones are established: *intensive management* (maximum recreation and tourism); *intermediate management* (low-impact tourism, but no hotels); *minimum management* (conservation given priority, four-wheel-drive access only); and *wilderness* (no permanent facilities).

12 *National Parks Act* ss 11(2a), 12. This contrasts markedly with SANP, which has no involvement by the government or parliament in approving any park's management plan. Kakadu's 1991 plan attracted 132 comments.

13 Elaborate provision is made for mediation. The Minister has other powers, such as approving contracts over a certain amount and resolving disputes between director and board. *National Parks Act* ss 11, 11a, 14, 17, and 21.

14 *National Parks Act* s 14.

15 Problems include lack of training, of senior Aboriginal staff and of clear understanding of the job of ranger: E Young, H Ross, J Johnson and J Kesseven (1991) *Caring for Country: Aborigines and Land Management*, Australian National Parks and Wildlife Service, p 147.

16 In Gurig National Park, 'despite a reasonable attempt . . . only a limited number of Aboriginal people ever worked at the resort': D Foster (1995) *Gurig National Park: The First Ten Years of Joint Management*, Australian Institute for Aboriginal and Torres Strait Islander Studies, p 64.

(6) Community members may reside in the parks,[17] and their privacy and some sacred sites are protected. At the same time they acknowledge that, to promote 'cultural tourism', the public should see at least some sites.

Joint management in South Africa

Introduction

The Makuleke are the first South African community to let their returned land remain in a national park in exchange for joint management.[18] When lodged in 1996, the Makuleke claim was seen as a 'test' for reconciling conservation with restitution of land rights, and a protracted and emotive dispute was expected. But the joint management model eventually agreed upon has been described as a 'turning point'.[19]

Background to the Makuleke claim

The Makuleke occupied the area until August 1969, when the then Department of Bantu Affairs forcibly removed them to include the area in the KNP. They were offered land in exchange, but received only 6,000 hectares – the rest (19,000 hectares) being given to other tribes.

Whether the Makuleke had a valid claim under the *Restitution of Land Rights Act* 1994 depended on four questions:

(1) Whether they occupied the land for at least 10 years before their dispossession. This was not disputed.

(2) Whether they were removed from land under discriminatory policies incompatible with the new South African Constitution. The Makuleke insisted that even though adding their land to a national park might seem a valid public purpose, it was done in a racist manner contrary to the new Constitution. The government concurred.

(3) Whether they received adequate compensation. The Makuleke argued that they did not receive the same as a White owner would have, under the *Expropriation Act* 1956, for their land, possessions and other consequential losses, nor did they receive adequate government assistance for their new settlement. The government agreed.[20]

(4) Whether restoration of the land is feasible and if not, what alternative compensation is available. Concerns were expressed that the land's

17 *National Parks Act* s 8c.

18 It is not clear how the government or SANP would have responded if the Makuleke had insisted on land use other than conservation.

19 Mavuso Msimang, SANP Chief Executive, at signing ceremony, 30 May 1998.

20 Record of Understanding, 8 January 1997.

conservation value would be eroded if it lost its national park status. (Although only 25,000 out of 1.5 million hectares, the region is one of the KNP's most bio-diverse.)[21] But the Makuleke did not want to use the land for residence, agriculture or mining, preferring instead to preserve the land's conservation status, with only eco-tourism allowed. This paved the way for agreement.

The Makuleke Agreement

After 18 months of intense negotiations, a settlement was reached. Described by both parties as a 'world-class agreement' and a 'breakthrough' for South African conservation, the Makuleke Joint Management Agreement was formally accepted by the Land Claims Court in December 1998, ratified by Parliament in April 1999, and signed on 30 May 1998. SANP's Chief Executive, Mavuso Msimang, described it as a 'breakthrough for conservation', in line with 'international precedents', one which 'ensures that the ecological integrity of the KNP is protected while the right to land restitution is accommodated'. The Agreement's main elements are:

(1) **Ownership of the land is returned to the Makuleke** via a Deed of Donation.[22] The Agreement subjects land use to certain limitations (eg, no mining, prospecting, residential or agricultural activities), and gives SANP right of first refusal to any sale.[23]

(2) **A contractual national park** is established. The Makuleke and SANP agreed to have the land declared part of the KNP (formally known as the 'Makuleke Region') for 50 years; the agreement may be unilaterally cancelled after 25 years, or extended by mutual agreement.[24]

(3) **A Joint Management Board** (JMB) is responsible for the Region's management. Both parties have six members each, the chair rotates annually, and decisions are by consensus. The JMB ensures that SANP performs its functions consistently with the Agreement, and that all tourism and commercial activities comply with environmental regulations and with the JMB's Master Plan.[25]

---

21 See de Villiers (1999), pp 51–7.

22 Sections 5 and 7. The Makuleke did initially claim mineral rights, but after negotiations accepted a compromise whereby such rights belong to the State, but no mining is allowed: s 14.

23 Section 12.

24 Agreement ss 23(3), 24. SANP and a private owner may have land included in a national park on agreed conditions: *National Parks Act* s 2b(1)(b). The name was chosen because (i) the area in itself does not qualify as a 'national' park; (ii) the name 'Kruger National Park' is known internationally; and (iii) it would be confusing if a new 'park' were established inside the KNP.

25 Agreement ss 25, 26, 27. Until the Master Plan is completed, relevant parts of the KNP's current Master Plan apply: s 2.

While conservation is SANP's responsibility (under the JMB's direction),[26] the Makuleke control the Region's commercial activities.[27] Commercial decisions are made by the Community Property Association (CPA), the legal entity representing the community, but are *deemed* to be decisions of the JMB once tabled at its next meeting.[28]

(4) **Transfer of skills and commercial activities.** One reason the Makuleke agreed to national park status was employment potential, in two areas. In the first, *conservation management*, the Makuleke community may nominate members to be trained by SANP to assist in day-to-day management. In the second area, *eco-tourism*, the Makuleke's Community Property Association has exclusive rights to undertake commercial activities, provided that the Master Plan's development constraints are followed; no activity contrary to the *National Parks Act* 1976 is undertaken; no human exclusion areas are created; and environmental constraints – including the implications of declaring the land a RAMSAR site under the *1971 Convention on Wetlands of International Importance* – are considered. The Makuleke may enter into partnership agreements with SANP or other developers.

(5) **Utilisation of natural resources** (eg, firewood, medicinal plants, hunting) is a difficult problem for conservation areas, given huge demand. The Agreement provides that:

- Community members have access to the Region on conditions determined by the JMB. So far, both parties agree in principle that members may freely enter the park for cultural and religious purposes; if they visit as ordinary tourists, a gate fee is payable.
- A traditional kraal shall be restored, and a research facility and a museum of Makuleke history established.[29]
- Controlled plant collection and limited hunting may be allowed but, but due to the Region's sensitivity animal migration and drought, would need restrictions.

(6) **The division of income and expenditure** was problematic. The Makuleke have few resources, but high hopes of economic benefit; while SANP must finance conservation management, but cannot

---

26 Some conservation decisions require a Regulation published in the government Gazette (*National Parks Act* s 29). The Makuleke may cancel the Agreement if non-publication leads to a 'fundamental deprival' of their rights: s 27(7).

27 *National Parks Act* s 12(2)(b).

28 Section 27(5). SANP insisted on a single management authority for the whole Region, to avoid jurisdictional conflicts.

29 Agreement s 33(2).

undertake commercial activities. All income, excluding gate fees (but including funds from research, filming or resource utilisation), accrues to the Makuleke. Fees from the Region's only gate are used to defray SANP's costs, although only partly, as few visitors use the gate. SANP is responsible for maintenance of conservation facilities, the Makuleke for tourism and other commercial infrastructure. For shared facilities, costs are apportioned by the JMB.[30]

(7) **Cancellation.** Both realised the need for resolving disputes amicably while recognising each party's right to cancel the Agreement. The Makuleke did not want to be locked into a situation where SANP could obstruct their commercial activities, while SANP could not afford to manage the park if occupants conducted activities against its ethos. So cancellation is allowed if either party's rights are 'fundamentally breached' in a manner not 'practically possible to remedy' and mediation fails.[31]

Reflections

Any comparison between Australian and South African experience must take account of vast differences between the countries. Some preliminary observations:

(1) Firstly, can traditional ownership and national parks co-exist at all? The answer seems a qualified 'yes'. In Australia the *Mabo* judgment means that declaring a national park does not extinguish native title – which implies both can co-exist, at least in principle,[32] although native title would be subject to park-related regulation.[33] In South Africa, the Makuleke's land use options are also subject to limitations on the Title Deed, which ensure that even if the land is not a national park, its conservation status remains. Because the Makuleke have an escape clause – they can terminate the agreement after 25 years – they may feel more secure than that Aboriginal owners of Kakadu and Uluru-Kata Tjuta.

---

30 Agreement ss 34, 35.

31 Agreement s 37.

32 Some dispute this conclusion, arguing that if a park was 'created to recognise Aboriginal interests' then co-existence was anticipated, and questioning 'whether traditional native rights of hunting and fishing or fire-lighting are compatible with national parks': MA Stephenson and S Ratnapala (eds) (1993) *Mabo: A Judicial Revolution*, University of Queensland Press, pp 209, 110.

33 The Federal Court of Canada has emphasised that 'numerous Canadian authorities... have held that the aboriginal right to hunt, even when confirmed by treaty, is subject to regulation by competent legislation': *Hamlet of Baker Lake v Minister of Indian Affairs* (1979) 107 DLR 513 per Mahoney J at 551.

(2) From a conservationist viewpoint, joint management is a revolutionary break from the 'museum-piece' approach to national parks which, for many years, regarded human presence as a nuisance.[34] Joint management seeks to reconcile conservation with Indigenous land use, but does not rule out the possibility of conflicts.[35] It must also cope with inevitable differences of views on what a national park is all about.[36] Notwithstanding criticisms, joint management at Uluru-Kata Tjuta and Kakadu is progressing well, while South Africa is still at an early stage.

(3) Although both countries have embraced a commitment to 'joint management', one could ask why traditional owners were not given the choice of '*self*-management'.[37] Being inherently discriminatory, mandatory leaseback should *not* be their only option. By contrast, the Makuleke Agreement provides that management may be taken over by the Makuleke community in time.

(4) Aboriginal commercial involvement in both parks has increased over the years, but there is still room for improvement. In Uluru-Kata Tjuta, the community benefits from a fixed percentage of gate fees, selling artefacts, and working as rangers and guides; the Kakadu community also manages accommodation and runs commercial boats. But despite this income, 'ownership of land does not necessarily lead to financial independence'.[38] The Makuleke's expectations of commercial development may be unrealistic: the region is not (yet) a major tourist destination. The future of joint management may suffer if commercial expectations are not met, especially when grazing offers more immediate profit than eco-tourism.

(5) Goodwill by staff and community members is essential, as is commitment 'from the very top of the agency and from the most senior people in the community'.[39] A paradigm shift by conservationists is needed. In the past conservation assets were protected *against* human

---

34 BJ Richardson, D Craig and B Boer (1994) 'Indigenous Peoples and Environmental Management: A Review of Canadian Regional Agreements and Their Potential Application to Australia (Part 2)' 11 *Environmental Planning Law Journal* 373.

35 'There is a damaging polarisation of views. . . . One extreme is a 'noble savage' view of Aboriginal people as archetypal conservationists; the others define Aboriginal people as careless and opportunistic exploiters': Woenne-Green et al (1992), p 36.

36 In the case of Gurig National Park 'informal power relationships were quite one-sided', resulting in complaints that 'the present situation makes a mockery of joint management': Foster (1995), p 13. This has changed over the years as traditional owners become more acquainted with the management of the park.

37 Queensland legislation creates a new category of 'Aboriginal National Park', where all management functions are the responsibility of the Aboriginal landowners. See also S Cowell, MB Lane and M McDonald (1998) 'Conservation, Indigenous Interests and Co-management: The Lawn Hill Case' 38(1) *Australian Parks and Recreation* 36.

38 Foster (1995), p 72 (discussing Gurig National Park).

39 AJ Press, DAM Lea, A Webb and A Graham (1995) *Kakadu: Natural and Cultural Heritage and Management*, Australian Nature Conservation Agency/ANU North Australian Research Unit, p 14.

involvement, but the contemporary trend is to protect *through* community involvement. This means a quantum leap for conservationists, who do not always have the skills needed for public accountability.

(6) Other practical issues include:

- The purpose of a national park. The traditional concept was a haven for wildlife and plants, with minimal human interference; but joint management may mean different expectations.[40]
- Differences in language, culture, and management style. Many South African and Australian Indigenous people, especially in remote areas, are not fluent in English – particularly conservation and business terminology.[41] Technical discussions may create feelings of disempowerment, not of participation,[42] while bureaucratic, often cumbersome management processes often cause frustration. Hence criticisms that 'traditional owners are coerced into engaging in the bureaucratic processes of the dominant society'.[43]
- Differing expectations of economic benefit – especially when alternatives like mining and agriculture are considered. Whereas conservation authorities, who receive government grants, may be satisfied with relatively low returns, Aboriginal and African communities may need higher profits if tourism is their main, even sole, source of income. If traditional owners consider other forms of land use after tourism turns out less profitable than expected, this may threaten the joint-management arrangement.
- Sustainable utilisation of natural resources. While conservationists may want to strictly control their utilisation, Aboriginal and African communities may have different priorities.

---

40 'The conservation lobby has often assumed that the Australian landscape . . . was largely unchanging and uncontaminated by human use. . . . Such a naïve view ignores both the previous impact of Aboriginal land management practices and the contemporary situation of Aboriginal people': Young et al (1991), pp 140–1.

41 A report on Gurig National Park found that 'several . . . [Indigenous] members cannot read English, hence the agenda and minutes have to be read to them':Foster (1995), p 12.

42 At least in the initial phase, board meetings 'were typically conducted in English and the same power relations that operated in the staff meetings applied. . . . Aboriginal people, despite their majority, were not necessarily in a position of power'. J Willis (1992) 'Two Laws, One Lease: Accounting for Traditional Aboriginal Law in the Lease for Uluru-Kata Tjuta National Park' in J Birckhead, T de Lacy and L Smith (eds), *Aboriginal Involvement in Parks and Protected Areas*, Aboriginal Studies Press, p 162.

43 A Moreton-Robinson and C Runciman (1990) 'Land Rights in Kakadu: Self-Management or Domination' 3 *Journal for Social Justice Studies* 75–88 at 75.

(7) The investment and allocation of money from tourism or mining, as in Kakadu, is potentially controversial. While the community's autonomy must be respected, so too must legislative or contractual requirements regulating use of funds.[44] Some Aboriginal communities complain that their tourism income goes to provide health and education facilities, normally the responsibility of State and federal governments.

(8) Residence within national parks is problematic. It creates risks of population increases exceeding the park's sustainable ability; for example, the number living in Kakadu rose from 50 in 1979 to 300 in 1992.[45] But traditional owners may be frustrated if their land title is restored but their access is not. The Makuleke Region does not allow permanent human residence; access for tourism and cultural purposes may still prove difficult to regulate.

(9) Despite the *ad hoc* joint management and consultation arrangements put in place, neither country has any general policy of Indigenous involvement in conservation matters generally – within and outside conservation areas – or in national park management in particular.[46] A 1993 report found 'a lack of strategic direction at the . . . [national] level concerning the involvement of Aboriginal people in the development and implementation of environmental policy'.[47]

Key issues for Australian Constitutional reform

In the longer term, reforms to the Australian Constitution should be considered over the next decade, along the following lines, to uphold the rights of Aboriginal and Torres Strait Islander people:

(1) Implementing an overarching system of minority protection. There are ample precedents in international law. Measures that could be considered at federal or State level include:

- Constitutional recognition of the diversity of the Australian population and a recognition that minority groups' cultures,

---

44 The East Kimberley Project (1985) 'Report of the Committee of Review of Aboriginal Employment and Training Programmes' (August).

45 D Gillespie (1988) 'Tourism in Kakadu National Park' in D Wade-Marshall and P Loveday (eds), *Contemporary Issues in Development*, ANU Northern Australia Research Unit, p 11. Reasons include desire to seek employment near one's place of birth.

46 Woenne-Green et al (1992), p 37, recommend the following minimum principles: freehold title; a negotiated long-term lease; rent paid; Indigenous majorities on management bodies; jointly prepared management plan; employment commitment; and residence rights (if applicable).

47 House of Representatives Standing Committee on the Environment, Recreation and Arts (1993) *Biodiversity: The Role of Protected Areas*, AGPS, p 62.

customs and beliefs should be taken into account when decisions are made and laws interpreted.

- Special constitutional arrangements to ensure direct Indigenous representation in legislative bodies, for example, changes to the electoral system so that more Aboriginal candidates are elected. Provision could also be made for a 'third' House of a State or Federal Parliament where Indigenous leaders discuss matters of direct importance to Aboriginal people.
- Power-sharing arrangements on executive bodies. Participation in executive policy formulation and implementation is no less important than representation in legislative forums.
- Self-governance on a local and community basis.

(2) Including 'second-generation' human rights in the Constitution – either as enforceable law or as 'directive principles of state policy'.[48] This may include special provisions or targets in housing, health, employment and education. Equality in formal procedures only is not sufficient; it must also be reflected in outcomes.

(3) Simplifying access to land, and restoring land rights. The complexity of the current *Native Title Act*, and its emphasis on historical connection to prove native title, make it virtually impossible to secure equitable access to land. Indigenous frustration with the slow pace of land reform should not be underestimated.

(4) Decentralising certain powers and functions – especially involving cultural and customary matters – to local, even communal, bodies, such as those set up as recognised native title bodies corporate.

---

48 B de Villiers (1992) 'Directive Principles of State Policy and Fundamental Rights: The Experience of India' *SA Journal of Human Rights* 29–49. See Klug, Chapter 16, p 195.

24

Constitutional Dreaming

Christine Morris[1]

In this chapter I argue that the constitution of Australia – the continent, not the post-1788 political entity – was established at the time of creation, with the Dreaming as its manifesto. I write from an Indigenous perspective and, so far as I can speak for others, I want to correct some common misapprehensions about what Indigenous Australians want when we demand that our law and our sovereignty be recognised.

Misconceptions

Mainstream White Australian law and constitutional theory are based on three assumptions:

(a) That justice consists of protecting individual rights, which 'trump' other values (even tangible collective goods like reducing pollution, let alone metaphysical values like harmony with the land) and are viewed almost as 'property' that individuals 'own' and may 'trade away'.

(b) That every country must have a single legal order with a top-down hierarchy of laws. Today's nation-states are jealous gods; they condemn as heresy anything that might disrupt their 'territorial integrity' – whether partitioning their lands, or exempting groups of their citizens from their control – even for the sake of protecting minorities against oppression.

(c) That Western law (based on Enlightenment culture, and embodying these two assumptions), if not perfect, represents the 'world's best practice' in governance.

Corrections

I challenge all three of these assumptions.

---

1 I would like to thank Tom Round and other members of KCELJAG, for their assistance with this chapter.

'What do we want?' – Indigenous law, not Indigenous rights

Indigenous conceptions of justice and governance embody two fundamental, and related, differences:

- Firstly, Indigenous governance focuses primarily on law and the duties it imposes, not on rights. Rights seem natural among people unwilling to share what they have. But Indigenous views place far greater importance on harmonious community relationships, and are less tolerant of individuals selfishly exploiting their own rights to the detriment of their community. Insofar as rights involve power to shut out one's fellow citizens, they are incompatible with Indigenous understandings of justice.

  Ironically, the 'rights industry' with which Indigenous claims are often linked is, in fact, foreign to Aboriginal and Islander traditions. Too often it is assumed that we agree with this 'industry' because we talk to the media in terms of 'rights' – land rights, native title, self-determination, racial non-discrimination, etc. We do this because these are terms that Westerners understand and Australian law recognises, not because they are our own. It is galling when Indigenous Australians are piously lectured on the ground we 'talk too much about rights but not enough about responsibilities'. Indigenous law is *founded* on responsibilities – to the land, to the community, to one's self.
- Secondly, fundamental to Indigenous law is a strongly felt presence of the sacred through the land. It must be respected, not treated as a disposable property or otherwise subordinated to individual rights. Only by recognising the sacred can a legal order aspire to be a 'full law', one that integrates both sides of the human person – physical and spiritual. Both seen and unseen reality are valid in the Indigenous worldview. The Law (as we name it) is based on the belief that humans must reciprocate every aspect of life on earth and in the spiritual realm. The penalty for a breach is termed 'payback'. Despite its colloquial overtones of revenge, this really derives from the guiding principle of reciprocity.

These two characteristics reinforce one another. Because the sacred and the land must be respected, individual rights are not paramount. Because individual rights do not reign supreme, the land cannot be treated as just another commodity in the marketplace.

By contrast, because it applies only to seen reality, Western law is a 'half law'. This is meant not to be derogatory, but rather a reflection of what the majority of Australians generally *want* their law to cover. This law derives from monotheistic belief centred on humankind's supremacy as owners of the earth. Breaches of this law carry loss of money or liberty as their penalty.

The guiding principle of Australian law is to protect individuals and their goods, so they can contribute effectively to the economic system.

Arguments for balancing individual rights with communitarian and sacred values receive a bad press in the West. Often they are dismissed as excuses used by dictators to evade international accountability for human rights abuses. However, Indigenous law cannot be so dismissed. Far from rejecting the world's scrutiny, Indigenous peoples in Australia and elsewhere welcome the domestic application of international law and human rights standards (indeed, implementing these wholeheartedly would require governments such as Australia's to accord Indigenous law far more respect). Further, experience shows that, by putting human beings in their rightful place within the natural order, Aboriginal and Torres Strait Islander law safeguards – not undermines – the respect individuals deserve:

> when one is subject to a law that dictates one's every waking moment and movement, one does not become a burdened ass but rather a refined and dignified human being . . . [who] sees a world constructed around a divine comedy in which humans are hapless actors believing in their own self-importance. I have observed . . . elders who take great delight in watching younger people come to terms with what the young think is the yoke of the laws. . . . These old people . . . wait in expectation for the day the young realise the Law is not their enemy . . . but the dreaming track that leads them to a world full of wonderment, challenges, opportunities and most importantly humour with which to bring out the best in themselves, so that they can be role models for the next generation, the next carers of the fertility of the Land.[2]

I have discussed more fully elsewhere the features of Indigenous law.[3] But a word of caution first. Despite the public prominence (and good intentions) of certain Indigenous spokespeople who happen to fit the media's image, it is the senior 'law men' and 'law women' who are best qualified to speak with authority on Indigenous law.[4] Some, like Galarrwuy Yunupingu, fall in both categories; but most other senior law men and women do not receive (or seek) media attention, as they do not fit the 'noble savage' stereotype. They may speak English as their fourth or fifth language, or not at all. But if White Australian leaders, students, academics and legal practitioners really want to learn the true nature of Indigenous law, they must approach these senior law men and women in a teachable frame of mind.

---

2 C Morris (1999) 'A Full Law' in DA Posey (ed), *Cultural and Spiritual Values of Bio-Diversity: A Complementary Contribution to the Global Biodiversity Assessment*, United Nations Environment Program (UNEP), pp 543–5.

3 Ibid.

4 I use 'law man' fully aware that it evokes the American 'Wild West'. In fact, the term is entirely appropriate; Indigenous law men operate in a milieu where lawlessness is a possibility at any time.

Western law has much to learn from Indigenous law

Western law would benefit greatly if it were to stop and listen to Indigenous perspectives, *on their own terms*. Indigenous perspectives are valuable not least because our law has something to say concerning a very wide range of constitutional and legal issues – indeed, on more issues than Western law does.

There is a real danger among well-meaning Whites that Indigenous perspectives may be 'ghettoised', ie, confined to relations between White and Indigenous Australia. It took 180 years just to accept that Indigenous people should be heard when Indigenous-specific policies are decided. That mainstream Australia might learn things *that would benefit itself* – insights useful for the general governance of the country – by studying Aboriginal law, is still a novelty, even to liberal-minded sympathisers.

No doubt we Indigenous will be consulted (however cursorily) over amendments to the *Native Title Act*; but would anyone think to seek Indigenous views on the *Trade Practices Act*? It's not an 'Aboriginal issue'. Yet we have things of value – particularly insights into intellectual property – to trade in a world market.[5]

Or take Federal–State relations. Few Australian commentators would think of linking this to Indigenous affairs, except to ask whether Commonwealth or States should have jurisdiction over 'Aboriginal natives'. But federalism itself, copied from the United States, owes a great debt to Indigenous peoples. The *Hau De No Sau Nee*, the 'Great Law of Peace' under which the Six Nations of the Iroquois confederated, had a well-documented influence on the United States Constitution. It was:

> a federal union of five (and later six) Indian nations that had put into practice concepts of popular participation and natural rights that the European savants had thus far only theorised. The Iroquois system . . . rested on assumptions foreign to the monarchies of Europe: it regarded leaders as servants of the people . . . and made provisions for . . . impeachment for errant behaviour. The Iroquois' law and custom upheld freedom of expression . . . [and] provided for political participation by women (women form the judiciary) and the relatively equitable distribution of wealth. These distinctly democratic tendencies sound familiar in light of subsequent American political history – yet few people . . . know that a republic existed on our soil before anyone here had ever heard of John Locke . . . the *Magna Charta*, Rousseau . . . or Jefferson.[6]

Before the United States Founders learned to copy the Iroquois precedent, attempts to unify formerly independent states had ended up as either loose leagues or centralised unitary monarchies. That the United States is federal

---

5 C Morris (1997) 'Indigenous Intellectual Property Rights: The Responsibilities of Maintaining the Oldest Continuous Culture in the World' 4(2) *Indigenous Law Bulletin* (available at http: //www.law.unsw.edu.au/centres/ile).

6 BE Johansen (1982) *Forgotten Founders: How the American Indian Helped Shape Democracy*, Gambit/Harvard Common Press.

while the United Kingdom is unitary shows the Iroquois Confederacy's value as a workable precedent for the American colonists.

Sovereignty

Copying federalism from the Iroquois was one step in leaving behind the shibboleth that has dominated Western governance since the Enlightenment – the idea that sovereignty must be indivisible within its own territory. The very concept of federalism challenges this: sovereignty is not vested exclusively in either the nation or the member states, but shared by both. Realising this helped the Americans address their very real post-1776 governance problems. It is time for Westerners to learn more from the Indigenous peoples they once dispossessed, whose insights are more relevant than ever in a globalised world where the old Westphalian model is less and less effective.

Lessons

The organic pre-1788 constitution

Before 1788, over 200 sovereign Indigenous nations co-existed on this continent, by means of an organic and trans-communicative federal model based on mutual respect, without needing organised state machinery. This system situated sovereignty within a multilateral system of communication, politics and trade. At its core was a concept of law based on the sacred and on community responsibility, rather than on individuals and their possessions. As Justice Blackburn said of the Gove Peninsula Aborigines:

> The evidence shows a subtle and elaborate system highly adapted to the country in which the people led their lives, which provided a stable order of society and was remarkably free from the vagaries of personal whim or influence. If ever a system could be called 'a government of laws, not men' it is that shown in the evidence before me.[7]

Margaret King-Boyes – an anthropologist who honoured her promise to Aboriginal tribal elders to explain their traditions to her 'own tribe' – praised the Aboriginal occupation of Australia for:

> the surprising uniformity of the basic philosophy, system of government and method of maintaining law and order which operated over the entire continent irrespective of very marked contrasts in climate and environment. There were variations in ceremonies and concrete expressions of belief but these were superficial, externalised variants and adaptations still stemming from a single fusion of sacred and secular concepts expressed in the Dreaming, the Foundation Drama expressive of their whole pattern of life.... These laws regulated trading

7 *Milirrpum v Nabalco Pty Ltd and Commonwealth* (1971) 17 FLR 141 at 267.

> practices between adjacent tribes, assisting the elimination of probable causes for dissent.[8]

King-Boyes' translations of what the elders taught her confirm my claim that the constitution of this continent was laid down at the time of creation – its manifesto being the Dreaming. Non-Indigenous Australians have not yet recognised this, because they approach the Dreaming from the perspective of their own law, not that of the Law of this Land. I say this not to confront my fellow citizens, but to offer them a deeper understanding. The Law of the Land speaks in poetic and subjective language, so as to reinforce that humans are interconnected with all of creation, and that knowledge comes from that interconnectedness, not from objective observation or even learning from a teacher. Because all life is one, this requires a new form of intellectual understanding. Its poetry does not invalidate this understanding; rather, it requires learners to extend themselves.

This understanding has powerful implications for how we govern ourselves. Mowalijarlai described the continent as a living body:

> The whole of Australia is *Bandaiyan*. The front we call *wadi*, the belly section, because the continent is lying down flat on its back. It is just sticking out from the surface of the ocean. Deep down underneath are the buttocks, *wambalm*, from where the leg joints run into the pelvis and right across to the other side.[9]

To extend Mowalijarlai's metaphor, Indigenous governance functions like the body's cellular formation. The cells, the Aboriginal nations, were each sovereign but not in the Westphalian sense; instead, they recognised that their existence required the co-operation of all. And this co-operation was facilitated through a dynamic trading system that traversed the country.

Just as a body has distinct parts, so does the Australian continent. Each clan, with its distinct language, personifies the body in its own part of the continent. There is another lesson from this analogy, often paid lip-service by politicians but soon learned if they fail to pay attention to their constituents: it is the body that tells the brain what to do. Those who use subjective research to 'prove' that the brain is the central focus, not just a relaying database, are often those who deny their bodies, feelings and experiential knowledge. The Indigenous understanding regards the body rather than the brain as the central focus for gathering knowledge – which comes from experience and from feeling the Law of the Land:

> Well, some people they say . . .
> 'Lovely tree, look!'
> But me . . . I think that story.
> This tree 'e stay . . . watching you.
> Something . . . this tree,

---

8 M King-Boyes (1977) *Patterns of Aboriginal Culture: Then and Now*, McGraw-Hill, p 63.

9 D Mowalijarlai and J Malnic (1993) *Yorro Yorro: Everything Standing Up Alive – Spirit of the Kimberley*, Magabala Books, p 191.

> If you go by yourself, lie down,
> That tree 'e can listen.
> Might be 'e might give you signal.
> Spirit . . . quiet 'e say . . .
> 'Oh, my man coming!'[10]

My use of organic rather than mechanical metaphors is deliberate. Parts of a machine are all expendable: when bulbs blow, you discard and replace them. Parts of an organism, though, each have intrinsic value. An unhealthy organ is to be cured if possible, not amputated except as a last resort. As Sahtouris argues, organic or bodily metaphors:

> are preferable to outdated and unrealistic mechanical metaphors of perfect societies that were supposed to run permanently and smoothly as well-oiled machines once we got them built correctly. The whole Cold War was rooted in competition over which side had that perfect social machinery![11]

Indigenous trade

The 'life-blood' circulating through this body was trade. Historian Jonathan Richards has found, through his extensive research into race relations in Colonial Australia, that robust trade flourished and proliferated. He also notes the importance of intellectual property as prominent factor of exchange.[12] Mowalijarlai used another metaphor – the criss-crossed strings of a fishing net – to explain the trading system:

> I want to show you something. I want show you how all Aboriginal people in Australia are connected in the Wunnan system. The squares are the areas where the communities are represented, and their symbols and the languages of the different tribes in this country from long, long time ago. The lines are the way the history stories travelled along these trade routes. The are all interconnected: it's the pattern of the Sharing system.[13]

To understand Indigenous trade requires an Indigenous perspective, one not so preoccupied with heavy metals as the post-1788 occupants of these shores. The British colonists found that the local peoples, like the Chinese, were not interested in acquiring such cumbersome wares lacking immediate use. What the traders did not understand is that most Indigenous were trading instead in intellectual property, based on something intangible – the sacred celebrated through ceremony and ritual.

---

10 B Neidjie (1989) *Story about Feeling*, ed Keith Taylor, Magabala Books, p 35.

11 E Sahtouris (1998) *The Biology of Globalisation: The Challenge of Evolution Symposium in Cagliari* (available at http://www.ratical.org/LifeWeb/Articles/globalize.html#ITAT, adapted from first publication in *Perspectives in Business and Social Change*, September 1997.

12 J Richards (forthcoming) '"A Question of Necessity": Queensland Native Mounted Police', PhD Thesis, Faculty of Humanities, Griffith University.

13 Mowalijarlai and Malnic (1993), p 190.

Trade and ceremony

Today's traders often dispense with formalities in order to speed up their transactions. But doing this has forged an unintended link between *speed* and *litigation*. The very purpose of ceremony and diplomacy was to raise a contract from a mere transaction for profit to the level of forging a relational link between diverse peoples, one incorporating political and social as well as economic ties. Today we reduce contracts to the level of mere 'exchanges', as though mixing ceremony with barter could not possibly be good business. And yet economic trade between nations is seen as desirable because it fulfils the same reasons.

Swain points out that the ceremonial element was of great importance. It would be seriously inadequate to suggest that the primary purpose of these exchanges was simply to obtain the items transferred. Instead, the value of the goods was 'enhanced and emphasised . . . by the elaboration of the ritual, which could transform even mundane items into worthy gifts'.[14]

The lesson of this is that pre-conquest Indigenous societies understood the importance of goodwill and interaction with their neighbours to supply themselves with goods. It also helped maintain peace, because the civilising force of ceremony and trade could pacify even would-be enemies. The late Wandjuk Marika, a senior law man in East Arnhem Land, described the importance of incorporating the enemy into a ceremony of friendship. (He is referring here to the *marrma* [two] laws; the Yolngu law is Djangkawu and Wawilak ceremony, and all the ceremonies practised before the missionaries came.)

> There is two – Djangkawu and Wawilak
> the first Christians [before missionaries], the first peacemakers.
> I'm telling you this
> that Djangkawu and Wawilak was the first Christians to make peace and make the friendship.
> No matter whoever got killed,
> who take miyalk from the other tribe.
> Djangkawu Wawilak made peace.
> My people, my father's grandfather and my grandfather used to have peace,
> my father's ceremony was for friendship.[15]

Wandjuk's behaviour throughout his life in the Balanda world aimed primarily to bring Balanda close to Yolngu, to teach them about Djankawu and Wawilak. His speeches, thinking and talking were consistent with this philosophy.[16]

Only an in-depth study by Indigenous people, under the tutelage of senior law men, could reconstruct the details of the pre-1788 constitution of

---

14 T Swain (1985) *Interpreting Aboriginal Religion: An Historical Account*, AASR, p 164.

15 W Marika and J Isaacs (1995) *Wandjuk Marika: Life Story*, University of Queensland Press, p 79.

16 Ibid, p 80.

this continent. But with these insights in mind, I offer the reader some sketchy points as to Indigenous lessons in governance, based on moving forward to build a partnership – as all the senior law men quoted in this chapter have recommended.[17]

There are hopeful signs of reconsideration by White Australians also. Scholars are beginning to question whether the present model of Australian federalism, with its arbitrary State borders, is ripe for constitutional revision:

> Constitutional proposals still boiling... include redrawing more rational, environment-focused state boundaries and a simpler, two-tiered federal system.... [R]estructuring government into a form that matches and serves Australian society and geography could include taking some account of natural bio-geographic regions. There are some 80 bioregions, *all of them clearly related to Australia's pre-European political structures*.[18]

Greens recognise the importance of basing governmental units around bioregions – geographical areas with boundaries determined by ecological and cultural similarities.[19] Bioregions offer the promise of governing ecologically attuned communities through principles learned from nature, rather than through coercive laws imposed by central governments.[20] Again the Enlightenment's chickens come home to roost. Two centuries after Europeans deemed Aborigines too primitive to be recognised as sovereign nations, their descendants learn that the earth-lines these 'savages' knew are more scientifically sustainable than the neat, straight lines demarcating the present States.

The two laws

Although some express alarm that recognising Indigenous law will lead to institutionalised civil war, I submit that Indigenous and White Australian law could in fact co-exist on this continent if proper protocols are instituted. Such protocols give both sides time and 'breathing space' to appraise the situation and come to terms with their own fears about control of the relationship. They also help those who do not share another people's perception of reality (here, the influence of the spirit world) to come to terms with the realisation that no one is asking them to believe in a spirit realm – only to accept the fact that others do.

---

17 See Kamali Council and P Neowarra (1997) 'Ngarinyin Response to the *Wik* Decision' 4(1) *Indigenous Law Bulletin* (available at http://www.law.unsw.edu.au/centres/ile); Mowalijarlai and Malnic (1993); Neidjie (1989).

18 AJ Brown (forthcoming) 'The Structure of Sub-National Government in a Global World', PhD thesis, KCELJAG, Griffith University, quoting I Macphee (1994) 'Challenges for 21st Century Australia: Politics, Economics and Constitutional Reform' 3 *Griffith Law Review* 245 (emphasis added).

19 F Capra and C Spretnak (1984) *Green Politics*, EP Dutton.

20 D Alexander (1990) 'Bioregionalism: Science or Sensibility?' 12 *Environmental Ethics* 161–73.

The clans who brought me up taught me that conciliatory, inclusive behaviour – especially respecting the law and customs of 'the other' – fosters a more aware society. However, Indigenous people are restricted by a 'half law' that prevents them from properly observing their own custodial duties and law. This tension arises from the incomplete nature of Australian law, not only from the fact that was imposed by those who invaded our continent.[21] The late David Mowalijarlai, senior law man of the Ngaringin people, emphasised the need for mutual understanding:

> What we see is, all the White people that were born in [this] country, they are missing the things that came from us mob, and we want to try and share it. And the people were born in this country, in the law country, from all these sacred places in the earth. And they were born on top of that. And that, we call '*wungud*' – very precious. That is where their spirit come from. That's why we can't divide one another, we want to share our gift, that everybody is belonging, we want to share together in the future for other generations to live on. . . . Because what we see is Western culture['s] law, . . . and we want to try and recognise the Crown law and they want to recognise our law too, and get it all evenly recognised. Then we all can share properly. But when one law want[s] to take over all the time, it makes us unhappy.[22]

Conclusion

I wrote this chapter primarily to emphasise that there are other ways of looking at the governance and the constitution of Australia. To understand this country's history, you must begin with the stories emanating from the Land itself, and passed down to its children through a *Yotha Yindi* (mother-child) relationship – not those imported by recent arrivals. Understanding such stories will soften the dualist antagonism between Black and White. And caring for land as a child cares for and respects its mother not only safeguards our sustainable future, but also gives *meaning* to the nation for its very being.

21 C Morris (1999), pp 543–5.

22 Interview with Susanna Lobez (1996) 'Law and Culture in the Ngarinyin Tribal Lands', *ABC Radio National Law Report*, 24 September. See also obituary by S Lobez (1997) *ABC Radio National Law Report*, 30 September.

Appendix 1

Promotion of the Right to Democracy

United Nations Commission on Human Rights Resolution 1999/57

The Commission on Human Rights,

Bearing in mind the indissoluble links between the principles enshrined in the Universal Declaration of Human Rights and the foundation of any democratic society,

Recalling that all peoples have the right of self-determination, by virtue of which they freely determine their political status and freely pursue their economic, social and cultural development,

Recognising that democracy, development and respect for all human rights and fundamental freedoms are interdependent and mutually reinforcing, and that democracy is based on the freely expressed will of the people to determine their own political, economic, social and cultural systems and their full participation in all aspects of their lives,

Recognising also the rich and diverse nature of the community of the world's democracies,

Recalling the large body of international law and instruments, including its resolutions and those of the General Assembly, which confirm the right to full participation and the other fundamental democratic rights and freedoms inherent in any democratic society,

Resolved, on the eve of a new century and millennium, to take all measures within its power to secure for all people the fundamental democratic rights and freedoms to which they are entitled,

1. Affirms that democracy fosters the full realisation of all human rights, and vice versa;
2. Also affirms that the rights of democratic governance include, *inter alia*, the following:
   (a) The rights to freedom of opinion and expression, of thought, conscience and religion, and of peaceful association and assembly;

(b) The right to freedom to seek, receive and impart information and ideas through any media;

(c) The Rule of Law, including legal protection of citizens' rights, interests and personal security, and fairness in the administration of justice and independence of the judiciary;

(d) The right of universal and equal suffrage, as well as free voting procedures and periodic and free elections;

(e) The right of political participation, including equal opportunity for all citizens to become candidates;

(f) Transparent and accountable government institutions;

(g) The right of citizens to choose their governmental system through constitutional or other democratic means;

(h) The right to equal access to public service in one's own country;

3. Notes that the realisation of all human rights – civil, cultural, economic, political and social, including the right to development – are indispensable to human dignity and the full development of human potential and are also integral to democratic society;

4. Urges the continuation and expansion of activities carried out by the United Nations system, other intergovernmental and non-governmental organisations and Member States to promote and consolidate democracy within the framework of international co-operation and to build a democratic political culture through the observance of human rights, mobilisation of civil society and other appropriate measures in support of democratic governance;

5. Requests the Office of the United Nations High Commissioner for Human Rights, in continuing and expanding its programmes and projects of technical co-operation to promote democracy and the Rule of Law, and in the context of the High Commissioner's activities in the promotion of human rights, to give priority assistance to such programmes and to promote democracy-related activities throughout the United Nations system;

6. Requests human rights treaty bodies, the Office of the United Nations High Commissioner for Human Rights and human rights mechanisms of the Commission on Human Rights and the Sub-Commission on Prevention of Discrimination and Protection of Minorities to pay due attention, within their mandates, to those elements of democratic governance outlined in paragraph 2 of the present resolution;

7. Requests the High Commissioner, in her report to the Commission at its 56th session, to reflect progress on the implementation of the present resolution;

8. Requests the Secretary-General to bring the present resolution to the attention of Member States, the competent United Nations organs and intergovernmental and non-governmental organisations and to disseminate it on the widest possible basis;

9. Decides to continue consideration of the matter at its 56th session under the same agenda item.

57th Meeting (27 April 1999)
Adopted by a roll-call vote of 51 votes to none, with 2 abstentions

Appendix 2

Items Proposed for Framework Agreement and Political Negotiations Process

From
Pat Dodson's Vincent Lingiari Memorial Lecture

(27 August 1999,
Northern Territory University, Darwin)

Text on-line at: *http://www.ntu.edu.au/cincrm/events/lectures/lectures/dodsonht.htm*

1. Equality

Aboriginal peoples have the right to all the common human rights and fundamental freedoms recognised in national and international law, as well as to our distinct rights as Indigenous peoples.

2. Distinct characteristics and identities

Aboriginal peoples have the right to maintain and develop our distinct characteristics and identities, whilst taking part in the life of the country as a whole. This includes the right to identify as Indigenous.

We shall not be subject to:

- actions which threaten our distinct cultures and identities;
- the removal of our children from our families and communities;
- taking of our lands and resources; or
- any other measures of assimilation.

3. Self-determination

Aboriginal peoples have the right to self-determination. A right to negotiate our political status and to pursue economic, social and cultural development.

4. Law

Aboriginal peoples have the right to our own law, customs and traditions, and equality before the National Law.

5. Culture . . .

6. Spiritual and religious traditions . . .

7. Language

Aboriginal peoples have the right to our languages, histories, stories, oral traditions and names for people and places. This includes the right to be heard and to receive information in our own languages.

In courts, other proceedings and in the criminal justice system, we shall have the right to understand and be understood, through interpreters and other appropriate ways.

8. Participation and partnerships

Aboriginal peoples have the right to participate in law and policy-making and in decisions that affect us. This includes the right to choose our own representatives. Governments shall obtain our consent before adopting these laws and policies.

Governments shall negotiate partnerships with Aboriginal peoples' representative bodies at local, regional, State and National levels.

9. Economic and social development . . .

10. Special measures

Aboriginal peoples have the right to special measures to improve our economic and social conditions. This includes the areas of employment, education and training, housing and infrastructure, and health.

11. Education and training . . .

12. Land and resources

Aboriginal peoples have the right to own and control the use of our land, waters and other resources.

This includes the right to return of land and resources taken without our consent. Where this is not possible, we shall receive just compensation.

Governments shall obtain our consent before giving approval to activities affecting our land and resources, including the development of mineral resources. We shall receive just compensation for any such activities.

13. Self-government

As a form of self-determination Aboriginal peoples have the right to self-government and autonomy in relation to our own affairs. This includes the right to determine the structure and membership of our self-governing institutions.

Governments shall facilitate the negotiation of self-government and regional agreements.

15. Constitutional recognition

The Federal Parliament shall initiate processes leading to concrete constitutional change to recognise and protect the special place and rights of the Aboriginal peoples in the Australian polity.

16. Treaties and agreements

The Federal Parliament shall enact legislation establishing a framework for the negotiation of agreements with the Aboriginal peoples.

Governments shall respect treaties and agreements entered into with Aboriginal peoples.

17. Ongoing processes

The Federal Parliament shall establish a discussion, research, information and negotiation forum to promote public awareness and to draft national legislation enacting principles of recognition, guidelines for public policy, and the framework for negotiation of agreements referred to above.

BIBLIOGRAPHY

'Alternative Governing Structure Program: Program Description and Funding Guidelines' (1996) 1 *Australian Indigenous Law Reporter* 675.

'FBI Kept Secret Files on the Supreme Court' (1988) *New York Times*, Nat Ed, 21 August, sec 1-13.

'Net-porn Law Faces Challenge' (1998) *Brisbane Courier-Mail*, 24 October.

'No Majority Best, Says Chaney' (1999) *Melbourne Age*, 7 August.

Aboriginal and Torres Strait Islander Commission (ATSIC) (1995) *Recognition, Rights and Reform: Report to Government on Native Title Social Justice Measures*, ATSIC.

Aboriginal and Torres Strait Islander Commission (ATSIC) (1999) *Aboriginal and Torres Strait Islander Peoples and Australia's Obligations under the United Nations Convention on the Elimination of all Forms of Racial Discrimination: A Report Submitted by the Aboriginal and Torres Strait Islander Commission to the United Nations Committee on the Elimination of Racial Discrimination*, ATSIC.

Aboriginal and Torres Strait Islander Commission (ATSIC) (1999) 'Indigenous Leaders Summitt [*sic*] Urges Federal Government Talks on Rights' Media Release, ATSIC, 15 September.

Aboriginal and Torres Strait Islander Commission (ATSIC) (1999) *Indigenous Peoples, Constitution and Treaties: A Paper for Presentation at a Dialogue on Indigenous Rights in the Commonwealth Institute of Commonwealth Studies (London)*, ATSIC.

Aboriginal and Torres Strait Islander Social Justice Commissioner (1995) *Indigenous Social Justice: Strategies and Recommendations – A Submission to the Parliament of the Commonwealth of Australia on the Social Justice Package*, ATSISJC.

Ackerman, BA 'The Rise of World Constitutionalism' (1997) 83 *Virginia Law Review* 771.

Albertyn, C (1994) 'Women and the Transition to Democracy in South Africa' *Acta Juridica* 39.

Alexander, D (1990) 'Bioregionalism: Science or Sensibility?' 12 *Environmental Ethics* 161–73.

Alfred, T (1999) *Peace, Power, Righteousness: An Indigenous Manifesto*, Oxford University Press.

Altman, J, F Morphy and T Rowse (eds) (1999) *Land Rights at Risk? Evaluations of the Reeves Report*, CAEPR Research Monograph No 14, ANU Centre for Aboriginal Economic Policy Research.

Aman, AC, Jr (1998) 'The Globalising State: A Future-Oriented Perspective on the Public/Private Distinction, Federalism and Democracy' 31 *Vanderbilt Journal of Transnational Law* 770.

ANC Land Commission (1991) *Land Manifesto for ANC National Conference*, July.

Anjum, S (1984) 'Land-use Planning in the North Slope Borough' in D Leamann (ed), *National and Regional Interests in the North: Third National Workshop on People, Resources, and the Environment North of 60°*, Canadian Arctic Resources Committee, pp 269–89.

Argy, F (1998) *Australia at the Cross-Roads*, Allen & Unwin.

Atkinson, R and N McWhirter (1995) *Treason at Maastricht: The Destruction of the Nation State*, Compuprint.

Attanasio, JB (1996) 'Rapporteur's Overview and Conclusions: Of Sovereignty, Globalisation and Courts' 28 *New York University Journal of International Law and Policy* 1.

Auerbach, J (1976) *Unequal Justice*, Oxford University Press, ch 8.

Austin, J (1832) *The Province of Jurisprudence Determined*.

Australian Greenhouse Office (1999) *National Carbon Accounting for Land Based Sources and Sinks* (available at: http://www.greenhouse.gov.au/ncas/).

Australian Law Reform Commission (1986) *Report No 31: The Recognition of Aboriginal Customary Laws*, AGPS.

Australian Surveying and Land Information Group, Department of Administrative Services (1994) *Indigenous Language Map*, in D Horton, *The Encyclopedia of Aboriginal Australia: Aboriginal and Torres Strait Islander History, Society and Culture*, Aboriginal Studies Press.

Australians for Native Title and Reconciliation (ANTaR) (1999) *Indigenous Social Justice: What It Means and How to Achieve It*, ANTaR Occasional Paper No 2.

Babbage, R (1990) *The Strategic Significance of Torres Strait*, ANU Strategic and Defence Studies Centre.

Ball, AR (1993) *Modern Politics and Government* (5th edn), Macmillan.

Ball, D (ed) (1991) *Aborigines in the Defence of Australia*, Australian National University Press.

Barber, BR (1995) *Jihad Versus McWorld*, Times Books.

Barber, K (1966) 'The Legal Status of the American Communist Party: 1965' 15 *Journal of Public Law* 94.

Barendt, E (1994) 'Free Speech in Australia: A Comparative Perspective' 16 *Sydney Law Review* 149.

Bartlett, R (ed) (1993) *The Mabo Decision: And the Full Text of the Decision in Mabo and Others v State of Queensland*, Butterworths.

Barton, G (1889) *History of New South Wales from the Records, Vol 1 (Governor Phillip)*, Charles Potter.

Bauman, RW (1992) 'Property Rights in the Canadian Constitutional Context' 8 *South African Journal on Human Rights* 344.

Bauman, Z (1998) *Globalisation: The Human Consequences*, Polity Press.

Beckett, J (1987) *Torres Strait Islanders: Custom and Colonialism*, Cambridge University Press.

Beer, LW (1992) *Constitutional Systems in Late Twentieth Century Asia*, University of Washington Press.

Bell, DA, Jr (1978) 'The Referendum: Democracy's Barrier to Racial Equality' 54 *Washington Law Review* 1.

Bell, P (ed) (1997) *The Making of the Constitution*, Churchill Murray.

Bennett, S (1999) *Should the Australian Electoral System be Changed?*, Current Issues Brief No 10, April, Politics and Public Administration Group, Department of the Parliamentary Library, Information and Research Services.

Bennett, TW (1985) *The Application of Customary Law in Southern Africa*, Juta.

Bennett, TW (1991) *A Sourcebook of African Customary Law for South Africa*, Butterworths

Bennett, TW (1995) *Human Rights and African Customary Law*, Juta.

Bennett, M and AC Castles (1982) *A Source Book of Australian Legal History*, LBC.

Berger, T (1985) *Village Journey: The Report of the Alaska Native Review Commission*, Hill and Wang.

Berman, S and K McNamara (1999) 'Central Banks: A Withdrawal of Accountability' *Australian Financial Review*, 14 May.

Blasi, V (1985) 'The Pathological Perspective and the First Amendment' 85 *Columbia Law Review* 449.

Blaustein, G (nd) *Constitutions of the World* (available at http://www.uni-wuerzburg.de/law/index.html).

Blay, S (1986) 'The International Covenant on Civil and Political Rights and the Recognition of Customary Law Practices of Indigenous Tribes: The Case of Australian Aborigines' 19 *Comparative and International Law Journal of Southern Africa* 199.

Bogart, WA (1994) *Courts and Country: The Limits of Litigation and the Social and Political Life of Canada*, Oxford University Press.

Boldt, M (1993) *Surviving as Indians: The Challenge of Self-Government*, University of Toronto Press.

Bollinger, LC (1986) *The Tolerant Society*, Oxford University Press.

Bontecou, E (1953) *The Federal Loyalty–Security Program*, Cornell University Press.

Boorstin, D (1941) *The Mysterious Science of the Law*, Beacon Press.

Brantenberg, OT (1993) 'The End of 13 Years of Silence: The Sami Land Rights Issue in Norway' *IWGIA Newsletter*, No 4/1993 (October–December).

Brantenberg, OT (1995) 'Murky Agenda in the Morketid: Norwegian Policy, Sami Politics and the Tromso Conference' in *Becoming Visible: Indigenous Politics and Self-Government*, The Centre for Sami Studies, University of Tromso.

Brennan, F (1996) 'An Australian Convert from a Constitutional Bill of Rights' 7 *Public Law Review* 132.

Brennan, F (1996) 'One Vote No' 6 *Eureka Street* 21.

Brennan, G (1997) 'Direct Democracy: The Case Against' *Policy* (Autumn) 32–4.

Brown, AJ (forthcoming) 'The Structure of Sub-National Government in a Global World' PhD thesis, KCELJAG, Griffith University.

Brown, RS, Jr (1958) *Loyalty and Security: Employment Tests in the United States*, Yale University Press.

Brown, H and D Pearce (1994) 'National Aboriginal Constitutional Convention Report' in C Fletcher (ed), *Aboriginal Self-Determination in Australia*, Report Series, Australian Institute of Aboriginal and Torres Strait Islander Studies, Aboriginal Studies Press.

Brownlie, I (1988) 'The Rights of Peoples in International Law' in J Crawford (ed), *The Rights of Peoples*, Clarendon Press.

Brundtland, GH (1987) 'Empowering Vulnerable Groups' in *Our Common Future: [Report of the] World Commission on Environment and Development*, Oxford University Press.

Bryce, J (1995) *The American Commonwealth*, Liberty Fund.

Budlender (1992) 'The Right to Equitable Access to Land' 8 *South African Journal on Human Rights* 295.

Buchanan, JM and G Tullock (1962) *The Calculus of Consent*, University of Michigan Press.

Burchill, S (1999) 'In-your-face Globalisation Yields "Democratic Deficit"' *Australian Financial Review*, 12 August.

Burdekin, B (1994) 'Foreword' in P Alston (ed), *Towards an Australian Bill of Rights*, ANU Centre for International and Public Law/Human Rights and Equal Opportunity Commission.

Burke, T (1982) 'Friends of the Earth and the Conservation of Resources' in P Willetts (ed), *Pressure Groups in the Global System: The Transnational Relations of Issue-Orientated Non-Governmental Organisations*, Frances Pinter.

Campbell, TD (1996) *The Legal Theory of Ethical Positivism*, Dartmouth.

Campbell, TD (1999) 'Human Rights: A Culture of Controversy' 26 *Journal of Law and Society* 6–26.

Capra, F and C Spretnak (1984) *Green Politics*, EP Dutton.

Carey, H (1996) *Believing in Australia: A Cultural History of Religions*, Allen & Unwin.

Carty, A (1991) 'English Constitutional Law from a Postmodernist Perspective' in P Fitzpatrick (ed), *Dangerous Supplements: Resistance and Renewal in Jurisprudence*, Pluto Press.

Castles, S (1995–6) *Research Paper No 16: Multicultural Citizenship*, Commonwealth Parliamentary Research Service.

Center for Development Studies (1991) *A Bill of Rights for a Democratic South Africa: Papers and Report of a Conference Convened by the ANC Constitutional Committee*, May.

Centre for Comparative Constitutional Studies (CCC) (1991) *Statement: Constitutional Centenary Conference* (Sydney) 5 April, University of Melbourne.

Cerny, PG (1996) 'Globalisation and Other Stories: The Search for a New Paradigm of International Relations' 51 *International Journal* 617.

Chafee, Z, Jr (1942) *Free Speech in the United States*, Harvard University Press.

Chafee, Z, Jr (1947) *Government and Mass Communications: A Report from the Commission on Freedom of the Press*, U of Chicago P.

Chanock, M (1991) 'A Peculiar Sharpness: An Essay on Property in the History of Customary Law in Colonial Africa' 32 *Journal of African History* 65.

Chesterman, J and B Galligan (1997) *Citizens Without Rights: Aborigines and Australian Citizenship*, Cambridge University Press.

Chopra, J and TG Weiss (1992) 'Sovereignty is no longer Sacrosanct: Codifying Humanitarian Intervention' 6 *Ethics and International Affairs* 95–117.

Choudhry, S (1999) 'Globalisation in Search of Justification: Toward a Theory of Comparative Constitutional Interpretation' 74 *Indiana Law Journal* 819.

Claassens, A (1992) 'Editorial' 8 *South African Journal on Human Rights* v.

Cleaver, HM (1998) 'The Zapatista Effect: The Internet and the Rise of an Alternative Political Fabric' 51 *Journal of International Affairs* 621.

Cohen, B (1997) *Whitlam to Winston*, Allen & Unwin.

Cole, T (1959) 'Three Constitutional Courts: A Comparison' 53 *American Political Science Review* 963.

Committee on the Elimination of Racial Discrimination (1999) *Decision on Australia*, CERD/C/ 54/Misc 40/Rev 2, 18 March, reproduced in (1999) 4 *Australian Indigenous Law Reporter* 140.

Condorcet, Marquis de (1795) *Sketch of the Intellectual Progress of Mankind.*

Constitutional Assembly (1995) Constitutional Committee, Documentation: Volume 2A Land Rights, 15 September.

Constitutional Assembly (1995) Theme Committee 6.3: Specialised Structures of Government: Documentation Volume 2A: Land Rights, 15 September.

Constitutional Assembly (1995) Constitutional Committee Subcommittee, Documentation: Land Rights, 9 October.

Constitutional Centenary Foundation (CCF) (1999) *1999 Referendum: A New Preamble*, CCF.

Constitutional Commission (1987) *Report of the Advisory Committee on Executive Government*, Canberra Publishing & Printing, June.

Constitutional Commission (1988) *Final Report*, AGPS.

Constitutional Convention (1998) *Communiqué*, 13 February.

Coonan, H (1999) 'The Senate: Safeguard or Handbrake on Democracy?' Address to the Sydney Institute, 3 February.

Coonan, H (1999) 'Survival of the Fittest' delivered at the Conference Marking Fifty Years of Proportional Representation for the Senate, Canberra, 6 August.

Coper, M (1983) 'Interpreting the Constitution: A Handbook for Judges and Commentators' in AR Blackshield (ed), *Legal Change: Essays in Honour of Julius Stone*, Butterworths.

Council for Aboriginal Reconciliation (CAR) (1993) *The Position of Indigenous Peoples in National Constitutions: Conference Report* (4–5 June), CAR and CCF.

Council for Aboriginal Reconciliation (CAR) (1993) *The Position of Indigenous Peoples in National Constitutions: Speeches from the Conference* (4–5 June), CAR and CCF.

Council for Aboriginal Reconciliation (CAR) (1995) *Going Forward: Social Justice for the First Australians – A Submission to the Commonwealth Government*, AGPS.

Council for Aboriginal Reconciliation (CAR) (1999) *Documents of Reconciliation*, CAR (available at http://www.austlii.edu.au/au/orgs/car/).

Cowell, S, MB Lane and M McDonald (1998) 'Conservation, Indigenous Interests and Co-management: The Lawn Hill Case' 34(1) *Australian Parks and Recreation* 36–8.

Craik, J, G Davis and N Sunderland (2000) 'Cultural Policy and National Identity' in G Davis and M Keating (eds), *The Future of Australian Governance: Policy Choices*, Allen & Unwin.

Cross, C (1992) 'An Alternative Legality: The Property Rights Question in Relation to South African Land Reform' 8 *South African Journal on Human Rights* 305.

Crough, G and C Christophersen (1993) *Aboriginal People in the Economy of the Kimberley Region*, Australian National University.

Dahl, RA (1957) 'Decision-Making in a Democracy: The Role of the Supreme Court as a National Policy-Maker' 6 *Journal of Public Law* 279.

Dahl, RA (1966) 'Epilogue' in RA Dahl (ed), *Political Oppositions in Western Democracies*, Yale University Press.

Dahlén, O (1982) 'A Governmental Response to Pressure Groups: The Case of Sweden' in P Willetts (ed), *Pressure Groups in the Global System: The Transnational Relations of Issue-Orientated Non-Governmental Organisations*, Frances Pinter.

Danayarri, H (1992) in D Bird Rose (ed), *Dingo Makes Us Human: Life and Land in an Aboriginal Australian Culture*, Cambridge University Press.

David, SR (1987) *Third World Coups d'État and International Security*, Johns Hopkins University Press.

Davidson, A (1997) *From Subject to Citizen: Australian Citizenship in the Twentieth Century*, Cambridge University Press.

Davies, J (1999) 'Of Caribou and Kangaroos: Agreements about Wildlife' 4 *Indigenous Law Bulletin* (June) 27–9.

Davis, G and M Keating (eds) (2000) *The Future of Australian Governance: Policy Choices*, Allen & Unwin.

de Lacy, T and B Lawson (1997) 'The Uluru-Kakadu Model: Joint Management of Aboriginal-owned National Parks in Australia' in S Stevens (ed), *Conservation through Cultural Survival: Indigenous Peoples and Protected Areas*, Island Press.

de Tocqueville, A (1835) *Democracy in America*, JP Mayer (ed) (1969) Anchor.

de Villiers, B (1992) 'Directive Principles of State Policy and Fundamental Rights: The Experience of India' *SA Journal of Human Rights* 29.

de Villiers, B (1999) *Land Claims and National Parks: The Makuleke Experience*, HSRC.

Deakin, A (1944) *The Federal Story*, Robertson & Mullins.

Debates of the Australasian Federal Convention (1891) Sydney, Government Printer.

Debelle, B (1983) 'Aboriginal Customary Law: Progress Report' in G Nettheim (ed), *Human Rights for Aboriginal People in the 80s*, Legal Books.

Democratic Party (1993) *Freedom Under the Rule of Law: Advancing Liberty in the New South Africa*, Draft Bill of Rights, May.

Desai, M (2000) 'The Left is Wrong about Free Trade' *New Statesman and Society*, 17 April.

Detmold, MJ (1985) *The Australian Commonwealth. A Fundamental Analysis of its Constitution*, LBC Information Services.

Detmold, MJ (1994) 'The New Constitutional Law' 16 *Sydney Law Review* 228.

Diamond, L (1996) 'Is the Third Wave Over?' 7 *Journal of Democracy* 20–37.

Dicey, AV (1885) *Introduction to the Study of the Law of the Constitution* (7th edn, 1915; Macmillan 10th edn, 1960).

Diggins, JP (1988) 'Class, Classical, and Consensus Views of the Constitution' 55 *University of Chicago Law Review* 570.

Dixon, O (1952) 'Address on Being Sworn in as Chief Justice' 85 CLR xi.

Dixson, M (1999) *The Imaginary Australian: Anglo-Celts and Identity – 1788 to the Present*, University of New South Wales Press.

Djerrkura, G (1999) 'Indigenous Peoples, Constitutions and Treaties' Speech, Chair of Aboriginal and Torres Strait Islander Commission (ATSIC) Dialogue on Indigenous Rights in the Commonwealth Institute of Commonwealth Studies (London) Canberra (available at http://www.atsic.gov.au/).

Djerrkura, G (1999) 'No Secret in Unfinished Indigenous Business' *Sydney Morning Herald*, 29 September.

Dodson, M (1999) 'The Human Rights Situation of Indigenous Peoples in Australia' 1 *Indigenous Affairs* 32.

Dodson, P (1999) *Until the Chains are Broken*, 4th Annual Vincent Lingiari Memorial Lectures, Northern Territory University, 27 August (available at http: //www.ntu.edu.au/cincrm/events/lectures/lectures/dodsonht.htm; or http://www.austlii.edu.au/au/special/rs.ct/rsjlibrary/car/lingiari/4dodson.html).

Dodson, M and S Pritchard (1998) 'Recent Developments in Indigenous Policy: The Abandonment of Self-Determination?' 4 *Indigenous Law Bulletin* 4.

Dorsen, N, P Bender and B Neuborne (1976) *Emerson, Haber, and Dorsen's Political and Civil Rights in the United States* (4th edn), Little, Brown, vol 1.

Dorsett, S and Godden, L (1998) *A Guide to Overseas Precedents of Relevance to Native Title*, Australian Institute of Aboriginal and Torres Strait Islander Studies.

Downing, J (1988) *Ngurra Walytia: Country of My Spirit*, North Australia Research Unit, Australian National University.

Dworkin, RM (1977) *Taking Rights Seriously*, Harvard University Press.

Dworkin, RM (1985) *A Matter of Principle*, Harvard University Press.

Dworkin, RM (1996) *Freedom's Law: The Moral Reading of the American Constitution*, Harvard University Press.

East Kimberley Project (1985) *Report of the Committee of Review of Aboriginal Employment and Training Programmes*, August.

Ecologically Sustainable Development Committee (1999) *Report: The Sustainability of Current Logging Practices*, tabled WA Legislative Council, December.

Editorial (1999) 'No Secrets' *Sydney Morning Herald*, 24 August.

Elliot, L (1994) *International Environmental Politics: Protecting the Antarctic*, St Martin's Press.

Elster, J (1995) 'Strategic Uses of Argument' in K Arrow, RH Mnookin, L Ross, A Tversky and R Wilson (eds), *Barriers to Conflict Resolution*, Norton.

Ely, JH (1981) *Democracy and Distrust: A Theory of Judicial Review*, Harvard University Press.

Ely, JW, Jr (1992) *The Guardian of Every Other Right: The Constitutional History of Property Rights*, Oxford University Press.

English, R (1996) 'Ubuntu: The Quest for an Indigenous Jurisprudence' 12 *South African Journal on Human Rights* 641.

Epstein, RA (1988) 'Modern Republicanism: Or the Flight from Substance' 97 *Yale Law Journal* 1633.

Epstein, L, JA Segal, HJ Spaeth and TG Walker (1994) *The Supreme Court Compendium: Data, Decisions and Developments*, Congressional Quarterly.

Erskine, H (1970) 'The Polls: Freedom of Speech' 34 *Public Opinion Quarterly* 483.

Eule, JN (1990) 'Judicial Review of Direct Democracy' 90 *Yale Law Journal* 1503.

Evans, G (1998) 'Intellectual Property Disputes and the Supercourt of the World Trade Organisation: The Case for a New Model of Dispute Resolution' 16 *Prometheus* 395.

Evans, H (1983) 'Questioning the Tyranny' *Quadrant* (April) 70–3.

Evans, H (1998) 'The Other Metropolis: The Australian Founders' Knowledge of America' 2 *The New Federalist* 30.

Fallon, RH (1989) 'What is Republicanism, and is it Worth Reviving?' 102 *Harvard Law Review* 1672.

Favoreu, L (1990) 'Constitutional Review in Europe' in L Henkin and AJ Rosenthal (eds), *Constitutionalism and Rights: The Influence of the United States Constitution Abroad*, Columbia University Press.

Fels, A (1998) 'Economic Globalisation: Creative Government Responses' 46(11) *Growth* 11–17.

Financial Times (1999) 'Democracy is a Very Nice Thing', 10–11 July, p viii.

Fine, B (1984) *Democracy and the Rule of Law: Liberal Ideals and Marxist Critiques*, Pluto Press.

Finn, PD (1995) '"The Forgotten Trust": The People and the State' in M Cope (ed), *Equity: Issues and Trends*, Federation Press.

Finn, PD (1995) 'A Sovereign People, A Public Trust' in PD Finn (ed), *Essays on Law and Government*, LBC.

Finnemore, M (1996) 'Norms, Culture, and World Politics: Insights from Sociology's Institutionalism' 50 *International Organization* 325.

Fishkin, J (1991) *Democracy and Deliberation*, Yale University Press.

Foster, D (1995) *Gurig National Park: The First Ten Years of Joint Management*, Australian Institute for Aboriginal And Torres Straits Island Studies.

France, A (1933) *Penguin Island*, Random House (first published 1908).

Franck, TM (1992) 'The Emerging Right to Democratic Governance' 86 *American Journal of International Law* 46.

Franklin, NE (1992) 'Initiative and Referendum: Participatory Democracy or Rolling Back the State?' in M Munro-Clark (ed), *Citizen Participation in Government*, Hale & Iremonger.

Freedom House, *Freedom in the World 1995* (available at http://freedomhouse.org/).

Frenkel, S (1994) 'Old Theories in New Places? Environmental Determinism and Bio-Regionalism' 46 *Professional Geographer* 289–95.

Friedman, T (1999) *The Lexus and the Olive Tree*, HarperCollins.

Funnell, W (1997) 'The Curse of Sisyphus: Public Sector Audit Independence in an Age of Economic Rationalism' 56 AJPA 87.

Galligan, B (1995) *A Federal Republic: Australia's Constitutional System of Government*, Cambridge University Press.

Galligan, B and J Chesterman (1999) 'Australia's Citizenship Void' in A Davidson and K Weekly (eds), *Globalisation and Citizenship in the Asia-Pacific*, Macmillan.

Galligan, B and C Walsh (1992) 'Federation: Yes or No?' in G Craven (ed), *Australian Federation: Towards the Second Century*, Melbourne University Press.

Garrow, DJ (1981) *The FBI and Martin Luther King Jr*, Penguin.

Giddens, A (1994) *Beyond Left and Right: The Future of Radical Politics*, Polity Press.

Gillespie, D (1988) 'Tourism in Kakadu National Park' in D Wade-Marshall and P Loveday (eds), *Contemporary Issues in Development*, ANU Northern Australia Research Unit.

Glendon, MA (1991) *Rights Talk: The Impoverishment of Political Discourse*, Free Press.

Global Development Finance (1999) World Bank Group (at http://www.worldbank. org).

Goldblatt, D, D Held, AG McGrew and J Perraton (1998) *Global Flows and Global Transformations: Concepts, Arguments and Evidence*, Polity Press.

Goldstein, RJ (1978) *Political Repression in Modern America from 1870 to the Present*, Shenkman.

Goodell, C (1978) *Political Prisoners in America*, Random House.

Goot, M and T Rowse (eds) (1994) *Make a Better Offer: The Politics of Mabo*, Pluto Press.

Gosovic, B (1992) *The Quest for World Environmental Cooperation: The Case of the UN Global Environmental Monitoring System*, Routledge.

Gray, J (1999) 'The Rise of Global Guardians' *Australian Financial Review*, 18–19 September.

Gray, R, D Lea and S Roberts (eds) (1994) *Constitutional Change in the 1990s*, Northern Territory Legislative Assembly Sessional Committee on Constitutional Development and North Australia Research Unit, Australian National University.

Grayson, I (1999) 'Future of Technology' *The Australian*, 12 October.

Grossman, LK (1995) *The Electronic Republic: Reshaping Democracy in the Information Age*, Penguin.

Gutmann, A and DF Thompson (1996) *Democracy and Disagreement*, Harvard University Press.

Gwyn, WB (1965) *The Meaning of the Separation of Powers*, Tulane University Press.

Gyngell, A and M Wesley (2000) 'Interweaving of Foreign and Domestic Policy: International Policy' in G Davis and M Keating (eds), *The Future of Australian Governance: Policy Choices*, Allen & Unwin.

Habermas, J (1996) *Between Facts and Norms*, Polity Press.

Hage, G and R Couch (eds) (1999) *The Future of Australian Multiculturalism: Reflections on the Twentieth Anniversary of Jean Martin's The Migrant Presence*, Research Institute for Humanities and Social Sciences.

Hamilton, C (1999) 'Native Wildlife under Threat' *Australian Financial Review*, 13 May.

Handford, P (1999) 'The Changing Face of Law Reform' 73 *ALJ* 503.

Hanf, K and A Underdal (1998) 'Domesticating International Commitments: Linking National and International Decision-Making' in A Underdal (ed), *The Politics of International Environmental Management*, Kluwer.

Hansen, A (1993) 'Greenpeace and Press Coverage of Environmental Issues' in A Hansen (ed), *The Mass Media and Environmental Issues*, Leicester University Press.

Haralambos, M and R Heald (1980) *Sociology: Themes and Perspectives*, University Tutorial Press.

Harrison, JFC (ed) (1965) *Society and Politics in England 1780–1960*, Harper & Row.

Hassall, G (1997) 'Constitutional Trends in Asia' in V Taylor (ed), *Asian Law through Australian Eyes*, LBC.

Heatley, A and P McNab (1999) 'The Northern Territory Statehood Referendum 1998' 10 *Public Law Review* 3.

Held, D (1989) *Political Theory and the Modern State*, Polity Press.

Held, D (1995) *Democracy and Global Order: From the Modern State to Cosmopolitan Governance*, Stanford University Press.

Henderson, G (1995) *A Howard Government? Inside the Coalition*, HarperCollins.

Henkin, L (1990) 'Introduction' in L Henkin and AJ Rosenthal (eds), *Constitutionalism and Rights: The Influence of the United States Constitution Abroad*, Columbia University Press.

Herron, J (1999) Speech to the United Nations, Minister of Aboriginal and Torres Strait Islander Affairs, Geneva, 29 July (available at http://www.atsia.gov.au/fr_press.html).

Hiebert, JL (1999) 'Why Must a Bill of Rights be a Contest of Political and Judicial Wills? The Canadian Alternative' 10 *Public Law Review* 22.

Hiley, G (ed) (1997) *The Wik Case: Issues and Implications*, Butterworths.

Hirst, P and G Thompson (1996) *Globalisation in Question*, Polity Press.

Hobbes, T (1973) *Leviathan*, Dent (first published 1651).

Holton, R (1998) *Globalisation and the Nation-State*, Macmillan.

Horwitz, MJ (1977) 'The Rule of Law: An Unqualified Human Good?' 86 *Yale Law Journal* 561.

Horwitz, MJ (1977) *The Transformation of American Law 1780–1860*, Harvard University Press.

House of Representatives Standing Committee on Aboriginal and Torres Strait Islander Affairs (1999) *Unlocking the Future: The Report of the Inquiry into the Reeves Review of the Aboriginal Land Rights (Northern Territory) Act 1976*, Commonwealth Parliament.

House of Representatives Standing Committee on the Environment, Recreation and Arts (1993) *Biodiversity: The Role of Protected Areas*, AGPS.

Howard, C (1980) *The Constitution, Power and Politics*, Fontana/Collins.

Howell, PA (1979) *The Judicial Committee of the Privy Council, 1833–1876*, Cambridge University Press.

Howell, PA (1999) 'Chamberlain' in H Irving (ed), *The Centenary Companion to Australian Federation*, Cambridge University Press.

Human Rights and Equal Opportunity Commission (HREOC) (1991) *Racist Violence: Report of the National Inquiry into Racist Violence in Australia*, Race Discrimination Commissioner, HREOC.

Human Rights and Equal Opportunity Commission (HREOC) (1995) *Indigenous Social Justice, Vol 1, Strategies and Recommendations*, Submission to the Parliament of the Commonwealth of Australia on the Social Justice Package by Michael Dodson, Aboriginal and Torres Strait Islander Social Justice Commissioner, HREOC (Vol 2, *Regional Agreements*, and Vol 3, *Resource Materials*).

Huntington, SP (1991) *The Third Wave: Democratization in the Late Twentieth Century*, University of Oklahoma Press.

Hyman, HH (1964) 'England and America: Climates of Tolerance and Intolerance' in D Bell (ed), *The Radical Right*, Anchor.

Ibrahim, A and MP Jain (1992) 'The Constitution of Malaysia and the American Constitutional Influence' in LW Beer (ed), *Constitutional Systems in Late Twentieth-Century Asia*, University of Washington Press.

Ignatieff, M (1998) *The Warrior's Honor: Ethnic War and the Modern Conscience*, Chatto & Windus.

Independent Commission on International Development Issues (Chair: Willy Brandt) (1980) *North–South: A Programme for Survival* (The Brandt Report), MIT Press.

Inglis, KS (1980) 'The Imperial Connection: Telegraphic Communication between England and Australia, 1872–1902' in AF Madden and WH Morris-Jones (eds), *Australia and Britain: Studies in a Changing Relationship*, Sydney University Press.

International Work Group for Indigenous Affairs (IWGIA) (1999) *Indigenous Affairs*, Special Issue for 50th Anniversary of the Universal Declaration of Human Rights, No 1/1999 (January–March), IWGIA, Copenhagen.

Irving, H (ed) (1999) *The Centenary Companion to Australian Federation*, Cambridge University Press.

Irving, H (1999) *To Constitute a Nation: A Cultural History of Australia's Constitution*, Cambridge University Press.

James, L (1995) *The Rise and Fall of the British Empire*, Abacus.

Joelson, MR (1963) 'The Dismissal of Civil Servants in the Interests of National Security' *Public Law* 51.

Joelson, MR (1963) 'Legal Problems in the Dismissal of Civil Servants in the United States, Britain, and France' 12 *American Journal of Comparative Law* 149.

Johansen, BE (1982) *Forgotten Founders: How the American Indian Helped Shape Democracy*, Gambit/Harvard Common Press.

Johnson, R (1999) 'The Challenge of the Knowledge Economy: Managing Knowledge' presented at Australia's Information Future Innovation and Knowledge Management for the Twenty-First Century, Australian National University, 3–4 March.

Joint Standing Committee on Treaties (1999) *Report No 18: Multilateral Agreement on Investment*, March.

Jokinen, P and K Koskinen (1998) 'Unity in Environmental Discourse? The Role of Decision-makers, Experts and Citizens in Developing Finnish Environmental Policy' 26 *Policy and Politics* 55

Judge, AJN (1994) 'NGOs and Civil Society: Some Realities and Distortions – The Challenge of "Necessary-to-Governance Organisations" (NGOs)', paper presented to a seminar on state and society at the Russian Public Policy Centre, Moscow, 6–8 December.

Jull, P (1981) 'Aboriginal Peoples and Political Change in the North Atlantic Area' 16 *Journal of Canadian Studies* 41.

Jull, P (1993) *A Sea Change: Overseas Indigenous-Government Relations in the Coastal Zone*, Resource Assessment Commission, Commonwealth of Australia, Canberra, September.

Jull, P (1996) 'An Aboriginal Policy for the Millennium: The Three Social Justice Reports' 1(1) *Australian Indigenous Law Reporter* 1.

Jull, P (1996) *Constitution-Making in Northern Territories: Legitimacy and Governance in Australia*, Central Land Council.

Jull, P (1998) 'Constitutional Work in Progress: Reconciliation and Renewal in Indigenous Australia and the World' (background paper for Indigenous Law Centre, University of New South Wales), Centre for Democracy, University of Queensland, Brisbane.

Jull, P (1998) '"First World" Indigenous Internationalism after Twenty-five Years' 4 *Indigenous Law Bulletin* 13.

Jull, P (1999) 'Constitutional Ambles and Preambles: With or Without the Country's Indigenous Peoples!?' Note, Department of Government, University of Queensland, Brisbane, 11 February.

Jull, P (1999) 'Reconciliation and Northern Territories, Canadian-Style: The Nunavut Process and Product' 4 *Indigenous Law Bulletin* 47.

Jull, P and H Kajlich (1999) 'A Reconciled Constitution and Reconciled Queensland: Opportunity for a Political Accord?', Brief to the Constitutional Reform Commission (Queensland) Department of Government, University of Queensland, Brisbane, 16 September.

Jull, P, M Mulrennan, M Sullivan, G Cough and D Lea (eds) (1994) *Surviving Columbus: Indigenous Peoples, Political Reform and Environmental Management in North Australia*, North Australia Research Unit, Australian National University.

Jupp, J (1999) *The Political Participation of Ethnic Minorities in Australia*, Centre for Immigration and Multicultural Studies.

Kairys, D (ed) (1998) *The Politics of Law: A Progressive Critique* (3rd edn), Basic Books.

Kalantzis, M (1995) *The New Citizen and the New State: An Australian Case for Civic Pluralism*, Occasional Paper No 9, Centre for Workplace Communication and Culture.

Kamali Council and P Neowarra (1997) 'Ngarinyin Response to the *Wik* Decision' 4 *Indigenous Law Bulletin* (available at http://www.law.unsw.edu.au/centres/ilc/).

Keck, ME and K Sikkink (1998) *Activists Beyond Borders: Advocacy Networks in International Politic*, Cornell University Press.

Kellow, A (1999) *International Toxic Risk Management: Ideals, Interests and Implementation*, Cambridge University Press.

Kellow, A (1999) '"No Representation Without Taxation": A Skeptical Look at the Case for Global Civil Society', paper presented to the 4th Annual Conference on International Trade Education and Research: 'The WTO Millennium Round' Melbourne, 16–18 September.

Kellow, A (2000) 'Norms, Interests and Environment NGOs: The Limits of Cosmopolitanism' 9(3) *Environmental Politics* (Autumn).

Kelly, P (1999) 'The New Social Glue' *Australia Unlimited* Conference, 4 May.

Kemp, R (1994) 'International Tribunals and the Attack on Australian Democracy' in *Upholding the Australian Constitution, Volume 4*, Samuel Griffith Society.

Keneally, T (1993) *Our Republic*, William Heinemman.

Kerr, AJ (1990) *The Customary Law of Immovable Property and of Succession*, Grocott & Sherry.

Kidd, R (1997) *The Way We Civilise: Aboriginal Affairs – The Untold Story*, University of Queensland Press.

Kidney, S (1999) *Knowledge Workers: Lessons from the Information Technology Revolution*, Brisbane Institute.

King-Boyes, M (1977) *Patterns of Aboriginal Culture: Then and Now*, McGraw-Hill.

Klotz, A (1995) 'Norms Reconstituting Interests: Global Racial Equality and US Sanctions against South Africa' 49 *International Organization* 451.

Klug, H (1996) 'Bedevilling Agrarian Reform: The Impact of Past, Present and Future Legal Frameworks' in J Van Zyl, J Kirsten and HP Binswanger (eds), *Agricultural Land Reform in South Africa: Policies, Markets and Mechanisms*, Oxford University Press, pp 161–98.

Klug, H (1996) 'Historical Claims and the Right to Restitution' in J Van Zyl, J Kirsten and HP Binswanger (eds), *Agricultural Land Reform in South Africa: Policies, Markets and Mechanisms*, Oxford University Press, pp 390–412.

Kobach, KW (1993) *The Referendum: Direct Democracy in Switzerland*, Dartmouth.

Komesar, NK (1984) 'Taking Institutions Seriously: Introduction to a Strategy for Constitutional Analysis' 51 *University of Chicago Law Review* 366.

Komesar, NK (1994) *Imperfect Alternatives: Choosing Institutions in Law, Economics, and Public Policy*, University of Chicago Press.

Komesar, NK (forthcoming) *Law's Limits: The Role of Courts, the Rule of Law and the Supply and Demand of Rights*, Cambridge University Press.

Kramer, DC (1982) *Comparative Civil Rights and Liberties*, University Press of America.

Krasner, SD (1995) 'Sovereignty and Intervention' in GM Lyons and M Mastanduno (eds), *Beyond Westphalia? State Sovereignty and International Intervention*, Johns Hopkins University Press.

Kuhn, T (1970) *The Structure of Scientific Revolutions* (2nd edn), University of Chicago Press.

Kundera, M (1991) *Immortality*, Faber and Faber.

La Nauze, JA (1972) *The Making of the Australian Constitution*, Melbourne University Press.

Lague, D (2000) 'Timor Call to Review Oil Treaty' *Sydney Morning Herald*, 8 May.

Lal, D (1995) 'Eco-fundamentalism' 71 *International Affairs* 515–28.

Lall, R (1999) 'Time to Get Wired' *Far Eastern Economic Review*, 19 August .

Lane, WB (1996) 'Reform of Administrative Law in Queensland' 79 *Canberra Bulletin of Public Administration* 174.

Latham, E (1966) *The Communist Controversy in Washington*, Harvard University Press.

Latham, M (MP) (1998) *Civilising Global Capital*, Allen & Unwin.

Latham, M (MP) (1999) Address to the Social Capital and Social Policy Conference, Canberra, 17 February.

Latham, RTE (1937) 'The Law and the Commonwealth' in WK Hancock (ed), *Survey of British Commonwealth Affairs*, Oxford University Press.

Leshy, JD (1990) 'The State of Constitutional Law in the States of the United States: Are There any Lessons for Australia?' 20 *UWA Law Review* 373.

Leveridge, V and D Lea (1993) *Takeback: Planning for Change in Aurukun*, North Australia Research Unit, Australian National University.

Levy, DL and D Egan (1998) 'Capital Contests: National and Transnational Channels of Corporate Influence on the Climate Change Negotiations' 26 *Politics and Society* 337.

Lieberman, L et al (1997) *Torres Strait Islanders: A New Deal – A Report on Greater Autonomy for Torres Strait Islanders*, House of Representatives Standing Committee on Aboriginal and Torres Strait Islander Affairs, Parliament of the Commonwealth of Australia, August.

Lijphart, A (1999) 'Australian Democracy: Modifying Majoritarianism?' 34 *Australian Journal of Political Science* 313.

Lindblom, CE (1977) *Politics and Markets*, Basic Books.

Linde; HA (1999) 'Structures and Terms of Consent: Delegation, Discretion, Separation of Powers, Representation, Participation, Accountability?' 20 *Cardozo Law Review* 823.

Lipschutz, RD (1992) 'Reconstructing World Politics: The Emergence of Global Civil Society' 21 *Millennium: Journal of International Studies* 389–420.

Lipsky, M (1968) 'Protest as a Political Resource' 62 *American Political Science Review* 1144.

Llewellyn, KN (1931) 'Some Realism about Realism: Responding to Dean Pound' 44 *Harvard Law Review* 1222.

Lobez, S (1996) 'Law and Culture in the Ngarinyin Tribal Lands' *ABC Radio National Law Report*, 24 September.

Lobez, S (1997) Obituary for David Mowalijarlai, *ABC Radio National Law Report*, 30 September .

Locke, J (1690) *Second Essay Concerning Civil Government*, ch V, § 26.

Lofton, J (1980) *The Press as Guardians of the First Amendment*, University of South Carolina Press.

Lowi, TJ (1964) 'American Business, Public Policy, Case Studies, and Political Theory' 16 *World Politics* 677.

Lui (Jr), G (1994) 'A Torres Strait Perspective' *Voices from the Land: 1993 Boyer Lectures*, Australian Broadcasting Corporation.

Lyons, GM and M Mastanduno (1993) 'International Intervention, State Sovereignty and the Future of International Society' 45 *International Social Science Journal* 519.

McAlpine, A (1997) *Once a Jolly Bagman*, Weidenfeld & Nicolson.

McBeath, GA and TA Morehouse (1980) *The Dynamics of Alaska Native Self-Government*, University Press of America.

McBeath, GA and TA Morehouse (1994) *Alaska Politics and Government*, University of Nebraska Press.

McCloskey, RG (1994) *The American Supreme Court* (2nd edn), University of Chicago Press.

McClosky, H and J Zaller (1984) *The American Ethos: Public Attitudes toward Capitalism and Democracy*, Harvard University Press.

McCormick, J (1993) 'International Non-governmental Organisations: Prospects for a Global Environmental Movement' in S Kamieniecki (ed), *Environmental Politics in the International Arena: Movements, Parties, Organisations, and Policy*, State University of New York Press.

Machiavelli, N (1975) *Discourse*, Routledge & Kegan Paul.

McKenna, M (1996) *The Captive Republic*, Cambridge University Press.

McLaughlin, R (1996) 'Some Problems and Issues in the Recognition of Indigenous Customary Law' 86 *Aboriginal Law Bulletin* 4.

Macphee, I (1994) 'Challenges for 21st Century Australia: Politics, Economics and Constitutional Reform' 3 *Griffith Law Review* 245.

MacQuarrie, R (1980) *Report of the Special Committee on Unity to the 3rd Session of the 9th Assembly at Frobisher Bay*, Tabled Document No 16-80, Legislative Assembly of the Northwest Territories, Yellowknife, 22 October.

McQueen, H (1976) *A New Britannia*, Penguin.

McRae, H, G Nettheim and L Beacroft (1997) *Indigenous Legal Issues: Cases and Commentary* (2nd edn), LBC.

Madden, AF and WH Morris-Jones (eds) (1980) *Australia and Britain: Studies in a Changing Relationship*, Sydney University Press.

Maddock, K (1984) 'Aboriginal Customary Law' in P Hanks and B Keon-Cohen (eds), *Aborigines and the Law*, George Allen & Unwin.

Madison, J, A Hamilton and J Jay (1987) *The Federalist Papers*, Penguin.

Mansell, W, B Meteyard and A Thomson (1995) *A Critical Introduction to Law*, Cavendish.

Marika, W and J Isaacs (1995) *Wandjuk Marika: Life Story*, University of Queensland Press.

Marsh, I (1999) 'The Senate, Policy-Making and Community Consultations' Senate Occasional Lecture, Canberra, 23 April.

Marshall, TR (1989) *Public Opinion and the Supreme Court*, Unwin Hyman.

Martin, H-P and H Schumann (1997) *The Global Trap*, Pluto Press.

Mason, A (1989) 'A Bill of Rights for Australia?' 5 *Australian Bar Review* 79.

Mason, A (1996) 'The Interpretation of a Constitution in a Modern Liberal Democracy' in C Sampford and K Preston (eds), *Interpreting Constitutions: Theories, Principles and Institutions*, Federation Press.

Mason, A (1998) 'The Constitution in a Contemporary Context' in *Selected Proceedings of the Federation into the Future: Government in a Global Era Convention*, Committee for Economic Development Australia.

Meggitt, MJ (1962) *Desert Peoples*, Angus & Robertson.

Métin, A (1977) *Socialism Without Doctrine*, Alternative Publishing.

Michelman, F (1988) 'Law's Republic' 97 *Yale Law Journal* 1493.

Mill, JS (1910) 'On Liberty' in *Utilitarianism, Liberty, Representative Government*, Dent (originally published 1859).

Miller, AS (1968) *The Supreme Court and American Capitalism*, Free Press.

Milner, A (1999) 'Why We Should Not Swagger in Asia' *Quadrant* (September).

Mollan, R 'Smith Act Prosecutions: The Effect of the *Dennis* and *Yates* Decisions' (1965) 26 *University of Pittsburgh Law Review* 705.

Montesquieu, C de (1989) *The Spirit of the Laws*, Cambridge University Press (first published 1748).

Moreton-Robinson, A and C Runciman (1990) 'Land Rights in Kakadu: Self-Management or Domination' 3 *Journal for Social Justice Studies* 75–88.

Morgan, E (1988) *Inventing the People*, WW Norton.

Morris, C (1997) 'Indigenous Intellectual Property Rights: The Responsibilities of Maintaining the Oldest Continuous Culture in the World' 4 *Indigenous Law Bulletin* (available at http://www.law.unsw.edu.au/centres/ilc/).

Morris, C (1999) 'A Full Law' in DA Posey (ed), *Cultural and Spiritual Values of Bio-Diversity: A Complementary Contribution to the Global Biodiversity Assessment*, United Nations Environment Program (UNEP).

Motshabi, KB and SG Volks (1991) 'Towards Democratic Chieftaincy: Principles and Procedures' *Acta Juridica* 104.

Mowalijarlai, D and J Malnic (1993) *Yorro Yorro: Everything Standing Up Alive – Spirit of the Kimberley*, Magabala Books.

Mulrennan, M and Hanssen, N (eds) (1994) *Marine Strategy for Torres Strait: Policy Directions*, ANU North Australia Research Unit, and Island Coordinating Council.

Murphy, J (1992) 'Insulating Land Reform from Constitutional Impugnment: An Indian Case Study' reprinted in 8 *South African Journal on Human Rights* 362.

Murphy, PL (1979) *World War I and the Origins of Civil Liberties in the United States*, WW Norton.

National Multicultural Advisory Council (NMAC) (1999) *Report: Australian Multiculturalism for a New Century – Towards Inclusiveness*, April.

Neidjie, B (1989) *Story about Feeling*, K Taylor (ed), Magabala Books.

Nettheim, G (1993) 'Judicial Revolution or Cautious Correction? *Mabo v Queensland*' 16(1) *University of New South Wales Law Journal* 1.

Nettheim, G (1999) 'Aboriginal Constitutional Conventions in the Northern Territory' 10 *Public Law Review* 8.

Nettheim, G (1999) 'Governance Bodies and Australian Legislative Provision for Corporations and Councils', Discussion Paper 7 for project: Governance Structures for Indigenous Australians, On and Off Native Title Lands, University of New South Wales.

Nettheim, G (1999) 'Indigenous Australians and the Constitution' 74 *Reform: A Journal of National and International Law Reform* 29.

Nettheim, G (1999) '"Retreat from Injustice": The High Court of Australia and Native Title' in M Gibney and S Frankowski (eds), *Judicial Protection of Human Rights. Myth or Reality?*, Praeger.

New South Wales Aboriginal Land Council (1992) *Annual Report*, NSW Aboriginal Land Council.

New York City Bar Association (1956) *Report of the Special Committee on the Federal Loyalty–Security Program of the Association of the Bar of the City of New York*, Dodd, Mead.

Nieuwenhuysen, J (1998) 'Commonwealth–State Cooperation: A Fresh Approach' in *Selected Proceedings of the Federation into the Future: Government in a Global Era Convention*, Committee for Economic Development Australia.

Nino, C (1994) *The Constitution of Deliberative Democracy*, Yale University Press.

Northern Land Council (1998) *Resolutions of the Northern Territory Aboriginal Nations Convention on Standards for Constitutional Development*, Batchelor, NT.

Note (1972) 'The National Security Interest and Civil Liberties' 85 *Harvard Law Review* 1130.

Note (1977) 'Implementation Problems in Institutional Reform Litigation' 91 *Harvard Law Review* 428, 463.

Nottage, L, Book Review (1998) 9 *Public Law Review* 78.

Nye, RB (1963) *Fettered Freedom*, Michigan State University Press.

Oakes, L (1999) 'Century-old Idea May Help Resolve Modern Problem' *The Bulletin*, 23 February.

O'Brien, P and M Webb (eds) (1991) *The Executive State: WA Inc and the Constitution*, Constitutional Press.

Office of Indigenous Affairs, Department of the Prime Minister and Cabinet (1994) *Aboriginal Customary Law: Report on Commonwealth Implementation of the Recommendations of the Australian Law Reform Commission*, AGPS.

Official Report of the National Australasian Convention Debates, 1891 (1986) Legal Books.

Official Report of the National Australasian Convention Debates, 1897 (1986) Legal Books.

Olivier, NJJ (1995) *Indigenous Law*, Butterworths.

OW Holmes Jr Papers, Harvard University, Boston.

Panyarachun, A (1999) 'Democracy in Thailand', CDI Annual Address, Parliament House, Canberra, 24 November (available at http://www.cdi.anu.edu.au).

Papadakis, E (1999) 'Constituents of Confidence and Mistrust in Australian Institutions' 34(1) *Australian Journal of Political Science* 1.

Paul, AM (1960) *Conservative Crisis and the Rule of Law*, Cornell University Press.

Pearsen, B (1999) 'Paying the Price over Rice' *Australian Financial Review*, 30 April.

Pearson, G (1976) 'Eighteenth-Century English Criminal Law' 3 *British Journal of Legal Studies* 115.

Peltason, JW (1954) 'Constitutional Liberty and the Communist Problem' in AH Kelly (ed), *Foundations of Freedom in the American Constitution*, Harpers.

People for the American Way (1989) *Democracy's Next Generation: A Study of Youth and Teachers*, People for the American Way.

Petersen, FJ (1998) 'The Façade of Humanitarian Intervention for Human Rights in a Community of Sovereign Nations' 12 *Arizona Journal of International and Comparative Law* 871.

Pettit, P (1997) *Republicanism: A Theory of Freedom and Government*, Oxford University Press.

Pettit, P (1992) 'Republican Themes' 6 *Legislative Studies* 29.

Pocock, JGA (ed) (1977) *The Political Works of James Harrington*, Cambridge University Press.

Posner, RA (1992) 'Legal Reasoning from the Top Down and from the Bottom Up: The Question of Unenumerated Constitutional Rights' 59 *University of Chicago Law Review* 433.

Press, AJ, DAM Lea, A Webb and A Graham (1995) *Kakadu: Natural and Cultural Heritage and Management*, Australian Nature Conservation Agency/ANU North Australian Research Unit

Preston, W, Jr (1963) *Aliens and Dissenters*, Harper & Row (on the 1903–33 period).

Prime Minister of Australia (1999) Media Releases, Prime Minister of Australia, Canberra (available at http://www.pm.gov.au/media/pressrel/index.htm).

Princen, T and M Finger (1994) *Environmental NGOs in World Politics: Linking the Local and the Global*, Routledge.

Pritchard, S (1998) 'Commission on Human Rights Working Group (CHRWG) Third Session 27 October–7 November 1997' 4 *Indigenous Law Bulletin* 4.

Pritchard, S (ed) (1998) *Indigenous Peoples, the United Nations and Human Rights*, Zed Books/ Federation Press.

Pritchard, S (1998) 'Recent Constitutional Developments in the Northern Territory: The Kalkaringi Convention' 4 *Indigenous Law Bulletin* 12.

Pritchard, S 'The Right of Indigenous Peoples to Self-Determination' in *The Laws of Australia*, Title 1, *Aborigines and Torres Strait Islanders*, 1.7 International Law, LBC Information Services.

Pritchard, S and C Heindow-Dolman (1998) 'Indigenous Peoples and International Law: A Critical Overview' 3 *Australian Indigenous Law Reporter* 473.

Puplick, C (1996) 'Citizen-initiated Referendums: The Case Against' in K Wiltshire (ed), *Direct Democracy: Citizens-initiated Referendums*, Constitutional Centenary Foundation.

Pyke, JR (1992) Submission 130 in Electoral and Administrative Review Commission (Queensland) (ed) *Review of the Preservation and Enhancement of Individuals' Rights and Freedoms, Public Submissions*, Vol 3, Queensland Government Printer.

Pyke, JR (2000) Submission to the Queensland Constitutional Review Commission (available at http://www.constitution.qld.gov.au/subs/sub_pyke.html).

Quick, J and R Garran (1901) *The Annotated Constitution of the Australian Commonwealth*, Angus & Robertson.

Rabban, DM (1981) 'The First Amendment in its Forgotten Years' (1981) 90 *Yale Law Journal* 514.

Rao, K and C Geisler (1990) 'The Social Consequences of Protected Ares Development for Resident Populations' 3(1) *Society and Natural Resources* 19–32.

Rawls, J (1974) *A Theory of Justice*, Oxford University Press.

Rawls, J (1993) *Political Liberalism*, Columbia University Press.

Rayner, M (1997) 'Watchdog on a Leash' *Eureka Street* (December) 24–5.

Redden, G (2000) '*The Beach*: A Tale of Two Freedoms' 19 *Social Alternatives* 30.

Redish, MH (1995) *The Constitution as Political Structure*, Oxford University Press.

Reeves, J, QC (1998) *Building on Land Rights for the Next Generation: The Review of the Aboriginal Land Rights (Northern Territory) Act 1976* (2nd edn), ATSIC.

Regulations and Ordinances Committee (1998) *Annual Report 1996–1997*, June.

Regulations and Ordinances Committee (1998) 'Statement of Work of the Committee during the Spring Sittings 1998' *Hansard*, 9 December.

Regulations and Ordinances Committee (1999) 'Statement of Work of the Committee during the Autumn and Winter Sittings' *Hansard*, 30 June.

Regulations and Ordinances Committee (1999) *Annual Report, 1997–1998*, March.

Reporters sans Frontieres (1999) Press Release, 9 August (available at http://www.rsf.fr).

Resource Assessment Commission (RAC) (1993) 'The Role of Indigenous People' in *Coastal Zone Inquiry: Final Report*, AGPS.

Reynolds, H (1987) *The Law of the Land*, Penguin.

Reynolds, H (1995) *Fate of a Free People*, Penguin.

Rhodes, RAW (1994) 'The Hollowing Out of the State: The Changing Nature of the Public Service in Britain' 65 *Political Quarterly* 138.

Rich, R (1998) 'Non-State Actors and Development Assistance' Australia New Zealand Society of International Law, Proceedings of the 6th Annual Conference, CIPL (available at http://www.law.anu.edu.au).

Richards, J (forthcoming) '"A Question of Necessity": Queensland Native Mounted Police' PhD Thesis, Faculty of Humanities, Griffith University.

Richardson, B (1991) *Flooding Job's Garden*, Video, Tamarack Productions and UNESCO, National Film Board.

Richardson, BJ, D Craig and B Boer (1994) 'Indigenous Peoples and Environmental Management: A Review of Canadian Regional Agreements and Their Potential Application to Australia (Part 2)' 11 *Environmental and Planning Law Journal* 357–81.

Rodman, KA (1998) '"Think Globally, Punish Locally": Nonstate Actors, Multinational Corporations, and Human Rights Sanctions' 12 *Ethics and International Affairs* 19.

Rosenberg, GN (1991) *The Hollow Hope: Can Courts Bring about Social Change?*, University of Chicago Press, ch 4.

Rosenberg, GN (1992) 'Judicial Independence and the Reality of Political Power' 54 *Review of Politics* 369.

Rosenberg, GN (1995) 'The Real World of Constitutional Rights: The Supreme Court and the Implementation of the Abortion Decisions' in Lee Epstein (ed), *Contemplating Courts*, Congressional Quarterly Press.

Rosenberg, GN (1998) 'The Irrelevant Court: The Supreme Court's Inability to Influence Popular Beliefs about Equality (or Anything Else)' in N Devins and D Douglas (eds), *Redefining Equality*, Oxford University Press.

Rosenberg, GN and JM Williams (1997) 'Do Not Go Gently into That Good Right: The First Amendment in the High Court of Australia' *Supreme Court Review* 439.

Royal Commission on Aboriginal Peoples (1996) *Report*, Vol 1, *Looking Forward, Looking Back*, Canada Communication Group Publishing.

Royal Commission on the Constitution of the Commonwealth (Chair: JB Peden) (1929) *Report*, Government Printer.

Rubin, EL and M Feeley (1994) 'Federalism: Some Notes on a National Neurosis' 41 *UCLA Law Review* 903.

Rubin, ER (1982) *Abortion, Politics, and the Courts*, Greenwood.

Sager, LG (1981) 'Rights Skepticism and Process-Based Responses' 56 *New York University Law Review* 417.

Sahtouris, E (1998) *The Biology of Globalisation: The Challenge of Evolution Symposium in Cagliari* (at http://www.ratical.org/LifeWeb/Articles/globalize.html#ITAT), adapted from first publication in *Perspectives in Business and Social Change*, September 1997.

Sampford, C (1989) 'Coups d'État and Law' 13 *Bulletin of the Australian Society of Legal Philosophy* 253.

Sampford, C (1991) 'Coups d'État and Law' in E Attwooll (ed), *Shaping Revolution*, Aberdeen University Press.

Sampford, C (1991) 'Dworkin's Claim to a Socialist Inheritance' 16 *Bulletin of the Australian Society of Legal Philosophy* 37.

Sampford, C (1992) 'Law, Institutions and the Public/Private Divide' 20 *Federal Law Review* 185

Sampford, C (1997) 'The Four Dimensions of Rights and Their Means of Protection' in B Galligan and C Sampford (eds), *Rethinking Human Rights*, Federation Press.

Sampford, C (forthcoming) *Dare to Call it Treason*, Dartmouth.

Sandbrook, R (1997) 'UNGASS Has Run Out of Steam' 73 *International Affairs* 641.

Sanders, AJGM (1990) 'The Role of Comparative Law in the Internal Conflict of Laws' in AJGM Sanders (ed), *The Internal Conflict of Laws in South Africa*, Butterworths.

Sassen, S (1996) *Losing Control? Sovereignty in an Age of Globalisation*, Columbia University Press.

Saunders, C (1995) 'Constitutional Arrangements of Federal Systems' 25 *Publius* 1–19.

Saunders, C (1998) 'Oration: Sir Daryl Dawson' 20 *Adelaide Law Review* 1.

Saunders, C (1999) 'In the Shadow of *Wakim*' 17 *Companies and Securities Law Journal* 507–17.

Saward, M (1997) 'In Search of the Hollow Crown' in P Weller, H Bavkis and RAW Rhodes (eds), *The Hollow Crown: Countervailing Trends in Core Executives*, Macmillan.

Scheingold, SA (1974) *The Politics of Rights*, Yale University Press.

Sen, AK (1999) 'Democracy as a Universal Value' 10(3) *Journal of Democracy* 3–17.

Shaffer, G (1999) 'International Decisions: United States – Import Prohibition of Certain Shrimp Products' 93 *American Journal of International Law* 507.

Shakespeare, W, *Richard II*.

Shapiro, M (1966) *Freedom of Speech: The Supreme Court and Judicial Review*, Prentice-Hall.

Shapiro, M (1981) *Courts: A Comparative and Political Analysis*, University of Chicago Press.

Sharman, C (1998) 'The Senate and Good Government' Senate Occasional Lecture, 11 December.

Sharp, N (1992) *Footprints along the Cape York Sandbeaches*, Aboriginal Studies Press.

Sharp, N (1993) *Stars of Tagai: The Torres Strait Islanders*, Aboriginal Studies Press.

Sharp, N (1996) *No Ordinary Judgment: Mabo, the Murray Islanders' Land Case*, Aboriginal Studies Press.

Shea, S (1998) *A State's Perspective on the Proposed National Carbon Accounting System*, Paper presented at the NCAS Expert Workshop June (at: http://www.greenhouse.gov.au/ncas/workshop/).

Sheldon, CH (1965) 'Constitutionalism: A Comparative Study of Communist Parties and High Courts' dissertation, University of Oregon.

Shnukal, A (1992) 'Pacific Islander Immigrants in Torres Strait' *Voices*, Winter, 5–14.

Singe, J (1989) *The Torres Strait: People and History*, University of Queensland Press.

Skinner, Q (1990) 'The Republican Ideal of Political Liberty' in G Bock, Q Skinner and M Viroli (eds), *Machiavelli and Republicanism*, Cambridge University Press.

Slaughter Burley, A-M and C Kaysen (1993) 'Introductory Note: Emerging Norms of Justified Intervention' in LW Reed and C Kaysen (eds), *Emerging Norms of Justified Intervention: A Collection of Essays from a Project of the American Academy of Arts and Sciences*, American Academy of Arts and Sciences.

Slaughter Burley, A-M, A Sweet and J Weiler (eds) (1997) *The European Courts and National Courts: Doctrine and Jurisprudence*, Hart.

Smith, A (1759) *The Theory of Moral Sentiments*.

Smith, A (1776) *The Wealth of Nations*.

Smith, J (1998) 'Global Civil Society?' 42 *American Behavioral Scientist* 93.

Smith, J and TP Moran (2000) 'WTO 101: Myths about the World Trade Organization' 47 *Dissent* (Spring) 66–70.

Soublière, M and G Coleman (eds) (1999) *Nunavut', 99: Changing the Map of Canada*, Nortext Multimedia and Nunavut Tunngavik. (available at http://www.nunavut.com/nunavut99/english/index.html).

South African Law Commission (1991) *Interim Report on Group and Human Rights* (August), South African Law Commission.

Standage, T (1998) *The Victorian Internet: The Remarkable Story of the Telegraph and the Nineteenth Century's On-Line Pioneers*, Weidenfeld & Nicolson.

Stephenson, M and S Ratnapala (eds) (1993) *Mabo: A Judicial Revolution*, University of Queensland Press.

Stone, J (1946) *The Province and Function of Law*, Associated General Publications.

Storing, HJ (ed) (1981) *The Complete Anti-Federalist*, Chicago University Press.

Stouffer, SA (1963) *Communism, Conformity, and Civil Liberties: A Cross-Section of the Nation Speaks its Mind*, Peter Smith.

Streeck, W (1998) 'The Internationalisation of Industrial Relations in Europe: Prospects and Problems' 26 *Politics and Society* 429.

Sullivan, JL, J Pierson and GE Marcus (1979) 'An Alternate Conceptualisation of Political Tolerance: Illusory Increases 1950s–1970s' 73 *American Political Science Review* 781.

Sunstein, CR (1985) 'Interest Groups in American Public Law' 38 *Stanford Law Review* 29–87

Sunstein, CR (1988) 'Beyond the Republican Revival' 97 *Yale Law Journal* 1539.

Sunstein, CR (1993) 'On Property and Constitutionalism' 14 *Cardozo Law Review* 907.

Sunstein, CR (1995) *Democracy and the Problem of Free Speech*, Free Press.

Sunstein, CR (1996) *Legal Reasoning and Political Conflict*, Oxford University Press.

Swain, T (1985) *Interpreting Aboriginal Religion: An Historical Account*, Australian Association for the Study of Religions.

Swanson, E (1992) 'A Land Claims Court for South Africa: Report on Work in Progress' 8 *South African Journal on Human Rights* 332.

Swinfen, DB (1987) *Imperial Appeal: The Debate on the Appeal to the Privy Council, 1833–1986*, Manchester University Press.

Swinford, B and EN Waltenburg (1998) 'The Consistency of the US Supreme Court's 'Pro-State' Bloc' 28 *Publius* 25.

Taylor, C (1992) *Multiculturalism and the Politics of Recognition*, Princeton University Press.

Taylor, J (1991) 'Alaska and the Northern Territory: Demographic Change' in P Jull and S Roberts (eds), *The Challenge of Northern Regions*, ANU North Australia Research Unit.

Teubner, G (ed) (1997) *Global Law Without a State*, Dartmouth.

Thayer, JB (1901) *John Marshall*, Houghton Mifflin.

Thompson, EP (1975) *Whigs and Hunters: The Origin of the Black Act*, Allen Lane.

Thompson, EV (1980) 'The Washminster Mutation' in P Weller and D Jaensch (eds), *Responsible Government in Australia*, Drummond.

Thompson, EV (1994) *Fair Enough: Egalitarianism in Australia*, University of New South Wales Press.

Tjamiwa, T (1991) '*Nganana Wirunya Tjunguringkula Waakarinyi:* We're Working Well Together' 19 *Habitat Australia* (June) 4–7

Toffler, A (1980) *The Third Wave*, Collins.

Toyne, P and R Johnston (1991) 'Reconciliation or the New Dispossession? Aboriginal Land Rights and Nature Conservation' 18 *Habitat* (June) 8–10.

Tully, J (1995) *Strange Multiplicity: Constitutionalism in an Age of Diversity*, Cambridge University Press.

Turner, T (1994) 'Anthropology and Multiculturalism: What is Anthropology that Multiculturalists Should be Mindful of It?' in DT Goldberg (ed), *Multiculturalism: A Critical Reader*, Blackwell.

Tushnet, MV (1999) *Taking the Constitution Away from the Courts*, Princeton University Press.

Uhr, J (1998) *Deliberative Democracy in Australia*, Cambridge University Press.

Vachon, C (1998) 'Sovereignty Versus Globalisation: The International Court of Justice's Advisory Opinion on the Threat or Use of Nuclear Weapons' 24 *Denver Journal of International Law and Policy* 691.

Vile, MJC (1967) *Constitutionalism and the Separation of Powers*, Clarendon Press.

Vines, KN and H Jacob (eds) (1976) *Politics in the American States: A Comparative Analysis*, Little, Brown.

Von Fritz, K (1954) *The Theory of the Mixed Constitution in Antiquity*, Columbia University Press.

Vonnegut, K (1982) *Palm Sunday*, Cape.

Waldron, J (1999) *Democracy and Disagreement*, Oxford University Press.

Walker, G de Q (1987) *Initiative and Referendum: The People's Law*, Centre for Independent Studies.

Walker, G de Q (1988) *The Rule of Law: Foundation of Constitutional Democracy*, Melbourne University Press.

Walker, RBJ (1994) 'Social Movements/World Politics' 23 *Millennium: Journal of International Studies* 669.

Wapner, P (1995) 'Politics beyond the State: Environmental Activism and World Civic Politics' 47 *World Politics* 311.

Wapner, P (1996) *Environmental Activism and World Civic Politics*, State University of New York Press.

Weiss, L (1998) *The Myth of the Powerless State: Governing the Economy in a Global Era*, Polity Press.

Weller, P, H Bavkis and RAW Rhodes (eds) (1997) *The Hollow Crown: Countervailing Trends in Core Executives*, Macmillan.

West, T (ed) (1990) *Algernon Sidney, Discourses Concerning Government*, Liberty Classic.

Westin, AF (1954) 'Constitutional Liberty and Loyalty Programs' in AH Kelly (ed), *Foundations of Freedom in the American Constitution*, Harpers.

Wheeler, F (1996) 'Original Intent and the Doctrine of the Separation of Powers in Australia' 7 *Public Law Review* 96.

Whipple, L (1927) *The Story of Civil Liberty in the United States*, Vanguard.

Willetts, P (1982) 'The Impact of Promotional Pressure Groups on Global Politics' in Peter Willetts (ed), *Pressure Groups in the Global System: The Transnational Relations of Issue-Orientated Non-Governmental Organizations*, Frances Pinter.

Willetts, P (1982) 'Pressure Groups as Transnational Actors' in P Willetts (ed), *Pressure Groups in the Global System: The Transnational Relations of Issue-Orientated Non-Governmental Organizations*, Frances Pinter.

Willetts, P (1988) 'The United Nations as a Political System' in Paul Taylor and AJR Groom (eds), *International Institutions at Work*, Pinter.

Willetts, P (1996) 'From Stockholm to Rio and Beyond: The Impact of the Environmental Movement on the United Nations Consultative Arrangements for NGOs' (22 *Review of International Studies* 57.

Williams, G (1995) 'A Republican Tradition for Australia?' 23 *Federal Law Review* 143.

Williams, JM (1995) '"With Eyes Open": Andrew Inglis Clark and Our Republican Tradition' 23 *Federal Law Review* 149.

Willis, J (1992) 'Two Laws, One Lease: Accounting for Traditional Aboriginal law in the Lease for Uluru-Kata Tjuta National Park' in J Birckhead, T de Lacy and L Smith (eds), *Aboriginal Involvement in Parks and Protected Areas*, Aboriginal Studies Press, pp 159–66.

Wilmer, F (1993) *The Indigenous Voice in World Politics: Since Time Immemorial*, Sage.

Wilson, HH and Harvey Glickman (1954) *The Problem of Internal Security in Great Britain 1948–1953*, Doubleday.

Wilson, R and M Dodson (1997) *Bringing Them Home: Report of the National Inquiry into the Separation of Aboriginal and Torres Strait Islander Children from Their Families*, HREOC, Commonwealth of Australia.

Winterton, G (1986) 'Extra-Constitutional Notions in Australian Constitutional Law' 16 *Federal Law Review* 223.

Woenne-Green, S, R Johnston, R Sultan and A Wallis (1992) *Competing Interests: Aboriginal Participation in National Parks and Conservation Reserves in Australia – A Review*, Australian Conservation Foundation.

Wollheim, R (1969) 'A Paradox in the Theory of Democracy' in P Laslett and G Runciman (eds), *Philosophy, Politics and Society*, Blackwell.

World Bank (1997) *World Development Report 1997*, Oxford University Press.

World Bank Group (1999) *Global Development Finance 1999* (available at http://www.worldbank.org).

World Trade Organisation (WTO) (1998) *Report of the Panel on United States: Import Prohibition of Certain Shrimp and Shrimp Products* 37 ILM 832.

Yandle, B (1989) *The Political Limits of Environmental Regulation*, Quorum Books.

Young, E, H Ross, J Johnson and K Kesteven (1991) *Caring for Country: Aborigines and Land Management*, Australian National Parks and Wildlife Service.

Yunupingu, G (ed) (1997) *Our Land is Our Life: Land Rights – Past, Present and Future*, University of Queensland Press.

Zdenkowski, G (1994) 'Customary Punishment and Pragmatism: Some Unresolved Dilemmas' 68 *Aboriginal Law Bulletin* 26.

Zines, L (1989) 'A Legal Perspective' in B Galligan (ed), *Australian Federalism*, Longman Cheshire.

Zines, L (1997) *The High Court and the Constitution*, Butterworths.

INDEX

1975 Whitlam Dismissal, 157; *see also* Senate, Australian

Aboriginal Constitutional Convention (Batchelor, NT, November 1998), 253, 261
Aboriginal and Torres Strait Islander Commission (ATSIC), 251, 252, 258, 264, 267
Aborigines and Torres Strait Islanders, Australian, 57, 60, 61, 179–80, 242–99
abortion, 218, 226
access and equity, 65–6, 186
accountability, 68, 97, 145, 174ff, 183
Aceh, 28
Ackerman, B, 193, 230
active citizenship, 61
activism, judicial, 7, 78, 81, 192–3, 232
adjudication, 9, 230ff
administrative law, 12
advantage, comparative *see* comparative economic advantage
Advisory Commission on Land Allocations (ACLA) (South Africa), 198
Advisory Opinion on the Legality of the Threat or Use of Nuclear Weapons, 33–4
affirmative action, 197, 201, 225–6, 254
Afghanistan, 18
Africa, 18, 29, 37, 99, 109, 243
African-Americans, 71, 219, 228
African National Congress (ANC), 72, 196ff
aggression, *see* intervention, international
agreement *see* disagreement; treaties
agriculture, 94, 287
Alaska, 259ff
Albertyn, C, 276
Albigenses, 111
Albright, M, 10
Alexander, D, 298
Alfred, T, 258
Algeria, 117
alliances, military, 116
Altman, JC, 252
Aman, Professor AC, Jr, 131–2
American Bar Association (ABA), 220–1
American Civil War, 110, 219
American War of Independence, 110
Americanisation, 29
Americas, 98
Amnesty International (AI), 71, 94
anarchy, 69, 71, 96
anthropology, 58, 272, 294
anti-monarchism, *see* republicanism, anti-monarchical
Antonios, Z, 186
apartheid, 196ff, 216, 225
Arctic Council, 258
Argy, F, 44
Aristide, J-B, 20
Aristotle, 116
Armenia, 99
Arrow, K, 83, 126
arts, 58
Asian Development Bank, 32
Asian financial crisis (1997), 96, 101, 103
Asian values, 101, 105, 163; *see also* universal values
Atkinson, REB, 3
Attainder, Bills of, 140
Attanasio, JB, 34
Atyeo, B, 179
Auditor-General, 208
Auerbach, J, 221
Aung San Suu Kyi, 20
Austin, JL, 2, 11
Australia Institute, 75
Australia, New Zealand and United States (ANZUS) Treaty, 112
Australia Unlimited Conference, 159
Australian Conservation Foundation (ACF), 75, 77
Australian Democrats, 167, 171
Australian Greenhouse Office, 151
Australian Labor Party (ALP), 60, 167
Australian Law Reform Commission (ALRC), 248, 270
Australian Nature Conservation Agency (ANCA), 280, 281

Australians for Native Title and Reconciliation (ANTaR), 264, 269
Azerbaijan, 99

Bakhtiar, Dr S, 110
Balanda (White Australians), 297
Balkans, 18, 30, 37
Ball, AR, 165
Ball, DM, 260
Bangkok, 71
banks and banking, 37, 50, 103
Banks, Sir J, 243
Barber, B, 4
Barber, K, 220
Barendt, E, 218
bargaining, 127
Barings Bank, 50
Bartlett, A, 7
Barton, E, 127
Barton, G, 243
Basel Action Network, 75
Basic Law of the Federal Republic of Germany, *see* Constitution, Germany
Batchelor, *see* Aboriginal Constitutional Convention
Bauman, RW, 199
Bauman, Z, 154–5
Bavadra, T, 20
Bavkis, H, 149
Beacroft, L, 246
Beazley, K, 170
Beckett, J, 260
Beer, LW, 105, 192
Belgium, 109, 110
Bell, D, 220
Bell, DA, 210
Bell, P, 194, 201
Bender, P, 220
Bennett, JM, 242
Bennett, S, 165, 167
Bennett, TW, 272–4, 276, 277
Bentham, J, 89
Berger, T, 259
Berlin Wall, 99, 108, 110, 184
Berman, S, 37
bicameralism, 113, 117, 134, 137, 156–63, 164–72, 289; *see also* House of Lords; Senate, Australian; Senate, United States
Bills of Rights (general), 8–9, 142, 144, 185, 188, 192ff, 209
Binswanger, HP, 198
biodiversity, 288
bioregions, 298
biotechnology, 149
Birckhead, J, 287
Black, Justice H, 219
Black Panthers, 221
Blackburn, Justice RA, 294
Blackshield, AR (Tony), 128
Blackstone, Sir W, 2, 178, 244
Blasi, V, 224
Blaustein, G, 191
Blay, S, 275
Bock, G, 123
Boer, B, 286
Bogart, WA, 215
Boldt, M, 258
Bollinger, LC, 221
Bolsheviks, *see* Marxism; Union of Soviet Socialist Republics
Bonaparte, N, 110, 118
Bondevik, Prime Minister KM, 262
Bontecou, E, 220
boomerang model (NGOs), 72
Boorstin, D, 178
Botany Bay, 243
Bradlow, D, 156
Brandeis, Justice LB, 219
Brandt Report, 18
Brantenberg, OT, 262
Brdaroska, V, 5
Brennan, Fr F, SJ, 227
Brennan, Sir G, 210
Brezhnev, L, 108
Bringing Them Home, *see* Stolen Generation
Britain, *see* United Kingdom
Britannia, Australia as 'new', 5
British Empire, 47ff, 55, 59, 243, 260
Brower, D, 74
Brown, AJ, 298
Brown, H, 261
Brown, RS, Jr, 220
Brownlie, I, 188
Brundtland, GH, 74
Brundtland Report, *see Our Common Future: Report of the World Commission on Environment and Development*
Bryce, J, 122, 127
Buchanan, JM, 86

Buchanan, P, 3
Budapest, 181
budgets, 238; *see also* fiscal federalism; supply bills
Budlender, G, 198
Bundy, C, 179
Burchill, S, 36
Burdekin, B, 215
Burgess, G, 222
Burke, T, 74
Burkina Faso, 99
Burley, A-M, *see* Slaughter (Burley), A-M
Burma, 20, 96
Business and Industry Advisory Committee (BIAC), 76

cabinet, *see* ministers, government
cable TV, 218
California, 212
Calvin, J, 111
Cameroon, 99
Campbell, T, 6, 81, 87, 126
Canada, 10, 108, 117, 121, 198–9, 215, 229, 241, 259, 263, 267–8, 285
capital flows, 49, 96, 102, 156
capital punishment, 81, 84
capitalism, 15, 118; *see also* free-market capitalism
Capra, F, 298
Carey, H, 2
Carnival Against Capitalism (London, June 1999), 71
Carty, A, 4
Castles, AC, 242
Castles, S, 64
catastrophe, 107
Catholic Church, 21, 111, 186
Ceausescu, N, 18
Cedras coup (Haiti), 20
Central Asia, 98
central banks, 37, 150
centralisation, *see* decentralisation
Centre for Applied Legal Studies (CALS), 198
Centre for Comparative Constitutional Studies (CCC), 263
Centre for Democratic Institutions (CDI), 100
Centre for Development Studies, 196
Cerny, PG, 13, 28
Chafee, Z, 224
Chamberlain, J, 51–2
Chaney, Senator F, 165
Chanock, M, 276
checks and balances, 12, 118, 144, 158ff
Chesterman, J, 59, 60, 260
chieftainship, African, 271, 276–7
Chile, 34
China, 96, 102, 104, 116, 184, 191
Chopra, J, 12
Choudhry, S, 120
Christophersen, C, 180
Churches, S, 7
citizenship, 16, 49, 55, 56ff, 65, 130, 212, 246, 272–3
civic republicanism, 120ff
civil society, 68ff, 94, 97, 104, 184ff, 226
civilisations, clash of, 95
Claassens, A, 198
Clark, A Inglis, *see* Inglis Clark, A
class, socio-economic, 60
Cleaver, HM, 149
Climate Action Network, 75
Clinton, WJ (Bill), 25, 28, 68
CNN, 27
Cockburn, Dr J, 52
Coffin, Rev WS, 221
Cohen, B, 174
Cold War, 15, 30, 98, 99, 116, 118, 129, 184, 219, 221ff
Cole, T, 224
Coleman, F, 267
collective action, 88–9
Colonial Office (UK), 52
colonialism, *see* imperialism
Commission on Government (WA, 1995), 176
Commission on Sustainable Development, 30, 75
Committee for Economic Development Australia (CEDA), 147, 148
committees, legislative, 161, 176
commodification, 90, 291
common law, 128, 189, 255
communications, 47
Communism, *see* Marxism; Smith Act; Socialism; Union of Soviet Socialist Republics
Communist Manifesto, 87, 116

Community Property Association (CPA) (Makuleke Region), 284
comparative economic advantage, 102ff
comparative institutional analysis, *see* institutions
competition, 36, 80, 131
complexity, 9, 230ff
Condlln, S, 11
Confucianism, 105
CONGO, *see* United Nations Committee on NGOs (CONGO)
conquest, 241
consequentialist morality, 79, 83
conservation, *see* environment
Conservative Party (UK), 51
Constitution
  Australia, 1, 45, 47, 119ff, 164–5
  implied rights, 120, 137, 139, 189
  Columbia, 194
  Germany, 194, 201
  India, 195
  Namibia, 195
  South Africa, 8, 195, 202–3, 277
  United Kingdom, 1, 113
  United States, 1, 114–15, 119, 125, 127, 132
Constitutional Assembly, South African, 200ff
Constitutional Centenary Foundation (CCF), 43, 266
Constitutional Commission (1985–8), 167, 254
constitutional interpretation, *see* interpretation, judicial
constitutionalism, 1, 105–6
constitutions, 72, 184–5, 191ff
consumerism, 29, 87, 89
contracts, governmental, 138
conventions, constitutional
  (1891), 50, 52–3, 121, 127, 210, 214
  (February 1998), 43, 210, 253, 265
  (March 1998), 43
Cook, Captain J, 242
Coonan, Senator H, 7, 161, 166
co-ordination, international, 9
Cope, M, 177
Coper, M, 128
copyright laws, *see* intellectual property
corporations, 23, 29, 38–9, 68, 69, 104, 138, 225
corporatism, 76
corruption, 90–2, 103, 170, 173–4
COSATU, *see* Council of South African Trade Unions
Côte d'Ivoire, 99
Council for Aboriginal Reconciliation (CAR), 246, 254, 263–5
Council of Australian Governments (COAG), 45
Council of Ministers, *see* European Union, Council of Ministers
Council of South African Trade Unions (COSATU), 21
coups d'état, 19–20, 93, 99, 110, 193
courts, *see* judiciary
Cowell, S, 286
Craig, D, 286
Craik, J, 148
Crawford, J, 188
Cromwell, O, 127
Cross, C, 198
Crough, G, 180
Crown, *see* executive power; monarchy
Crown immunity and privilege, 140, 174, 178–80, 208
cruel and inhuman punishment, 275
Cuba, 102, 110
culture, 8, 15, 95, 119, 190, 216, 223–5, 248, 287
currencies, 28, 96; *see also* European Single Currency
custodianship, Indigenous, 265
Cyberworld, 156
Czechoslovakia, 98, 110, 213

Daes, Professor E-I, 264
Dahl, RA, 217, 222
Dahlén, O, 74
Dallas, 18
Darwin, C, 3, 111
David, SR, 24
Davidson, A, 59, 60
Davies, J, 280
Davis, G, 6, 148
Davos, 71
de Lacy, T, 280, 287
de Tocqueville, A, 122, 223
de Vattel, E, 244
de Villiers, B, 10, 259, 280, 283, 289
Deakin, A, 50, 51
Deane, Sir W, 206

death penalty, *see* capital punishment
Debelle, B, 278
debts, international, 21–2
decentralisation, 6, 70, 106, 130–2, 135–6, 153, 289
decision-making, 36, 39, 71, 156, 159
Declaration of Independence (USA, 1776), 14, 25
Declaration of the Rights of Man and of the Citizen (France, 1791), 14
defence, *see* military
deficit, democratic, *see* democratic deficit
deliberation, *see* democracy, deliberative
democracy
  correlation with economic success, 98, 101ff, 113, 117
  definitions, 60, 69ff, 78, 93, 108
  deliberative, 90ff, 123, 125–7, 161
  direct, 16, 87, 91, 157, 210; *see also* referenda
  illiberal, 96
  representative, 16
  survival and spread, 78, 95–100, 163
democratic blockage, 72ff
democratic deficit, 36, 37, 41, 44, 69ff, 147, 151
Democratic League, 22
Democratic Party (South Africa), 197, 201
Democrats, Australian, *see* Australian Democrats
Denmark, 109, 112, 213
Denning, Lord AT, 179
deontological morality, 79, 83
Department of Foreign Affairs and Trade (DFAT), 43
Department of Immigration and Multicultural Affairs (DIMA), 63
depressions, economic, 50; *see also* recessions, economic
deregulation, *see* globalisation; economic rationalism
Desai, M, 4
Detmold, M, 121, 253
Devins, N, 218
dialogue, 82, 83
Diamond, L, 96–100
Dicey, AV, 124, 206, 209
dictatorships, 93
Diggins, JP, 223
dinosaurs, 107
directive principles of state policy, 199, 289
disagreement, moral and political, 83, 91
disallowance
  of colonial legislation, 48, 51–3
  of delegated legislation, 161, 177–8, 281
  of executive decisions, 137, 161, 177–8
  of treaties, 42, 151, 162
discourse democracy, 82–4; *see also* democracy, deliberative
discrimination, 80, 86, 91, 97, 231–4, 236, 254, 276–7
  gender, 276–7
disease, 41, 107
Disraeli, B, 48
dissent, political, 218
diversity
  cultural, 56, 61, 266
  diversity, 64
Dixon, Sir O, 120
Dixson, M, 57
Djangkawu, 297
Djerrkura, G, 267
Dodson, M, 249, 263, 264
Dodson, P, 255, 266
domestic politics, 71
Dorsen, N, 220, 221
Dorsett, S, 245
Douglas, DM, 218
Douglas, Justice WO, 219
Downer, A, MP, 42, 162
Downing, J, 259
Dreaming, the, 290, 294–5
Drittwirkung, 195
Dworkin, RM, 18, 81, 86, 211, 226
Dynasty, 18

East Germany, 186
East Kimberley Project, 288
East Timor, *see* Timor
Eastern Orthodox Church, 186
Ecologically Sustainable Development (ESD) Committee (WA), 177
ecology, *see* environment
Economic and Social Council, *see* United Nations Economic and Social Council (ECOSOC)
economic nationalism, 61

economic rationalism, 3, 28, 44, 59, 61; *see also* free-market capitalism
economic success, correlation with democracy, 98, 101ff, 113, 117
economics, 9, 233ff
Economist, 37, 213
economy, *see* economics; knowledge economy; economic rationalism
education, 58, 190, 209, 218, 228
Egan, D, 70
Egypt, 111
elections, 85, 88–9
elective dictatorship, 80, 96
Electoral and Administrative Review Commission (EARC), Queensland, 205
electoral democracy, 96
electoral systems, 80, 97, 115, 157, 164–72, 163, 206, 225, 289
Elliot, L, 75
Elster, J, 83, 126
Ely, JH, 81, 233
Ely, JW, 204
Email (corporation), 213
English, R, 277
Enlightenment, 11, 14, 17, 21, 25–6, 290ff
entrenchment of laws, 12, 113, 205ff, 224–5
environment, 29, 40–1, 69ff, 94, 146ff, 150ff, 156
Environmental Liaison Centre (ELC), 73
epistemology, 82–4, 126, 174
Epstein, L, 217, 227
Epstein, RA, 126, 237
Equal Opportunity Commission, *see* Human Rights and Equal Opportunity Commission
equality, 58–9, 65, 83, 86, 97, 126, 186, 192, 210, 211, 231, 250, 276
equity, *see* access and equity
Erskine, H, 223
Ethiopia, 99
ethnic inclusivity, 59, 61
ethnicity, 56
ethnocentrism, 276; *see also* Asian values; universal values
Eule, JN, 210
Europe, 37, 98
Eastern, 184ff
European Central Bank, 37
European Commission, 34, 76
European Court of Human Rights (Strasbourg), 188, 194
European Court of Justice, 34, 194
European Parliament, 44, 115
European Single Currency (Euro), 37
European Union (EU), 15, 34, 136, 149, 213; *see also* Treaty of Rome
Eurosceptics, 3, 34
euthanasia, 81
Evans, G, 40
Evans, H, 1, 122, 164–5
evolution, 111
exchange rates, *see* currencies
excises, 139–40; *see also* Constitution, Australia
executive power, 144, 149, 164ff, 177, 207, 289
external affairs power, *see* Constitution, Australia
extinction, 107

Fallon, RH, 126
famine, 101, 107
FastWorld, 160
Favoreu, L, 215
Federal Bureau of Investigation (FBI), 221, 222
Federal Court of Australia, 141
Federal Reserve Bank (United States), 27
federalism, 6, 42, 45, 106, 113, 123, 125, 129–45, 146–55, 193–4, 207, 208, 212, 251, 261, 293
Federalist Papers, 121, 124, 224–5
Feeley, M, 132
Fels, A, 147
Fiji, 20
finance, 49
Financial Times, 37
Fine, B, 124
Finger, M, 74
Finn, Justice PD, 176–7
Finnemore, M, 70
First World, 154, 256, 260, 268
fiscal federalism, 135–6, 170
fishing rights, 268, 285
Fishkin, J, 87

Ford Foundation, 191
foreign aid, 103, 163
Fortress Australia, 2
Foster, D, 281, 286, 287
France, 71, 109, 221–2
France, A, 241
Franck, TM, 230
Franklin, NE, 210
Frankowski, S, 250
Fraser, JM (Malcolm), 60, 146, 167
free trade, 32, 40, 84, 96, 127, 134; *see also* Constitution, Australia; economic rationalism; tariffs
freedom, 60, 82, 142
  of association, 104
  of information (FoI), 45, 104, 207
  of speech, 89, 97, 142, 293
  see also secrecy, official
Freedom House, 97
free-market capitalism, 13, 17, 118, 128, 209–10, 225
free-riding, 234
Friedman, T, 160
Friends of the Earth (FOE), 74–5
Fuchs, K, 222
Fulbright Commission, 11
Fulbright, Senator JW, 10
full law, 291–2, 299
funding, international, 73
Funnell, W, 208

G-77 nations, 75
Galbraith, JK, 18
Galen, 174
Galligan, B, 12, 59, 60, 125, 161, 216, 260
Galtieri, General, 108
Garran, R, 48
Garrow, DJ, 221
Geisler, C, 280
General Agreement on Tariffs and Trade (GATT), 38
General Assembly (United Nations), *see* United Nations General Assembly
Geneva, 111
genocide, 18, 216
geographical isolation, 111–12
Ghana, 99
Gibney, M, 250
Giddens, A, 70
Gillespie, D, 288
Glendon, MA, 226
Glickman, H, 223
global governance, *see* world government
Global Village, 29, 95
globalisation, 12, 28ff, 44, 55, 59, 72, 93, 95, 119, 129, 143, 270
  inevitability of, 10, 36, 87–8, 213–14
globo-sceptics, 35
Goddard, Lord Chief Justice R, 181
Godden, L, 245
Goldberg, DT, 58
Goldblatt, D, 80
Goldfields Land Council, 279
Goldstein, RJ, 219
Goodell, Senator C, 221
Goods and Services Tax (GST), 135
Goot, M, 246
Gosovic, B, 73
governance, 14
Governor-General, 207
grants, federal, 135–6, 170
Gray, R, 261
Great Britain, *see* United Kingdom
Greece, 93, 109
greenhouse gases, 83, 94, 146, 150ff
Greenland, 241, 260, 267
Greenpeace International, 68, 70–1, 74–6, 94
Greenspan, A, 27
Grey, Sir G, 53
Griffith, Sir S, 121, 122
Groom, AJR, 68
gross domestic product (GDP), 117
Grossman, LK, 157
Gummow, Justice W, 206
Gurig National Park, 281, 286, 287
Gutmann, A, 83
Gwyn, WB, 124
Gyngell, A, 148, 152
Gypsies (Roma), 186

Habermas, J, 82
Habibie, BJ, 106
Haiti, 20
half law, *see* full law
Halls Creek (WA), 179
Hamilton, A, 121, 224–5
Hamilton, C, 41

Hancock, WK (Keith), 127
Hanf, K, 71
Hanks, P, 278
Hansard, 42, 165, 168, 182, 183
Hansen, A, 75
Hanson, P, 3, 265
Harrington, J, 123, 125
Harris, B, 10, 259
Harrison, JFC, 48
Hassall, G, 105
Hawke, RJL (Bob), 146
Haysom, Professor N, 194
He, B, 72
health, 40, 58, 61, 180, 288
Heatley, A, 253
Heindow-Dolman, C, 248
Held, D, 80, 88
Henderson, G, 266
Henkin, L, 215
Herron, Senator Dr J, 266
heterogeneity, *see* homogeneity
Hiebert, JL, 229
Hiley, G, 265
Hill, MA, 280
Hindmarsh Island Bridge, 251
Hinze, R, 174
Hirst, P, 49
Hitler, A, 108, 109, 116
Hmong, 94–5
Hobbes, T, 2, 11
Hollywood, 2, 221
Holmes, Justice OW, 128, 219
Holton, R, 17
Home, H, 244
homogeneity, 71, 119, 126
homosexuality, 84, 149
Horwitz, MJ, 217
House of Commons (UK), 160, 243
House of Lords (UK), 49, 52, 113, 160, 168
House of Representatives (Australia), 164ff, 252
House of Representatives (United States), 172
House Un-American Activities Committee (HUAC), 220
Howard, C, 1
Howard, JW, 165, 170, 265
Howell, PA, 49, 51
human rights, *see* rights, human
Human Rights Commission, *see* Human Rights and Equal Opportunity Commission (HREOC)
Human Rights and Equal Opportunity Commission (HREOC), 8, 63, 184, 264, 266
Hungary, 30, 98, 181
hunting rights, 285
Huntington, SP, 95, 99
Husites, 111
Hyman, HH, 220, 222

Ibrahim, AN, 192
Iceland, 241
ideal speech situation, 83
Ignatieff, M, 17
illiberal democracy, 96
immigration, 59ff, 129, 212
impartiality, 82–4, 91, 126
imperialism, 47ff, 66, 108, 241, 246, 260
implied rights, *see* Constitution, Australia
incompletely theorised agreement, 82
Independent Commission on International Development Issues, *see* Brandt Report
independent MPs, 157ff, 166–7, 207
India, 40, 111, 117, 199
Indiana, 220
Indigenous Constitutional Reform Conference (Adelaide, February 1996), 264
Indigenous peoples, 9, 10, 69, 243ff; *see also* Aborigines and Torres Strait Islanders, Australian
Indigenous rights, 247–8
Indonesia, 30, 96, 100, 106, 111, 147
information, 86, 177; *see also* freedom, of information (FoI)
Inglis Clark, A, 6, 122, 128
Inglis, KS, 47
institutions, 9, 14, 16, 25, 217, 238ff
integrity, governmental, *see* corruption
integrity, territorial, 25, 249
intellectual property, 28–30, 156, 293, 296
intention, original, *see* interpretation, judicial
interest groups, 68, 158, 168, 234
intergovernmental co-operation, 45, 144
Intergovernmental Maritime Consultative Organisation (IMCO), 74

International Court of Justice, 22, 34
International Criminal Court (ICC), 33, 38
International Institute for Democracy and Electoral Assistance (IDEA), 22
International Labor Organisation (ILO), 70
international law, *see* law, international
International Monetary Fund (IMF), 32, 38, 156
International Union for the Conservation of Nature, 74
International Whaling Commission, 74
International Work Group for Indigenous Affairs, 257
Internet, 29, 39, 63, 94, 96, 104, 154–5, 156
interpretation, judicial, 127, 179–80, 225, 266
intervention, international, 11, 14, 19, 25, 73
invasion, 111–12; *see also* intervention, international
investment, 102
Iran, 85, 110
irony, postmodern, 81
Iroquois, Confederacy of the Five (later Six) Nations of the, 10, 293–4
Irving, H, 4, 51, 243
Isaacs, J, 297
Isaacs, Justice Sir I, 175
Islam, 105, 111, 117
isolation, geographical, *see* geographical isolation
Italy, 109

Jacob, H, 214
Jaensch, D, 7
Jain, MP, 192
Jakarta, 187
Japan, 38, 54, 109
Japanese-Americans, wartime detention of, 216; *see also Korematsu v US*
Jay, J, 121
Jefferson, T, 293
Jenkins, Lord R, 171
Jihad, 4
Joelson, MR, 222
Johansen, B, 293
John Lewis department stores, 223
John Paul II, Pope, 111
Johnson, J, 281
Johnston, R, 30–1, 280
Joint Standing Committee on Treaties (JSCOT), 42, 162
Jokinen, P, 71
Judge, AJN, 73
judges, *see* judiciary
judicial activism, *see* activism, judicial
Judicial Committee of the Privy Council, *see* Privy Council
judicial independence, 140–1
judicial restraint, *see* activism, judicial
judicial review, *see* scrutiny, by judiciary,; interpretation, judicial
judicialisation, *see* activism, judicial
judiciary, 97, 116, 134, 140, 217, 293
Jull, P, 10, 256, 260, 263, 267
Jupp, J, 62
jurisdiction, courts and tribunals,, 34, 35, 44, 49, 134, 194, 217
justice, 290–2

Kairys, D, 217
Kajlich, H, 10, 268
Kakadu National Park, 2780ff
Kalantzis, M, 58, 63
Kalkaringi Statement (August 1998), 253, 261
Kamali Council, 298
Kamieniecki, S, 74
Kant, I, 108
Karamanlis, C, 93
Karasjok, 262
Kaysen, C, 11
Kazakhstan, 99
KCELJAG, 1, 13
Keating, Dr M, 148
Keating, P (MP), 252, 263
Keck, ME, 72
Kellow, A, 5, 69, 75
Kelly, AH, 219, 220
Kelly, P, 159
Kemp, Senator R, 14
Keneally, T, 122
Kennedy, JF, 25
Kennett, J, 160
Kenya, 99
Keon-Cohen, B, 278
Kerensky, A, 109

Kerr, AJ, 276
Kesteven, J, 281
Key Centre for Ethics, Law, Justice and Governance (KCELJAG), 1, 13
Khomeini, Ayatollah, 110
Kidd, Dr R, 266
Kimberley region (WA), 179–80
King Canute, 213
King James II, 177
King, ML, Jr, 25, 221
Kingaroy, Queensland, 213
King-Boyes, M, 294–5
Kingston, M, 267
Kirby, Justice M, 119
Kirsten, J, 198
Klotz, A, 71
Klug, H, 8, 16, 120, 198, 203, 259
knowledge, *see* epistemology
knowledge economy, 31
Kobach, KW, 213
Komesar, NK, 9, 16, 231, 233–4
Korea, North, 96, 101
Koskinen, K, 71
Kosovo, 27, 29, 30, 34, 186; *see also* Balkans
Kramer, DC, 220
Krasner, SD, 13, 15, 19, 24
Kruger National Park (KNP), 279ff
Kuhn, T, 178
Kundera, M, 189
Kuwait, 117
Kyoto Protocol on Greenhouse Gas Emissions (April 1998), 30, 75, 151ff; *see also* greenhouse gases

La Nauze, JA, 122
Labor Party, 60, 167
labour, 103, 112, 150; *see also* trade unions
Lague, D, 21
laissez-faire, *see* free-market capitalism
Lal, D, 71
Lall, R, 95
Lamer, Chief Justice A, 215
land, *see* land rights; territorial integrity
Land Claims Commissions (South Africa), 203
Land Claims Court (South Africa), 203, 283
Land Manifesto (African National Congress), 197ff
land rights, 196ff, 245ff
Lane, MB, 286
Lane, WB, 208
Langa, Justice PN, 278
languages, 57, 61, 65, 248, 287, 292
Laos, 94–5, 105
Lapps, *see* Sami
Laslett, P, 88
Latham, E, 220
Latham, RTE, 127
Latin America, 98, 108
Law Lords, 52; *see also* House of Lords (UK)
law
  Aboriginal and Torres Strait Islander, *see* law, Indigenous
  administrative, 12
  Indigenous, 248, 271–8, 290ff
  international, 8, 21, 23, 32, 64, 88, 250, 272–3, 292
  men (Indigenous), 292
  natural, 192, 278
  women (Indigenous), 292
law, Western, 290ff
Lawn Hill, 286
Lawson, B, 280
Lawson, H, 127
lawyers and legal profession, 173, 220–1
Lea, D, 261
lease-back, 280
leases, pastoral, 245
Lebanon, 56
Lee Kuan Yew, 96
legal ethics, *see* lawyers
legal realism, 128
legitimacy, 19, 23, 155, 163, 228
Leshy, JD, 210
Leviathan, 2, 11
Levy, DL, 70
lex mercatoria, 194
liberal democracy, 96
Liberia, 99
libertarian capitalism, *see* free-market capitalism
liberty, *see* freedom
Liechtenstein, 117
Lijphart, A, 37, 169
Lincoln, A, 25
Lindblom, CE, 69
Linde, HA, 208

Lipschutz, RD, 68
Lipsky, M, 69
Llewellyn, KN, 128
loans, international, 22, 136
Lobez, S, 299
local governments, 235, 289
localism, 130, 150
Locke, J, 12, 211, 244, 293
locus standi, 276
Lofton, J, 227
London, 71, 154
Loveday, P, 288
Lower House, *see* House of Representatives (Australia); House of Commons (UK)
Lowi, TJ, 76
Lumina, Dr C, 11
Luxembourg, 109
Lyons, GM, 11, 12

Maastricht Treaty (1992), 3, 213
McAlpine, Lord A, 173
McBeath, GA, 259
Machiavelli, N, 123, 125
McCloskey, RG, 217
McClosky, H, 223
McCormick, J, 74
McDonald, A, 179
McDonald, M, 286
McGrew, AG, 80
McHugh, Justice M, 206, 239
McKenna, M, 127
McLaughlin, R, 275
MacLean, D, 222
McLuhan, M, 29, 95
McNab, P, 253
McNamara, K, 37
Macphee, I (MP), 298
MacQuarrie, R, 262
McQueen, H, 5
McRae, H, 246, 247, 248
McWhirter, N, 3
McWorld, 4
Madden, AF, 47
Maddock, K, 278
Madison, J, 121, 124, 125–6, 212, 225
Magga, OH, 262
Magna Charta, 293
majoritarian bias, 233ff
majority rule, 84–5, 88, 211
Makuleke region, 282ff
Malaysia, 109, 192
Maliseets, 268
Malnic, J, 295, 298
mandate theory of democracy, 46, 168
mandatory sentencing, 142
Mandela, President N, 194, 203
Manila, 187
Manne, R, 208
Mansell, W, 21
Mao Zedong, 96, 108
Maori, 212
Marcos, F, 99
Marcus, GE, 224
Marika, W, 297
markets, 44, 78ff, 83, 150, 231
Marsh, I, 161
Marshall, Chief Justice J, 244, 269
Marshall, TJR, 217
Martin, H-P, 29
Marx, K, 84, 87, 116
Marxism, 107, 108, 112–13, 116, 124, 184, 220–2
Mason, Sir A, 4, 28–46, 121, 146–7, 150, 151, 155, 206, 218, 239
Mastanduno, M, 11, 12
Meagher, Justice R, 175
media, 27, 58, 97, 126, 148, 150, 258
medical profession, 181
Meggitt, MJ, 278
Mein Kampf, 116
mentally impaired, 232–3, 235
Meteyard, B, 21
Métin, A, 121
Michelman, F, 127
Micmac (Mi'kmaq), 268
middle classes, 116
Middle East, 37, 95
military, 93, 97, 99, 113, 163
Mill, JS, 82
Miller, AS, 217
Milner, Professor A, 163
mining, 287
ministers, government, 164ff, 175, 179, 207
Minnesota, 220
minor political parties, 157ff, 160, 166–7
minoritarian bias, 233ff
minorities, 58, 80, 84–5, 89, 97, 186, 194, 225, 250; *see also* majority rule

Mnookin, RH, 83
mobility, *see* movement
Mokgoro, Justice Y, 277–8
Mollan, R, 219
monarchy, 117, 134, 206, 293; *see also* republicanism, anti-monarchical
Mongolia, 98
Montana, 209
Montesquieu, Baron CL de, 121, 124
morality, 79, 83
Moran, TP, 213
Morehouse, TA, 259
Moreton-Robinson, A, 287
Morgan, E, 205–6, 208
Morphy, F, 252
Morris, C, 10, 243, 292, 293, 299
Morris-Jones, WH, 47
Motshabi, KB, 277
movement, 33, 58, 104, 129
Mowalijarlai, D, 295–6, 298–9
Msimang, M, 282
multiculturalism, 56ff, 60
Multilateral Agreement on Investments (MAI), 36, 93–4, 149, 162
Multilateral Environmental Agreements (MEAs), 76–7
Munro, J, 50
Munro-Clark, M, 210
Murphy, J, 199
Murphy, PL, 219
Mussolini, B, 109, 110

National Interest Analysis (NIA), 42–3, 151
National Labor Relations Board, 220
National Multicultural Advisory Council (NMAC), 61, 63, 65
national parks, 10
  joint management, 280ff
National Party (South Africa), 199, 200
nationalism, *see* economic nationalism; xenophobia
nation-building, 59
nation-states, 12, 13, 33, 51, 55, 130, 193
Native Americans, 242, 245, 259, 293–4
native title, 245ff, 271; *see also* Aborigines and Torres Strait Islanders, Australian
natural resources, 152, 284
natural selection, 111
naturalisation, *see* citizenship
nature, 278
naval power, 116
Neidjie, B, 296
neo-protectionism, *see* economic nationalism
Neowarra, P, 298
Netherlands, 109, 110
Nettheim, G, 9, 246, 247, 250, 253, 257
Neuborne, B, 220
New Deal, 128
New Delhi, 100
New Order (Indonesia), 96
New South Wales
  Aboriginal Land Council, 280
  Parliament, 182
New York, 154
New Zealand, 108, 112, 117, 243, 256, 260, 268; *see also* Treaty of Waitangi
Newcastle disease, 41
Newfoundland, 213
Nicaragua, 21
Nieuwenhuysen, J, 148
nineteenth century, 47, 107
Nino, C, 82
non-English-speaking-backgrounds, *see* languages
non-government organisations (NGOs), 5, 22, 68–77, 94, 105, 143, 149
North American Free Trade Agreement (NAFTA), 32, 34, 194
North Atlantic Enlightenment, *see* Enlightenment, the
North Atlantic Treaty Organisation (NATO), 34, 38, 112, 116
Northern Land Council, 261
Northern Territory, 142, 253, 259–60
Norway, 109
Nottage, L, 105
November 1975 Whitlam Dismissal, *see* 1975 Whitlam Dismissal
nuclear power, 153
nuclear weapons, *see* weapons, nuclear
Nunavut, 267
Nye, RB, 219
Nystø, SR, 262
Ó Dálaigh, Justice C, 178
Oakes, L, 164–5
O'Brien, P, 209
Oceania, 98
oil, 96, 117, 158
Olivier, NJJ, 276

ombudsmen, 185
One Nation Party (ONP), 160, 186, 265; *see also* Hanson, P
Orange, NSW, 213
Organisation for Economic Cooperation and Development (OECD), 33, 36, 76, 93–4
originalism (constitutional interpretation), 8, 127
Our Common Future: Report of the World Commission on Environment and Development (Brundtland Report), 74
ozone layer, *see* greenhouse gases

Pakistan, 109
Palestine Liberation Organisation (PLO), 73
Panyarachun, A, 106
Papadakis, E, 155
Papadopoulos, G, 93
Papua New Guinea, 99, 190
Parkes, Sir H, 127
parks, national, *see* national parks
parliamentarians, 175
parliamentary supremacy, *see* sovereignty, legislative
parties, political, 90–1, 97, 141, 159
patents, 40; *see also* intellectual property
Paul, AM, 217
Pearce, D, 261
Peltason, JW, 219, 224
People for the American Way (PAW), 218
People's Global Action, 71
Perraton, J, 80
Peru, 99
Petersen, FJ, 20
petitions, *see* referenda, citizen-initiated
Pettit, P, 122, 123
Philippines, 99, 105–6
Phillip, Governor A, 243
Piddington, Chief Commissioner AB, 128
Pierson, J, 224
Pinochet, A, 34, 108
Planning Law Journal, 357–81
pluralism, 65, 81, 97, 111, 185, 272
Pocock, JGA, 123, 126
Pol Pot, 108
Poland, 21, 98, 186
pollution, *see* environment
Pontecorvo, B, 222
popes, 111
populism, 212, 262, 269
Portugal, 99, 109
Posey, DA, 292
Posner, Judge RA, 120
postmodernism, 81
Pound, R, 128
poverty, *see* wealth disparities
Preamble, to Australian Constitution, 253, 265–6
Preece, A, 5
preferences
  external, 86
  voting, 167
pre-modernism, 84
Press, AJ, 280, 286
Preston, K, 121
Preston, W, Jr, 219
Priestley, Justice LJ, 175
Prime Minister, 164ff
Princen, T, 74
Pritchard, S, 248, 249, 250, 253, 261
privatisation, 28, 148, 166, 208
Privy Council, 49, 51
procedural rights, 81, 83, 90
Promotion of the Right to Democracy (United Nations Commission on Human Rights resolution, April 1999), 100, 101
property, private, 196–204, 237, 249
proportional representation, *see* electoral systems
protectionism, *see* economic nationalism
protest, political, 69, 218
Protestantism, 111–12
protocols, 298
public choice theory, 86, 88
public trust, 176–7
public/private distinction, 23, 38, 40, 94, 131, 144, 145, 195, 215–16, 276
Puplick, C, 209
Putin, V, 28
Pyke, J, 8, 24, 126
quarantine, 40

Quebec, 108
Queensland, 147
Quick, J, 48

Rabban, DM, 219

Rabuka, S, 20
racism, racial discrimination, 212, 282
Rao, K, 280
rational choice theory, *see* public choice theory
Ratnapala, S, 246, 285
Rawls, J, 82, 84
Rayner, M, 208
Reader's Digest, 15
realism, international politics, 68
realism, legal, *see* legal realism
recessions, economic, 49–50; *see also* depressions, economic
Reconciliation, Aboriginal and Torres Strait Islander, 261
Redden, G, 4
Redish, MH, 125
Reed, LW, 11
Reeves, J (QC), 252
referenda, 209–14, 253
  citizen-initiated, 8, 209–14
  convention-initiated, 8, 209–14
Reformation, Protestant, 111–12
regionalism, within nation-states, 150
religion, 57, 85, 111–12, 218, 227, 290ff
representation, 66
republicanism
  anti-monarchical, 6, 122, 127, 128, 160
  civic, 120ff
resources, 9, 186–7, 238
Reynolds, H, 243, 260
Reza Pahlevi, Shah, 110
Rhode Island, 213
Rhodes, RAW, 148, 149
rice, Australian growers of, 38
Rich, R, 5, 94, 107, 110
Richards, J, 296
Richardson, BJ, 286
rights
  human, 23–4, 61, 70, 88, 188, 202, 237
  judicial enforcement of, 137
  natural, 8
  political, 83
  talk, 8, 10, 189, 226, 290–2
Roberts, S, 261
Rodman, KA, 70
Romania, 18, 186
Roosevelt, FD, 25
Rosenberg, GN, 8, 120, 126, 217, 218, 225, 227
Rosenthal, AJ, 215
Ross, H, 281
Ross, Lee, 83
Rousseau, J-J, 60, 87, 293
Rowse, T, 246, 252
Royal Commission into the Commercial Activities of Government (WA, 1992), 176
Royal Commission on the Constitution (Cth, 1929), 133
royal prerogative, 116, 140
Rubin, EL, 132, 227
rule of law, 34, 61, 86, 91, 97, 102, 103, 123–4, 187, 191, 230, 294
Runciman, C, 287
Runciman, G, 88
Russia, 15, 99, 109, 112, 116
Rwanda, 18

Sachs, A, 199
sacred, the, 10, 291, 294–5
Sager, LG, 211
Sahtouris, E, 296
salmon import case, 40
Sami (Lapps), 258, 262–3
Sami Parliament, 262
Sampford, C, 4, 12, 20, 23, 24, 121, 216
sanctions, *see* trade sanctions
Sandbrook, R, 74
Sassen, S, 78
Saunders, AJGM, 273
Saunders, C, 6, 119, 130, 138, 264
Saward, M, 149
Scheingold, S, 229
Schumann, H, 29
science, 83, 174, 178ff
Scott, L (MP), 176
scrutiny
  international, 250, 266, 292
  by judiciary, 192, 232ff
  by legislature, 42, 169, 183
Seattle, 71, 76, 94, 149
secession, 213, 249
Second Vatican Council (Catholic Church), 111
secrecy, official, 31, 41, 43–5, 86, 177
Segal, JA, 217
self-determination, 9, 61, 79ff, 247, 249, 286
self-interest, 86, 163

self-protection, democracy as, 79ff
Semmelweiss, I, 181
Sen, AK, 100
Senate,
Australia, 7, 141, 156–63, 164–72, 207
United States, 7, 12, 172
Senegal, 99
separation of powers, 12, 97, 123–4, 137, 193
Serbia, 30, 186
Shaffer, G, 41
Shakespeare, W, 111, 182
Shapiro, MM, 217, 222
Sharman, Dr C, 168–9
Sheldon, CH, 224
Shreiner, Justice OD, 272
Sicily, 109
Sidney, A, 123
Sierra Leone, 99
Sikkink, K, 72
Singapore, 96, 109, 213
Skinner, Q, 123, 125
Slaughter (Burley), A-M, 11, 194
SLORC (Burma), *see* State Law and Order Restoration Council (SLORC)
Slovakia, 213
Smith, A, 3, 84
Smith, J, 149, 154, 213
Smith, L, 287
social democracy, 15
social justice package, 253, 254
social security, *see* social welfare
social services, 58
social welfare, 81, 150, 185, 195, 266, 288
Socialism, 15, 30
without doctrine, 121
Solicitor General, United States, 217
Soublière, M, 267
South Africa, 10, 21, 72, 187, 194–204, 215, 259
Agricultural Union, 200
Law Commission, 197
National Parks, 279ff
South Carolina, 213
South-East Asia Treaty Organisation (SEATO), 112, 116
Southern (Confederate) States (USA), 213, 228
sovereign, *see* monarchy
sovereign immunity, 140–1, 245; *see also* Crown immunity and privilege
sovereignty
Aboriginal and Torres Strait Islander, 244, 247, 271
Australia, 137, 205
legislative, 35, 141, 206ff
nation-states, 1–3, 10–11, 19, 23–4, 31, 35, 51, 78, 87–8, 107, 137, 205, 211, 290–2
popular, 205ff
see also Treaty of Westphalia
Spaeth, HJ, 217
Spain, 34, 99, 109, 243
speech, freedom of, *see* freedom of speech
Spigelman, Chief Justice J, 175
Spock, Dr B, 221
Spretnak, C, 298
Sri Lanka, 29
Stalin, J, 105, 108, 111, 184
Standage, T, 47
standing, *see locus standi*
Starke, Justice Sir H, 182
state action, *see* public/private distinction
State Law and Order Restoration Council (SLORC) (Burma), 20
Stephenson, MA, 246, 285
stock exchange, 27
Stockholm, 75
Stolen Generation, 62, 265; *see also* Aborigines and Torres Strait Islanders, Australian
Stone, J, 128
Storing, HJ, 126
Stouffer, S, 223
Sudan, 18
suffrage, universal adult, 96–7, 102, 206
Suharto, 96, 106
Sullivan, JL, 224
Sultan, R, 280
Sunderland, N, 6
Sunstein, CR, 82, 92, 125, 126, 230
supply bills, 165; *see also* Senate, Australia
supply and demand, 9, 230ff
Supreme Court, *see* United States Supreme Court
survival of democracy, *see* democracy, survival and spread
Swain, T, 297
Swanson, E, 198

Sweden, 74, 108, 110, 113, 116, 117
Sweet, A, 194
Swinfen, DB, 52
Swinford, B, 132
Switzerland, 108, 110, 116, 117, 210, 212, 213

tabling, *see* disallowance
Tajikistan, 99
tariffs, 28, 38; *see also* free trade
taxation, 6, 29, 33, 69, 72, 135–6, 138, 139–40, 156, 169; *see also* Goods and Services Tax (GST)
Tay, AE-S, 8
Taylor, P, 68
Taylor, V, 105
technology, 10, 64
telegraph, 47
Templeman, Justice T, 179
terra nullius, 244
territorial integrity, 25, 249
Teubner, G, 194
Thailand, 100, 105–6
Thayer, JB, 226
third wave of democratisation, 96–100
Third World, 154
Thomas, Justice C, 225
Thompson, DF, 83
Thompson, EP, 124
Thompson, EV, 7
Thompson, G, 49
Thomson, A, 21
Timor, 18, 21, 28–30, 106
Tito, 108
Tjamiwa, T, 281
Toffler, A, 9
Togo, 99
tolerance, 184, 221ff
Toohey, Justice J, 206
Torres Strait Islanders, *see* Aborigines and Torres Strait Islanders, Australian
torture, 275
tourism, 279ff
Toyne, P, 280
trade, 156, 243, 244, 296–7
  sanctions, 72, 129
  unions, 112, 219–20, 222
  see also labour
Trade-Related Aspects of Intellectual Property Rights (TRIPS) Agreement, 28, 40
Trade Union Advisory Committee (TUAC), 76
traditions, 113, 117
transnational social movement organisations (TSMOs), 149, 154
transparency, *see* corruption
transportation, 47
treaties, 31–2, 34, 42, 54–5, 129, 137, 143, 162, 239, 250
Treaties Council, 42
Treaty
  of Rome (25 March 1957), 32, 34; *see also* European Union
  of Waitangi (1840), 243, 256
  of Westphalia (1648), 1, 26, 211
treaty-making, *see* treaties
tribalism, *see* xenophobia
tribunals, international, 38
trust, 176–7
Tullock, Gordon, 86
Tully, J, 268
Turkey, 27, 111, 117
Turkmenistan, 99
Turner, T, 58
Tushnet, MV, 226
Tversky, A, 83
Twain, M, 221
two-force model of political bias, 233–4

ubuntu, 277–8
Uhr, J, 126
Uluru-Kata Tjuta National Park, 280ff
Underdal, A, 71
unemployment, 63, 247
Union of Soviet Socialist Republics (USSR), 30, 105, 109, 184, 195
United Kingdom (UK), 34, 108, 113
  Consitution, 1, 113
United Nations (UN), 31, 37, 70, 73, 101–2, 156, 162, 213, 248
United Nations Centre for Human Settlements, 73
United Nations Commission on Human Rights (UNCHR), 102, 248
United Nations Committee on the Elimination of Racial Discrimination, 251

United Nations Committee on NGOs (CONGO), 74
United Nations Economic and Social Council (ECOSOC), 73, 74
United Nations Environment Program (UNEP), 73, 74
United Nations General Assembly, 22, 101–2
United Nations High Commissioner for Human Rights (UNHCR), 187
United States (USA), 108, 119
  Agency for International Development, 191
  Constitution, *see* Constitution, United States
  State Department, 110
  State Constitutions, 208
  Supreme Court, 132, 216–28, 244–5
universal values, 8, 15, 56, 100, 126, 201–2, 278
universalism, *see* universal values; Asian values; Western values
upper houses, *see* bicameralism; House of Lords; Senate, Australian; Senate, United States
Uruguay Round (1994), 39; *see also* General Agreement on Tariffs and Trade
USA, *see* United States
utilitarianism, 79

Vachon, CJ, 33, 34
values, 13, 17
Van Zyl, J, 198
Venezuela, 99
Vesalius, A, 174
veto, 52; *see also* disallowance
Victor Emmanuel II (King of Italy), 109
Vientiane, 94
Viet Cong, 108
Vietnam War, 221
Vile, MJC, 124
Vincent Lingiari Memorial Lectures, 255, 266, 267
Vines, KN, 214
Viroli, M, 123
Volks, SG, 277
voluntary euthanasia, *see* euthanasia
Von Fritz, K, 124
Vonnegut, K, 181
voting, *see* elections
voting systems, *see* electoral systems

Wade-Marshall, D, 288
Walbiri, 278
Waldron, J, 80
Walker, G de Q, 124, 210
Walker, RBJ, 70, 71
Walker, TG, 217
Wallis, A, 280
Walsh, Justice B, 178
Walsh, C, 161
Waltenburg, EN, 132
Wapner, P, 70, 74
War Crimes Tribunal, 33
Warren, E, 25
Washminster mutation, Australian Constitution as, 7
Wawilak, 297
wealth disparities, 29, 85, 225
weapons, 18, 226
  nuclear, 33, 34
Webb, M, 209
Weber, M, 51
Weekly, K, 59
Weiler, J, 194
Weiss, L, 150, 152
Weiss, TG, 12
welfare, *see* social welfare
Weller, P, 7, 149
Wesley, M, 148, 152
West, T, 123
Western Australia, 173ff, 183
Western values, 290ff
Westin, AF, 220
Wheeler, F, 122
Whipple, L, 219
White Man, 260, 268
Whitlam Dismissal, *see* Senate, Australian
Whitlam, EG (Gough), 166
Whitlam Government (1972–5), 166
wildlife, 41
Willetts, P, 68, 73, 74, 75
Williams, G, 122
Williams, J, 6, 83, 120, 122, 126, 225
Willis, J, 287
Wilmer, F, 257
Wilson, HH 223
Wilson, R, 83
Wilson, Sir R, 265
Wilson, TW, 25
Wiltshire, K, 209
Winterton, G, 120

Witwatersrand, University of, 198
Woenne-Green, S, 280, 281, 286, 288
Wollheim, R, 88
Wong, Peter, 5
Work, 64
World Bank, 32, 33, 38, 156, 191, 200
world government, 14–15, 44
world heritage listing, *see* environment
World Intellectual Property Organisation (WIPO), 32
World Movement for Democracy, 100
World Trade Organisation (WTO), 38–40, 68, 76, 143, 194
World War
  First, 55, 219
  Second, 95, 99, 109
World Wildlife Fund (WWF), 70, 74–5

xenophobia, 8, 17, 61, 211–12

Yandle, B, 69
Yolngu, 297
Young, F, 281, 287
Yugoslavia, *see* Balkans
Yunupingu, G, 292

Zaire, 99
Zaller, J, 223
Zapatistas, 149
Zdenkowski, G, 275
Zimbabwe, 99, 279
Zines, L, 125

Also available from The Federation Press:

Disrupted Families: The Law

Stephanie Charlesworth, J Neville Turner and Lynne Foreman

All these [significant changes] are explained clearly and their particular significance is placed into the current context of family law systems. . . . Disrupted Families *recognises the diversity of family disputes, the variety of means by which they may be resolved and the importance of interdisciplinary skills in that process.*

Alastair Nicholson
Chief Justice, Family Court of Australia

Disrupted Families covers family law and other law, State and federal, with which disrupted families become entangled. It is written firmly in the belief that clients from such families will almost invariably be best served by professionals, be they lawyers, counsellors, social workers, psychologists or other behavioural scientists, working separately but co-operatively and interdependently.

The book provides a detailed map of the legal areas concerned and its focus is on important practical aspects of the way the law applies. Important themes are changes in the concept of parental responsibility; the wider child welfare jurisdiction of the Family Court; recognition of the financial consequences of family violence; provision to identify and deal with the neglect and abuse of children; recognition of the significance of superannuation and spousal maintenance; and the implications of the new, independent summary jurisdiction of Federal Magistrates' Courts. Mediation is also given considerable prominence throughout the book.

Contents:

- Law and Social Work Issues
- Professional Responsibility and Accountability in Family Matters
- Family law and its Implementation
- Separation and its Aftermath
- Family Law and State Jurisdictions
- State Law and Children
- Family Violence and Child Welfare
- Mediation
- Professional Training and Roles

2000 ISBN 1 86287 361 5 Paperback 360 + xxi pages $49.50

Through the World's Eye

Michael Kirby

Once we saw issues and problems through the prism of a village or nation-state, especially if we were lawyers. Now we see the challenges of our time through the world's eye.

So Justice Michael Kirby AC CMG introduces this book which fuses his belief in human rights and, in the words of Geoffrey Robertson QC, his demonstration 'that law really can be of help. He shows this time and again in the chapters of a book which makes you proud to be a lawyer.'

Writing with facility and power, drawing on polymathic learning, he devotes the first half of the book to major human rights issues in which he has been involved, and the second to the law and its institutions. The result is a book in which, Sir Zelman Cowen says, 'Michael Kirby demonstrates this extraordinary breadth of thought, humanity and insight into contemporary issues.' Justice Edwin Cameron of South Africa notes the 'sublime combination of intellectual brilliance, emotional depth and a nearly inexhaustible capacity for human engagement'.

Lord Cooke of Thorndon writes in his foreword: 'Michael Kirby is a most distinguished citizen and servant of Australia. Yet it is his international impact that has most marked him out. There is not a paper in this book that can be read without interest and at least some degree of enlightenment. We can be disturbed but never bored.'

Contents:

- Non-Violence, Compassion and Visions for the 21st Century
- Refugees: Their Need Has Never Been Greater
- Cambodia: The Struggle for Human Rights
- The Human Genome
- Privacy in Cyberspace
- Same-Sex Relationships: Some Australian Developments
- HIV/AIDS: Anger, Hope and Love
- Civil Liberties: Early Days and Days Ahead
- Judicial Activism
- The Mason High Court: A Study in Change in Judicial Technique
- The Power of Lionel Murphy's ideas
- Popular Sovereignty and the True Foundation of the Australian Constitution
- Attacks on Judges: A Universal Phenomenon
- Judicial Stress
- Has the Legal Profession Lost its Soul?

2000 ISBN 1 86287 347 X Hardback 229 + xxv pages $43.94

Human Rights in Australian Law

David Kinley, Editor

This book details the impact, and potential impact, of human rights law in the major areas of Australian legal practice – criminal law, administrative law, constitutional law, immigration law, family law, labour law, and environmental law. It also includes chapters on researching human rights laws and on using them in litigation.

This book chronicles nothing less than a legal revolution. Every chapter records the growing impact on Australian law of international human rights law. . . . It demonstrates, in a way that even sceptics cannot ignore, that human rights law is now permeating the nooks and crannies of Australian substantive and procedural law. . . .

The special value of this book is that it demonstrates this fact in a multitude of practical instances where courts and tribunals, faced with difficult decisions, have looked beyond the hitherto orthodox sources of legal reasoning. . . .

Scarcely a week goes by in a sitting of the High Court of Australia that a case does not present which involves, in some way or other, an international treaty to which Australia is a party or values that find reflection in the principles of international law. . . .

The most striking feature of these essays is that they demonstrate beyond argument what a practical subject the study of human rights jurisprudence is now becoming for the judge and lawyer in Australia.

Justice Michael Kirby AC CMG, High Court of Australia

Systematically analyses the way human rights principles are implicated across the Australian legal system. The book is an innovative blend of theory and practice and is a most valuable addition to the Australian literature on human rights.

Professor Hilary Charlesworth, Australian National University

This work is a major contribution to the development of human rights law in Australia. It will be of enormous assistance to judges, practitioners, teachers and students.

Ron Castan AM QC, Melbourne

1998 ISBN 1 86287 306 2 Paperback 366 + xxxiii pages $66.00

Controversies in Health Law

Ian Freckelton and Kerry Petersen, Editors

What are the significant legal concerns of health care professionals? What is the law on the difficult issues that relate to health care practice? To what extent can legal rules and informal codes of practice provide effective regulation of the health care community? This book debates the core areas of Australian health law likely to confront health care and legal practitioners in the coming years. The authors include medical and legal practitioners, and bureaucrats and academics, who reflect the diverse range of interests and expertise represented.

Medical decision-making is no longer shrouded in privilege and privacy. Courts are now paying more attention to human rights and patients' rights in medico-legal dilemmas, as is clinical practice through its accountability procedures.

Controversies in Health Law exposes the legal system as often fettered by a brace of formal rules of proof and procedure, out of step with public opinion and practice. It also takes stock of the ramifications of the new information that is becoming available, and the constructive contribution the legal system can make in regulation, governance and supervision.

A must for lawyers in the medico-legal area and health care professionals generally, in particular, medical practitioners, nurses, physiotherapists, psychologists and health care managers and administrators. In addition, is it a valuable collection for students of law and medicine and health law courses.

Contents:

Legal Regulation of Clinical Decision-Making
Special procedures on children, including sterilisation; criminal abortion laws; withdrawal of life support: prosecution issues; end of life: legal framework.

Litigation Issues
Consent to treatment; doctors as witnesses; malpractice actions against health care providers; confidentiality; medical records; health disputes and alternative dispute resolution; continuing legal education for medical practitioners.

Technology issues
The challenge of human genetics; regulation of assisted reproductive technology; why legislate on assisted reproduction?

Health law and ethics issues
Moral frameworks in health care; health care resource allocation; organ donation and transplantation in Australia; future directives.

1999 ISBN 1 86287 331 3 Cloth 334 + xxix pages $71.50

Native Title Corporations: A Legal and Anthropological Analysis

Christos Mantziaris and David Martin

In their thorough and comprehensive study [the authors] have explained the intricacies of the legislative scheme and its implications. . . . They have identified practical problems and their sources [and] suggested solutions. . . . This book contains an extended analysis of the legal and anthropological issues. . . . It has been written with the needs of legal practitioners, policy makers, courts and other commentators in mind.

Graeme Neate, President, National Native Title Tribunal

This book combines 'black letter law' with policy-oriented anthropology to offer an original interdisciplinary account of the complex and unstable body of law and policy surrounding Australia's native title corporations, and of features of the intercultural domain within which they will be situated.

Part I develops a systematic account of native title, which is conceived as the product of a 'recognition space' in which indigenous relations to 'country', ordered under traditional law and custom, are 'translated' into legal rights and interests. Part II offers a legal analysis of the title management system informed by an anthropology of contemporary indigenous societies. Particular attention is given to indigenous representational politics and problems generated by the interaction of traditional law and custom and the management relations established under the *Native Title Act* and the general law. Part III provides an innovative design process for native title institutions, which takes account of both the features of indigenous polities and the legislative objectives of title protection and transaction security.

The work has both practical and theoretical dimensions. On the one hand, it combines conventional legal analysis with 'hands-on' anthropology and corporate governance know-how to provide practical guidance on these issues. On the other hand, these proposals are developed on a firm theoretical footing. The book develops a legal theory of the content of native title, an anthropologically informed theory of institutional design, an analysis of legislative policy, and a critical examination of the use of the legal forms of corporation, trust and agency in the service of indigenous groups. The theoretical dimension of the work also provides the background for a set of suggestions on law reform.

Published with the National Native Title Tribunal

2000 ISBN 1862873720 Cloth 400 + xxxiv pages $99.00

The High Court at the Crossroads: Essays in Constitutional Law

Adrienne Stone and George Williams, Editors

Between 1995 and 1998, five of the seven judges of the High Court resigned or retired. The Court today is therefore a very different institution to that under Chief Justice Mason. However, the Court has not just seen a change in personnel. A shift in approach by the Court is evident in its interpretation of the Australian Constitution.

The High Court at the Crossroads contains a series of essays and commentaries by leading Australian practitioners and academics. Each essay takes a critical look at an aspect of interpretation of the Constitution by the High Court. This book marks a very important point in the work of the Court. Most members of the current Court are apparently unwilling to embrace the more policy-oriented approach that characterised the Court under Chief Justice Mason. However, a coherent replacement for the adventurism of the Mason Court has not yet emerged. The recent decisions therefore reflect new and, at times, contradictory approaches to constitutional interpretation.

These essays have a particular focus on issues raised by Chapter III of the Constitution, which establishes the separation of judicial power and which has been the subject of intense attention over the last few years. These cases have not yet received sustained analysis and are of great interest to lawyers as the High Court continues its activity in this area. The cases dealt with include the recent controversial decision in the *Cross-venting Case*. Other essays discussing recent developments in doctrine and methodology provide a broader context for the analysis of Chapter III.

This book covers the most important topics in contemporary constitutional law, and contains new insights and fresh approaches from leading writers from around Australia. Each chapter deals with a topic of great contemporary interest and is written in a form that will appeal to practising lawyers as well as academics.

Foreword: The Hon Justice Ronald Sackville

Contributors: Adrienne Stone, Nicholas Aroney, Bradley Selway, Simon Evans, Anne Twomey, Chris Horan, Linda J Kirk, Henry Burmester, MA Perry, George Williams, Dennis Rose, Brian R Opeskin, Leslie Zines.

2000 ISBN 1 86287 371 2 Cloth 242 + xxii pages $99.00